W9-BRN-071

ATLANTA RISING

ATLANTA RISING

The Invention of an
International City
1946 - 1996

FREDERICK
ALLEN

LONGSTREET PRESS
Atlanta, Georgia

This book is dedicated to my wife, Linda,
who is my best friend (and, I hope, severest critic).

Published by
LONGSTREET PRESS, INC.
A subsidiary of Cox Newspapers,
A subsidiary of Cox Enterprises, Inc.
2140 Newmarket Parkway
Suite 118
Marietta, GA 30067

Printed in the United States of America

1st printing 1996

Library of Congress Catalog Card Number: 95-822237

ISBN 1-56352-296-9

Book design by Jill Dible
Jacket design by Neil Hollingsworth
Jacket photography courtesy of *The Atlanta Journal-Constitution*

Digital film prep and imaging by Advertising Technologies, Inc., Atlanta, GA

CONTENTS

AUTHOR'S NOTE

One afternoon in the summer of 1994, I sat at a table in the reading room of Emory University's Special Collections Department, on the school's leafy, not-so-quiet campus in suburban Atlanta, awaiting a box of materials from the archives. Ordinarily, the arrival of a couple of cubic feet of documents does not occasion much excitement. But this was different.

The cardboard carton that was placed in front of me contained the private papers and memorabilia of Calvin Craig, former grand dragon of the Ku Klux Klan in Atlanta. The collection had been on Emory's restricted list, unavailable for review, until I appealed to the head of the department and gained permission to examine the contents. The box that emerged from the stacks was lighter than I expected, and I lifted off its top with considerable curiosity, wondering what I would find. I looked inside and jumped. There, loosely folded — coiled may be the better word — was the serpent-green satin robe and hood that Craig had worn on so many memorable occasions in Atlanta's past.

My surprise wore off quickly, and I spent the next few minutes contemplating the irony of the situation. As Klansmen go, Craig had not been especially hateful. In his heyday in the late 1950s and early 1960s, as one of a handful of rivals hoping to unite the KKK's various splinter groups, he was best known for renouncing violence. His public career had ended in 1968, a few days after the assassination of Martin Luther King, Jr., when he called a press conference to announce that he had experienced an epiphany. He was quitting the Klan, he said, because he now believed that blacks and whites should work together in harmony. He seemed to mean it, too. A few weeks later he joined a biracial steering committee in the Model Cities program and made a point of befriending his black colleagues.

In a sense, Craig's robe was like a museum piece, a relic of bygone days, a mark of progress. One of Emory's archivists, Ellen Nemhauser, helped me shake out the hand-stitched garment, and we marveled together at its fine embroidery and elegant purple tassels. We found a pair of Klan cufflinks, or "kufflinks," in Ellen's suggested spelling, along with a few old George Wallace buttons that said "Our Kind of Man." We laughed. It occurred to me that only in Atlanta, a city whose capacity for self-examination and self-absorption knows few bounds, would the grand dragon of the Ku Klux Klan donate his personal effects for scholarly research and the edification of later generations.

Yet the robe also left me uneasy. Modern Atlanta was built, in large part, on the amazing grace of its race relations in the pivotal decades after World War II. In the grand phrase of its longtime mayor, William Hartsfield, Atlanta was "a city too busy to hate." It had escaped the riots and ugliness that engulfed so many other Southern cities in the '60s, and the rewards were enormous: rapid growth, corporate and individual wealth, a profusion of cultural amenities, the arrival of major league sports, recognition as the unquestioned capital city of the region. How much of that bounty was due to virtue, I found myself asking, and how much to blind luck?

One of the instructive episodes of Atlanta's early history, now nearly forgotten, was the day William Tecumseh Sherman made a return visit to the city he'd burned to the ground during the Civil War. The old general arrived back in town on the afternoon of Wednesday, January 29, 1879, at the invitation of the city fathers. It was an unseasonably warm day, and quite a few citizens gathered outside the railroad depot. Their mood was one of edgy, brittle humor, as if they were torn between old bitterness and the newer exhilaration of greeting a celebrity. "Ring the fire bells!" a man shouted as the train pulled in. "The town will be gone in forty minutes!"

During his stay, Sherman granted an interview to Clark Howell, a young reporter from the *Atlanta Constitution*, who asked him why he had destroyed the city. Sherman reached over, took Howell's hand, and turned it palm up. "Young man," he said, "when I got to Atlanta, what was left of the Confederacy could be roughly compared to your hand. Atlanta was the palm, and by destroying it I spared myself much further fighting. But remember, the same reason which caused me to destroy Atlanta will make it a great city in the future."

Many years later, the story became a favorite of Ralph McGill's. The celebrated editor of the *Constitution* told it over and over, as an explanation for Atlanta's remarkable flowering. Yet to a skeptic, Sherman's gesture was really little more than a gentle way of saying that Atlanta owed its being to an arbitrary act of topography. Sitting on the first stretch of level ground south of the Appalachians, the city had begun as an inevitable nexus for the railroad cars that clacked back and forth from the Tennessee Valley to the seaports of the Atlantic coast, trading crops for finished goods. Atlanta had not existed, and so it had become necessary (in 1837) to invent her. Couldn't it be said that the very same forces were at work in the air age? How much of Atlanta's glory was deserved, and how much of it derived from the centrality of the city's airport? The old joke, that to get to heaven or hell you had to change planes in Atlanta, was not so funny if it reduced Atlanta's exalted position to that of a regional switching station.

And what of the "power structure," that self-ordained group of powerful white businessmen who ran the city during its golden era? Were they really so enlightened? Or did a local cynic have it right, that their legacy was merely "a triumph of Babbittry over bigotry?" The city, inexorably associated with the courtly, hoop-skirted, antebellum glories of the Old South by the book and movie *Gone With the Wind*, was actually nothing of the sort. The nearest cotton field was twenty miles to the south. Tara was fiction. The grandest mansion in town, the Swan House, had been built by a cotton broker — a financier — and not by a planter. White Atlantans had sentiment for the Confederate past, but a far higher yearning for Yankee capital.

Everyone remembered Henry Grady's declaration of a New South, where sharecroppers were ready to leave the farm and work for good wages in factories built by northern industrialists. Few recalled that the idea originated with Benjamin Harvey Hill, a Georgia politician and orator who traveled north to New York City's Tammany Hall in 1866, just a year after the war ended, and proclaimed, "There was a South of slavery and secession — that South is dead. There is a South of union and freedom — that South, thank God, is living, breathing, growing every hour." Had he spoken those eloquent words, in effect, for money?

Finally, what verdict would historians return on the twenty-plus years of black political rule in Atlanta? In an uncomfortable number of instances, *real* juries had been finding some of the city's black officeholders guilty of acts of corruption. Was Julian Bond right? He'd once said half-jokingly that the good government reforms of the post-Watergate era were a bane to the black community because they slammed the door on old-fashioned graft at the precise moment blacks were poised to take advantage. The "talented tenth" had become a talented half, but what of the rest? Was the black political elite gaining any ground for those left behind in the projects?

As I packed Craig's robe back into its keeping place, I thought about the approach of the Summer Olympic Games in 1996 — an event with the potential to certify Atlanta forever as the international city it has long claimed to be. An army of journalists would be arriving to see if Atlanta lived up to her boasts, and there was no telling what boxes they would open and what surprises would jump out. It was a safe bet that no small number of reporters would discover after brief tours of the downtown streets that there were "pockets of poverty in the shadows of the gleaming skyscrapers," and they might conclude that Atlanta's brightly burnished image was a fraud. Yet that is not so.

I've undertaken this book with the goal of lending some perspective to the forces that shaped the city in the half-century from 1946 to 1996. I gained a unique, detailed view of the activities of Atlanta's white power structure during the two years I spent researching *Secret Formula*, a history of the Coca-Cola Company and its longtime leader Robert W. Woodruff. Before that, I covered the advent of black political power as a reporter and columnist for the *Atlanta Journal-Constitution* from 1972 to 1987. And I've discovered fresh material in the newly released personal papers of Klansman Craig, civic leader John A. Sibley, and sociologist Floyd Hunter. Among other newsworthy items, I've unearthed what an archivist at the Atlanta History Center calls "the smoking gun" — a file of confidential reports on the activities of a shadowy city official who worked behind the scenes in the 1950s and 1960s to control "blockbusting," the explosive transition of neighborhoods from white to black.

In almost every instance, I've found that the clichés about Atlanta mask a far richer truth — that for all of the city's good fortune, it could not have risen to become the foremost metropolis of the American South without the hard work, hard-headedness, forward thinking, bluster, and occasional sheer brilliance of its leaders, black and white. Atlanta's history is a tale of clever, ambitious men and women who exploited their natural advantages while leaders in other Southern cities failed to do so.

Time and again during the past half-century, Atlanta's pathfinders managed to pick the right fork in the road. The airport would not have become the travel hub of the South without Bill Hartsfield's "airmindedness" in the early days of commercial aviation. Race relations would not have been calm without the willingness of both "sides" to negotiate, not fight. The explosion of wealth that built Atlanta's skyline and sodded the lawns of her suburbs would not have occurred without robust capitalism

— and huge grants of the taxpayers' money secured by City Hall from the federal government. The Olympics would not have arrived without the wild-eyed, impractical aspirations of Billy Payne and the international diplomacy of Andrew Young.

Some criticism of Atlanta is perfectly valid. Certainly the old claim of a "moderate" climate, with an average summer temperature of 78 degrees, will seem an outrageous lie to visitors melting in the steam-cooker heat of a July afternoon. (As a matter of fact, a meteorologist's report from 1940 indicated that the summers were growing hotter, but the news was kept under wraps.) The civility of race relations in the 1990s is more tenuous than thirty or forty years ago. Even the *memory* of race relations has grown turbulent, typified by the controversy over the Georgia state flag. Adopted in 1956 to incorporate the St. Andrew's cross from the Confederate battle pennant, the flag reminds blacks of the era of massive resistance, while many white Georgians revere it as a symbol of their heritage. There *are* pockets of poverty — whole census tracts of poverty, uncured by decades of ministration by private charity and the programs of the federal, state, and local governments.

Still, Atlanta emerged as the capital of the New South for a reason, and that reason was a willingness to embrace change. As much as anyone else, Atlanta's spirit was embodied by McGill, whose column appeared on the front page of the *Constitution* for twenty years and chronicled the growing pains of his conscience. Many people who know that McGill earned a Pulitzer Prize for his writing on race assume that he spoke as a liberal from the outset. It comes as a surprise to learn how gradually he accepted the idea of full integration, how he initially opposed many of the laws that gave blacks equal rights, and how he once remarked bitterly, when Martin Luther King moved back to Atlanta from Montgomery, "I feel like a citizen of a medieval walled city who has just gotten the word that the plague is coming."

Some of McGill's defenders thought he deliberately held himself in check, not wanting to get too far ahead of his readers, but they missed the point. He struggled with change, just as so many other white Southerners did. He did not start off "better"; he bettered himself along the way. Change did not come easily to him, which made his evolution all the more admirable.

And the same was true of Atlanta. As World War II ended, the city was blessed with potential but no guarantee of success. To reach its goal of primacy, it would have to change, and to do that it would have to go to work.

ATLANTA RISING

CHAPTER 1

1946

The political turmoil and racial violence that convulsed the state of Georgia in 1946 and sullied its image for years afterward began with an entirely commonplace event. Atlanta's congressman resigned to take a job for more money working as a lobbyist.

Robert Ramspeck was a moderate Democrat who had served in Congress from the city's Fifth Congressional District for nearly two decades. On the first day of January 1946, he gave up his seat to join the Air Transport Association of America — a career switch that made sense, reflecting as it did the growing importance of aviation and the emergence of Atlanta's airport as a vital regional hub.

When a special election was called to fill the vacancy, Helen Douglas Mankin decided to run. She was far from an orthodox politician. "She was a cussin', whiskey-drinking, cigarette-smoking lawyer," in the words of one colleague, "and she could give it to you in kind." A stocky ex-tomboy who stood five-foot-nine and weighed 148 pounds, Mankin knew how to shoot a pistol, play baseball, and fix a flat tire on a truck. Her blue-gray eyes, in the description of one newspaperman, could "look a hole through a concrete wall." She won a race for the Georgia General Assembly in 1936 as an unabashed New Dealer and supporter of child labor reform, and ten years later, at the age of fifty-two, she had become a seasoned campaigner eager to carry her liberal convictions to Washington. Her enemies called her a communist and whispered that she was a lesbian.

Ordinarily, Mankin would not have had much chance of winning. But through a stroke of sheer carelessness, the leaders of the Democratic

Party failed to call the customary whites-only primary. They scheduled a general election instead, which meant the polling booths would be open to black registered voters. At a time when restrictive primaries were under legal attack all across the South, the special election in Atlanta's Fifth District would serve as a sort of test-case, demonstrating for an audience of anxious whites the changes that might be in store once blacks began participating in politics.

The significance of the opportunity at hand was not lost on Atlanta's black leaders. A few thousand blacks already were registered to vote, and by the eve of the election their numbers had swelled to nearly 7,000. All of the candidates were invited to the Butler Street YMCA, a rambling, Victorian-era brick structure in downtown Atlanta, where the top men in the black community hoped to conduct question-and-answer sessions and solicit commitments for help in the coming struggle for civil rights. The stakes were considered so high that the two leading political rivals of the day, Democrat A. T. Walden and Republican John Wesley Dobbs, put aside their partisan differences in the interest of unifying the black vote behind a single candidate. Largely because she was the only one of the seventeen hopefuls who bothered to show up, Mankin turned out to be their choice.

The meetings Mankin held with the black leaders were kept a strict secret. Walden and Dobbs understood the likelihood of a white backlash should their plans become known, as did newspaper publisher C. A. Scott, whose *Atlanta Daily World* teasingly admitted, "There is one candidate we favor . . . but we think it will be unwise to express our preference in these columns."

On the night before the election, the black leaders gathered at Wheat Street Baptist Church, which had one of the largest and most prosperous congregations in the city. Waiting cautiously until the final radio news broadcast of the night was over, at 11:15, Dobbs and Walden finally made their endorsement official. "Vote for the woman," they said. Word of the "ticket" went out from Wheat Street along the grapevine, and by morning every black voter in Atlanta knew which candidate to pick. The white community was oblivious.

When the polls closed at seven o'clock the following evening and the vote-counting began, it became clear that Mankin was locked in a see-saw battle with Thomas L. Camp, the outgoing congressman's executive secretary and heir-apparent. Eventually every precinct but one was accounted for, and Camp held a precarious advantage of 156 votes. But the remaining polling place turned out to be the largest black precinct in Atlanta, Number 3-B, at the E. R. Carter School on Ashby Street. It had yet to report because black voters were still standing in line an hour after the official closing time, waiting to cast their ballots. More than a thousand people had turned out. Many others had been turned away when the doors closed at seven.

As word spread that the ballots at 3-B were uncounted, newspaper and radio reporters raced to the school and began banging on the front door, shouting to the poll watchers inside that their ballots would be the deciding factor in the race. Clarence Bacote, a professor from Atlanta University who was serving as an election supervisor that night, later recalled his surprise at the unfolding events. He had no idea the Carter School would determine the outcome of the race. But he was pleased. He and his colleagues sent out for sandwiches, relaxed for five minutes, and then began counting. In all there were 1,039 ballots, and Mankin got 963 of them, giving her a come-from-behind victory.

The melodramatic outcome of the special election captured national attention. "The Negro vote did it," *Time* reported, and *Newsweek* carried an item as well. Georgia had elected its first female member of Congress. For the black community and the small corps of liberal whites who believed the day of equal citizenship for blacks was at hand, Mankin's victory stood as a triumph. That it occurred on February 12, Lincoln's birthday, seemed a fitting coincidence.

Yet for hundreds of thousands of white Georgians, looking ahead to the regular election scheduled for the summer of 1946, the result was nothing less than a piercing alarm, a warning of the nightmare world just around the corner when blacks would invade the polling place, vote in lockstep in huge numbers and send radicals to high office. White leaders would do almost anything to prevent it.

The most powerful politician in Georgia, Eugene Talmadge, looked upon Helen Mankin with deep distaste. Known as "the wild man from Sugar Creek," Talmadge was one of the South's most notorious demagogues and race-baiters, a former three-term governor who wanted desperately to return to office in 1946.

Talmadge had lost the governor's chair in 1942 after making the worst political miscalculation of his career. Largely for the sport of it, he purged some of the faculty at the University of Georgia, accusing them of advo-

cating race-mixing. When they fought back, he packed the Board of
Regents with puppets and made the firings stick, a bit of ham-fisted med-
dling that cost the state's colleges their accreditation.

Talmadge learned the hard way that his natural constituents, the
rural poor, who tolerated and often appreciated his antics — including
his use of the state militia to rough up his political enemies — would
not stand for an act that injured their beloved university. On Georgia's
farms, mothers and fathers who scratched around in the harsh red clay
to eke out a living had always been able to take comfort knowing their
sons had a path to a better life through a degree from the state college.
The writer Sherwood Anderson, traveling by train through north
Georgia in the 1940s, described passing mile upon mile of unpainted
shacks, until he came to the campus in Athens and found "this magnificent institution upon her hill." He realized that the people in the
shacks had built it. No governor could survive an act that rendered its
diploma worthless.

In the election of 1942, Talmadge was defeated by the state's attorney
general, a chunky, balding young man named Ellis Arnall, who promised
reform. Beginning in January 1943, Arnall's administration was marked
by a burst of progressive legislation — giving 18-year-olds the vote, ending the poll tax, abolishing chain gangs, restoring the university system's
accreditation — that earned him national attention. "While old Gene
Talmadge sits sourly down in Sugar Creek, still a-wonderin' what hit
him," *Collier's* magazine reported, "his young successor has been doing a
job of fumigating America's worst state government."

With Arnall prohibited by law from seeking a second consecutive
four-year term, Talmadge stood a good chance of recapturing the governor's office in 1946, but he needed a popular issue to pump fire into his
campaign and draw attention away from his missteps in the past. Mankin
made the perfect target. After she won the special election, Talmadge
heaped scorn on her. In his weekly broadsheet, the *Statesman*, he charged
that she had "campaigned with colored folks . . . and won the Darktown
votes in a canter." He gave her the sarcastic nickname "the belle of
Ashby Street," which stuck.

Mankin tried her best to discount the importance of the black vote in
her victory, calling the timing of the report from the last precinct a piece
of "unfavorable publicity," but of course there was no escaping the fact
that black votes had decided the outcome. As he began his own campaign for governor, Talmadge set out to tar Mankin as an advocate of

civil rights and to exploit her as a symbol of white voters' fears. To a large extent, he succeeded.

The prospect of Talmadge returning to the governor's mansion left a great many Georgians feeling intensely uneasy. His behavior during three previous terms had turned him into a caricature and secured him a place in the same rogues' gallery with Huey Long and Theodore Bilbo — fire-brand Southern populists whose violent rhetoric appalled the rest of the nation, and whose cornpone sentiments often embarrassed fellow South-erners. In Atlanta, especially, where so many people hungered for the trappings of big-city sophistication, Talmadge's conduct was considered boorish because it reinforced the state's Tobacco Road image. Among his other colorful habits, Talmadge had kept a cow on the grounds of the governor's mansion, where it grazed in bovine bliss and made Ansley Park, one of Atlanta's fingerbowl neighborhoods, look like a farm. The sullen indignation of his neighbors delighted him.

During an up-and-down career, Talmadge had lost two bids for the U. S. Senate, in 1936 and 1938, mostly because he made the mistake of opposing President Roosevelt. The New Deal, Talmadge once said, brought Georgia nothing but "liquor, popcorn, rat traps, skates, and bicy-cles, all furnished by the taxpayers' money." His refusal to appreciate how desperately his fellow Georgians wanted and needed the largesse of the federal government — paved roads, bridges, hospitals, electrification, farm and business loans — cost him the elections. There were many peo-ple, inside Georgia and out, who believed the state's voters were simply too proud to send him to Washington.

On the issue of race, Talmadge had been damaged by the same ques-tion of comportment. In the better social circles, a politician who shouted "nigger" and stirred up racial animosities tended to be held in contempt for bullying a helpless minority whose members represented no real threat at all to the South's "way of life." From the late 19th cen-tury to the eve of World War II, blacks were so utterly and completely disenfranchised by the Jim Crow laws that attacking them was thought to be the equivalent of going to a cockfight — a cruel, lower-class amuse-ment. Talmadge made a point of saying he had never joined the Ku Klux Klan, but in the same breath he would boast cheerfully to friends that he "used to help out with a little whipping" from time to time.

What made Talmadge's attitude even more galling to liberals in Atlanta was the feeling that he deliberately enjoyed putting on a show. His demeanor on the stump — ripping off his coat to reveal the trade-

mark red suspenders beneath, the ranting that always sent a forelock of
hair tumbling down over his brow — was at odds with his college education and sharp mind. One wit dubbed him a "self-made illiterate." For
all his antagonism toward the city of Atlanta, including his famous vow
that he never wanted to carry the vote in any county that had streetcars,
Talmadge often sided with big business on matters of taxes and regulation. In private, he tried to cultivate cordial relations with even his
harshest critics. "I believe in white supremacy," he once wrote Ralph
McGill, the editor of the *Atlanta Constitution* and a leading voice for
racial moderation. "Your compromising position would say that you do
not. But I am going to pray for you anyway, Ralph."

In the governor's race of 1946, the banter and occasional goodwill
disappeared. Thanks to World War II, blacks were no longer tucked
snugly in their place. After joining the armed forces and fighting for the
United States, black GIs had returned home shed of their old deference.
Many of them placed double-V signs, which stood for the slogan "Victory for Democracy at Home and Abroad," in the front windows of their
homes. On a Monday afternoon in March 1946, three weeks after
Mankin's victory, a group called the United Negro Veterans marched on
Atlanta City Hall carrying flyers that proclaimed, "The average Negro
Veteran has given about three years of his life to fight Hitler and returns
to find Hitlerism, Racial Bigotry and White Supremacy facing him at
home. We demand Negro Policemen."

That new word — *demand* — became part of the black voter's vocabulary. In an episode that typified the change of attitude, the head of the
NAACP chapter at Morehouse College wrote a letter to the manager of
the city-owned Municipal Auditorium withdrawing a request for reno-
vation of the seats in the balcony. Since black patrons would now insist
on full integration, he said, they would be able to sit in the good seats
reserved for whites. Making his point explicitly, he warned that
"Negroes in Atlanta will be voting in large numbers in forthcoming
elections. . . ."

Blacks' patience was wearing thin. Precisely one half-century after the
U. S. Supreme Court upheld the concept of "separate but equal" in the
landmark decision *Plessy* v. *Ferguson*, per capita spending on black pupils
in Atlanta schools was a third the level for whites. Most black children
in Atlanta were stacked in so-called "double sessions," attending classes
only half the day because of overcrowding, while white kids got a full six
hours of schooling.

Nothing pressed more severely on Atlanta's black community than the need for housing. The return of black veterans, the influx of rural blacks fleeing the poverty of the sharecropper's life, the decline of live-in domestic work in white households, all combined to choke the city's black neighborhoods, where tiny frame houses stood so closely side by side their roofs looked like a single tar-paper canopy. Inside, according to one observer of the period, were "sour mattresses, clothing, refuse in sleeping rooms, unscreened doors, windows, newspaper 'wallpaper,' coal-burning stoves, fumes" — in short, the elements of squalor.

Desperate for space, blacks were beginning to encroach on white neighborhoods, where the threat of "blockbusting" triggered episodes of panic. A group of working-class whites who styled themselves the Columbians (and who considered the Klan's methods too timid) banded together one night in a vacant lot at the corner of Cooper and Glenn streets, vowing to hold the blacks at bay. When "For Sale" signs went up in border neighborhoods, the two sides occasionally confronted each other, milling around in knots on the sidewalk, glaring and muttering threats back and forth.

In the midst of this volatile season, on April 1, 1946, the U. S. Supreme Court abolished the whites-only Democratic primary in Georgia. Reacting fiercely, some of the hard-liners at the Capitol wanted to convene a special session of the Legislature and defy the federal courts. But Governor Arnall refused. Now a lame duck, casting a hopeful eye on national office, he did not wish to repudiate the law of the land. "I will not be a party," Arnall announced, "to any subterfuge or 'scheme' designed to nullify the orders of the courts." Blacks, who formed roughly a third of Georgia's population, would be allowed to vote in the upcoming statewide primary.

Talmadge seized the opportunity for a furious counterattack. Making his formal announcement for governor two weeks later, he proclaimed a platform of white supremacy and vowed that his top priority would be to restore the restrictive primary, "unfettered and unhampered by radical communist and alien influences." Given the wrath unleashed among many white Georgians by the court's ruling and Arnall's capitulation, the direction Talmadge took seemed unsurprising. Yet in truth his strategy was a dangerous indulgence.

In the view of the state's more sophisticated segregationists, the key to maintaining white supremacy in Georgia was not the whites-only primary, but rather the state's unique county-unit system, a strange, decades-

old method of counting votes that gave immensely more clout to people
in small, rural counties than those in big cities like Atlanta. Georgia primaries were not settled by popular vote. Instead, like a grossly unbalanced electoral college, each of Georgia's 159 counties was assigned
either two, four or six unit votes, depending on its population, and those
unit votes (like electoral votes) were awarded to the candidate who won
a countywide plurality. The result could hand victory to a politician who
carried numerous tiny counties while trailing in the popular vote.

The blatant unfairness of the system lay in the fact that Fulton
County, which contained most of the city of Atlanta, had a hundred
times more people than the smallest county in the state, Echols, yet
cast only three times as many unit votes.

As an illustration of the way the rules operated — and why they put
such a blemish on Georgia's reputation — one had only to look at the
mischief Democratic Party leaders inflicted on Helen Mankin. Her congressional district consisted of Fulton and two neighboring counties,
DeKalb and Rockdale. Fulton and DeKalb had six unit votes each;
sparsely settled Rockdale had two. Quick calculation with a pencil
showed that on a county-unit basis, Mankin could be beaten by an opponent who carried DeKalb and Rockdale and their combined eight unit
votes, no matter how many popular votes she might pile up winning the
six unit votes of Fulton.

Mankin was standing for re-election to a full term in the July primary,
and by late May the number of registered black voters in Atlanta had
more than tripled, from 7,000 to 24,000. But Mankin's enemies decreed
that the outcome in July, unlike the earlier special election, would be
governed by county-unit rules. They recruited an opponent, James C.
Davis, a granite-faced, archconservative judge from DeKalb County,
whose campaign flyer listed his qualifications: "true Georgian, fervent
Southerner, loyal American." Davis called himself the "fearless, red-
blooded, able and energetic type of *man* we need to give us *real representation* in Washington." He would not be competing for black votes. He
would not need them.

It was the county-unit system, not the whites-only primary, that gave
Talmadge his real strength. Trying to revive the restrictive primary not
only was unnecessary, in the thinking of many members of his inner circle, it was dangerous. Defying the Supreme Court on the primary might
jeopardize the county-unit system as well, which thus far had survived
repeated legal challenges. Better to leave well enough alone.

But Talmadge could not help himself. "I was raised among niggers and I understand them," he explained from the stump one day. "I want to see them treated fairly and I want to see them have justice in the courts. But I want to deal with the nigger this way: He must come to my back door, take off his hat, and say, 'Yessir.'"

A recording survives of one of Talmadge's speeches from late in the campaign. He stood one afternoon on the lawn in front of the Muscogee County courthouse in Columbus, Georgia, trying to speak as a dark, towering storm came racing toward the stage, shaking him with gusts of wind and interrupting his words with sharp cracks of thunder. He would obey the courts on the primary law this one time, he said. "Some of the Nigras will vote — the fewer the better — but I add to it this: If I'm your governor, they won't vote in our white primary the next four years!" The applause that followed was cut short by a fierce, ear-splitting thunderclap, very nearby, that left Talmadge muttering fearfully under his breath. Portent was in the air, literally, as if he were about to reap the whirlwind.

As the primary approached, the activities of the Ku Klux Klan began to pick up. Moribund for nearly two decades after its heyday in the '20s, the Klan signalled its "rebirth" on the night of May 9, 1946, with a cross-burning atop Stone Mountain, the giant dome of granite east of Atlanta. How potent a force the Klan represented remains a matter of some dispute. A reporter from the *Constitution* who was present that night mocked the tattered clothing and obvious poverty of the few hundred men who gathered, noting that a shortage of sheets required some of the new members to cover themselves with paper and handkerchiefs.

Furthermore, the swift, thorough infiltration of the new Klan by state investigators, the FBI and the media — even by agents of the Internal Revenue Service — often lent a comic aspect to the group's activities. Using an alias, an enterprising writer named Stetson Kennedy joined the Klan and began filing weekly reports to the authorities and to Ralph McGill, Drew Pearson, Walter Winchell, and other columnists, who gleefully published detailed accounts of the not-so-secret meetings. In one memorable instance, Kennedy supplied all of the Klan's secret passwords to the producers of "Superman," the radio serial, and they broadcast the information over the airwaves.

Two days after the bonfire on Stone Mountain, Kennedy sat down with McGill and briefed him on the Klan's plan to recruit all the Yellow

Cab drivers in Atlanta so they could provide transportation in the event of a race war. On another occasion, Kennedy revealed, the Klan leadership grew agitated over a rumor that the British government was planning to sneak 5,000 racially mixed babies, the wartime offspring of black American GIs and English mothers, into the United States.

At such times the "Invisible Empire" seemed laughable. So did its grandiose titles of investiture: the exalted cyclops and his various deputies — the kligrapp, kladd, klabee, and kludd (respectively the secretary, ritualist, treasurer, and chaplain) — who met in their clandestine klaverns. What wasn't so funny was their capacity for sudden, unspeakable violence. One of Kennedy's reports described the rage of Dr. Samuel Green, the Atlanta Klan leader, over the presence of the traitor in their midst. Should they discover his identity, Green announced, they would "split his tongue, strip him naked and nail his penis to a log, set fire to the log at both ends and give him a straight razor and tell him to cut it off or burn up." No one could read Kennedy's matter-of-fact recitation of this threat against him, made as he sat in the room listening, without recoiling.

The undercover agents discovered that one of the Klan leaders, Sam Roper, had served as head of the Georgia Bureau of Investigation under Gene Talmadge. A big, slow-talking man, Roper later joined the Atlanta Police Department, where he began recruiting members to the Klan's cause. At a klavern meeting a few nights after the cross-burning, according to an informant from the state attorney general's office, Roper discussed the question of abducting and killing A. T. Walden, the black leader who had helped deliver the vote to Helen Mankin. Roper also outlined a plan to trigger a race riot on the eve of the primary by snatching a black victim from the bus station in downtown Atlanta for a flogging. Once Talmadge was elected, Roper continued, the Klan planned to place a member in every Georgia county and pay him $125 a month to "assist" the local sheriff.

No one could say how much of this was real menace and how much just talk. Very few white Georgians advocated violence against blacks. Yet neither were many whites enthusiastic about blacks gaining the vote or achieving other civil rights. Hughes Spalding, the senior partner in Atlanta's most powerful law firm, King & Spalding, admitted the Talmadge crowd frightened him. "It is the Negro issue with them from now on," he wrote a friend, "and inasmuch as we Georgians are ignorant, bigoted, prejudiced and biased — so say the Yankees — it is a dangerous issue." Poking fun at himself, he continued, "One of my reasons for saying it is dangerous is because I have mixed feelings on the subject myself, and I am enlightened, educated, broad minded and unprejudiced. So I am worrying about what effect this issue will have upon those who are less enlightened than I am."

Talmadge's main opponent, James V. Carmichael, was scarcely a beacon of advanced thinking. Using polite language that echoed the feelings of most white voters, he vowed never to permit the mixing of the races or other violations of "our Southern traditions." A successful businessman and patron of the arts, Carmichael offered a progressive alternative to Talmadge for white voters, but it is hard to imagine his words exciting much support among blacks. Talmadge portrayed him as a liberal anyway and passed out a card that asked in dialect, "Honey, is you bin down to de Cote House and relished [registered], so's we kin vote fer Jimmy Comical for Guvner?" Playing a dirty trick, Talmadge hired a substitute who looked like Carmichael and paid him to ride around the state in a car with two well-dressed black men who puffed big cigars and grinned broadly while "Carmichael" introduced himself at filling stations.

At many campaign stops, an unwary voter might have thought Talmadge's opponent was Helen Mankin. Over and over, he denounced her as the "nigger candidate," who could never be trusted to look after white interests in Washington. When some of her advisers urged her to repudiate the black vote, Mankin refused. "They call me the belle of Ashby Street," she told a group of Atlanta policemen. "Well, I am proud of every one of those votes and I hope I'll get more!"

She did get more. Stirred by the ugly rhetoric and the specter of social change, blacks and whites alike rushed to the polls on July 17 in record numbers. When the ballots were counted, Mankin had 53,882 votes, with nearly half coming from the black precincts in the city of Atlanta, and she led Judge Davis in the popular vote by more than 10,000 votes. As expected, though, he carried DeKalb and Rockdale counties and "won" the primary, eight unit votes to six. Mankin's political career was abruptly over.

A similar pattern occurred in the governor's race. Amid a heavy turnout, Carmichael carried the statewide popular vote, with 313,389 ballots to 297,245 for Talmadge. But Talmadge took more than a hundred of the state's small counties and won the county-unit contest handily, 242 to 146, thereby becoming the Democratic nominee and, in effect, governor-elect for a fourth term.

In a strange concluding episode late on primary night, Talmadge

arrived at the *Atlanta Constitution* building, where candidates tradition-
ally spoke to the public by radio, and strode down a hallway to McGill's
office. He barged in and found the editor sitting with Governor Arnall,
commiserating over the outcome of the election. "Ralph," Talmadge said,
taking the cigar out of his mouth, "I gave you a good whippin' this time,
didn't I?" Barely paying attention to Arnall, who seemed physically
cowed at the intrusion, Talmadge reached across the desk and shook
McGill's hand. In what passed for a light mood with Talmadge, he spent
a few minutes reminiscing about old campaigns. Of the one that had just
ended, he sighed and said, "This has been a rough 'un, Ralph. The way I
feel now, it took about fifteen years off my life." Then he turned on his
heel and left.

Nationally, the reaction to Talmadge's victory, and its reflection on
the state, was every bit as harsh as McGill and others feared. The *New
York Times* offered its condolences for "Georgia's misfortune." Herblock,
the *Washington Post*'s cartoonist, drew Talmadge as an angry father drag-
ging a schoolboy labeled "Georgia" down Tobacco Road for a switching.
"Thanks, Mr. Arnall," the caption said. "Thanks for everything!"

But the worst was yet to come. On Thursday, July 25, 1946, nine
days after the primary, a terrible lynching took place in Walton County,
on the banks of the Appalachee River fewer than 50 miles east of
Atlanta. The details of the incident became widely known very quickly.
Several days earlier, a white farmer named Barney Hester had tried to
break up a domestic fight between one of his black tenants, Roger
Malcolm, and Malcolm's wife. In the course of the struggle, Malcolm
had accidentally stabbed his boss, seriously injuring him. The sheriff,
E. S. Gordon, arrested Malcolm and locked him up in the Walton
County jail.

The dismal situation took an even worse turn when another white
farmer, a prosperous and influential man named Loy Harrison, decided
to intervene. Harrison had a big farm across the Appalachee in
Oconee County, where he employed Malcolm's mother-in-law and
several more of his relatives, who swore that Malcolm was a good man.
It was Harrison's idea, born of a mind-set a century old, that he could
pay for Malcolm's freedom and bring him to live on his farm. Accordingly, Harrison persuaded Sheriff Gordon to release Malcolm on $600
bail — a shockingly small amount under the circumstances. Malcolm's
family told some friends about their good fortune and when word got
out many of the white men of Walton County were outraged.

Late on the Thursday afternoon in question, Harrison drove to the Walton County jail to pick up Malcolm. He had Malcolm's wife and her sister in the car with him, along with the sister's husband. After posting bond, Harrison and the two black couples drove back toward Harrison's farm. When they reached the one-lane iron bridge that crossed the Appalachee River, they found their way blocked by a car. As they came to a stop, another car pulled up and parked behind them. A group of rifle-toting white men, unmasked, walked up to Harrison's car, seized the two black men, tied their hands behind them, and marched them down to the bank of the river, out of sight. The two women began crying and wailing, and one of them made a fatal mistake. She recognized one of the white men and blurted out his name.

The mob now moved to seize the women as well. Medical examinations later showed that both women suffered fractures of their arms, a result of the white men using the butts of their rifles to break their desperate clutching at the car. Harrison, covered at gunpoint, made no move to interfere. The women were taken down to the riverside with the men. Harrison heard a voice count out sharply, "One! Two! Three!" Then he heard a loud volley of rifle fire and shotgun blasts. A few moments later, the leader of the mob walked back up from the river and asked Harrison if he recognized any of them. "No," Harrison said. He left the scene and drove home.

News of the killings made headlines across the United States. Reporters descended on the small town of Monroe, the Walton County seat. One interviewed Sheriff Gordon, who shook his head and said quietly, "They hadn't ought to have killed the two women." The *Washington Post*, which had poked fun at Georgia just a week earlier, now denounced "mobocracy" and spoke of the "sickness" that pervaded the state's body politic. Eleanor Roosevelt wrote in her syndicated column that the killings left her "seething with righteous indignation."

PM magazine ran a long story called "Portrait of a Lynch Town," followed by another article that asked in all seriousness, "Should Negroes Abandon Georgia?" In fairness, *PM* took note that many white citizens of Walton County were appalled by the killings, and that the congregations of Monroe's two biggest white churches voted to condemn the incident. One unnamed businessman was quoted as saying, "I hold Eugene Talmadge guilty of murder." Overall, though, the national coverage was scathing. One columnist dismissed Georgia as "that red-soiled desert of pine scrub, swamps, sandy land, mules, ramshackle shacks . . . and just

plain white trash." He concluded, "Brother, you go out of that state
thanking heaven you're a Yankee!"

It seemed the coolest heads belonged to Georgia's black leaders.
Responding to the suggestion of leaving the state, the great educator
Benjamin Mays replied staunchly, "Negroes have been battling things
worse than Talmadge since they hit America. Talmadge will try to take
the vote away. He will give courage to the Klan. He will wave the red rag
of race. But any governor would hold to segregation. We don't win the
fight by running away." A. T. Walden, unaware that his name had come
up in a Klan meeting as a possible assassination target, took a practical
view. "If Talmadge is too bad," Walden said, "he will ruin the state and
white folks will turn against him, too."

Talmadge did not get the chance to govern again. The weariness he
described to McGill turned out to be the ravages of cirrhosis of the liver.
He had other internal problems as well, the consequences of a career of
heavy drinking and a poor diet on the campaign trail. He suffered a ruptured blood vessel in his stomach a month after the primary, and by
autumn he was dying.

With Talmadge stricken, common sense seemed to dictate that his
place be taken by the man who had just won the Democratic nomination
for lieutenant governor, a mild-mannered school superintendent named
M. E. (for Melvin Ernest) Thompson. But Thompson was a protegé of
Governor Arnall and thus a mortal enemy in the eyes of Talmadge's followers. So they staged what amounted to a palace revolution.

In one-party Georgia, the Democratic primary in the summer had
always determined who would take office, as the Republicans did not
even bother to field candidates in the November general election. This
tradition now yielded an opportunity. Combing the fine print of the state
constitution, the Talmadge crowd found an oddly worded clause that said
if no candidate for governor gained a majority of votes in the November
general election, the Legislature would meet and choose between the two
top vote-getters. Making a highly inventive interpretation, Talmadge's
backers reasoned that if their man died, he could not very well be cho-
sen governor, which meant the Legislature should select one of his two
nearest rivals as his replacement. Since Talmadge was the only candidate

on the ballot, a last-minute write-in campaign was organized to give a designated successor enough votes to qualify for consideration. On election day, to fulfill their scheme, several hundred of the faithful dutifully marked their ballots by pencil — and wrote in the name of Talmadge's son, Herman.

Gene Talmadge breathed his last as dawn broke on Saturday, December 21, 1946. One of his final visitors, McGill, learned of the succession plan and disclosed it on the front page of the *Constitution*, saying it seemed likely to go through. Jimmy Carmichael, who had earned several hundred write-in votes of his own in the general election, announced that he had no intention of competing with Herman Talmadge for the Legislature's designation.

But to the surprise of many, meek M. E. Thompson refused to play along. A few days after Gene Talmadge's funeral, Thompson declared that the governor's chair properly belonged to him. Taking his side, Governor Arnall vowed to remain in office until Thompson was sworn in. Herman Talmadge, a young lawyer and Navy veteran, promptly accused Thompson and Arnall of plotting to steal his father's rightful office.

The devilment passed from artful sophistry to physical mayhem on January 14, 1947, when Georgia's legislators gathered in joint session to try to sort things out. Hundreds of Talmadge supporters, some armed, some drunk, descended on the state Capitol in Atlanta and began choking the aisles of the House chamber, jeering and yelling, refusing repeated orders to clear out. The presiding officer banged his gavel for nearly an hour, trying to silence the throng, only to give up and call a recess until the afternoon. Herman Talmadge set up shop in the speaker's suite just off the House floor, where one of his friends, a judge, relied on a pair of .45-caliber revolvers to help keep the peace.

At length the legislators were brought to order, and a committee was named to tabulate the votes in the governor's race. The paper ballots were carted into the House in a large laundry hamper and two cardboard boxes. Five hours later, as expected, the late Gene Talmadge was certified as the first-place finisher with 143,279 votes. But in a totally unexpected development, Herman Talmadge was not among the two nearest runners-up. Carmichael had received 699 write-in votes, and a perennial also-ran, a tombstone salesman from north Georgia named D. Talmadge Bowers, had finished next with 637 votes. Herman had failed to garner enough ballots. His total was only 617. His strong-arm grab for power threatened to collapse under the weight of ridicule.

Wild rumors began spreading through the Capitol, most of them ema-
nating from Governor Arnall's office a floor below the House chamber.
Jimmy Carmichael was reconsidering his decision, Arnall suggested, and
might compete for the governorship after all. The legislators would have
to pick Carmichael in preference to the hapless tombstone salesman,
Arnall told an ally, although "if they are stupid enough to elect Bowers,
I think I'll surrender the office to him."

As midnight approached, with his prospects eroding, Talmadge
became the beneficiary of a famous piece of luck. The delegation from
tiny Telfair County, his home, discovered that their votes had been mis-
counted. An additional 58 write-in ballots were discovered in an enve-
lope that somehow had been overlooked earlier in the day. (More
remarkable still, as an enterprising newspaperman discovered several
weeks later, most of these new votes had been cast, in alphabetical order,
by dead people.) With his new total of 675 write-in votes, Talmadge
now stood atop the list of contenders, and his gambit enjoyed new life.
Carmichael sealed the outcome when he contradicted Arnall and
repeated that he did not wish to serve.

Just before two o'clock the next morning, a weary, boozy General
Assembly voted to install Talmadge as governor. He took the oath of
office and delivered a brief, impromptu inaugural address from the well of
the House, then marched down the Capitol's marble staircase with an
entourage that included his mother, Miss Mitt, to claim his father's office
on the ground floor. He found the outer doors locked. Two of his supporters smashed them open, and Talmadge stood face-to-face with
Arnall. Each picked his words with care.

"I presume you've been informed," Talmadge said, "that I've been
elected governor by the General Assembly."

"The General Assembly cannot elect a governor," Arnall replied. "I
refuse to yield the office to you. I consider you a pretender."

As a gauge of the potential for violence, it is worth noting that
several dozen newspapers had dispatched reporters, including seasoned
war correspondents, to cover the confrontation. They now watched as
Talmadge and Arnall exchanged claims of authority. With a body of
men behind him straining to seize Arnall and throw him out of the
room, Talmadge ended the showdown by choosing a strategic retreat. If
Arnall wished to stay in the governor's office that night, Talmadge said,
he would defer. His followers protested. One, his father's former body-
guard, got in a scuffle with Arnall's chauffeur and broke his jaw with a

roundhouse punch. Talmadge urged calm. Eventually, about three in the morning, he led his supporters out of the Capitol.

But young Talmadge was not giving up. He returned to the Capitol the next morning, armed with a .38-caliber Smith & Wesson pistol, and set up shop in the vacant executive secretary's office in the governor's suite. All that day, he issued orders and made appointments, while Arnall sat nearby in his private office performing his own set of duties. Lending a chilling aura to an otherwise slapstick situation, the two men gave conflicting orders regarding control of the National Guard.

A day later, Talmadge resolved the impasse by the simple expedient of getting to the Capitol earlier than Arnall, taking over his office and changing the locks on the door. Arnall arrived to find Talmadge's top aide, Benton Odum, blocking his way. After an exchange of insults, Arnall was reduced to setting up a desk in the Capitol rotunda, where Talmadge's supporters took glee in taunting him. One tossed a firecracker at his feet from a railing on the floor above, scaring everyone. The same fellow occupied the desk during the lunch hour and refused to get up when Arnall returned, explaining, "It's my turn to play governor." Finally Arnall staged a strategic retreat of his own, back to his private law office, to pursue the matter in court.

The "two governors" fiasco, as the affair was dubbed, brought Georgia's image to a new low. Predictably, the press excoriated Talmadge. His actions constituted a *coup d'état*, in the ominous phrasing of many editorial writers. The *Washington Post* speculated that the federal government might have to intervene to restore lawful rule. In cities and small towns across Georgia, people rallied in support of one side or the other, trading bitter insults. Arnall labelled Talmadge "King Herman" and accused him of seizing the governorship by means "that would have shamed the German Third Reich."

At last, two months later, the Georgia Supreme Court resolved the stalemate in favor of Thompson, the lieutenant governor, and he assumed the powers of the governorship. To his credit, Talmadge accepted the court's ruling. He and his wife, Betty, and their two sons moved out of the governor's mansion after a stay of 67 days. A measure of calm was restored, but not before serious, permanent damage had been done to Georgia in the eyes of the nation. A Gallup poll found that 84 percent of the American people had heard about the debacle, and it seemed safe to say most of them were shaking their heads.

The tumult of 1946 had a dramatic impact on one man in particular —
William Berry Hartsfield, the mayor of Atlanta.

Like Gene Talmadge, his longtime nemesis, Hartsfield was a grizzled
veteran of the political wars, a former city alderman and state legislator
now serving his third term as mayor. Unlike a governor, Hartsfield faced
no limit on the number of times he could run for re-election. Only the
voters could defeat him, a prospect that filled him with deep concern
when blacks were given the ballot.

By one account, Hartsfield spent the early weeks of 1946 prowling the
state Capitol, entreating his former colleagues in the Legislature to think
of a way to outfox the Supreme Court and keep blacks out of the city's
Democratic primary. Roy Harris, a guileful lawyer and ardent segregationist who was then serving as speaker of the Georgia House, claimed
that Hartsfield frequented his suite at the Henry Grady Hotel, "urging
that something be done to protect the city of Atlanta from the onslaught
of Negro registration and Negro voting."

Like most white men of his time and place, Hartsfield viewed blacks
as different beings who occupied a lesser rung in human society. Though
he was not an overt hater, he had a well-known, visceral dislike for white
activists, especially those from the North, who were busy "stirring up
racial questions in the South." He had his police department keep an eye
on the activities of the NAACP office in Atlanta, which he suspected of
funneling money to "missionaries and agitators, who make a sensible
solution of our race problems so hard." Twice, in 1943 and again in 1944,
he asked Congress to investigate the NAACP.

The elections of 1946 changed Hartsfield's tune. Much to Roy Harris's
disgust, Hartsfield "deserted" the cause and quickly accepted the futility
of trying to revive the whites-only primary. The 25,000 black voters who
turned out for Helen Mankin in the July primary all lived within the city
limits of Atlanta, and Hartsfield understood immediately that they would
be the swing vote when the next mayor's election took place in 1949.
Agile politician that he was, he set out to woo them.

When the Klan began acting up in the summer of 1946, Hartsfield
got a briefing from investigators in the state attorney general's office
and learned that his own police department was riddled with members.
An informant counted 38 Atlanta policemen, some of them high-rank-
ing, attending a klavern a few days after the Stone Mountain bonfire.
Hartsfield's response was a confidential memo to Police Chief Marion
Hornsby telling him to warn his men "that such activity will embarrass

them and eventually the city government, and further that any overt acts of lawlessness will be dealt with sternly." Mild as it might sound by today's standards, and even though it seemed to put a higher priority on the city's image than the civil rights and safety of its black citizens, Hartsfield's memo nonetheless was a pivotal document that placed City Hall firmly on the side of racial moderation. Not long afterward, one of the city's aldermen, O. B. Cawthon, advised his fellow Klansmen against burning crosses inside the city limits, lest they rile up the "city fathers."

In 1945, the story went, Hartsfield had received a visit from C. A. Scott, the black newspaper publisher, and the Reverend William Holmes Borders, pastor of Wheat Street Baptist Church, who urged him to hire black police and integrate the force. Declining, the mayor observed tartly that the city would be ready for black officers about the same time Wheat Street began appointing white deacons.

Three years later, eight black patrolmen were walking the beat.

CHAPTER 2

"AIRMINDEDNESS"

Bill Hartsfield's career as an air show promoter lasted only one performance.

In the 1920s, as he later told the tale, he invested his net worth of $6,000 in a barnstorming demonstration at Candler Field, the tiny, two-mile dirt racetrack that served as Atlanta's airport. Ticket sales were flat and ruin beckoned until the Society for the Prevention of Cruelty to Animals somehow got word that Hartsfield planned to drop a dog wearing a parachute out of his airplane. As animal lovers rallied in protest, the story made page one, and the show sold out. The dog landed safely, as did Hartsfield's nest egg.

Such a stunt might have suited P. T. Barnum, but for a budding politician the idea of making money by scaring and outraging large numbers of voters held little long-range appeal. Hartsfield gave up his dream of striking it rich and returned to public service, much to Atlanta's good fortune. Today, millions of air travelers know that the giant airport just south of downtown Atlanta is named for Hartsfield, but few understand just how richly and thoroughly he deserved the honor.

Hartsfield was born in 1890, the son of a tinsmith whose work with acids left his fingers burned and discolored. Determined to find a better line of work, young Hartsfield trained as a male secretary and became known for his lightning-fast typing. Later he "read" the law, passed the bar, and opened a legal practice in downtown Atlanta. His first bid for public office, a successful run for the city's Board of Aldermen in 1922, coincided with the early stirrings of interest in commercial aviation.

Airplanes had been buzzing in and out of Atlanta for years, ever since

Asa Candler, Jr., son of the founder of the Coca-Cola Company, built a raceway on 300 acres of land south of the city in 1909. Though the oval track was meant for automobiles, pilots often showed up to put on demonstrations and sell rides. Hartsfield recalled seeing a Frenchman named Moisant race his monoplane against a field of autos the year the track opened.

No one could figure out how to turn flying into a regular, profitable business until Congress authorized the postmaster general to begin awarding contracts for airmail service. In Atlanta, on the afternoon of September 8, 1924, Lieutenant Colonel Charles H. Danforth, the commander of the Army Air Corps in the eight-state Southeast region, got a cable from his superiors in Washington asking what preparations the city of Atlanta had made to compete for designation as a site along the proposed federal route from New York to Miami. The answer, in a word, was none.

Danforth was a great believer in Atlanta's future as an aviation hub. Within days of receiving the cable, he persuaded the Fulton County Commission and the Atlanta Board of Aldermen to join forces and start the search for an airfield to buy and spruce up. Direct, overnight access to New York would give Atlanta's banks and brokerages a huge advantage over other Southern cities, Danforth argued, if only the local politicians would act quickly. His urgency proved contagious, as the commissioners and aldermen agreed to split the costs of acquiring the necessary property. Spurning the Candler track, which needed extensive grading and sodding, they settled instead on a nearby parcel of land with a flat, dry creekbed that formed a natural runway. The asking price was $65,000.

The deal was all set to go through when Atlanta's mayor, Walter Sims, suddenly balked. A staunch conservative when it came to the city's finances, Sims saw no reason to buy the site unless and until Atlanta gained designation as part of the federal route. If a different city were picked, Sims figured, his administration would be out its half of the $65,000 purchase price, stuck with a useless piece of land. Accordingly, on December 7, 1924, he vetoed the appropriation.

Danforth was furious. He found Sims's decision impossibly shortsighted. While Atlanta dithered, other Georgia cities — Decatur, Athens, Macon — were hastening to develop airfields. One of them might very well nudge Atlanta out of its rightful place as the aviation nucleus of the region. Danforth carried a map showing how Atlanta sat at the dead center of the eight states of the Southeast, the perfect crossroads for air transportation. But the map meant nothing without an airfield on it.

Determined to find a way around Mayor Sims, Danforth ventured one afternoon to see Bill Hartsfield in his law office. Pacing back and forth, pouring out his frustration, Danforth lit into the city of Atlanta as if it were a human being with a flawed personality. Atlanta was all talk and no action, he said, and would never do anything about aviation.

Hartsfield, who had a sharp temper of his own, responded defensively, just as Danforth hoped. "He got my goat," Hartsfield admitted later, and he vowed to prove Danforth wrong. After winning a second term as an alderman in the fall of 1924, Hartsfield took office at the first of the year with enhanced clout, serving as mayor pro tem. He appointed himself chairman of a special committee on aviation and set out to revive plans for the airfield. The skies would be to the 20th century what the seas had been in centuries past, Hartsfield began preaching, and "the city that makes its port on this new ocean [will] be the city of the future."

As his first order of business, Hartsfield went to inspect the Candler track. He arrived to find two local barnstormers, Doug Davis and Lawrence "Beeler" Blevins, using the raceway as their base of operations for a hand-to-mouth existence. The lone physical structure on the property was a wooden shack, five feet square, where the two pilots padlocked their barrels of gas and oil. The need for grading and other improvements made the track a less-than-ideal site, even though Asa Candler, Jr., was offering to give the city free use of the land for five years if his property taxes were forgiven.

Hartsfield decided to use Davis and Blevins for guides as he checked out other possible venues. Instead of driving from place to place, he flew in Davis's Waco or in Blevins's Lincoln Standard, with the result that he got a bird's-eye perspective others failed to appreciate from the ground. The problem with the creekbed property, Hartsfield soon recognized, was the limitation it placed on future expansion. With higher ground on either side, the runway could not be lengthened. Had he listened to the real estate agents, Hartsfield said later, he might have picked a site that would have doomed Atlanta forever to a tiny airport. As it was, he came to appreciate Candler's racetrack, which sat on level terrain that stretched for miles around.

With Hartsfield pushing the issue, the Board of Aldermen agreed to lease the track, and Hartsfield was given the new assignment of getting the land graded as cheaply as possible. Mayor Sims, meanwhile, appointed a delegation to begin lobbying in Washington for designation of Atlanta as part of the federal airmail system for the eastern United States.

In Hartsfield's mind, a crucial moment arrived in the spring of 1925 when his fellow aldermen grudgingly approved a budget of $5,000 for grading the track. Up to then, in spite of all the talk, not a cent of the taxpayers' money had actually been spent on the airport. Once he got his colleagues to invest in the project, Hartsfield reasoned, retreat would be difficult. In his eagerness to cinch the commitment, he had a crew working on the site eight hours before their wages were legally appropriated. Later he completed the job using an old steam shovel and convict labor borrowed from Fulton County.

Mayor Sims, for his part, turned into an enthusiastic advocate of aviation. On a Saturday in May 1925, the old man held on for dear life behind Beeler Blevins in his Lincoln Standard as they flew straight through a cloud. Though the rest of the sky was clear and sunny, "I had the experience of riding through a rainstorm," the mayor marveled after they landed.

Hoping to prod the federal government into action, Sims personally led a group to the White House and called on President Coolidge. Perhaps if the president would visit the Southeastern Fair in Atlanta in October, Sims suggested, he could see for himself the progress at the Candler track. But Coolidge was non-committal. Sims also asked the Army and Navy to designate the new airport as a regional base, another request that was placed on hold.

Hartsfield worked at transforming the raceway into a real airfield. He and the city's chief of construction, W. A. Hansell, brought in several truckloads of manure to sod the landing grid, which led in turn to vigorous complaints from the residents of the nearby town of Hapeville, who were downwind. Another neighbor, a dairy farmer, complained that the droning of the airplanes had ruined his cows, drying up their milk. He offered to sell out and move for $1,000, but Hartsfield couldn't pry the money out of the Board of Aldermen. (Many years later, as Hartsfield took satisfaction pointing out, the city had to pay $400,000 for the same piece of land as part of a highway interchange.)

Next Hartsfield turned his attention to the question of gaining clear title to the Candler property. As things stood, the city had free use of the land for five years, but to keep it after that would cost $94,500, an amount that seemed beyond the city's means. Thinking a bit of flattery might help, Hartsfield had the Board of Aldermen adopt a resolution naming the infant airport Candler Field. It was his hope, Hartsfield admitted later, that the tribute would persuade the Candlers to give the land to the city as a gift, and to that end he lavished the family with praise. Its members, he wrote, "have builded unto themselves monuments more endurable than eternal granite, and have reflected by their works great glory upon this said and throbbing city."

Unhappily, Hartsfield's throbbing prose failed to achieve its purpose. Asa Candler, Sr., the patriarch of the clan, one of Atlanta's great philanthropists, had indeed given away millions of dollars of his Coca-Cola fortune for the betterment of the city. But it was his son, Asa Jr., who owned Candler Field, and Asa Jr.'s many eccentricities — keeping a menagerie of wild animals on the grounds of his mansion, for instance — did not include wanton generosity. He made it clear he would demand his money, in full, when payment came due.

In the early part of 1926, Hartsfield's excitement over his new airfield gave way to worry. After months of dawdling, Congress finally gave formal authorization for the New York-to-Miami airmail route. But much to Hartsfield's consternation, officials in Birmingham, Alabama, put in a bid for designation in Atlanta's place. "We looked at a map," Hartsfield said later, "and saw the Shenandoah Valley — good ground under you was important in those days — headed straight for Birmingham, and from Birmingham through Tampa was an excellent route to Miami. It scared us."

The stakes could hardly have been higher. Birmingham was Atlanta's natural regional rival, a city of similar size just 150 miles to the west. Lose out to Birmingham on the federal airmail route and Atlanta's dream of supremacy in the Southeast might be gone for good. To make sure that did not happen, Hartsfield arranged to have an assistant postmaster general visit Atlanta and inspect Candler Field. The fellow was greeted upon his arrival by an eight-motorcycle escort, driven up Peachtree Street in a motorcade, and given a sumptuous dinner by John K. Ottley, dean of Atlanta's bankers, with Mayor Sims, Governor Clifford Walker, and other worthies in attendance. Then he was cosseted in a deluxe hotel suite overnight. "No east Indian potentate ever got the attention he did," Hartsfield crowed later.

There is no record of the assistant postmaster general's impressions of Candler Field, if any, but a week later the Commerce Department designated Atlanta as a stop on the federal airmail route, crushing Birmingham's hopes.

Atlanta's eclipse of the other cities of the Deep South had begun.

At times it seemed Hartsfield lived two lives.

So long as he applied his jitterbug energy and fevered imagination on Atlanta's behalf, success followed success. The city bought Candler Field (and renamed it Atlanta Municipal Airport), put in lighting, built hangars, gained airmail and passenger traffic, and by 1930 ranked third in the nation with 16 scheduled flights a day, trailing only Chicago and New York. Recognizing his efforts, the Atlanta Chamber of Commerce gave Hartsfield its Distinguished Achievement Award.

When it came to his own fortunes, though, Hartsfield proved utterly inept. He made very little money from his legal practice. His side ventures, including an amusement park supply business he started with his brother, went bankrupt. He spent thousands of dollars drilling for oil and investing in other mining operations that never made a dime. He and his wife, Pearl, and their two children lived with Hartsfield's widowed mother in her home, a domestic arrangement that rubbed on everyone's nerves. He often escaped at night and drove around the city streets listening to the police radio, tending to the voters he considered his true family. With his wide brow, bright blue eyes, and big, toothy grin, he gave the impression of having a sunny disposition, when underneath he was a restless soul with an often quarrelsome temperament.

After three terms as an alderman and two more in the state Legislature, Hartsfield made his first race for mayor in 1936. Riding around in a borrowed sound truck, he accused the incumbent, James L. Key, of growing lazy in office and running a "one-hour-a-day administration." Furthermore, Hartsfield said, the mayor and his top police officials were guilty of winking at illegal liquor sales and lottery operations, "the despair and shame of all Atlanta." Actually, Key was not notably corrupt, but he'd served off and on for ten years, and with the city suffering a budget deficit, voters were ready for a change.

Hartsfield's only bad moment during the campaign came when Key unearthed some of his business records and accused him of failing to pay his debts, including an $86 doctor's bill. Flipping the attack neatly on its head, Hartsfield asked everyone in Atlanta who owed money to a doctor to vote for him. In the lingering days of the Depression, he found many voters in his corner and won election to a four-year term.

As mayor, Hartsfield was in his element. He balanced the budget, instituted civil service reform, cleared slums, built public housing (after insisting the federal government pay 90 percent of the cost), and appointed a new police chief who rousted moonshine runners and "bug" operators alike. He raised water, sewer and tax rates, and pushed through a $4 million bond issue for schools and hospitals. He opened Hurt Park, a grassy triangle across from the Municipal Auditorium, the city's first new public plaza since the Civil War.

Hartsfield reveled in taking action and getting publicity, so much so that his relations with the press occasionally turned prickly. One of the *Journal's* editors, Harllee Branch, Sr., was serving on the Civil Aeronautics Board, and Hartsfield made sporadic trips to Washington to browbeat him into doing favors for the city. As Hartsfield saw it, Branch's duty was to pursue Atlanta's interests and make sure the city was awarded the lion's share of new domestic air routes. But Branch thought he was acting in a judicial role, with a moral obligation to give fair, unbiased consideration to bids from all cities. He would object and complain of impropriety when Hartsfield came to see him. Hartsfield, amazed, would try to explain: "I'm just working for the town. It means nothing to me personally." Their misunderstanding was the origin of Hartsfield's chronic exasperation with the Atlanta newspapers, whose reluctance to play unquestioning cheerleader for him and the city mystified and angered him.

In Hartsfield's view, anything that promoted Atlanta was a brilliant, sure-fire idea. Not content with a rapidly expanding airport, he wanted to dredge the Chattahoochee River and make it navigable all the way south to Columbus, Georgia, so that Atlanta would be the head port on a waterway reaching the Gulf of Mexico. He wanted to dam the Chattahoochee north of Atlanta, to create a reservoir that would guarantee an adequate water supply for the city no matter how big it grew. And he launched a campaign to annex Buckhead, the wealthy suburb just north of Atlanta, as a way of "preserving the town for decent folks," by which he meant well-to-do white people.

The mayor's ambitions for Atlanta were illustrated perfectly by his attitude toward *Gone With the Wind*. The phenomenal success of Margaret Mitchell's novel, first published in 1936, meant little to Hartsfield. As a piece of literature, full of longing for an imaginary South that never existed, it filled him with contempt. "So many speak of magnolias and beautiful ladies and soft nights," he once explained, "and so many of them had only hookworm and poverty." Like the vast majority of white Southerners, Hartsfield came from a family that had not owned slaves, had not grown cotton, and certainly had not lived on a grand plantation like Tara. He revered the "Lost Cause" as most Southerners did, for reasons of regional pride and sacrifice on the battlefield, not economics.

Yet there was money to be made from *Gone With the Wind*, and Hartsfield meant for modern Atlanta to get its share. As soon as plans for a movie version were announced, Hartsfield began lobbying producer David O. Selznick to stage the world premier in Atlanta. The Junior League promised to hold a costume ball for the visiting cast, including the stars, Vivien Leigh and Clark Gable. When Hartsfield heard a rumor that the event might be held in New York instead, he "leapt eight feet in the air," Margaret Mitchell recalled, and told reporters it was "the worst outrage since Sherman burned the town." His bluster paid off, as Selznick arranged for the movie to open on December 15, 1939, at Loew's Grand Theater on Peachtree Street.

The ensuing events are remembered to this day as a high point in Atlanta's history: the motorcade of arriving celebrities, the grand ball with its program broadcast live over NBC radio, the showing of the movie the next night while spotlights bathed the facade of the theater and tens of thousands of people lined the streets. "It was," an insightful observer noted, "as if two shows were being presented simultaneously — the fictional *Gone With the Wind* on the screen and the factual 'Biography of Gone With the Wind' in the seats and the aisles, as well as upon the screen, of the theater. News, history, was being made, and everybody knew it."

Hartsfield, Atlanta's ringmaster, placed himself at the center of it all. He promoted the festivities on WSB radio. He invited hundreds of guests, including the governors of Florida, South Carolina, Alabama, and Tennessee, and played the genial host when they arrived. He brought in a photographer from *Life* magazine to capture the sights. He rode in a limousine next to Vivien Leigh. Before the costume ball, he stood on a platform outside the Municipal Auditorium and introduced the movie's actors and actresses to a cheering crowd. Even his misadventures turned out nicely. When the clasp on Hartsfield's white tie broke in the theater just before the premier, Clark Gable sent a messenger hurrying back to his suite at the Georgian Terrace Hotel to fetch a replacement.

If Hartsfield was bothered by the falsity of the movie's images and ideas, he never let on. Hollywood might have distorted the Atlanta of the Civil War era, but at least its impresarios and stars were endorsing the Atlanta of 1939 as a place of glamour and cosmopolitan taste — not so bad a bargain. The invitations Hartsfield sent out were embossed with

Confederate flags over the words, "Furled But Not Forgotten," as if Atlanta's past and present could be reconciled with a facile phrase.

The rebuke Hartsfield suffered a few months later, when he lost the only election of his career, had no direct link to the hoopla over the premier. Most contemporary accounts blamed his defeat on a single issue, the use of so-called "hiding police" — motorcycle cops who concealed themselves behind billboards to catch unsuspecting speeders and feed their fines into the city coffers. But there was more to the 1940 mayoral election than a rebellion by angry motorists. Hartsfield's hell-bent insistence on growth and glory, no matter the price, made voters uneasy, as did their suspicion that he was letting his ego get the better of him.

An associate with an acid wit tried to warn the mayor he was headed for a fall. "I have seen so many bright careers of public officials dimmed by friendship," Clint Hager wrote in a personal note to Hartsfield. "It so often happens that a public official's vision is obscured by the interest of friends or that such public official's actions are influenced by selfish and designing friends. It is generally recognized that President Harding's public career was influenced and ruined by his friends. I find you in the happy and fortunate position of being unhampered by such impediments to your career, because you have no friends." The hike in taxes and water rates, the crackdown on the lottery, tougher regulations on cab drivers — all these things, Hager warned, were alienating important segments of the electorate.

On September 4, 1940, by the slender margin of 111 votes, Hartsfield lost to Roy LeCraw, an insurance executive, lawyer, and former Chamber of Commerce president. Stunned by the outcome, Hartsfield angrily claimed voting irregularities and briefly threatened to contest the election before conceding. It could hardly be said that the loss humbled him. He blamed the voters. "You could pave the streets with gold, reduce taxes to a nickel a year, and scent the sewers with Chanel No. 5," he complained, "and they wouldn't remember you unless you reminded them." He felt he simply hadn't campaigned adequately.

Still, Hartsfield's behavior changed in subtle but important ways after his comeuppance. For one thing, he faced financial hardship. Teasing aside, Hartsfield did have friends, and he now turned to one of them, Robert Woodruff, the chairman of the Coca-Cola Company, for help. The two men had known each other since childhood and had formed a special bond years earlier when Hartsfield worked for Woodruff as a male secretary. Woodruff arranged to give Hartsfield a retainer of $6,000 a year as legal counsel for one of Coca-Cola's subsidiaries and also cut him in on a lucrative private investment pool.

Even before the bailout, Hartsfield had treated Woodruff with great deference, as did many Atlantans who were awed by Coca-Cola's corporate wealth and Woodruff's personal magnetism. Afterward, Hartsfield grew almost worshipful, calling Woodruff "my number one friend on Earth." Part of the reason for Hartsfield's loss had been a coolness toward him on the part of some members of Atlanta's business community, who disliked the new taxes and water rates. Officials of the Georgia Power Company, the giant electric utility, complained that Hartsfield allowed jitney buses to operate in competition with their streetcars. In the future, if he could revive his political career, Hartsfield vowed he would never again make a decision without clearing it first with Woodruff and securing the full backing of the city's business leadership.

He also resolved to be more careful about his personal life. One subterranean element of the mayor's race was gossip about an incident during the campaign when the police pulled over a car going too slowly — 25 miles per hour on busy Buford Highway — and discovered Hartsfield at the wheel with a young woman as his companion. No charges were filed, but LeCraw's camp had the police report photocopied and distributed in select quarters.

Hartsfield stayed active politically during his exile from office. Among other things, he continued to push the cause of aviation. With American involvement in World War II rapidly approaching, he helped talk the Roosevelt administration into placing a giant Bell Bomber plant outside Marietta, Georgia (where 30,000 defense jobs were eventually created with a monthly payroll of $15 million). Then he argued that the federal government ought to lengthen the runways at Atlanta Municipal Airport so they could serve as an alternate landing site for the B-29s.

The chance for political redemption arrived quickly. Mayor LeCraw resigned in May 1942 to serve in the Army, and a slightly chastened Hartsfield, using a campaign consultant for the first time, stumped actively in defense of his record. He swept to easy victory in a field of nine candidates, taking more votes than the others combined.

Back in office, with his spirits revived, Hartsfield traveled around town with a hand-held 16-millimeter camera making home movies to send to GIs serving abroad. And for soldiers from other cities who passed through Atlanta, he made sure the night life was safe. "A soldier could come into Atlanta with a few dollars in his pocket, looking for a few beers and some pleasant companionship," one observer noted, "and be pretty well assured that he would not be robbed, rolled, ripped off or served a Mickey in any of the local bars and pleasure palaces."

The mayor's thirst for news coverage was not entirely slaked. In the fall of 1942, when his name had not appeared for several days in the *Atlanta Journal*, he picked up the phone, called the city desk and tartly reminded the editor who answered that he was back in office. But he'd learned a lesson. He got the federal War Production Board to waive its wartime restrictions and allow the city to complete repairs to the Municipal Auditorium; then he persuaded the *Journal* and the *Constitution* not to report the story, since other cities might complain about the preferential treatment and hurt Atlanta's chances for favors in the future.

The war years accelerated Atlanta's bid for regional primacy. Fulfilling Colonel Danforth's vision, the government designated Atlanta as the military supply center for the eight states of the Southeast, inspiring the nickname "Little Washington of the South." Dozens of federal agencies made Atlanta their regional headquarters. The population of the metropolitan area swelled to 500,000.

The Bell plant, which later became a giant Lockheed complex rolling out C-5A cargo planes, proved to Northern investors that Southern workers could perform well on a demanding assembly line, leading Ford and General Motors to build automobile factories near Atlanta after the war. Atlanta led the South in bank clearances, thanks to the presence of a regional Federal Reserve Bank, and bragged of having the largest telephone exchange in the South, the third largest in the world.

Roy LeCraw returned from military service and tried to reclaim the mayor's office in the summer of 1945 by promising to make Atlanta the next great city of the South; Hartsfield trounced him, largely because Atlanta already had achieved that goal.

But Atlanta was not yet the cosmopolitan oasis so many of its citizens liked to think. The High Museum of Art still allowed wealthy dowagers to donate paintings of their loved ones to be hung in a gallery called "Memory Lane." With an annual budget of $25,000, the Atlanta Art Association could barely afford to conduct classes at the museum school. When a professional museum director was hired, the association could not afford to pay his initiation fee of $600 to join the Capital City Club — which worked a considerable hardship on the man, since Atlanta had almost no decent public restaurants. (One of the few was called "Mammy's Shanty.")

The lone civic gathering place was the Municipal Auditorium, where the walls were famous for the rich tapestry of odors they had accumulated over the years, courtesy of the circus animals, professional wrestlers, roller derby rowdies, and other performers who took turns sharing the stage. The custodians rigged up a "fogging machine" that swished deodorant around the hall, but by all accounts it operated without much efficiency in the days before air-conditioning. When the symphony played, wooden planking would be installed temporarily over the concrete floor, and conductor Henry Sopkin would stop his baton in mid-air and glower at latecomers who made the boards creak.

The high point of the city's cultural life was the annual spring visit of the New York Metropolitan Opera company, whose members toiled in the same venue. One year Hartsfield unveiled a bust of the great tenor Enrico Caruso and declaimed at length about the honor of having a bust of Caruso in the auditorium. Later one of his listeners — a roller derby fan, Hartsfield guessed — approached him in the lobby and asked, "Who in the heck is this Buster Caruso?"

The most recent of the town's modest skyscrapers, the 16-story William-Oliver Building, had gone up years before, in 1930, on the eve of the Depression. Cars choked the downtown streets, since very few parking lots existed. Traffic lights, unbeholden to any master system, turned red and green at their own individual intervals, making driving a stop-and-go nightmare. The city's budding convention business was in its infancy, with only 50,000 people visiting during all of 1946 — a smaller number than can fit in today's Georgia Dome.

The city's limitations showed their tragic side on December 7, 1946, when fire gutted the Winecoff Hotel, killing 119 people, many of them youngsters attending a YMCA and YWCA meeting. Built in 1913, the hotel lacked fire escapes and a sprinkler system. As news photographers arrived to capture the horrific sight in the middle of the night, guests fleeing the flames leaped out of windows to their deaths on the sidewalks of Peachtree Street. It was the worst hotel fire in U.S. history.

Almost by definition, Atlanta was provincial, the capital city of a region that continued to lag far behind the rest of the United States. By one estimate, the South had emerged from the Civil War with no more than $7 million in banking capital in all the states of the Confederacy combined. Not until 1946, one historian estimated, had the South regained the economic ground it lost during the Civil War, meaning, in effect, that the region entered the second half of the 20th century in little better shape than it had left the first half of the 19th.

The South's cotton economy had been a disaster. In 1908, in South Carolina, "Cotton Ed" Smith campaigned for a seat in the U.S. Senate riding a mule wagon, perched atop a bale of cotton, stroking the cotton boll he wore in his lapel, chanting, "My sweetheart, my sweetheart, others may forget you, but you will always be my sweetheart." Forty years later, the boll weevil had devastated cotton, and cotton in turn had exhausted the soil across a wide band of the South, denuding the ground and exposing it to direct sunlight that baked it dry and rain that washed it away by the square mile. By 1946 erosion had carried off enough of the South's topsoil to cover the entire surface of Ed Smith's home state.

With the decline of cotton, the South's primary export had become people: the sharecroppers, black and white alike, who abandoned their flimsy shacks and headed north to find industrial jobs in Detroit or Chicago or Akron. During a single decade, from 1928 to 1939, one million farm families in the South had pulled up stakes and moved north. The state of Georgia, by one account, had expended nearly $1 billion educating 400,000 young people who left the state as soon as they finished school.

The consequences of the South's poverty included an illiteracy rate twice that of the rest of the nation. During World War II, 14 percent of the South's white draftees had failed the Army intelligence test, compared with one percent of Ohioans. Wages had doubled in the region during the war, but even so the state of Mississippi was paying its school-teachers only $517 a year in 1946.

Atlanta was the capital of the region by default, in a sense, the one-eyed king in the land of the blind. The demise of the plantations and their barter system gave rise to country stores and a retail economy, with Atlanta as the natural distribution point, the commercial center of an agrarian hinterland. It seemed entirely appropriate when Delta Air Lines, which began life as a crop-dusting service fighting the boll weevil in rural Louisiana in the 1920s, moved its headquarters to Atlanta in 1941, established a hub operation and began transforming itself into a hugely successful passenger carrier connecting the cities of the South.

Transportation was Atlanta's lifeblood. More than two hundred passenger and freight trains still passed through the city every day. In February 1946, the same month he was quaking at the prospect of blacks gaining the vote, Hartsfield convened his fellow local officials for a formal dinner at the Henry Grady Hotel, where he unveiled a road map drawn by an engineering consultant. It showed ambitious plans for a "Downtown Connector," as the broad ribbon of interstate highway was christened (and as it is still known today), running through the middle of Atlanta, serving as the main north-south thoroughfare of the region. Another highway, running east and west, would make Atlanta the cross-roads of the South.

Above all, in the nice coinage of *Atlanta Journal* editor Jack Spalding, Hartsfield had a sense of "airmindedness." The mayor remained convinced that aviation was the key to the future. On May 9, 1948, he presided as the city opened its first airport terminal, an oversized Quonset hut fashioned from war surplus materials for a bargain price of $270,000, with the name Atlanta Municipal Airport written in big block letters on the side.

The ceremonies were less than a rousing success. Rain turned the grounds into a muddy mess because the access road, owned by Fulton County, had not yet been paved. But the problem was quickly rectified. Borrowing a page from Hartsfield's book of political tricks, airport manager Jack Gray arranged to put up a large sign in the middle of the airport road paying tribute (and thus assigning blame) to the county commissioners. Within days they sent the asphalt trucks.

By law, Hartsfield served as a so-called "weak" mayor, with little direct power over the committees on the Board of Aldermen. City employees reported directly to the board, with predictable results. For years, the chairman of the Police Committee, G. Dan Bridges, ran a supermarket in the Grant Park neighborhood, and most of the city's men in blue understood that their careers would benefit if they bought groceries there. Bridges finally died in 1944, but the same kind of old-fashioned graft still existed in many areas of city government.

Rather than clean house, Hartsfield tried to shape the system to suit the city's needs. A decade after denouncing Mayor Key for allowing illegal lottery operations and liquor sales, Hartsfield became a convert to the idea that many voters liked to drink and play the bug (and would be more likely to keep him in office if he accommodated those vices). At his behest, the police relaxed their vigilance. They also winked at mixed drink sales in the bars and restaurants of most of Atlanta's big hotels, which pleased visiting businessmen. For "newcomers" who didn't belong to private clubs, Hartsfield claimed later, Atlanta's liberal policy on drinking was a welcome change from the rest of the blue-nose, Baptist South, and helped attract branch offices of national companies.

Hartsfield's indulgence extended to the Capital City Club, where some of Atlanta's leading citizens, including the mayor's patron, Bob Woodruff, liked to gamble after hours with their friends. The club was notorious for its slot machines, which brought in as much as $50,000 some years and kept down the need for dues. Police would raid the club from time to time, but only after a warning call was made well in advance. (The hiding place for the machines, club officials confided years later, was on top of the elevator cars, the one spot police never looked.)

The mayor wanted a city with an atmosphere conducive to business. While he tolerated petty sins, he prided himself on keeping organized crime out of Atlanta. He curtailed traffic arrests but insisted on safe streets. He supported segregation but disapproved of police mistreatment of blacks. His was a balancing act that required just the right sort of person to run the Police Department, and when his longtime chief, Marion Hornsby, died in early 1947, Hartsfield gave careful thought to picking a successor. The choice he made, Herbert Jenkins, proved to be a stroke of genius.

With his ruddy complexion, open features and stocky frame, Jenkins looked every bit the stereotype of the beat-walking, club-twirling cop, but he brought a new level of sophistication to the department that was sorely lacking. Working with the FBI, he instituted a three-month training program for recruits. He established a mandatory retirement age of 65. And he discouraged membership in the Klan, which came as a surprise to fellow officers who remembered when he'd been a member himself in the 1930s. He turned out to be a progressive on race, determined to quell police brutality in the black precincts.

A farm boy from Lithonia, Georgia, Jenkins had begun his career during the Depression as a $75-a-month cadet assigned to drive Mayor Key around town. One of his vivid memories was the day a dozen black leaders, including "Daddy" King, the father of Martin Luther King, Jr., called on the mayor at City Hall and asked him to hire black police. Like Hartsfield a few years later, Key declined, saying the city wasn't ready yet. What amazed Jenkins was how politely Key treated his callers. "I wanted you to meet these people and hear the conversation," Key told Jenkins afterward, "because I'm getting to be an old man. I'll never live to see nigger police in Atlanta, but someday you'll have to work with 'em."

Once Jenkins became chief, that someday arrived. Looking ahead to the next election, Hartsfield was ready to break the barrier and hire black patrolmen. The old chief, Hornsby, had been unable to contemplate the idea, finding it so offensive he threatened to resign rather than carry it out. Jenkins had no such qualms. He asked the aldermanic Police Committee for permission to begin hiring, and the committee handed the hot potato right back to him, leaving the decision in his hands. Jenkins picked eight black recruits — their names were Johnnie P. Jones, Willard Strickland, John Landers, Jr., Willie T. Elkins, Robert McKibbens, Henry H. Hooks, Ernest Lyons, and Claude Dixon, Jr. — and put them on active duty on April 4, 1948.

Years later, Jenkins laughed about the ensuing outcry. His phone rang at home one night, he said, and an angry white man demanded, "Do you want a Negro policeman to arrest your wife?" After a pause, Jenkins answered, "Hell, no — not a white one either!" At the time, the atmosphere was not so lighthearted. Some of his fellow officers called the chief "nigger lover" to his face. Showing his tough side, he busted one of his fiercest detractors, the president of the powerful Police Union, and sent him out to walk the early morning foot patrol in Pittsburgh, a black neighborhood.

Atlanta's black community responded to the black police with unbridled pride. Hundreds of black citizens lined the sidewalks to watch the officers on their first day, cheering wildly as they passed by. The NAACP staged a formal celebration one Friday a few weeks later at Greater Mount Calvary Baptist Church, where Daddy King led the singing of "My Country 'Tis of Thee." Jenkins and Hartsfield attended as guests.

Most historical accounts have emphasized the restrictions that were placed on the black officers' authority: They had to change into their uniforms at the Butler Street YMCA instead of police headquarters and were instructed not to arrest whites. But Jenkins actually gave the black officers confidential permission to stop any crime they discovered in progress, no matter the color of the perpetrators. And though they dressed separately for the sake of decorum, the black officers took the same oath, wore the same uniform, and carried the same equipment and guns as their white counterparts. They made the same pay, too — $196 a month. By the standards of the day, they enjoyed near parity.

As he headed toward the 1949 mayor's election, Hartsfield tried to walk a political tightrope. He wanted the 25,000 black votes that A. T. Walden and John Wesley Dobbs had proven they could deliver with their "ticket." But he could not afford to alienate too many whites, who after all remained a clear majority of the electorate. In hindsight, it may seem surprising that Hartsfield did not attract opposition from an arch segregationist, who might have lambasted him for getting too cozy with the Negro leadership.

The mayor's salvation lay in the relative goodwill that then existed between the races. In the thin slice of Southern history that occurred between the era of absolute subordination of blacks under the Jim Crow laws and the bitter, hard-fought gains of the civil rights movement, a smart politician like Hartsfield could play to both sides. Blacks were grateful for almost any gesture, while whites were not yet panicky about losing the racial sanctity of their buses, golf courses, theaters and schools. Integration was a distant threat.

During the half-century that "separate but equal" was the law of the land, blacks in Atlanta had built a remarkably vibrant business district of their own, centered on Auburn Avenue — "Sweet Auburn," as they fondly called it, because money was sweet — where black-owned drug stores, restaurants, theaters and even a bank, Citizens Trust, thrived, creating a black middle class. Alonzo Herndon, an ex-slave turned barber, took the profits he made cutting white men's hair and started an insurance company exclusively for blacks; by the 1940s Atlanta Life had 1,500 employees in nine states, with $12 million in assets. People could stand on the sidewalk in front of the Atlanta Life building on Auburn Avenue and watch Herndon's neatly dressed clerks scurrying around inside. Across town, Atlanta University and its affiliated colleges produced a steady stream of black graduates ready for white-collar work.

The attitude of many white Atlantans toward this mecca of black enterprise could be captured in two words: proud paternalism. One of the black community's most familiar figures, home-builder Walter H. "Chief" Aiken, who liked to ride around surveying his building sites on horseback, got a letter of praise one Christmas from a white supplier: "Although your skin may be unbleached," the man wrote, "I can sincerely say your heart is as white as any human I ever met." It was meant as a warm compliment.

Far from being a matter of shame, the caste system in place in Atlanta and the rest of the South struck many well-meaning whites as an enviable situation. The Negro, as Archibald Rutledge, the poet laureate of South Carolina, put it, "had a secure, if secondary, place. In it he was happy." Allowing blacks to police their own neighborhoods seemed reasonable enough, a modest advance that would not undermine (and might even strengthen) the American version of apartheid.

Hartsfield faced a lone serious opponent in 1949, a Fulton County commissioner named Charlie Brown, who, like his cartoon namesake, often seemed the butt of misfortune. A progressive, well-meaning fellow, Brown tried to do to Hartsfield what Hartsfield had done to Mayor Key 13 years earlier by suggesting that the incumbent had "grown old and tired in office." Only Hartsfield wasn't tired. He campaigned non-stop. And he parried Brown's every thrust.

Brown got hold of a letter Hartsfield had written to white leaders in the suburbs north of Atlanta urging them to accept annexation as a means of keeping blacks from gaining political power. Putting the matter directly, Hartsfield had warned that "the time is not far off when they [blacks] will become a potent political force in Atlanta if our white citizens are just going to move out and give it to them." Brown publicized the letter in the black community, thinking it would gain him votes. But Hartsfield went directly to Auburn Avenue's leading merchants and explained in all candor that he wanted to bring "the best kind of white folks, not the Ku Kluxers," inside the city limits. "I asked them," he explained later, "if they would like to inherit an abandoned shell of a town — what the white man threw away." The black leadership stood by him.

Race was not the only issue. Knowing that the railroads employed upwards of 8,000 workers, many of whom lived in the city, Brown attacked Hartsfield for spending too much money on his "pet project," the airport. When Hartsfield traveled, Brown charged, he flew instead of taking the train. The attack fell flat, because Atlantans had embraced the air age. One day while Hartsfield was addressing an outdoor rally, Brown sent a plane of his own flying overhead with banners and a loud-speaker. As the noise died down, the mayor shouted, "Look up in the air and see promises. Then look down here with me and see performance."

A not-so-subtle subtext of the campaign was the question of social standing. Despite his chummy-sounding name, Charlie Brown had a dignified air about him. A graduate of Georgia Tech and the president of a large mop and broom factory, he couldn't help looking down his nose at Hartsfield, who had flunked out of Boys High and never succeeded in business. Brown recalled with contempt how Hartsfield once abandoned a car, a broken-down Hupmobile with four flat tires, on the street outside his law office, where it sat accumulating dust and parking tickets. Hartsfield's legal career, Brown scoffed, had never elevated him above the level of a police-court "fixer." But Brown misunderstood the empathy of the

voters. Hartsfield had devoted untold hours to educating himself — he
solicited reading lists from college presidents and studied books at the
public library — and by middle age he had become knowledgeable on a
number of subjects. His rough edges did not offend voters; on the contrary, he had a common touch people recognized and appreciated. Hartsfield considered Brown too eager to curry favor — the sort of politician,
he once sniffed, who would "go to a funeral to shake the corpse's hand."

As canny as ever, Hartsfield sent a memo to the city's chief of construction directing him to suspend heavy construction a week before the
September election. No point irritating the voters, the mayor wrote,
adding that "pneumatic hammers" in particular were to be silenced. On
a related note, Hartsfield kept his own explosive temper in check, heeding an adviser's admonition to "keep on an even keel, and let's don't get
mad at anybody, including your opponent." And he displayed a ripened
sense of humor. Hartsfield told an inquiring journalist that as a matter of
policy he did not give away keys to the city, but instead made a point of
personally greeting any and all important visitors — including Bess, the
MGM wonder horse, "which was the first time I'd ever had a *whole* horse
in my office."

By far the most dramatic moment of the campaign came on August 11,
1949, when Margaret Mitchell, trying to cross Peachtree Street with her
husband, John Marsh, was struck by a speeding taxi. She died five days
later. When reports came out that the off-duty cab driver, Hugh Gravitt,
had been charged with drunken driving, and furthermore that he had a
record of 24 previous arrests for traffic violations, Hartsfield faced an
angry public reaction and charges that his administration was too lax
toward dangerous drivers. An ad in the *Atlanta Journal* all but accused the
mayor of murder.

Writing in the *Constitution*, McGill rallied to Hartsfield's defense,
pointing out the irony that overzealous ticketing had been the leading
reason for his loss at the polls nine years earlier. The business community,
led by Woodruff and banker James D. Robinson, Jr., stayed firmly in the
mayor's corner. So did black voters and organized labor.

In the end, not even the death of Margaret Mitchell could halt Hartsfield's bid for a fourth term. Brown's slogan, "We Need a Change," failed
to articulate much of a vision for the city's future, and on election day
Hartsfield swept to victory.

CHAPTER 3

"UNDER THE CRUST"

The man who did the most to glorify Atlanta's business leaders of the 1950s, who nicknamed them the "power structure" and chronicled their use of the carrots and sticks of capitalism as they built the city into an important regional hub, was actually a fervent admirer of Vladimir Lenin.

Floyd Hunter arrived in Atlanta during World War II to run the city's USO Clubs and stayed on afterward as director of the Social Planning Council of Atlanta, a liberal outfit dedicated to improving living conditions for blacks and poor whites. For two years, Hunter published his impressions of the city and his pleas for social reform in a monthly bulletin, the *Atlanta Letter*, until his support for Henry Wallace and the Progressive Party in the 1948 presidential election finally brought him to grief with the council's moderate elders. Out of work, he looked around for a dissertation subject and settled on the idea of dissecting the elite group of businessmen who pulled the city's strings.

Late one weekday afternoon, Hunter was shown into the law offices of Hughes Spalding, the senior partner in Atlanta's most prominent law firm, King & Spalding, where the client list included the Coca-Cola Company, Trust Company of Georgia, and (as one partner gleefully put it) "a lot of wealthy widows." Hoping to find common ground, Hunter described his upbringing on a small farm in Kentucky and was gratified when Spalding said his father, Jack, the firm's founder, had grown up in rural Kentucky, too. Naturally, Hunter did not dwell on his socialist politics.

What Hunter failed to appreciate was that Spalding, then in his early

sixties and at the height of his influence, required no guile or cajoling to
open up. Spalding adored gossip and routinely unburdened himself of
juicy tidbits about the city's leading citizens to almost anyone willing to
listen. This was especially true toward the end of the day, when he liked
to have a drink or two.

As Hunter scribbled notes, thrilled at the candid details he was hearing, Spalding rambled on for an hour, fleshing out the roles played by various prominent Atlantans. Like a therapist and patient engaging in free
association, Hunter would name a name and Spalding would set him
straight about the person's true standing in the community. "You fellows
who make these surveys," Spalding said, "most of the time you do not get
'under the crust.' I'm going to take you under the crust."

Hunter's influential book, *Community Power Structure*, was born during that one long session with Spalding, as the lawyer patiently laid out
the tiles that formed the mosaic of Atlanta's hierarchy. Published in
1953, the book gained renown for its sophisticated analysis of the way
wealthy businessmen acted behind the scenes and ran the politics and
civic affairs of the city. Following the conventions of scholarly writing
at the time, Hunter declined to identify Atlanta by name, instead placing his study in an anonymous "regional" city. And he used pseudonyms
for all of the characters, thereby frustrating several generations of
Atlantans who have spent years trying to discern the actual identities of
the dramatis personae.

Happily, Hunter's notes survive, as does a trove of Spalding's private
correspondence, making it easy to sort out the players and restore a portrait of the times. On the day of their interview, Hunter expressed his surprise that Spalding would speak so frankly when second-tier men typically were more guarded. Spalding laughed with delight. "Maybe it is
security of position," he said, "but probably it is that some of them don't
want to admit they're stooges. I *know* I'm a stooge." His boss, he said, was
Robert Woodruff, the head of the Coca-Cola Company and, through
cross-ownership and a web of interlocking boards of directors, the final
authority in several other institutions in Atlanta as well. "I guess I'm a
top stooge," Spalding explained, "but I don't mind admitting it. When
Mr. Woodruff wants something done, and I can possibly do it, I do it!"

Spalding described Woodruff's place atop the heap. Through various
family trusts, Woodruff single-handedly controlled the Coca-Cola Company, Atlanta's flagship enterprise, then worth half a billion dollars, and
oversaw the affairs of his late father's bank, Trust Company of Georgia.

His influence extended to Emory University, where he underwrote the expenses of the medical school out of his own pocket and helped establish a U.S. Public Health Service research laboratory that later became the Centers for Disease Control. As a member of General Electric's board of directors, Woodruff arranged to have a GE plant built in Georgia, and he served on the board of Southern Railway, where he worked to persuade Ford and General Motors to build plants in the suburbs of Atlanta.

Other important "crowds," Spalding continued, were the leaders of the city's two other major banks, Citizens & Southern and First National Bank of Atlanta, the executives of Rich's department store, and the top men at the Georgia Power Company, the giant electric utility. The railroads still had power, too. "If you want to know what is going on," Spalding lectured his socialist guest with breezy good cheer, "you have to be where the money is. It is capitalism, I suppose you'd say."

On one level, of course, Spalding could be faulted for stating the obvious as if delivering revelation. A glance at the newspaper, where Mayor Hartsfield was shown pouring a two-foot bottle of Coke over the nose of a Capital Airlines passenger plane before its inaugural flight to New York, spoke volumes about Atlanta's pecking order. Hartsfield's fealty to Woodruff was well advertised. He kept a large portrait of Woodruff on the wall of his office at City Hall and regularly introduced himself as the mayor of "Coca-Cola City." He told people without prompting that he never made a decision without clearing it first with Woodruff. If anyone missed the point, Ralph McGill would occasionally hint at the extent of his friend Woodruff's power in his column on the front page of the *Atlanta Constitution*.

What remained a mystery, though, was Woodruff's relationship with the governor of Georgia, Herman Talmadge. After the "two governors" fiasco of 1947, young Talmadge had bided his time until a special election the next year, when he narrowly defeated the acting governor, M. E. Thompson, and won the right to serve out the final two years of his father's term. To this day, historians have struggled to understand why Woodruff, so eager to put a progressive stamp on Atlanta, allied himself with Talmadge, an ardent segregationist and champion of the "wool hat" rustics in Georgia's rural counties.

A clue to the answer lay in the hard days of the Great Depression, when Georgia law allowed the state and its cities and counties to levy stiff taxes on securities held by the wealthy. By one account, a stockholder could be forced to surrender as much as $428 of a $600 dividend, if all the levels of government applied the maximum rate. The full tax was never imposed, but in 1934, late in his first term as governor, Gene Talmadge threatened to raise the state's tax bite, which sent rich Atlantans fleeing in droves to other states. Woodruff moved Coca-Cola's headquarters to Wilmington, Delaware, where the company was chartered, and took up official residency there himself.

One of Spalding's early assignments for Woodruff, in the days when they were first getting to know each other, was to lobby Gene Talmadge and the Georgia Legislature for a change in the law. At the time, Spalding held Woodruff and the city's other skittish, absentee millionaires in mild contempt. "All of these rich people are so tax conscious," Spalding told his father, "that all you have to do is mention taxes and they immediately fling a fit and look for some haven of refuge." Spalding nevertheless carried out his task, and Talmadge, who was shaken by the exodus of wealthy Atlantans, agreed to curtail the tax.

For the remainder of Gene Talmadge's political career, he enjoyed Woodruff's grudging respect. Contrary to some accounts, Woodruff was not an enthusiastic backer. During the summer of 1946, after his victory in the Democratic primary, Talmadge flew out to Los Angeles for a rest and encountered one of Coca-Cola's West Coast executives. What could he do, Talmadge asked, to get back in Woodruff's good graces? The executive passed the message along, and Woodruff responded tersely that Talmadge was "pretty much" in his good graces by the simple expedient of having won the election. As long as Talmadge held office, Woodruff said, he would manage to get along with him.

Spalding, however, came to have a much warmer affection for Gene Talmadge, one he was never fully able to explain. Partly it was a matter of temperament. A devotee of the rough and tumble of politics, Spalding admired Gene's fighting spirit. And certainly Talmadge had grown friendlier toward Spalding's clients over the years. "He would have been economical and would have held the boodlers in line and would have frowned on a lot of extra taxes," Spalding told Woodruff shortly after Talmadge died. "There is no telling what we will have now." Spalding had been present at Gene's deathbed and promised him he would look after Herman. According to McGill, who also admitted a fondness for Gene Talmadge, Spalding came to view the younger Talmadge "almost as a foster son."

Whatever the reasons, Spalding developed a great deal of faith in Herman Talmadge and supported him openly in the special election of

1948. He tried to get Woodruff to share his enthusiasm. Shortly after Talmadge was sworn in, Woodruff invited him to lunch in his private dining room at the Coca-Cola Company for a get-acquainted session, and later they hunted quail together at Woodruff's plantation in southwest Georgia. But they did not grow comfortable with each other. Talmadge recalled many years later that he offended Woodruff and the staff at Ichauway by showing up with a powerful automatic rifle, when guests were expected to use light-gauge shotguns. He was treated, he said drily, "as if I'd taken advantage of a girl below the age of consent." On a more fundamental level, Woodruff was accustomed to subservience, especially from younger men, while Talmadge, the son of a legendary figure, exuded an air of princely self-assurance and rarely deferred to anyone. Woodruff was 59 years old when they met, Talmadge just 35.

With their relationship off to a cool start, Woodruff and Talmadge relied on Spalding as their go-between, which suited Spalding perfectly. At Woodruff's request, Talmadge appointed Spalding to the board of regents, which oversaw the University of Georgia and the state's other public colleges. In turn, Spalding kept Woodruff closely apprised of Talmadge's progress in office. Though he won with the votes of rural whites who were dead-set against giving black Georgians the vote or any other civil rights, Talmadge spurned the Klan and discouraged its members from acting up. He offered the help of the Georgia Bureau of Investigation to any sheriff who had trouble handling the Klan in his county. And he stopped the Legislature from carrying out a wholesale purge of newly enfranchised black voters.

Oddly enough, given his fierceness in seeking the job, Talmadge's first few months as governor saw him stricken by a mood of lassitude and depression. He went through several bouts of heavy drinking. "He is today, for example, holed up on his farm getting over a binge brought on by frustrations," McGill wrote a friend in the spring of 1949. Spalding reported to Woodruff that the governor "is not as circumspect about his highballs as he should be." Yet his performance was encouraging. McGill urged an editor at the *New Republic*, the liberal weekly, to let him write an anonymous article praising Talmadge as a politician wholly unlike his father. "He has never been as violently anti-Negro as his father," McGill reported. "He has never shouted, 'Nigger! Nigger!' as did his father."

Such praise, thin gruel by later standards, reflected the attitudes of the time. McGill had yet to take more than a few halting steps on his long road to enlightenment about race. He had grown up in a rural area of eastern Tennessee, near the mining town of Soddy, where only a few blacks lived. One of them, a roofer, hired McGill as an apprentice one summer and later gave him the money for his train fare to Vanderbilt University. The gesture made a lasting impression, and McGill displayed an empathetic attitude toward black people. But he could not bring himself to the view that their civil rights extended to the private sector.

Woodruff, meanwhile, believed that blacks had enjoyed dramatic advancement during World War II and were like an army that needed a rest before their next campaign. As a businessman, his main goal was to curtail the episodes of racial violence and ugly name-calling that sullied Georgia's image and, by association, his company's. Woodruff wanted to see improvements in the lives of black and white Georgians alike, but he had no thought that those lives would be lived together. Spalding, arguably the most liberal of the group, was concentrating his efforts on the construction of a hospital for the exclusive use of Atlanta's blacks (later named the Hughes Spalding Pavilion in his honor). Except in radical circles, paternalism was the order of the day, not enthusiasm for civil rights.

So it was that in his conversation with Floyd Hunter, Spalding struck a defensive note when the subject turned to Herman Talmadge. "You probably do not like our governor," Spalding said, "but he is a man dedicated to raising Georgia by the bootstraps in industrial development and agriculture." Hunter confessed he had never met Talmadge and quickly dropped the subject, when a little digging might have produced quite a scoop. It turned out that Spalding and Talmadge were negotiating a political deal that would transform the state.

Unhappy in the governor's office, Talmadge had turned his sights on the U.S. Senate, where Walter F. George, Georgia's courtly senior senator, was standing for re-election in 1950. Talmadge's father had tried in vain to unseat George in 1938, and this was a chance for the son to avenge the loss (while scoring an oedipal victory of his own).

Talmadge's ambition put a scare into Woodruff. Senator George was Coca-Cola's man in Washington, a faithful ally who had rescued the company from many an undesired tax, tariff, and federal regulation over the years. At age seventy-one, George wanted another term, and Woodruff wanted him to have it. Accordingly, Spalding invited Talmadge to his farm outside Atlanta and spent an afternoon discussing the problem. "I told him as frankly and firmly as I could that he could not afford to run against Senator George," Spalding reported back to Woodruff. By dusk they had reached an accommodation.

Unlike his father, Talmadge took no pleasure in running a government based on stinginess. The younger Talmadge yearned to build roads, hospitals, and schools, and to elevate Georgia's citizens from their lingering poverty. He confided in Spalding that he would be willing to run for governor again, but he wanted to sponsor a sales tax that would give him enough revenue to do a proper job. Talmadge believed that pushing through a major new tax would damage his popularity, and he asked for Spalding's guarantee that Woodruff and his circle would back him when Senator George's seat came open again in 1956, or earlier if George retired or died.

As it happened, a sales tax suited the Coca-Cola Company's purposes ideally. For years, the company had been fending off attempts by the Georgia General Assembly to levy a one-cent soft-drink tax that would have hiked the retail price of a bottle of Coke from its traditional nickel to six cents. A general sales tax, on the other hand, would be imposed only on items that cost more than a dime. Coke would be spared. With the most rudimentary of special interests in mind, Spalding told Talmadge they had a deal. Woodruff and his crowd would promote Talmadge for governor in 1950, and would support his sales tax the next year and work to put him in the Senate in 1956. In a rare public utterance soon afterward, Woodruff praised Talmadge as "the best governor Georgia ever had, sired by the second best."

Talmadge won the 1950 governor's race easily in a rematch with M. E. Thompson, and early the next year he pushed a three-percent sales tax through the Legislature. The resulting flow of new revenues was dramatic — the state budget nearly doubled overnight, from $100 million to $200 million — but the real significance was that Talmadge now had the money to try to put the "equal" in "separate but equal."

In the late summer of 1950, a group of 200 black plaintiffs filed suit in federal court against the Atlanta Board of Education, charging gross racial inequities in the city's public schools. The point, one of them explained, was "the growing belief that the 'separate but equal' theory is a myth." Similar suits were being filed in city after city across the South, part of a strategy pursued by the National Association for the Advancement of Colored People.

Speaking at the lone biracial forum available in Atlanta at the time —
the "Hungry Club" luncheon in the gymnasium of the Butler Street
YMCA — Benjamin Mays, the president of Morehouse College, tried to
allay white fears. The black plaintiffs did not want to force wholesale
integration just for the sake of mixing the races, he said. But it had
become obvious that segregated schools would never be equal. On a
statewide level, Mays estimated that bringing all of Georgia's public
schools up to the "white" standard might cost as much as $100 million,
perhaps more. White politicians, he said, would never agree to spend the
money unless the courts forced them.

Six months later, with the passage of the sales tax, the kind of money
Mays was discussing suddenly became available. Whatever his other limitations, Herman Talmadge had a first-rate mind and a lawyer's training.
Seeing that blatant inequality threatened the survival of segregated facilities, he embarked on the greatest spending binge in state history. He
later calculated that during his six years as governor, from 1949 to 1955,
he spent $452 million on public education — more than all the gover-
nors who had served before him combined. He started construction on a
thousand school buildings, bought a thousand school buses, doubled teachers' salaries, doubled spending on vocational education and extended the
school year to nine months. He raised the salaries of black teachers
almost to the level of whites.

Rather than seeing Talmadge's efforts as too little, too late, Woodruff
and his associates applauded the burst of social spending. The idea that
"separate but equal" could be saved by a last-minute flurry of catch-up
restitution after half a century of neglect did not seem at all outrageous
to them. The notion of widespread desegregation as a remedy simply
hadn't entered their thinking. Confronted with a lawsuit filed by black
players who wanted access to the city's whites-only Bobby Jones Golf
Course, Mayor Hartsfield, a progressive by the standards of the day,
responded by pushing through a $200,000 appropriation to build a sepa-
rate black course instead.

McGill, already under fire from some of his readers for supporting the
hiring of black policemen in Atlanta and for denouncing the Klan and
mob violence, reassured a friend that he would not go so far as supporting President Truman's call for a Fair Employment Practices Commission
that would outlaw job discrimination by race. It was an employer's right,
McGill said, "to hire whom he pleases." To a liberal newspaper friend, he
explained that it would be impossible for the *Constitution* to hire a black

reporter. "He would not have a desk at the office," McGill said. "We are not ready for that."

There is a lasting misconception, fostered in part by McGill himself in later years, that he was held in check by the paper's conservative management when he would have preferred taking a more liberal stance. But the truth is that in the early 1950s, like many other Southern white men of decent heart, McGill was poking along at a measured gait, taking time to become accustomed to ideas he found revolutionary. If anything, McGill stood to the right of his boss, James M. Cox, Sr.

Cox, the publisher of the Dayton *Daily News* and a former governor of Ohio, had been the Democratic nominee for president in 1920, when, with Franklin D. Roosevelt as his running mate, he lost to Warren Harding. Later, looking south, Cox devoted himself to building a media empire. In 1939, he bought the afternoon *Atlanta Journal* and its radio station, WSB (whose call letters, some said, stood for "Welcome South, Brother"). His first item of business, he said at the time, was to hire a top editor to carry the fight against Gene Talmadge. By 1950, when Cox consolidated his monopoly in Atlanta by acquiring the morning *Constitution*, his distaste for the elder Talmadge had been transferred to Herman, and the editorial pages of both papers frequently disparaged the young governor.

For McGill, who liked Talmadge and thought he was doing a good job, the situation proved extremely uncomfortable. Cox accused McGill of "conniving to put over a political deal" by supporting Talmadge, a rebuke that upset the high-strung McGill so much he came down with a painful case of shingles. An ex-Marine with a barrel chest and gravelly voice, McGill often surprised friends by fretting excessively over his job, when it was not actually in jeopardy. In the end it fell to Woodruff to arrange a private party where he talked to Cox and smoothed over his differences with Talmadge, who began to enjoy friendlier coverage. That was how the "power structure" worked.

Yet it was not in Herman Talmadge's nature to forge permanent alliances. Because they had so little personal rapport, Woodruff and Talmadge rarely met face-to-face. When Woodruff wanted to do business, he typically sent Spalding in his place. Only once, perhaps because it was such a small matter, did Woodruff ask a direct favor of Talmadge. The state road that passed through Woodruff's plantation in south Georgia was unpaved and Woodruff, who craved privacy, asked Talmadge to make sure it stayed that way. When he heard the request, Talmadge laughed out loud. "Most folks *want* roads," he said. "I ought to be able to accommodate you pretty easily." But he didn't. A local political crony asked Talmadge to pave the road, and soon Georgia Highway 200 was a two-lane blacktop running through the heart of Ichauway.

It was in 1917 that H. L. Mencken published his acid essay indicting the American South as "the Sahara of the Bozart," a desolate region utterly lacking in culture.

In an area as vast as Europe, Mencken wrote, memorably and mercilessly, "there is not a single picture gallery worth going into, or a single orchestra capable of playing the nine symphonies of Beethoven, or a single opera house, or a single theater devoted to decent plays, or a single public monument worth looking at, or a single worship devoted to making beautiful things."

Despised everywhere in Dixie, Mencken's screed was especially hurtful to Atlantans because he singled out Georgia as the worst Southern state of all, with a landscape bereft of any notable characteristics save "worn-out farms, shoddy cities and paralyzed cerebrums."

Georgians could answer — and repeatedly did — that the War Between the States and the subsequent wretched privations of Reconstruction were the cause of whatever shortcomings they might suffer, but by the midpoint of the 20th century those excuses, however valid, had begun to grow threadbare. Some progress had been made, notably by the Atlanta Symphony, whose growing national reputation was cinched with a live concert broadcast on the NBC radio network. But the Municipal Auditorium continued to be an embarrassment with its meager capacity of 5,000 seats and its strange mix of concerts, trade and auto shows, animal acts, basketball games, conventions and pro "rasslin."

In the way of civic activities, Mayor Hartsfield's Parks and Recreation Department sponsored a kite contest, a tulip festival, a lantern parade, an arts and crafts fair, and a Festival of Nations — nice events all, but hardly what Mencken had in mind. In the spring of 1952, the Kress Foundation, parceling out one of the nation's great art collections, offered to give the city twenty-five Italian Renaissance paintings, but the Atlanta Art Association had to decline the gift because its museum, the High family's decaying old mansion, lacked air-conditioning and wasn't fire-proof.

As members of the arts association bickered over a campaign to raise money for a new building (one accused another of having "the mentality of a four-year-old child"), it seemed inevitable that for Atlanta, as for some individuals, refinement would have to await the attainment of wealth. Without money, the city's cultural ambitions would have no means of flourishing. To this day, critics chide Atlanta for lacking a top-drawer cultural tradition, when the real culprit is a historical lack of families with vast fortunes, guilty consciences, and spare time. Aside from Coca-Cola wealth, which the Candlers and later the Woodruffs funneled mostly into health and education, Atlanta's well-to-do made their money in banking, commerce, and transportation, not in oil, steel, automobiles, or other giant industries, and as a result, the city's elite tended to be millionaires rather than billionaires — modest patrons rather than benefactors.

One of the mistakes Floyd Hunter made in an otherwise brilliant study was to think cities everywhere must be very much like Atlanta, with "power structures" that behaved similarly. He missed the point that Atlanta had missing ingredients. Along with rich families and powerful corporations, it lacked organized crime, powerful unions, immigrant factions, and an active Catholic church, to name some of the things found in the typical municipal stew. Atlanta's political machine consisted of the personal clout of Hartsfield, who operated without a genuine patronage system. The mayor and his businessman friends exercised power largely in a vacuum. Atlanta could be dismissed as a city led by its Chamber of Commerce — "a city of salesmen," in the phrase of one contemporary journalist — but what other source of leadership was there?

In Hartsfield's view, only growth could provide the wealth the city needed to become great. Liberals might disagree, but their voices were faint. Student editors at the Georgia Tech *Engineer* ran an editorial deploring the city's spending on parks, roads, and conventions when it should be cleaning up slums, then recanted under alumni pressure and apologized in the next issue for the "grave injustice" they had done the mayor.

A showman by instinct who yearned to lift the curtain on new attractions, Hartsfield made the most of the opportunities for glory that came along. In 1950, he served as master of ceremonies at the groundbreaking of Buford Dam, a huge federal project on the Chattahoochee River north of Atlanta that eventually created Lake Lanier and guaranteed the city an adequate water supply for decades to come. (When the dam was finished seven years later, Hartsfield watched from his office on the second floor of City Hall as dozens of dignitaries boarded the bus for the hour-long ride to the dedication. After waiting exactly ten minutes, he saun-tered downstairs and conspicuously took the last seat. Being late, he con-fided to an aide, was the way to ensure getting attention.)

In 1951, with Hartsfield leading the charge, voters in Atlanta and its northern suburbs agreed to triple the area of the city to 118 square miles, thereby adding 100,000 citizens, most of them white, to the pop-ulation. Not all of the new Atlantans were thrilled at their status. To sell the plan, Hartsfield promised a wide array of city services to those in the annexed neighborhoods, but some white suburbanites objected to the very idea of coming under the same civic roof with Atlanta's black community. One of Hartsfield's friends reported that he was accosted physically by the retired school teacher who lived next door when he tried to defend the new system. "I asked [her]," he said, "how often her garbage was taken up under the old plan and if she had ever seen a street sweeper before. [My wife] had to pull us apart. Her cry is 'nigger, nigger, nigger.'"

As the mayoral election of 1953 approached, the strain of Harts-field's balancing act between the races began to show. Most black lead-ers had endorsed the annexation plan, even though it diluted their growing political strength, because they believed a wider tax base would benefit them in the long run. And they appreciated the gradual easing of Jim Crow practices that Hartsfield undertook through a pol-icy he called "go slow, go easy, but go." At the mayor's behest, clerks at City Hall began addressing mail to black citizens as "Mr." and "Mrs." instead of using their first names. The signs on the doors of the airport's segregated restrooms were left unpainted until the word "Colored" faded and nearly disappeared.

But to increasing numbers of blacks, the changes seemed not so much gradual as glacial. John Wesley Dobbs, the old Post Office Republican known as "the mayor of Auburn Avenue," broke with Hartsfield over the issue of hiring black firemen and garbage collectors. Hartsfield tried to explain that garbagemen had to work together in teams and firemen had to live and sleep together, side by side, making integration a far more difficult challenge than it had been with the police. The city, he said, simply wasn't ready.

As if to prove him right, flyers began appearing in white, working-class neighborhoods accusing the mayor of plotting to fire white firemen and give blacks their jobs. On the pretext that communists must be plotting against him, Hartsfield assigned a sergeant in the Police Department's vice squad to track down the source of the flyers. The perpetrator, discovered driving along Moreland Avenue in a 1947 Dodge passing out circulars, turned out to be a garden-variety Klansman exercising his rights under the First Amendment, trying to stir up political opposition. After questioning, the police let him go with a warning.

Gearing up for another campaign, Hartsfield anticipated the fight of his career, and he pulled every trick he could think of to keep office. He persuaded his allies in the Legislature to advance the date of the election, ordinarily held in September, so that the balloting would take place before a convention of 6,000 Negro Elks came to town in August. He planned to greet the visitors in person, which might further enflame the segregationists. As an added benefit, the early election, set for May 14, 1953, would allow him to face the voters before they received their annual property tax bills.

Calculating that the black vote would be decisive in the coming campaign, Hartsfield's advisers shaped their politics accordingly. With the blessing of Woodruff and others in the power structure, Hartsfield threw his support behind a black man, Dr. Rufus Clement, the president of Atlanta University, for a seat on the Atlanta Board of Education. When opponents smeared Clement with a charge of "un-American" activities, Hughes Spalding came to his aid with a ringing public defense. As one of the mayor's strategists noted in a confidential memo, the "really bigoted [sic] vote" had long since been lost, "and no concession should be made to it."

As a piece of luck, the only opponent Hartsfield faced in 1953 turned out to be Charlie Brown, repeating his challenge of four years earlier. To his credit, Brown refused the temptation of running a segregationist campaign. Some of Brown's friends sounded out Governor Talmadge about help in unseating Hartsfield, but Talmadge turned them away, saying, "Gentlemen, I would not take part in any such thing. I personally don't like Bill Hartsfield, but he would get my vote if I lived in Atlanta." He praised the city's growth during Hartsfield's tenure.

Once again, the mayor's innate political cunning helped settle the outcome. He and Brown held a first-ever TV debate, broadcast live, and for years afterward, Hartsfield delighted in describing how he waited for the cameraman to close in for a tight solo shot on Brown. Hartsfield leaned over, stepped on Brown's foot and elbowed him sharply in the ribs,

making the poor man appear unhinged to the viewers at home. The final
result, though, was largely a matter of numbers. Blacks gave Hartsfield
more than 95 percent of their ballots, whites about half of theirs, and he
won comfortably by a 7,000-vote margin. Dr. Clement prevailed, too,
thanks to white support, becoming the first black in modern times to
gain a citywide post.

As if to reward the city for a job nicely done, the national media began
paying attention to the signs of biracial progress. *Newsweek* lauded
Atlanta as "a showcase and the nerve center of the New South," a place
with "more hum than drawl." Others, including Carson McCullers in an
article for *Holiday*, pointed out how different Atlanta seemed from the
rest of Georgia, an old point newly made. The Negro Elks arrived as
scheduled and held a parade up Peachtree Street without incident.

In the same month as the election, Delta Air Lines merged with
Chicago and Southern Airlines, becoming the nation's fifth largest carrier, and soon afterward the word "Municipal" — now outgrown — was
dropped from the name of Atlanta Airport. When drought struck the
farms of south Georgia, Atlanta's C&S Bank lent huge sums of money for
irrigation and rounded up used tank cars to send water for the parched
livestock. Mills B. Lane, Jr., the head of the bank, explained that he felt
a "semi-public" responsibility toward the region as a whole.

Ralph McGill reached an important milestone in December 1953
when he concluded that segregation imposed by law had become inde-
fensible and was "finished," a conclusion so stark and dramatic coming
from a Deep South spokesman that it merited an item in *Time*. In many
ways, it seemed, Atlanta was preparing to lead the South into a new era.
Like most observers, McGill anticipated a ruling from the U.S. Supreme
Court attacking the foundations of segregation, but as he confided in a
friend, the one area he hoped the court would avoid was the public
schools. Integrating children, he warned, "would give the fanatics too
much opportunity."

————————

Governor Talmadge was just starting a speech in Lafayette, Georgia, on
May 17, 1954, when an aide came hurrying up and told him an *Atlanta
Journal* reporter was trying to reach him on the phone. "I knew what it
was," he said later. Talmadge borrowed a DC-4, flew the 118 miles back

to Atlanta and in less than an hour stood on the lawn of the Governor's Mansion reading a formal statement.

The Supreme Court's decision in *Brown v. Board of Education*, he said, was an outrage and a recipe for social disaster. The people of Georgia "will not tolerate the mixing of the races in the public schools," he warned, firmly vowing defiance. He did not, as his father might have, raise his voice or launch an angry attack on Negroes. "I get along with colored people fine," he said, "but we don't mix socially, and a judicial decree can't change it."

All across the South, white political leaders reacted to the ruling with anger and dismay. They knew a decision on segregation was coming, but the Warren Court's unanimous vote and sharp, unequivocal language attacking the doctrine of "separate but equal" took them by surprise and left many of them genuinely rattled. As one Georgia historian put it, "The Constitution had not been amended to bring this about; Congress had passed no law requiring it; nor had the President, by following the precedent of Lincoln's Emancipation Proclamation in 1863, decreed it." In the period of uncertainty that followed, Talmadge's calm, adamant demeanor and lawyerly way of talking set him apart and gained him national attention.

Appearing on network television on "Meet the Press," Talmadge denounced *Brown* on constitutional grounds and gave a spirited defense of segregation rooted in his interpretation of Christianity. "The Lord made all of us," the governor intoned, "some white, some black, some red, some yellow. He put the white people in Europe, the black in Africa, the red in the Americas, and the yellow in Asia. If He had wanted one race and one color He would have created them. When He segregated them, it was good enough for me." He left the panel of reporters speechless.

Coming so soon on the heels of the accolades the city of Atlanta had won for its modest advances on race, Talmadge's sudden emergence as a leading advocate for preserving segregation caused widespread consternation. "The fact that Talmadge's 'Retreat, hell!' pronouncements are usually issued from downtown Atlanta — often hailed as the South's most progressive city — bewilders people outside the region and makes them wonder if Georgia and the South are really changing as fast as they have been led to believe," *Harper's* magazine chided. Talmadge took it all in stride. Answering the phone himself at the Governor's Mansion, he would sit in an overstuffed maroon armchair in his den chatting amiably with reporters from around the country, championing segregation. When he got tired of talking, he would ask his wife, Betty, to tell callers he was outside reviewing the Confederate troops.

Some historians, borrowing from the psychology textbooks, have contended that Southerners went into denial after *Brown* was handed down, refusing to accept the inevitability of the collapse of legal segregation. Certainly the region's political leaders, including Talmadge, did their share of posturing about resistance, tossing off old notions of interposition and nullification as if John C. Calhoun were still alive and the Civil War had had a different outcome. But a fairer interpretation may be that people in the South were dazed. The gulf between the slow changes of the previous decade and the idea of swift, complete desegregation, starting with schoolchildren, made it hard for anyone — white or black — to think clearly or know the wisest course. Dr. Clement, the newly elected black member of Atlanta's school board, borrowed Mayor Hartsfield's motto and advocated that all concerned "go slow, go easy."

A genuine puzzlement — one that remains unanswerable to this day — was why white Southerners responded to the idea of desegregation with such revulsion when so many of them dealt on a friendly, often intimate basis with black people in their daily lives. To say simply that racism was at work was to shortchange the rich and wicked history of a relationship built on enslavement, liberation, subordination by force, interdependence — literally on love and hate.

The sexual tension and guilt white men felt toward blacks was at the root of much of the agitation, of course. A brochure of the period called "The Pending Tragedy in the South," distributed by a Presbyterian minister named George Cheek from Selma, Alabama, survives as a remarkable study of one white man's thinking:

> My earnest prayer is that nothing I write here, or hereafter, will offend any of my friends, thanks to God's grace Who has given them to me in the past by the hundreds, nor would I insult my foes or enemies, if I have any, be they white, black, red or yellow. My relationship to the Negro race has been extremely friendly across the span of many years, and my devotion to them has mellowed with the passing years. I have never intentionally injured one of them, and I have been very impatient with those who have regarded them as less than a creation of God, with a soul in God's image. . . .

[But] it is crystal clear that the native and naive longing of the ordinary Negro is to enter the bedroom door of white women. . . . Just wait till one of them, possessing a veneer of civilization, asks you for the hand of your daughter in marriage, or from lurking in a dark corner suddenly seizes your wife or daughter, pulls her into the dark and brutally assaults her. Then you will wake from your lethargy!

It should not have been necessary to point out that when it came to longing and lurking, white men had held the monopoly since the days of slavery. The *New York Times Magazine* estimated that 70 to 90 percent of American blacks had a white ancestor, almost invariably male. When white fathers vowed that black men would not marry their daughters, one black observer answered tartly, "You mean Negroes aren't going to be marrying your *wife's* daughters. We've been marrying *your* daughters for a long time."

Perhaps, as the cliché went, whites' fears of integration sprang from the question, "What if they do to us what we did to them?" Yet, in truth, there were very few instances of black men turning the tables and consorting with white women, either consensually or by force. Answering a critic who accused him of advocating race-mixing, McGill wondered pointedly about "those who . . . seem to be willing to insult the people of the South by insisting that only a law prevents them from rushing into intermarriage with the black race."

The real fear experienced by many whites went beyond sexuality and was far more nebulous. The segregated South gave white people a wide array of advantages, tangible and otherwise, that they enjoyed without wishing to suffer continual pangs of conscience. The central lie many of them told was that they did not believe in white supremacy. In fact, they did, in large part to justify a system that kept blacks subordinated. The most striking thing about the South of the 1950s was the number of intelligent, well-meaning whites who turned a completely blind eye on the deprivations suffered by blacks, and who persuaded themselves that blacks must be content with their second-class status.

No less a humanitarian than Jimmy Carter has admitted that he failed to notice the glaring disparity in the public schools in his native Sumter County until he became president of the school board. "As we began to go around and inspect the school facilities," he said many years later, "the whites were in brick buildings with adequate seats, new school books, buses to take them to school, and it dawned on me, quite belatedly, that the black kids were still walking to school."

That they were walking to school while white children rode by in buses certainly had dawned on the black children. Hosea Williams, who later became a fiery street protester and one of Martin Luther King's lieutenants, grew up in the southwest Georgia countryside, not too far from Sumter County, and recalled ducking along the roadside as white kids sped past in their bus tossing rocks and bottles and spitting at him. It was customary, Williams added, for white tobacco and peanut farmers to enter his school at harvest time and take the black children out to work in the fields.

Depending on their social position, whites had different ways of dealing with blacks, and the central irony was that the higher up the ladder a white person climbed, the easier it became to ignore the cruel underpinnings that held the system of segregation together. A wealthy white matron in one of Atlanta's upscale neighborhoods might have a warm, loving relationship with a black nanny she trusted enough to rear her children. Robert Woodruff had a valet, James Roseberry, and a chauffeur, Lawrence Calhoun, who revered him so deeply that they kept a small savings account for him in case he went broke giving away his fortune to good causes. After more than two centuries, there were members of both races who had learned to play the roles of master and servant with utter perfection, and who knew the elaborate rituals of their relationships as well as actors schooled in Kabuki theater.

It was at the bottom end of the social scale that the mask of gentility slipped off. It was no accident that so many members of the Klan were policemen, sheriffs' deputies, and police court bailiffs and judges. They were the ones charged with the responsibility of enforcing the positions of the two races. Lonnie King, one of the plaintiffs in Atlanta's school desegregation suit, described walking home from school one afternoon when he was 12, cutting through property owned by a truck dealer. A white watchman spotted him and let loose a guard dog that snarled at him and snagged his pants leg. When King kicked at the dog, the overseer "punched me and smashed me down like I was a piece of dirt, and just beat me." That night King went back and broke every window in the building.

No one could predict what might happen, what forces might be let loose, if segregation came to an end. The greatest fear, as always, was of the unknown. Woodruff and one of his closest associates, John Sibley, the chairman of Trust Company of Georgia and a former general counsel of Coca-Cola, talked at length about the prospects of the *Brown* decision and concluded that the races should live separately, as a matter of "natural" segregation.

Forcing black and white children together in school struck Sibley as a terrible risk, with unforeseeable consequences. "If a close contact between the children accentuates racial differences," he wrote Georgia's senior congressman, Carl Vinson, "then we kindle the fires of dislike and hatred and place a burden on the police power of the state to keep order that it cannot adequately carry." But a peaceful outcome scared Sibley even more: "If by throwing the races together, racial differences are eliminated and the boys and girls fall in love with each other, the result will be a mongrel race of lower ideals, lower standards and lower traditions. . . ."

A few months after the court's decision, McGill boarded a private railroad car in Atlanta for an off-the-record luncheon with Talmadge. Though he did not name the nine other men present, it is probable that Woodruff, Sibley, and Hughes Spalding were among them. The Atlanta power structure wanted to pick the governor's brain about the future. "The path we are going to have to travel has been laid down for us," Talmadge told the group. "My position will be to delay as long as possible." McGill recorded no expressions of dissent.

One theory of history holds that if President Eisenhower had given quick, enthusiastic endorsement to the court's *Brown* decision, and had Southern governors and congressmen led their constituents to recognize that desegregation was now the "law of the land" and as such inescapable, there might have been widespread, albeit sullen acceptance. In Little Rock, for instance, the local school board met just five days after the ruling and issued a statement saying it intended to comply. Perhaps others would have followed suit.

But it seems likelier that any attempt to impose swift, sweeping desegregation would have triggered violence, or at least the wholesale abandonment by whites of the South's public schools and other institutions. A *Newsweek* correspondent traveling around the South in the autumn of 1954 found most of the seasonal rituals unchanged, with men in a "football-watching, deer-hunting, car-buying mood," and many rural whites convinced they would somehow escape the court's reach. In cities like Atlanta, though, he found poor whites "greasing their guns."

Whatever might have been, the justices of the Supreme Court them-

selves clearly appreciated the threat of disorder and issued their own version of a "go slow, go easy" policy, amending *Brown* with a subsequent ruling in 1955 that called for "all deliberate speed" — a deliberately vague
oxymoron — as the timetable for compliance. As a measure of the confusion sowed by the court, it is noteworthy that the NAACP said it was
"gratified" by the ruling, even though others saw it as the excuse for delay
it proved to be. The *Atlanta Constitution* called the cooling-off period "a
relief," and McGill wrote personally to Chief Justice Earl Warren con-
gratulating him.

Given an indefinite reprieve, the South's leaders might have devoted
their attention to working out practical solutions to the challenge of dis-
mantling the framework of their segregated society. Instead they chose up
sides for a fight.

CHAPTER 4

BATTLE FLAG

In downtown Atlanta, the gold-domed state Capitol and neo-gothic City Hall sit a block apart, facing adjacent sides of a leafy central square. During the second half of the 1950s, they might as well have been on different planets.

The governor's race of 1954 was captured by Marvin Griffin, a man of prodigious charm and wit and also one of the most corrupt public officials ever to hold office in Georgia. His platform — "I take my stand with the white people" — swept him past nine opponents to easy victory with the blessing of the incumbent, Herman Talmadge.

Griffin hailed from the tiny city of Bainbridge, in the far southwest corner of Georgia, where gospel music spanned the radio dial and live oaks with beards of Spanish moss shaded the roadsides from the hot sun. He published a weekly newspaper, the *Post-Searchlight*, from a cluttered office whose back wall was covered by a large picture of an astonished-looking Grant surrendering to Lee at Appomattox. "It could've been," Griffin would tell visitors wistfully.

To understand Griffin, to begin trying to reconcile his personal warmth with the virulent strain of racism he espoused, it helped to know the story of the relationship he and his brother enjoyed with Hosea Williams, the black activist who came from the nearby community of Attapulgus. Williams had served with distinction in the Army during World War II, suffering wounds at the hands of the German infantry. After recuperating in a military hospital, he went home and graduated from high school at the age of 21. Williams was elected president of the black American Legion post in Bainbridge at the same time R. A.

"Cheney" Griffin, Marvin's brother, became president of the corresponding white post. They grew friendly.

As things happened in those days, Williams went to work as the headwaiter at a private club in Bainbridge, where he often found himself serving at Cheney Griffin's parties. A naturally ebullient sort like his brother, Griffin would invite friends to join him for dinner on the weekends, and the affairs usually involved many courses and several bottles of liquor. Griffin enjoyed playing host and at the end of the meal would call grandly to Williams, "Boy! Bring me the bill!" White napkin folded neatly over his arm, Williams would approach with the check, get within two or three feet of Griffin and then veer off suddenly. "No, suh!" he would announce. "You been pickin' up too many of these lately!" Then he would hand the check to one of Griffin's unsuspecting guests.

Many years later, long after he had marched side by side with Martin Luther King, Jr., and made a name for himself as a fearless civil rights leader, Williams still delighted in recounting the story. He and the Griffin brothers had become friends, and the Griffins helped put him through college, where he earned a degree in chemistry and later landed a job with the U. S. Department of Agriculture.

The point, of course, was that the men shared a sense of humor. As governor, Marvin Griffin did vigorous battle against the cause of desegregation and had a wonderful time of it, enjoying himself thoroughly. Williams and other black leaders saw him for what he was, a fierce political foe who would fight them without hating them personally.

One of Griffin's quirks was his habit of being candid about his vices. "I plan to fire hell out of my enemies and take care of my friends," he announced upon taking office, and he made good on his word. He appointed his brother chief of staff, and together they combed the state's books, trying to learn the secrets of the Capitol. In one celebrated episode, they discovered that the state owned a small office building near the airport, where a dozen secretaries were on the payroll with no apparent duties. The Griffins decided to fire the women, just to see what would happen. Cheney hid behind a column outside the governor's office and watched as a succession of state senators came racing down the marble staircase to complain about the sacking of their mistresses. The women were quickly rehired, and the Griffins could count twelve key legislative votes in their pocket.

Governor Griffin did not devote much time to the issue of race in the early days of his administration, in part because it hardly seemed necessary. In November 1954, Georgia voters agreed in a statewide referendum to turn the public schools private rather than submit to desegregation. And in February 1955, with Griffin's approval, the Legislature made it a crime — a felony punishable by two years in prison — for any state or local official in Georgia to spend tax money on an integrated school. The debate appeared to be closed, at least for the time being.

The governor occupied himself arranging state contracts for his cronies. The chairman of the highway board sold the state car pool $33,000 worth of "gas savers" that didn't work because they turned out to be shut-off valves for motor boats. Another official, who was not in the paint business, bought center-line paint for $2 a gallon at retail and resold it to the state at $4 a gallon. With a nice sense of symmetry, the administration bought boats that wouldn't float and shipped them to lakes that had gone dry. "Never in Georgia history had so many stolen so much," the *Reader's Digest* reported later, when the excesses came to light. Griffin personally visited Cuba and went into business with Fulgencio Batista's brother running rum and cigars to Florida.

When the press exposed his various schemes, Griffin grew exasperated. He nicknamed investigative reporters "jorees," explaining that these were small birds that lived near stables and lived off horse droppings. Some observers thought he turned up the volume on his segregation speeches whenever he needed a convenient distraction from the scandals.

Toward the end of Griffin's first year in office, on November 7, 1955, the U. S. Supreme Court tipped over another set of dominoes and outlawed segregation in public parks, playgrounds, and golf courses. The governor announced the next day that the state would stop operating its parks rather than comply. But as he was soon to discover, absolute defiance in racial matters did not automatically earn popular support with white voters.

In early December 1955, Georgia Tech was practicing for the upcoming Sugar Bowl when word got out that the opposing team, the University of Pittsburgh, had a black player on its roster. The governor ordered Tech to boycott the game, which caused him to learn an important lesson about college football in the South. Tech's Yellow Jackets, then in their glory years, had no intention of missing the prestigious Sugar Bowl, the annual New Year's Day game in New Orleans, just because Pitt had a lone black on the team — a reserve running back at that. Tech students took to the streets of Atlanta in two days of raucous protest, burning

Griffin in effigy on the Capitol grounds at one point, and the alumni applied political pressure on the Board of Regents, whose members voted 14-1 to allow Tech to play. Griffin had to back down.

In the same month, Atlanta Mayor Bill Hartsfield came to a turning point that set him at odds with the governor. The Supreme Court's ruling on public golf courses arose from an Atlanta lawsuit and thus applied directly to the city. It could not easily be defied, and Hartsfield gave close thought to the wisest response. As long as segregation was legal, he tended to favor it: When A. T. Walden and other black leaders pushed to desegregate the downtown library in the summer of 1955, the library board, with the mayor's blessing, voted instead to acquire a bookmobile and send it around to Atlanta's black neighborhoods. Such were the final throes of "separate but equal." After the court's ruling on public facilities, however, Hartsfield could see no way to continue enforcing segregation in those places without putting himself and the city's employees in serious legal jeopardy.

Hartsfield decided to obey the court, and as always he displayed an enviable sense of cunning. The way the mayor saw it, the idea of shutting down the city's golf courses was foolish, because only a tiny handful of black players had any design on using them. If he could arrange the token desegregation of the courses without triggering a violent protest, he figured the controversy would die out quickly. So he devised a strategy based on stealth.

First, Hartsfield arranged to meet privately with the hundred-plus employees, all white, who worked at the city's courses. He asked them if their belief in segregation extended to sacrificing their jobs, which they would lose if the courses were closed. Seeing his point, they agreed to accommodate the occasional black foursome that might turn up. Next, the mayor talked with the group of black golfers who intended to test the court's ruling.

The black men wanted to play at the city's premier public course, named for Bobby Jones, the celebrated native son who won golf's Grand Slam in 1930. Thinking the Jones course would be too visible a target for protest by angry whites, the mayor concocted a diversion. He notified the newspapers and television stations that the city planned to desegregate the course on December 22, 1955, three days before Christmas. Then he asked the black golfers to show up at a different course, North Fulton, on the morning in question.

"They told me they had promised the television people they would appear," Hartsfield recounted later. "I said, 'Those TV boys aren't interested in watching you hit the ball — they want to get pictures of you getting beat up!'" The black golfers, Dr. H. M. Holmes and his sons and some friends, reluctantly acquiesced.

Before dawn on the 22nd, Hartsfield sent a maintenance crew out to the Jones course, where they removed several racial epithets that had been scrawled on the pavilions and benches in yellow paint during the night. When the TV camera crews and newspaper photographers arrived, they found nothing to cover — no vandalism, no black golfers, no white protesters. Several miles away, meanwhile, the North Fulton course was peacefully desgregated that morning. In the afternoon, Dr. Holmes and his group arrived unannounced at the Jones course and played a round without incident.

It was only several days later, after Christmas, that Hartsfield disclosed to the press what had happened. Angry editors at the *North Side News*, a weekly that catered to white neighborhoods, labeled the mayor's stratagem a "Pearl Harbor attack." Governor Griffin was furious, telling reporters that if the decision on Atlanta's golf courses had been up to him, "I'd have plowed them up the next morning and planted alfalfa." The state's attorney general, Eugene Cook, who often complained that the goal of the Supreme Court was "intermarriage" of the races (and who seemed to believe what he said), denounced Hartsfield as well. Yet they could not undo his actions.

Atlanta's boardroom oligarchs gave Hartsfield their full backing. As the *Atlanta Journal* argued in an editorial, the court's attempt to end segregation might be a "fundamental error," but it nonetheless stood as the law of the land. No one played a more significant role than Coca-Cola's Robert Woodruff. So far as is known, the only black people Woodruff ever met personally were his own servants and the sharecroppers on his plantation, and the only blacks he ever saw on a golf course were caddies. He never once talked with A. T. Walden, William Holmes Borders, "Daddy" King, John Wesley Dobbs, or any other black leader. In every sense of the term, he was an old-fashioned Southerner. But the Coca-Cola Company simply could not afford to be associated with die-hard segregation — not with 15 million black Americans and millions more people of color around the globe as potential customers. Woodruff let it be known that he supported the mayor's position.

The nature of the civil rights movement began to change in fundamental ways, driving the city and state apart. Under pressure, Atlanta showed it would make concessions. But in the countryside, it seemed, whites could resist desegregation with impunity. The Klan was relatively quiet during the mid-1950s, for the most part because white people felt no need to conceal their activities. White Citizens Councils and States' Rights Councils sprang up in almost every Georgia county, with leading citizens as their top officers and massive resistance to integration as their openly stated mission.

The Georgia General Assembly, overloaded with rural members because of the county-unit system, approved a package of doomsday laws meant to preserve segregated schools at all costs. Governor Griffin, Attorney General Cook, and other state officials began traveling to other parts of the South urging defiance of the Supreme Court, promising that Georgia would lead the way.

It is a matter of some irony that four decades later, the keenest focus has fallen on one of the minor footnotes of that period. In February 1956, the Legislature adopted a new design for the state flag, incorporating the "rebel" cross of the Confederate battle flag. Understandably, a great many black Georgians (and others) have grown to detest the flag, with its X-shaped Saint Andrew's cross of blue stripes and white stars on a red field, seeing it as a symbol of unapologetic contempt for civil rights.

In the years since then, the instigators of the change have insisted, sometimes under oath, that their motivation was not to signal defiance of the Supreme Court or to create a banner for massive resistance, but rather to honor the Confederacy on the eve of the Civil War centennial. They have come to see protests against the flag as an assault on their heritage.

As it happens, neither side is entirely right. Interviews and research undertaken for this book disclose that *both* sides of the great flag debate have been mistaken about the circumstances of the change of design, and thus have overlooked a possible resolution of their differences. Because the symbolism of the Civil War remains intensely potent to this day — and because the state flag continues to spur violent argument — it seems worthwhile to examine the actual background of the matter.

Until 1956, Georgia flew a state flag modeled on the "Stars and Bars," commonly considered the first flag of the Confederacy. When leaders of the seceding Southern states met in Montgomery, Alabama, in February 1861 to form a Confederate government, one of their immediate tasks was to adopt a new national flag. A dispute broke out between proponents of a distinctive design that would signal complete separation from the Union, and others who believed that the South was just as "American" as the North, with an equal claim on the American flag, the Stars and Stripes. Alexander Stephens, the widely respected Georgian who served as vice president of the Confederacy, belonged to the latter group and argued successfully for a design that resembled Old Glory.

Accordingly, on March 4, 1861, at the precise hour President Lincoln was being inaugurated in Washington, the Stars and Bars was raised over the capitol building in Montgomery. It had white stars on a blue field beside horizontal bars of red and white. The problem with the new

flag, as General Beauregard and others soon discovered in the smoky haze of battle, was that it looked *too* much like the Stars and Stripes, threatening deadly confusion among troops in the field. In its place, the Confederate generals devised a special battle flag, using the Saint Andrew's cross, for use in combat.

Stars and Bars, 1861

Confederate Battle Flag

After flying in the field throughout the four years of a civil conflict that took 600,000 American lives, the battle flag was retired, revered in the South and ignored, for the most part, in the North. Its revival as a political emblem began many years later, in 1948, when the "Dixiecrats" broke from the regular Democratic Party and ran Strom Thurmond for president. Afterward, the battle flag gained widespread popularity across the South and eventually turned into a craze, appearing on neckties and bumper stickers, flying from car antennas, even forming the pattern for beach blankets. As symbols go, it conveyed approximately the same sentiment as the phrase, "Fergit, hell!" and bespoke equal parts pride and prejudice. Only later was it misappropriated by the Klan and other hate groups as a different kind of symbol.

Had they been consulted in the mid-'50s, black Georgians might have found scant significance in the distinction between the Stars and Bars and the battle flag, neither having much intrinsic appeal for them. But at the time, the sensibilities of black Georgians mattered not a bit to the state's political leaders. The argument was among white Georgians over the propriety of tampering with their heritage.

The man who designed the new flag, John Sammons Bell, the chairman of the state Democratic party, was a proud descendant of Confederate warriors and a true believer in the sanctity of the blood they had shed. He could speak movingly, and often did, of the sacrifices his family endured during Reconstruction. But by his own admission, he knew very little about the history and symbolism of the confederate flag. Since boyhood, Bell had admired the battle pennant, and in the fall of 1955, he used it in designing the prototype of a new state flag. He considered the existing flag "meaningless," he conceded later, having no idea it was based on the Stars and Bars. Bell showed his creation to friends and gained an enthusiastic response. Cheney Griffin, the governor's brother, made a large reproduction and hung it on the wall over his desk at the Capitol.

When the General Assembly convened for its 1956 session, Bell persuaded two state senators (one of them the aptly named Jefferson Lee Davis) to introduce legislation adopting his new flag. Their stated goal was to honor the memory of their ancestors on the eve of the Civil War centennial by embracing a new design that looked more obviously "Confederate."

But Mrs. Forrest Kibler of the United Daughters of the Confederacy promptly weighed in with an objection. No individual state, in her view, had the right to appropriate a sacred emblem of the Lost Cause for use in a contemporary flag. Other patriotic groups expressed similar concerns. After swift passage in the Georgia Senate, the bill ran into trouble in the state House. Siding with the UDC, several of the lower chamber's most ardent segregationists announced opposition to the bill.

The debate then turned to the question of esthetics. The editors of the *Atlanta Constitution* complained that the old state flag appeared "very much run of the mill," but warned that the new one "may be a little overdone." Groping for safe artistic ground, the newspaper concluded, "Perhaps the subject should be studied by a committee of experts."

There were other problems. The new flag had to be described in words, since the Legislature could not legally enact a drawing, and Bell pored through old descriptions of Confederate flags until he found the proper heraldic names for the various components. Unfortunately, it turned out that the five-pointed stars in the cross were known technically as "mullets." When the bill was read aloud by the House clerk, several startled members had to be reassured that the new flag did not have fish on it.

On a more serious note, Bell's search for a legal description of his new flag led him to make a mistake of great symbolic importance. Contrary to widespread belief, the Stars and Bars was never formally adopted by the Confederate congress. Even though it flew for years over Southern courthouses and capitols, it was never the "official" flag of the Confederacy. Neither was the battle flag, whose use was military. The first *legal* flag of the Confederacy was a pure white pennant, twice as long as wide, with a Saint Andrew's cross in the upper lefthand corner. This strange design, known as the "Stainless Banner," was approved by the Confederate congress on May 1, 1863. It proved to have serious shortcomings. Because of its unusual length, it tended to droop, even in a brisk wind, and its color made it appear to be a flag of surrender. It got dirty easily. One critic said it looked like a tablecloth. Its first public display was at the funeral of General Stonewall Jackson, where it draped the coffin, an ominous sign. Little used, it was quickly forgotten.

By modern standards, the greatest flaw of the "Stainless Banner" was its other popular nickname, bestowed by William T. Thompson, editor of the *Savannah Daily Morning News,* who called it "the White Man's Flag" and argued that it represented "the cause of a superior race and a higher civilization contending against ignorance, infidelity and barbarism" — a bit of racist rhetoric that is plainly unacceptable in current public discourse. "As a people," Thompson wrote, freighting the historical record with a smoking gun, "we are fighting to maintain the Heaven-ordained supremacy of the white man over the inferior or colored race. A white flag would thus be emblematical [*sic*] of our cause."

As it happened, the wording that Bell found for the legal description of his new state flag came directly from the act of the Confederate congress adopting the Stainless Banner. Thus, though he was entirely ignorant of its burdensome legacy, Bell managed to invest the new state flag with elements and echoes that were dismaying to all Georgians, black and white alike.

Today, many people believe the Georgia General Assembly of 1956 took up the new flag as a gesture of defiance aimed at the U.S. Supreme Court and the cause of integration. At the time, however, those questions, along with the issues of heritage and Confederate history, took a back seat to concern about corruption. In light of the ethics of the governor and his crowd, many members of the Legislature wondered who stood to profit if the old state flag had to be replaced in every schoolroom and courtroom in Georgia. Charles Pou, the *Atlanta Journal's* political editor, wrote a story speculating that change might be costly, since there were nearly 3,000 public schools in the state. Bell was sitting in the balcony of the House gallery watching when the bill came to the floor for debate, and he was deeply offended when a member asked pointedly if he held a copyright on the new design. He did not.

In lobbying for adoption of the new flag, Bell eventually admitted the political purpose he had in mind. The Democratic national convention was scheduled for the summer of 1956, and party rules forbade the use of protest signs on the floor. The only way to get the rebel cross in front of the TV cameras was to make it part of the state flag, which had to be allowed in the hall.

Thus prodded, the House passed the flag bill, but only by the slimmest of margins. At a time when bills and resolutions that openly defied the federal government were regularly approved with only one or two dissenting votes, the flag bill attracted 32 "nays" and 66 abstentions, passing with only four votes to spare. Soon afterward, the leaders of the Democratic Party held a ceremony and presented the new flag to their Republican counterparts to take to the GOP convention in San Francisco.

Many years later, Bell maintained that honoring the Confederacy was his only purpose in changing the flag. He had gone on to enjoy a distinguished career on the bench, rising to become chief judge of the Georgia Court of Appeals, and, like many Southerners, he eventually conceded that he had been wrong about segregation. He did not wish to be remembered as a racist, which was fair enough. But he and his flag had been part and parcel of the times. As one of the flag bill's supporters put it during floor debate in the House, "This will show that we in Georgia intend to uphold what we stood for, will stand for, and will fight for."

There was, that is, more than a whiff of defiance in the air — enough to give opponents of the flag a strong debating point. Forty years later, changing the flag seems a prudent course of action. For white Georgians proud of their ancestry (and fearful that all traces of the Confederacy will someday be eradicated from the landscape), the acceptable solution might be to restore the pre-1956 flag, the one that expressed the philosophy of Alexander Stephens, who saw himself as a patriotic American as well as a rebel. For black Georgians, removing the Saint Andrew's cross ought to suffice as a symbol that the battle is over — and won.

Atlanta in 1940, on the verge of momentous change.

The congressional campaign of liberal Helen Mankin (*left*) inspired thousands of black Atlantans (*below*) to register to vote in 1946.

2

3

4

5

Above: Black gains triggered a revival of the Ku Klux Klan in Georgia, led in the 1940s by Grand Dragon Dr. Samuel Green (center).

Left: Despite their wholesome appearance, the Columbians were even more violent than the Klan. The young man in the tie wears a medal he won in 1946 for flogging a black man.

Firebrand Gene Talmadge (*right*) won a fourth term as governor of Georgia in 1946 by race-baiting. The nation was horrified when two black couples (*below*) were lynched in Walton County just after the election.

6

7

Left: Witness Loy Harrison describes the scene of the lynching to Sheriff J. M. Bond (*holding rope*) of Oconee County. Note the blood stain in the foreground.

Below: When Gene Talmadge died before taking office, his son Herman (*left*) tried to take his place as governor. On the night of January 14, 1947, Herman's mother (*center*), wife (*right*), and sister (*far right*) confronted outgoing Governor Ellis Arnall (*lower right*), triggering Georgia's notorious "two governors" controversy.

8

9

10

Above: Atlanta airport in the barnstorming 1920s.

Facing: Mayor William Hartsfield loathed the novel *Gone With the Wind* for giving a false portrait of the South. But he exploited the excitement of the movie's premiere in Atlanta in 1939 by welcoming star Vivien Leigh and orchestrating the program on opening night at Loew's Grand Theater.

New arrivals were welcomed in Atlanta's white neighborhoods (*above*).

But Atlanta's swelling black population faced a desperate need for new housing to replace over-crowded slums (*below*).

Black Atlantans, demonstrating here in front of City Hall, wanted the city to hire black police.

In 1948, the first eight officers were sworn in. *Seated, left to right*: Henry H. Hooks, Claude Dixon, Jr., Ernest H. Lyons. *Standing, left to right*: Robert McKibbens, Willard W. Strickland, Willie T. Elkins, Johnnie P. Jones, John Landers, Jr.

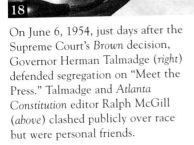

On June 6, 1954, just days after the
Supreme Court's *Brown* decision,
Governor Herman Talmadge (*right*)
defended segregation on "Meet the
Press." Talmadge and *Atlanta
Constitution* editor Ralph McGill
(*above*) clashed publicly over race
but were personal friends.

Though he was a virulent racist, Georgia Governor Marvin Griffin (*above, left*) had a keen sense of humor. But he was not amused when Georgia Tech students (*above, right*) hanged him in effigy in 1955 for trying to keep their football team out of the Sugar Bowl, where opponent Pitt had a black player on the roster.

Nor did Griffin approve when the Reverend William Holmes Borders (*right*) was quickly and quietly bailed out of jail after challenging segregated seating on city buses.

22

By the mid-1950s, Atlanta's streets were jammed with traffic. And its glowing reputation as "the nerve center of the New South" was proclaimed by *Newsweek* magazine.

Facing: Bill Hartsfield, Atlanta's "airminded" mayor, often christened flights with a big bottle of Coca-Cola, showing his loyalty to the city's premier corporation.

24

Right: Governor Ernest Vandiver won office in 1958 vowing that "no, not one" black child would integrate Georgia's public schools.

Below: Many whites expected him to keep the promise.

25

27

26

Hearings chaired by elder statesman John Sibley (*above, right*), here holding a child while his mother testifies, helped persuade Georgians to keep the public schools open. So did revulsion at the bombing of an Atlanta elementary school (*above*), and protests over the ham-fisted treatment of Martin Luther King, Jr., (*right*) after a sit-in arrest at Rich's department store.

28

29

Above: Charlayne Hunter (*inside car, left*) and Hamilton Holmes integrated the University of Georgia in 1961, setting the stage for peaceful desegregation of Atlanta's Murphy High School (*below*) later in the year.

30

Any doubt that the vast majority of white Southerners remained adamantly opposed to desegregation was swept away in the elections of 1956, when hard-line candidates won governorships and congressional seats all across the South.

Completing the deal he'd struck six years earlier, Herman Talmadge pushed the genteel Walter George into retirement and ran successfully for his U. S. Senate seat. Georgia sent a high-profile, vocal segregationist to Washington to replace a bashful one.

But in Atlanta, things were different. Some of the city's biggest companies were experimenting with integrated work forces and finding a productive fit. The giant Lockheed plant had all-black crews working alongside all-white crews, and the executives of Scripto, the pen and pencil manufacturer, made a point of hiring black women for their assembly line. Eighty of Atlanta's most prominent white ministers issued a "manifesto" calling for racial tolerance.

Atlanta's wealth set it apart from the rest of the South. Workers in the metropolitan area shared in the national economic boom. Mechanics, carpenters and telephone linemen could afford to buy sport boats. Trolley riders were overheard discussing the stock market. In Montgomery, Alabama, Martin Luther King, Jr., had just shown with a successful bus boycott that in the cities of the South, black dollars could be withheld from white enterprises with real impact. Mayor Hartsfield did not want King proving the same point in Atlanta, his hometown.

"We're too busy to hate," Hartsfield told an audience at a National Toastmasters Club meeting, giving birth to the city's slogan. In a single year, the mayor's beloved airport doubled the number of passengers it handled, from one million to two million. New interstate highways opened and attracted more traffic in 1956 than had been projected for 1970. Plans for a perimeter highway, I-285, were unveiled. A giant new public hospital, Grady Memorial, went up, along with the city's first new skyscraper in a quarter-century, the 25-story Fulton National Bank building. Parking lot space grew by 72 percent in a year and a half.

The convention business blossomed. Ten thousand Jaycees gathered, firing off pistols, dropping dummies out of their hotel windows, and generally having "a helluva time," by one account. Air-conditioning became commonplace in offices and hotel rooms. The population of the metropolitan area surged toward the million mark, as newcomers — two of every five of them from outside the South — continued to arrive in droves. An ambitious civic leader, architect Cecil Alexander, proposed holding a World's Fair in Atlanta.

Given the climate of progressive boosterism enveloping the city, Governor Griffin's affinity for out-of-state travel was not surprising. On the second anniversary of the *Brown* decision, he gave a stirring speech on massive resistance to a White Citizens Council meeting — in New Orleans. The governor's brand of politics was unwelcome in Atlanta because racial disarray represented the one real threat to continued prosperity. The question was how to keep him away.

On January 9, 1957, shortly after the success of the Montgomery bus boycott, William Holmes Borders announced on the front page of the *Atlanta Daily World* that he and other black ministers intended to challenge the law that required segregated seating on the city's buses. Seeing the article, Hartsfield exploded in anger, complaining that Borders had not seen fit to warn him of his plans or discuss strategy. Civil disobedience and mass arrests would smudge Atlanta's image, Hartsfield feared, and might give the governor an opening to crack down in the city.

Understandably, the Reverend Borders no longer felt it his duty to obtain the mayor's permission to challenge a system that relegated his people to the back of the bus. If he and other respected Negro ministers were handcuffed and shoved into a paddy wagon, Borders figured the news — and especially the pictures — would bring segregated seating to a swift end.

Hartsfield wasn't so sure. The Atlanta Transit Company's bus drivers had the authority to arrest blacks who refused to obey the seating law. But when Borders and his group made their first attempt to provoke an incident, by boarding a bus in downtown Atlanta and sitting in the white section, the driver merely got out, pulled down the electric trolley wires and pretended the bus was disabled. He sent for a second bus, which picked up the white riders. Then, with his bus segregated anew, he reattached the wires, scrolled up a "Special" sign, and finished his route. No one was arrested.

When they got word of the episode, Griffin and Attorney General Cook vowed to call out the National Guard to ride the city's buses and make arrests. The charge, they added, would be disturbing the peace. Since the Supreme Court had overturned Alabama's segregated busing laws, a test-case in Georgia would almost certainly yield the same result. But if the riders were accused of criminal misconduct, the federal courts would have no jurisdiction and no opportunity to rule on the constitutionality of the seating law. The ministers might find themselves stuck in jail for a long time.

The state's adjutant general, George J. Hearn, paid a visit to see Atlanta Police Chief Herbert Jenkins. "Chief," Hearn asked, "if I have to take over those buses, can I count on you to help me?"

"General," Jenkins replied, "that depends on whose side you're on. I'll be on the side of the federal courts."

With a showdown brewing, Hartsfield arranged another of his artful solutions. He agreed to have the Reverend Borders and his colleagues arrested, as they wished, on charges they could appeal in the federal courts. Then he sent a black detective to take them into custody. They were booked, bonded, and out of jail in two hours flat. The door of the detention room was never locked. No one bothered to notify the governor.

Hartsfield had prevailed again. His reward came quickly, with victory in the 1957 mayoral primary over a weak opponent, a white moderate named Archie Lindsey. Hartsfield deflected questions about his age, 67, by likening himself to President Eisenhower, and survived the puzzlement of voters baffled by his adamant refusal to allow fluoride in the city's water supply. (Like many other staunch anti-communists of the day, Hartsfield believed fluoridation was a plot to poison red-blooded Americans.)

Hartsfield's biggest scare came when an intrepid *Atlanta Constitution* reporter, Jack Nelson, exposed the cozy relations between the Atlanta Police Department and the city's most notorious lottery kingpin, Horace Ingram. Nelson spent weeks holed up next door to Ingram's Garage, spying on the gambling activities inside, and helped set up a raid that uncovered a $2 million-a-year numbers racket. Three Atlanta policemen were charged with accepting bribes. But the scandal died down quickly. Years later, after becoming Washington bureau chief of the *Los Angeles Times*, Nelson still complained about the lack of support he got from Ralph McGill, his editor, who pooh-poohed the affair in his column. The power structure was happy to wink at the lottery because its great popularity in the black community meant votes for Hartsfield.

While fluoride and the "bug" were the main topics of open debate, race became the great unspoken issue of the campaign. After years of tolerating Hartsfield's mild concessions to the black community, many white voters had grown alarmed at the quickening pace of change. Large numbers of them defected to Hartsfield's opponent, Lindsey, even though Lindsey refused to pander to them. Hartsfield won by nearly 4,000 votes, but when the numbers were analyzed the degree of erosion in his white support became evident. Of his final tally of 37,612 votes, Hartsfield got fully half from the black community. Without the support of black voters, the mayor would not merely have lost, he would have been routed.

The fragility of the bond between the white power structure and the black leadership was exposed three weeks after the primary, in a runoff election for one of the seats on the Board of Aldermen. Hoping to duplicate their success of four years earlier, when they put a black on the school board, the business leaders had recruited a candidate to break the color line as an alderman.

Their choice seemed ideal. T. M. (for Theodore Martin) Alexander had grown up in Alabama as an enterprising youngster who made money selling fruit and vegetables from his family's garden and running a sidewalk candy and soft drink stand. He kept his profits in a baking powder can before opening his first bank account at age 14. After moving to Atlanta in 1931, Alexander waited on tables at a private, whites-only club on weekends and sold insurance policies to black clients during the week. By the late 1950s, his insurance agency was prospering. He earned a spot in civil rights history by arranging for Lloyd's of London to provide liability coverage during Dr. King's Montgomery bus boycott.

"Atlanta Negroes want to see signs of progress," Alexander told a reporter, "but we are not trying to ram it down the white man's throat. The beauty of Atlanta is that there is a liaison between the Negro and the better class of the white community." Such sentiments earned Alexander the backing of Woodruff's crowd, but not enough white votes to win an outright majority in the primary. Alexander had to face a white barber, Jack Summers, in a runoff, and Governor Griffin seized the opportunity to inflict a lesson on the "Big Mules," as he called Atlanta's businessmen. Griffin jumped into the campaign, openly urging Atlanta's white voters to support the white candidate, and took immense satisfaction when Alexander was beaten.

For the first time in his two and a half years in the governor's chair, Griffin had flexed his political muscle inside the city of Atlanta. There was no telling what he might try next.

On August 20, 1957, a deeply worried Orval Faubus placed a phone call to Georgia. Marvin Griffin was due in Little Rock in two days to speak at a Capital Citizens Council dinner. The audience would be made up of ardent segregationists, and Faubus feared Griffin might whip them into violence. He asked Griffin not to come.

For three years, moderates in Little Rock had been preparing for the desegregation of their public schools. As a border state, Arkansas had not experienced the same widespread mood of defiance that gripped Georgia and the rest of the Deep South. The Little Rock school board had voted to comply with the *Brown* decision and was ready with a plan to integrate Central High School.

As the opening of the school year approached, opponents of desegregation worked belatedly to get organized. They scheduled a $10-a-plate dinner to raise funds and invited Griffin and Roy Harris, the former speaker of the Georgia House, to give speeches. As a founder of the States' Rights Council of Georgia and publisher of the *Augusta Courier*, a belligerent weekly broadsheet that trumpeted its pro-segregation headlines in bright red ink, Harris was one of the best-known white supremacists in the South, a propagandist who skirted close to the views of the Ku Klux Klan.

Faubus, the governor of Arkansas, was trying to straddle the fence. Facing re-election in 1958, he had no wish to identify too closely with either side. The idea of Griffin and Harris coming to town, ratcheting up the tensions, filled him with apprehension. He phoned Griffin, who reassured him that no one would be encouraging trouble. "Naw," Griffin said. "I'm gonna give 'em hell on the Constitution, and Roy's gonna give 'em hell on the civil rights thing. But nobody'll advocate violence." In that case, Faubus said, Griffin and Harris would be welcome. For reasons he never fully explained, out of courtesy perhaps, or in hopes of keeping an eye on them, Faubus invited the two Georgians to stay in the guest house next to the Governor's Mansion.

When Griffin told him about the invitation, Harris was gleeful. "Why, having us at the mansion is the worst thing that could happen to Faubus," he predicted. "It'll ruin him with the integrationists and the liberals." Actually, it was Griffin and Harris who had to fend off criticism, as their hard-core supporters questioned their willingness to hobnob with a man of Faubus's moderate reputation.

Any doubts about their commitment to the cause were dispelled on the night of the dinner, when Griffin told the audience of about 350 that the public schools in Georgia would never, ever be integrated. Harris, a lawyer by training, said Georgia would call out the National Guard and the State Patrol to prevent Negroes from attending white schools, and would even resort to mobilizing posses of private citizens if necessary. The message was one of complete, unyielding resistance, and the endorsement of violence was plain. The audience roared with approval.

After the dinner, Griffin and Harris returned to the governor's guest house for the night. Faubus left word that they were to join him for breakfast. The next morning, as he stood in the bathroom shaving, Griffin called out to Harris: "What the hell are we gonna talk about that won't embarrass us and won't embarrass him?" They decided not to discuss the dinner or their speeches at all. Faubus said he'd heard they had a good meeting. "And we said, 'Yessir, we did,' and that's all we said about it," Harris recalled later. With no more conversation than that, they left the mansion and returned home.

Within the week, energized opponents filed suit seeking to delay the desegregation plan, and Faubus testified that it was "the worst possible time" to try integrating Central High because of the threat of violence. He blamed Griffin for assuring the hard-liners they could resist successfully. "He told them there was no integration in Georgia," Faubus complained, "and people are coming to me saying, 'Why does Arkansas have to have it?'"

What once seemed likely to be a smooth operation now turned into a high drama, one of the pivotal moments of the civil rights era. A federal judge rejected Faubus's request for postponement and ordered the desegregation of Central High to proceed. Members of the Little Rock school board met with the governor and came away with the deeply upsetting impression that he might be planning to defy the judge's order.

Like Atlanta, the city of Little Rock had an elite group of top businessmen whose views on race tended toward the pragmatic. One of them, Winthrop Rockefeller, the head of the state's Industrial Development Commission, asked for a meeting with Faubus. In a private session in a room at the Albert Pike Hotel, the grandson of John D. Rockefeller pleaded with Faubus to obey the law. Faubus was non-committal.

On the afternoon of Monday, September 2, 1957, the day before the school year was scheduled to begin, Faubus sat in a high-backed leather chair behind a plywood veneer desk in his office at the state Capitol, worrying, he said, about the heightened climate of violence. Toward dusk, he decided to call out the National Guard. He told the state's adjutant general to secure Central High, and by nine o'clock that night troops were ringing the school. Faubus went on television and announced that the soldiers were there to keep the peace and prevent vandalism.

As yet, no one could tell what hand Faubus had decided to play. Back home in Georgia, Roy Harris heard the news that Faubus had called out the guard. Later he took a bath, he said, "and I sat there in the tub just scratching my head and wondering if he called 'em out *for* us or *agin'* us."

The next morning, filled with uncertainty, black leaders decided to keep the nine black children who had been selected to desegregate the school at home. The day afterward, September 4, armed with a new federal court order, the children finally tried to enter the school, and it was then that they learned what Faubus had in mind. The National Guard turned them away. Harris was ecstatic. "If the Yankees keep trying to integrate us," he warned a reporter, "there's gonna be a war between the whites and the niggers."

The mayor of Little Rock, Woodrow Wilson Mann, denounced Faubus in the strongest terms. The governor had fabricated the threat of violence, Mann said, and if blood flowed it would be on the governor's hands. At the time (and for almost 40 years afterward, until his death in 1994), it was impossible to say whether Faubus had been stampeded by Griffin and Harris or simply inspired by their example. Faubus's father, "Uncle Sam" Faubus, a mountain populist from the tiny Ozark town of Greasy Creek, openly criticized his son for picking the wrong side of the racial divide. "I told Orval not to hate anybody of any race," his father said. "I told him people would think he was narrow-minded and look down on him."

Most historians believe Faubus acted deliberately for his own political gain, and it is true enough that he went on to win re-election, not just in 1958 but three more terms as well. However genuine his fear of violence, he plainly exploited the situation to make himself a martyr in the eyes of white segregationists, polarizing a state that might have led the way in racial adaptation.

From the vantage point of Atlanta, Faubus's motives were of little significance. The important thing was that the governor of Georgia, by a stroke of fate, had managed to export his politics of massive resistance to another state. The doctrine that the federal courts could be defied would be tested in Little Rock, not Atlanta, and the penalty for guessing wrong would be paid by the people of Arkansas, not Georgia.

Faubus's gambit led quickly to a showdown with President Eisenhower. For three long years, progressives had waited in vain for Eisenhower to give a clear signal that he intended to enforce the *Brown* decision. He did so now. An intermediary arranged a private meeting between Faubus and the President in Newport, Rhode Island, and when Faubus asked for a year's delay in integrating Central High, the President refused, saying the authority of the federal courts had to be recognized. In apparent surrender, Faubus issued a statement saying the "law-abiding" people of Little Rock would comply.

But Faubus soon went back on his word. Returning to Little Rock, he renewed his claim that desegregating Central High would result in chaos. After holding hearings on the matter, a federal judge ruled that Faubus's concerns were exaggerated and ordered the desegregation plan to go forward. A defiant Faubus replied that since the court was so confident of a peaceful outcome, he would withdraw the National Guard entirely and let matters unfold as they might.

The integration of Central High was scheduled for Monday, September 23. Over the weekend, Faubus abandoned Little Rock and flew to Sea Island, Georgia, for a meeting of the Southern Governors' Conference. Stopping in Atlanta on the way, he predicted rioting and disorder and urged black parents to keep their children away from the school. He seemed to be hoping for bloodshed, just to prove his point.

Early Monday morning, a mob of about a thousand whites gathered at Central High, churning and shouting taunts. Just before nine o'clock, three black newspaper reporters arrived on the scene and walked toward the front door of the school as if they planned to go inside. Someone yelled, "Get the niggers!" A burly white man rushed up and punched one of the reporters, Earl Davey of the Little Rock *State Press*, knocking him to the ground. Another of the reporters had his camera smashed. While the crowd swarmed around the newsmen, nine black children were slipped into the school through a side entrance. For the moment, Central High was desegregated.

Soon, however, Little Rock's police chief, Marvin Potts, found his forces overwhelmed. When they learned the black students had gone into the school, the white protesters surged against the police lines and almost broke through. Most of the school's white students walked out and joined the throng. At noon, the black children had to be removed for their own safety. Network television captured all of it. From Sea Island, Faubus issued a statement observing smugly that it would be in poor taste to say, "I told you so."

For the President, the scenes of rebellion in Little Rock were the final straw. He told McGill later that he had to call upon all of his experience as a military commander to hold his temper in check, he was so furious with Faubus. When the same mob gathered again on Tuesday morning, Eisenhower federalized the Arkansas National Guard and ordered the riot-trained paratroopers of the 101st Airborne Division into Little Rock. The next morning, with 1,100 soldiers looking on, Central High was desegregated for good.

Faubus did not give in gracefully. Returning home, he accused the paratroopers of "bludgeoning innocent bystanders" and prodding school-girls in the back with their bayonets. He said the FBI was holding white students incommunicado, a charge J. Edgar Hoover hotly denied. At his lowest point, Faubus made the lurid, absolutely false allegation that fed-eral soldiers had invaded the girls' locker room while they were dressing.

In the days just after the crisis, Governor Griffin and other Georgia officials fancied that their position had been strengthened. "Naked bay-onets were held against the throats of teenage girls," Attorney General Cook wrote Griffin, "and American blood was spilled upon the soil of a sovereign state by a posse comitatus under order of the President of the United States." Roy Harris told a reporter the events at Little Rock were helpful, since Georgians were now "more determined than ever to fight integration." If blacks in Georgia tried to go to white schools, Harris added, "there'll be some beatings at night, and then they'll get the idea."

Griffin sounded almost as bellicose. Rather than integrate, he said, Georgia would close its schools. "And if anyone tried to federalize the guard," he continued, "I could just discharge it, then form a state militia under the Second Amendment to the Constitution, the right to bear arms. No Georgia boy can be made to turn his bayonet against a fellow Georgian. These people just won't do it. I know these people. Georgia will never be integrated. The people won't stand for it."

Harris and the governor were entirely correct that many thousands of Georgians had reacted radically against the forced desegregation in Lit-tle Rock. A Gallup poll taken two weeks after Eisenhower sent in the troops found that half the people of the South opposed the action. Remarkably, though, more than a third of Southerners — 36 percent — said they agreed with the President. Attitudes were not as one-sided as Griffin and Harris thought.

In Atlanta, Mayor Hartsfield saw the events of Little Rock as a sign that it was time to take on the segregationists directly and settle the issue. He told

McGill he wanted "to call for a showdown between the better element of this town and those who would throw us into violence and anarchy."

He got his wish. Because of the narrowness of his victory in the 1957 mayoral primary, Hartsfield at long last appeared vulnerable. His rivals were kicking themselves for having skipped the race, and for the first time in decades there was talk of challenging Hartsfield in the rarely contested general election in December. Several politicians, including Hartsfield's old sparring partner, Charlie Brown, considered running, but in the end it was a 41-year-old restaurant owner named Lester Maddox who entered the fray.

Maddox ran a family-style place called the Pickrick on Hemphill Avenue, in a white, working-class neighborhood about five blocks north of Georgia Tech. The skillet-fried chicken was considered first-rate and a bargain at 45 cents. Servings were generous. As Maddox explained in the ads he placed in the Atlanta Constitution, the "rick" in the restaurant's name came from a verb that meant "to pile up or to heap, to amass. You PICK it out — We'll RICK it up."

As the rest of the nation would discover in the years to come, Maddox was quite a character. Unlike some professional politicians who engaged in race-baiting as a calculated campaign tactic, Maddox genuinely believed in the separation of the races. "We have a divine right to discriminate," he once explained. His fundamentalism sprang from his mother, Flonnie Castleberry Maddox, who spent years studying biblical prophecy and believed the Second Coming was near. "It could happen any minute," she liked to say. Lester was one of seven children she bore to Dean Maddox, a roll-turner at the Atlantic Steel plant who lost his job during the Depression and ended up doing odd jobs and selling vegetables from the family garden.

Lester dropped out of school in the eleventh grade, worked for a while at the steel mill and saved up $400 to buy a "hole-in-the-wall beaner," as one journalist described it, that he gradually built into a successful business. His newspaper ads, a mix of orthodox menu items and passionate sermons against the "amalgamation" of the races, turned him into a minor local celebrity. Governor Griffin, a college-educated former teacher, often quoted an imaginary friend he called Willie Highgrass to articulate the sentiments of blue-collar Georgians; one observer of the period noted that in many ways Maddox *was* Willie Highgrass.

Unlike Roy Harris and other ardent segregationists, Maddox did not aim violent words at blacks. He never uttered the word "nigger," and even in private conversation the ugliest epithet he used was "jigaboo." Under the prodding of reporters, he would confirm his belief in white supremacy, but in his ads and later in his speeches he stuck to the idea that separation of the races was a Christian ideal and an American right, good for black and white alike. This did not exonerate him from charges of racism, of course, but it made him a more complicated figure than some historians like to recall.

Maddox was an improbable politician. With a bald head and florid face, and with his wide-set, berry eyes magnified by spectacles, he looked quite a bit like an angry chicken. His voice had a redneck twang, ill-suited to oratory. He couldn't remember names to save his life. He irritated many of the men he encountered (and who contributed money to him) by calling them "buddy boy," even after repeated introductions. He completely lacked the sort of dignity that Mayor Hartsfield, who came from a similar background, had spent so many years trying to cultivate. Maddox's one great gift, the flip side of his limitations, was the aura of guilelessness he exuded, the sense that he would always tell the truth as he saw it.

For Hartsfield, Maddox represented a model opponent, a figure with no constituency beyond his stance on race. Even though Maddox talked about other issues, notably the need to clean up the lottery and close the liquor stores, the election would be a referendum on how Atlantans wished to handle race relations. "I'm proud of the fact that in the face of race trouble all over the South, you have seen none in Atlanta," Hartsfield told a civic group.

Belying the deadly serious stakes of the contest, Maddox campaigned cheerfully. On a Friday morning a month before the election, he arrived at City Hall with a list of 6,200 signatures on petitions, rushed up the stairs to the second floor with a coterie of press and supporters in his wake, barged into the mayor's office, and demanded that Hartsfield sign the papers to put him on the ballot. Rattled, Hartsfield lost his composure and threw Maddox out. Undaunted, Maddox went back downstairs and filed his papers with the city clerk, securing his spot as the challenger. On his way out the door, he made a show of taking his hat with him. "I guess I could get it when I come in on January first," he said, "but I'd better take it now."

For the first time in his career, Hartsfield opened an official campaign headquarters. He found nothing amusing in Maddox's hijinks. Abandoning his usual guise of the happy warrior full of political pranks, Hartsfield ran as if his life were on the line, which in a way it was. Toward the end of the campaign, in an act that bordered on the foolhardy, Hartsfield agreed to debate Maddox face-to-face in front of a group of working-class whites who were known to be violently racist.

Helen Bullard, a political adviser, accompanied Hartsfield to the event and later recalled the scene vividly. The mayor arrived at the hall a few minutes late and quietly took a seat in the back. Maddox spoke first and had the crowd stomping and cheering. When Hartsfield's turn came, he rose and started slowly up the aisle to the front. Only then did most of the men in the audience realize he had come. "Nigger lover!" someone hissed in a loud stage whisper. Then others began yelling the words, over and over, until the crowd was chanting "Nigger lover! Nigger lover!" at deafening volume. The mayor tried to speak, only to have his words drowned out.

Hartsfield stood for a moment, silent. He had scattered a handful of undercover police around the room, but he refused to call on them for help. He straightened his spine, and something in his voice changed. Bullard had the thought that Hartsfield's friends in the city's boardrooms would not recognize the man who now spat out his words with a hard edge of raw fury. "You invited me to come here," he began, his face dark. "I didn't want to come. *Are you going to listen to me or act like a bunch of bums?*" The crowd quieted. The mayor waited until they were listening.

"Now," he continued, "you seem to be very interested in the business of my being a 'nigger lover.' Well, let's talk about my being a 'nigger lover.' What would you want me to do as mayor of your town?" He paused. "Do you want me to put on a sheet and burn down a few houses? Do you want me to plant a few bombs and blow a few porches off people's homes? *Do you want me to kill a few?*"

The room was utterly silent. "Now look," Hartsfield said, "this is evidently on your mind. Come on, tell me. What do you want? Surely you must have some plan." No one said a thing, and at length Hartsfield lapsed back into his more familiar persona, ticking off his administration's accomplishments.

Later, driving back downtown, he told Bullard he hadn't wanted to rely on the police. "I've always wanted to know if I could control a mob," he said evenly. He had.

On election day, Hartsfield won his sixth term as mayor of Atlanta. The numbers seemed to vindicate him, at least at first glance, as he took more than 41,000 votes to Maddox's 24,000. On close inspection, though, it was evident that black voters had provided the margin of victory once again. Hartsfield had lost the white vote to a man whose only qualification for office was his implacable opposition to civil rights for blacks.

What made the outcome especially discouraging was that for all the hoopla about the city's progress — "Atlanta: Smart Politics and Good Race Relations," trumpeted a headline in the magazine *The Reporter* — very little actual integration had occurred as yet. Indeed, since the buses remained segregated while the Reverend Borders and his group pursued their appeals in court, the stark reality was that in all of Atlanta only the public golf courses had been legally desegregated. And that had been enough to push half the city's white voters into Maddox's camp.

Underscoring the persistence of separate but equal thinking, the new quarters for the city's premier charity hospital, Grady Memorial — a $26 million, 21-story mountain of yellow brick — had been scrupulously divided into two identical, independent wings for black and white patients.

Hartsfield's victory gave the city some breathing room, little more. Governor Griffin, nearing the end of his term and sinking further into scandal, decided to keep his nose out of the city's affairs. With a cloud of unresolved racial tensions clinging overhead, Atlantans went about their business. The airport grew to 5,000 employees with a $25 million annual payroll, and planning began for a new, modern terminal. The first jet arrived, a French Caravelle flown in from Washington by Delta pilots. The municipal bon mot, "If you are going to heaven or hell, you have to go by way of Atlanta," was placed in the minutes of a meeting of the Atlanta Chamber of Commerce by an unnamed board member.

On the white northside, the bustling economy created a new level of wealth. While older Southern cities like Savannah and Charleston gave off the perfume of languid aristocracy, Atlanta gladly reeked of the nouveau riche. As one matron explained, "It doesn't matter who you were. You could be a ditch digger or a bootlegger, and if you came to Atlanta and could hold your liquor, if you used decent English, you were accepted." Then as now, status symbols were a 233 (for CEdar-3) telephone exchange, membership in the Piedmont Driving Club and a house in Buckhead. The Cadillac dealer prospered. He gave everyone who bought a new model a free Zippo lighter embossed with the Cadillac crest, as if they had earned a small coat of arms.

Wealthy blacks created a mirror society, albeit much smaller, across town. Hartsfield often picked up visiting journalists at the airport and drove them through Collier Heights, casually pointing out the fine brick houses, many in the $75,000 range. "These are some of our Negro homes," he would say matter-of-factly.

A handful of black families lived like exiled nobility. Henry Rucker, who served as Atlanta's collector of internal revenue after the turn of the century, built a big house and installed a full-sized soda fountain in it, just so his children would not have to go downtown and experience the humiliation of the Jim Crow laws. One of his daughters, Lucy, who married the prominent builder Walter "Chief" Aiken, recalled many years later that she had lived her whole life in Atlanta without once riding a streetcar or going to the theater.

The governor's race of 1958 looked like a cut-and-dried affair. Griffin was barred by law from seeking a second consecutive term (which was just as well, with a grand jury poking into his administration's excesses), and the state's lieutenant governor, Ernest Vandiver, emerged as the odds-on favorite. Never very close to Griffin to begin with, Vandiver had broken completely with the governor and was campaigning on a promise to clean up state government. A 40-year-old lawyer from the north Georgia town of Lavonia, Vandiver qualified as a "moderate" as the term was then understood — a proponent of segregation, but not a race-baiter, a man who would pursue economic development without getting bogged down by bigotry. Married to a niece of the highly respected U. S. Senator Richard Russell, Vandiver had an impeccable pedigree.

Unhappily, Vandiver proved to be an antsy candidate. With no serious opposition, facing only the Reverend William T. Bodenhamer, an arch-segregationist preacher from the tiny hamlet of Ty Ty, Vandiver felt it necessary to reassure the state's white voters that not one black child — "no, not one" — would attend a white school while he was governor. Thus cementing an already sure victory, he captured 156 of Georgia's 159 counties and won in a landslide. But he prepared to take office saddled with an ironclad vow that would be very hard to break.

Just as Vandiver was uttering his memorably defiant phrase, the state of Virginia provided a laboratory test of the consequences of massive resistance. In a case similar to Little Rock's, a federal judge ordered the all-white public schools in Norfolk to begin admitting black children. Rather than comply, Virginia Governor J. Lindsay Almond invoked a new state law forbidding integration and closed the schools. Ten thousand students were sent home.

In Atlanta, some of the members of the power structure recognized that Georgia eventually would confront the same hard choices. "Aren't we lucky in Georgia," Hughes Spalding wrote Robert Woodruff, "that all this stink is happening in Virginia and Arkansas! It could have happened here. . . . It is good for us to be by-passed in this connection."

Atlanta was not spared for long. In the small hours of Sunday morning, October 12, 1958, a bomb ripped open a gaping hole in the side of the Temple, the premier house of worship for Atlanta's large, well-established Jewish community. No one was injured, but the power of the blast — 30 to 40 sticks of dynamite, the police estimated — shook buildings and broke windows for a radius of several blocks. The psychological impact was even greater. Random bombings had pockmarked the South for years, but rarely in Atlanta. The city's confident, almost carefree presumption that it stood above the vulgar violence of the rest of the section — an attitude conveyed nicely by Alfred Uhry in his play *Driving Miss Daisy* — was rattled to the bone.

That Jews were the target rather than blacks fueled a sense of hatred billowing out of control. Arriving home from a speaking engagement late that Sunday, McGill was greeted at the door by his wife, Mary Elizabeth, who gave him the news. He went straight to his office at the *Constitution* and in 20 minutes of furious writing composed the editorial that won him a Pulitzer Prize.

"Let us face the facts," he wrote. "This is a harvest. It is the crop of things sown. It is the harvest of defiance of courts and the encouragement of citizens to defy law on the part of many Southern politicians." Though he did not single out Marvin Griffin by name, McGill added that it would be the height of irony if any of several Southern governors deplored the bombing. His scorn seemed prophetic when Griffin issued a statement calling the act "despicable" and saying, "I cannot conceive of any Georgian participating in a thing of this kind."

The police, it happened, could conceive very easily of certain Georgians participating in the crime: Four suspects, one of them a state employee, were arrested the next day. The first defendant was tried quickly, and though he avoided conviction courtesy of a hung jury, the vigor of the prosecution left no doubt that the authorities in Atlanta meant to discourage similar acts in the future. Led by McGill and Mayor Hartsfield, Atlantans raised a convincing chorus in damning the bombing. President Eisenhower praised Hartsfield for his swift, decisive response, telling him, "You have set an example for the entire nation." The city's reputation actually gained luster as a result of the incident.

One minor act by a federal bureaucrat toward the end of 1958 brought Atlanta closer to a dream long held by Hartsfield and his friends at the Chamber of Commerce. The U. S. Census Bureau added Gwinnett County to the official metropolitan area, bringing the population count to 960,000 and rapidly advancing the arrival of "M Day," when greater Atlanta would become the first city in the Southeast with a million people.

A countdown was begun with a dramatic flourish, as Atlanta entered a touch-and-go race to reach the million mark before the end of 1959. The idea of starting the decade of the '60s as a certified metropolis took on a sense of urgency, one more deadline in a place that suddenly seemed to be full of ticking clocks.

In a city obsessed with image, the proliferation of the suburbs took on great symbolic importance. If attention could somehow be drawn away from the federal courthouse and shifted to the green lawns and station wagons of suburbia, the emphasis would be on Atlanta's wealth and its commonality with the urban centers of the rest of the nation — not on the slow, grudging pace of change in race relations. The issue was more than a question of cosmetics. Hartsfield and Woodruff and the other city fathers wanted the city to look good to outsiders, but an even greater imperative was to look good to the governor and the members of the Legislature. For all their allegiance to segregation, the men at the Capitol might hesitate to do damage to Atlanta if it meant shutting down an indispensable economic engine.

It did not escape anyone's notice that in the year and a half after Orval Faubus's infamy, the city of Little Rock paid a high price for the violent pictures that appeared on the nation's television screens. Plans for five new plants were scrapped, by one account, costing Arkansas $1 million in capital investment and 300 jobs. Not a single new factory had opened. Atlanta could not afford a similar fate.

On May 10, 1959, Hartsfield testified before the federal Commission on Civil Rights that Atlanta was moving — slowly — to desegregate. "I have often said to my Negro citizens," he explained, "that the important thing is the direction in which we are moving, and not always the speed with which we are moving." A federal judge had ended segregated seating on the city's buses in January, and in May the libraries were desegregated without incident.

Then, in June, as if to test the mayor's cautious pace, U. S. District Judge Frank Hooper asked the city to present a plan for the integration of its public schools.

Recognizing the thorniness of the situation, Hooper granted the city a one-year grace period. It would be necessary, he noted, for the Legislature to revoke its newly enacted laws that required the immediate shutdown of any white school that admitted a black student. Since the Legislature was not scheduled to reconvene until January 1960, there would be time to work out a solution. But it was hard to see how Governor Vandiver could reconcile his "no, not one" pledge with the judge's order. It was equally hard to imagine the judge backing down.

Against this backdrop of impending collision, a developer named Ed Noble presided over the opening of Lenox Square, the South's first regional shopping mall. Built along Peachtree Road on a 74-acre site that had once been the country estate of banker John Ottley, the mall served as vivid proof that Atlanta was growing beyond the old conceptions of what it meant to be a Southern city. Rich's, the legendary department store in downtown Atlanta, opened a big, three-story branch at Lenox, joining the hunt for suburban customers. With 53 stores and 6,000 parking spaces, Lenox quickly began drawing immense crowds — 65,000 shoppers in one day — with many of them coming from other Georgia cities and towns, even other states.

At the Chamber of Commerce, statisticians designated October 10, 1959, as "M Day." Elaborate plans for a celebration were drawn up, calling for widespread noise at high noon: "Whistles, fire and civil defense sirens, church bells, school bands. General rejoicing at our achievement." Hartsfield printed a million dollars in simulated Confederate currency, which he called a tribute to the "real" money Yankees had invested in the city over the years. He sent the bills all over the world, including a dollar to the Soviet premier, Nikita Khrushchev. The *Journal* and *Constitution* collaborated on a three-part special section, "Atlanta: The First Million." A recent émigré from Cincinnati, Don Smith, was picked out and honored as the official millionth citizen.

It was all a matter of guesswork, of course. Fulton County had about 575,000 people at the moment, DeKalb 237,000, Cobb 104,000, Clayton and the new addition, Gwinnett, some 37,000 apiece. The total, for those finicky enough to do the addition, appeared to fall about 10,000 short of the mark. But when "M Day" arrived, nothing could dampen the spirits of the celebrants, not even the rain and gloomy overcast of a chilly autumn Saturday.

Atlanta had reached critical mass.

CHAPTER 5

"NOT ONE"

Ernest Vandiver had a promise to break. His stark vow, "no, not one" — meaning not a single black child would attend a white school in Georgia while he was governor — placed him directly at odds with the federal courts bent on desegregating Atlanta's public schools.

U. S. District Judge Frank Hooper had ordered the city to prepare a desegregation plan in time for the opening of the school year in the fall of 1960. And the judge had warned the Georgia General Assembly that it must repeal its laws forbidding any and all integration. Otherwise the likely outcome would be the forced closing of every public school in Georgia.

Naturally the governor did not wish to humiliate himself by publicly renouncing the oath that had helped elect him. But neither did he want to be remembered as the man who destroyed public education in Georgia. What he needed was an escape hatch, and courtesy of a bright young adviser, Griffin Bell, he found one.

A sly lawyer with a molasses drawl who later gained the nation's respect as President Carter's attorney general, Bell at the time had just taken over as managing partner of King & Spalding, the big Atlanta law firm that seemed to have a hand in every facet of the state's political life. Bell supported Vandiver for governor and was rewarded with the honorary post of chief of staff.

As the legislative session drew to a close in February 1960, Vandiver's anxiety deepened. In spite of the building pressure, the General Assembly showed no intention of revoking its segregation laws. If it adjourned without taking action, Judge Hooper would be sure to press ahead with his order, and autumn would bring crisis.

At first glance, the solution Bell crafted looked like a mere gimmick. He suggested the appointment of a blue-ribbon commission to study the problem — one of the oldest devices known in politics, a transparent method of gaining time in a pinch. But the commission Bell had in mind would be unusual. Its members would not seek advice or explore alternatives or even try to keep an open mind. Bell's commission would be a propaganda machine, bent on instructing Georgians about the futility of resisting the law of the land. Its purpose would be to get Vandiver off the hook by persuading voters that he *ought* to break his promise.

To serve as head of the commission, Bell required someone of exceptional public standing and political skill, a man who could hold hearings, handle angry crowds, soothe explosive tempers, and deliver some harsh truths without losing his composure. He picked one of his mentors, John Sibley, the embodiment of Atlanta's business elite.

With his rounded features and soft voice, Sibley gave the impression of a Dutch uncle, gentle and wise. Underneath, he could be as hard as dried Georgia clay. An alumnus of King & Spalding, where he had served as general counsel to the Coca-Cola Company, Sibley was a charter member of Robert Woodruff's inner circle. At Woodruff's insistence, he had quit the law to become chairman of Trust Company of Georgia, the so-called Coca-Cola bank, where he oversaw millions of shares of Coca-Cola stock and made sure they were voted as Woodruff wished.

At the time Bell approached him, Sibley had just turned 71 and was partly retired. Though he still chaired Trust Company's executive committee, he preferred spending time on his 1,300-acre farm outside Atlanta, where he liked to pull on a windbreaker and muddy boots and perform physical labor. He was reluctant to accept Bell's summons. It took a personal meeting with Governor Vandiver to bring him around. Given assurances that he could help name the other members of the commission, he agreed to serve.

Even then, the undertaking faced roadblocks. As a measure of the tensions of the time, the governor proved too skittish to propose the commission himself. Instead, he got a little-known legislator from south Georgia named George Busbee to introduce the measure, as if it had nothing to do with the Vandiver administration. An innocuous sounding General Assembly Commission on Schools was created, and 19 white men — no blacks, no women — were appointed as members.

For all the stealth, Georgia's hard-line segregationists saw through Vandiver's game instantly. Roy Harris, the white supremacist who had helped trigger Little Rock's troubles, held a rally just outside Atlanta on February 16, 1960, the evening before the commission's first meeting, and vowed a "holy crusade" to fend off integration. While Harris could not be certain just who was behind the commission — he blamed "Rastus" McGill, the editor of the *Atlanta Constitution*, among others — he recognized its purpose.

The next morning, the commission convened and elected Sibley as its chairman. From the outset, he made it plain that he did not intend to listen to anguished sermons or wishful thinking. A segregationist himself, he denounced the Supreme Court's *Brown* decision as "devoid of legal reasoning" and poor sociology as well. Nevertheless, he said, it was the law. The Atlanta public schools were going to be desegregated, and the only important question was how the state government would respond.

Sibley announced a schedule of 10 hearings, one in each of Georgia's congressional districts, to gauge the will of the people. He gaveled the first session to order on Thursday, March 3, 1960, in the Sumter County courthouse in Americus, a stronghold of segregationist passion in southwest Georgia. He picked Americus, he said later, because he thought it was the most dangerous spot in the state. If the commission could get through the first hearing without a riot, he figured the rest would be easier.

Sibley's performance was masterful. He began by explaining the dilemma that confronted the state, couching the discussion in terms that allowed him to control the debate. In his analysis, only two outcomes were possible. If current state law remained in effect, Atlanta's public schools would have to be shut down the minute a black student integrated a white school. Then *all* of the state's public schools would have to close, because the federal courts would not allow some public schools to remain open while others were closed.

On the other hand, Sibley continued, state law could be amended to allow schools to desegregate by local option. Only Atlanta would be affected, he predicted, and only a handful of black students would participate. The odds were that a generation might pass before the courts tried to integrate schools in the rest of the state. Life would go on pretty much as it had in the past.

Having spun this one-sided scenario, Sibley took testimony. "I made up my mind there would be no speeches," he said later. He asked the witnesses which of the two outcomes they preferred and gently but firmly insisted that they be recorded one way or the other before they made additional remarks. Historians have credited the Sibley Commission with acting as a release valve — "the opening of a steamcock in the boiler of emotion," in one writer's phrase — and it is true that hundreds of Georgians turned out and got to speak their minds. But the key to the outcome was Sibley's unyielding adherence to the idea that Georgia faced a stark, yes-or-no choice.

Not everyone agreed with Sibley's assessment of the situation, of course. Roy Harris came to one of the early meetings and argued forcefully that integration in Atlanta's schools would be widespread rather than token, that it would provoke white flight to the suburbs, and that desegregation would follow swiftly in the rest of Georgia's schools. In rural Georgia, where there were no suburbs to absorb fleeing whites, Harris said, the school systems would break down. "So we have to stand," he vowed, "and stand adamant."

That Harris's prophecy might be accurate did not trouble Sibley in the least. He listened politely and even allowed Harris to take more than his allotted time. The worst pain known to man, Sibley remarked genially, was that of an undelivered speech.

At the root of Sibley's strategy lay a simple premise. Anything was better than shutting down the schools. As in other instances, Georgians could look elsewhere and see examples at work. In Norfolk, where 10,000 children had been turned out into the streets, efforts to operate segregated private schools had failed miserably. After a single semester, at the pleading of Norfolk's business community, the public schools had reopened on an integrated basis.

Over the course of a month, Sibley called upon all of his considerable wiles to placate the frightened, angry people who came before him. Once he held a woman's baby in his lap while she testified. His good humor never flagged. When a black witness said he wished Sibley could have the experience of being black for half an hour, Sibley answered, "I might not mind if I could take my half-hour on Saturday night." The only threat of violence came toward the end of the tour, in Atlanta, when a white plumber named Jack Dorsey swore he would rather die fighting integration than live under it. His simple, passionate words electrified the room and spurred wild applause. Sibley had to pound his gavel repeatedly to maintain order, and at one point, he fended off a man who clung to his sleeve while trying to reach the microphone. The peace held.

When the last hearing ended, Sibley and his fellow commissioners counted up the responses. A majority of the witnesses had said they would rather close the public schools than allow integration, but thanks to Sibley's persuasiveness the margin was surprisingly close, three to two. In making a final report, Sibley got ten other members to join him in recommending that the schools remain open.

The Sibley Commission's vote in favor of limited integration made headlines around the state and nation. Judge Hooper, the target of the enterprise, announced in May 1960 that he was impressed with the signs of progress and would give the state another year to revoke its segregation laws. He called it "one last chance."

Those who believed that Atlanta's glowing reputation owed more to luck than design could point to the events of 1960 as evidence. Nearly six years after the *Brown* decision, with federal judges elsewhere in the South losing patience and accelerating the laggard pace of change, Atlanta was given the luxury of holding back once again. When it came to "all deliberate speed," a liberal critic noted, Atlanta's speed seemed to be the most deliberate in all of Dixie.

The city's good fortune extended beyond an indulgent judge. With blacks across the region growing increasingly restive and discovering newer, more aggressive forms of protest, Atlanta remained a place of calm in the eye of a storm. When Martin Luther King, Jr., moved back home from Montgomery in January 1960 to expand his crusade for civil rights, the event filled even the most progressive of Atlanta's white leaders with uneasiness. "I must say," Ralph McGill remarked, "I feel like a citizen of a medieval walled city who has just gotten word that the plague is coming."

But King's presence actually worked to inhibit the protest movement in Atlanta. Not content to be rid of him, the state of Alabama indicted King for tax evasion, and though it was plainly a political case, King worried about the damage a conviction could do to his moral authority. Just when the sit-in phenomenon was spreading from Greensboro, North Carolina, to other cities in the South, King found himself preoccupied, meeting with accountants and lawyers to prepare his defense. He didn't have time to participate in civil disobedience at lunch counters.

Citing the need to spare King from additional controversy in his hometown, the presidents of Atlanta's black colleges moved to discourage their students from staging repeated sit-ins. Julian Bond and other student leaders organized a single, day-long series of arrests at several establishments in downtown Atlanta on March 15, 1960, and then reluctantly agreed to an armistice. Other cities witnessed violent clashes, not Atlanta.

Atlanta's police chief, Herbert Jenkins, reciprocated by adopting a live-and-let-live policy toward King. One day, Jenkins recalled, a pair of Alabama state patrol captains showed up at his office and said they were investigating reports that King was not who he claimed to be but rather an African secret agent. Concealing his mirth, Jenkins replied that he had known King since birth and would be happy to have Grady Memorial Hospital provide a footprint as proof of his identity. On several occasions, the FBI asked Jenkins to raid hotel rooms, claiming King was having assignations. Each time Jenkins replied, "If you want to raid him, raid him yourselves." The relationship between Jenkins and J. Edgar Hoover grew chilly as a result.

The most serious threat to the placid surface of the city's race relations came on the sixth anniversary of the *Brown* decision, when the students at the Atlanta University complex made plans to march on the state Capitol. Governor Vandiver responded that he would ring the grounds with state troopers to keep them out. Shortly after dawn on May 17, 1960, a hundred troopers in full riot gear were deployed to repel the marchers by force.

The students spent the morning on campus, listening to pleas from their college presidents not to proceed, before hundreds of them shrugged off the warnings, formed columns and headed for downtown Atlanta. The delay had the effect of raising the potential for violence even higher, as the day turned unseasonably hot and the troopers began sweating under their helmets and protective equipment. By mid-afternoon, when 2,000 black collegians surged up Hunter Street toward the gold dome of the Capitol, the troopers had been standing in baking heat for nearly eight hours and were itching for trouble.

Recognizing the dangerous mood of the troopers, Chief Jenkins intercepted the students before they reached the Capitol grounds and urged them to stop. They refused at first, but Jenkins had earned a degree of their trust. "Believe me," he warned, "this is really going to cause trouble." At the last moment, a block from the Capitol, they turned aside. The procession went on to Wheat Street Baptist Church, where King was waiting for them. He greeted them in triumph, praising their nonviolence.

While much of Atlanta's racial melodrama unfolded in public view, Mayor Hartsfield operated behind the scenes to keep a lid on the most explosive issue of all — blockbusting. Between 1950 and 1960, the city gained 38,000 new black residents, whose desperate need for housing pushed them toward white neighborhoods. The same pattern was occurring in several different parts of the city. Unscrupulous real estate agents, black and white, would pay a sky-high price for a white family's house, then make a show of parading black families around to look at buying it. Some agents went so far as to pass out printed cards that asked ominously, "Who will be your new neighbors?" The remaining whites would panic, and some would sell at distressed prices. Others would resist, at times violently. In April 1960, a house was dynamited in Adamsville, one of the city's transitional neighborhoods.

The mayor came to detest blockbusting, so much so that at one point he petitioned the Georgia Real Estate Commission to prohibit the placement of "Sold" signs in front of houses, a novel idea that was voted down unanimously. A far more effective tactic was Hartsfield's employment of a so-called "housing coordinator" who helped decide which neighborhoods should stay white and which should undergo an orderly conversion to black.

To protect himself politically, Hartsfield paid the coordinator's salary out of a secret fund in the city budget and gave him an office outside City Hall. When angry groups of white homeowners descended on him and demanded relief, Hartsfield would throw up his hands, saying there was little he could do, and send them to see the coordinator.

"That was when I learned to pray," recalled T. M. "Jim" Parham, who served in the post during the summer of 1960. A sociologist by training, Parham's job was to listen to the furious outbursts of the whites and then try to talk them into negotiating a settlement. On one occasion his reward was a rock that came sailing through the window while he spoke. Typically the situation was complicated by the divergent wishes of the white neighbors. Some would agree to band together, pool their resources, and buy every house that came on the market for resale to whites only. More often, though, white families in a transitional neighborhood simply hoped to recoup enough to pay off their mortgages and move away. They would sell to anyone.

Parham sent questionnaires to the residents of troubled neighborhoods, asking confidentially if they wanted to stay or sell. Their replies were tabulated, and their remarks were kept in a restricted file. "We are willing to sell or rent our house to colored," one respondent from the Kirkwood section of east Atlanta answered, "and would like to close a deal as soon as possible." Another homeowner complained that he wanted to sell, "but the people on other streets, farther away, want us to hold the line for them. They do not want to live next to colored people, but they want us to. I feel that if they want to control my house, they should buy it themselves. I will be happy to sell it to any of these people who are nailing up the 'WHITE AREA' signs."

If most of the residents wanted to sell, Parham and Hartsfield would try to negotiate a deal with the Empire Real Estate Board, a group of top black real estate agents, to buy out the whole neighborhood at once at fair market value. Empire would guarantee the prices and coordinate the transition, so that the whites all moved out and the blacks all moved in at the same time.

By and large, the system worked. As always, the mayor's goal was peace, not integration. But as Parham looked ahead to the rest of the 1960s, he could see far greater demands — "insatiable" was the word he used — for black housing. Urban renewal was wiping out slums and displacing thousands of families without providing replacement homes. New highways were cutting through parts of existing black neighborhoods. "Time and imaginative thought should be given to ways of making it easier for whites to give up their homes to Negroes," Parham advised Hartsfield. "This may sound screwballish, but necessity is the mother of invention, and almost anything is preferable to racial violence."

The city would have to take a more active role, Parham argued, possibly by paying whites a guaranteed minimum price for their homes. The newspapers, he said, should be encouraged to promote the "civic virtue" of whites selling to blacks. "For the die-hard race haters," he added, "the idea might be sold negatively, in terms of saddling Negroes with old houses and big mortgages." If the coordinator sounded a little desperate, he had reason. By today's standards, his activities might be considered improper. At the time, they prevented bloodshed.

The Atlanta of 1960 was a cosmopolitan, enlightened city, but as the New York Times pointed out, it was one where black college graduates often had to find work as postal clerks, where supermarkets would not hire black workers even in black neighborhoods, and where "a Negro may not ride in a 'white' taxi or eat in a downtown restaurant or see the touring company of 'Sunrise at Campobello' except from a segregated seat."

Schools, neighborhoods, shops, theaters, and lunch counters all remained strictly separated by race. The city that called itself too busy to hate seemed to be too busy to integrate. Deadlines of one sort or another loomed on every front. Black students ached for a showdown. Sooner rather than later, a major institution somewhere in Atlanta would have to be desegregated.

Atlantans had a longstanding love affair with Rich's department store.

Founded by Morris Rich in 1867, two years after the end of the Civil War, the business had grown from a modest drygoods outlet that specialized in corsets to become the largest retail emporium south of New York City. The main downtown store covered a million square feet, offered everything from wedding cakes to carpets, and enjoyed sales of $75 million a year. Rich's had a policy of allowing customers to return absolutely anything for a full refund (including the occasional cocktail dress, the day *after* a society ball), which helped explain the store's enduring popularity. And it gave easy credit. Some 400,000 Atlantans held Rich's charge plates. "You're nobody," an Atlanta matron assured a writer from *Holiday* magazine, "if you owe Rich's less than $300."

As far as corporate citizenship went, Rich's had an exemplary record, dating back to the great Atlanta fire of 1917, when store employees helped shelter and clothe hundreds of homeless families. During the Depression, Rich's joined the Coca-Cola Company in honoring the scrip the city issued to meet its payroll, in effect underwriting the salaries of Atlanta's policemen, firemen, and teachers. Members of the Rich family were among Atlanta's most generous philanthropists.

Under Frank Neely, the store's top executive from the 1920s to the 1940s, and later under Morris Rich's grandson, Richard Rich, blacks were welcomed as customers at the store and treated with a degree of courtesy rare for its time. Clerks addressed blacks as "Mr." and "Mrs." Since they were accorded the same liberal credit terms as whites, thousands of black Atlantans opened Rich's accounts and took pride in carrying a Rich's card.

Nonetheless, the store was rigidly segregated. Blacks were not allowed to try on shoes or clothes before buying them. If a black shopper needed a bathroom, she had to use a shabby facility in the basement or go to the nearby Terminal Station. Blacks could eat in the Hunter Room, but not in any of the other snack shops or cafeterias, and certainly not in the Magnolia Room, Rich's upscale restaurant.

No other establishment in Atlanta illustrated the vast gulf in black and white perceptions as well as Rich's. Richard Rich considered himself a liberal and thought he had earned the loyalty of his store's black clientele. Blacks wondered with increasing frustration why their dollars did not entitle them to the same treatment as whites. At the Atlanta University complex, Julian Bond and Lonnie King, two of the leaders of the newly formed Student Nonviolent Coordinating Committee (called "Snick" after its acronym, SNCC), began to see Rich's as an inviting target.

"Rich's was the gem," Bond explained years later. "Rich's was the pinnacle." If Rich's could be forced to desegregate, other retailers in town — Davison's, W. T. Grant, Woolworth's, Kresge's, Sears-Roebuck — would have to follow suit. So would the drugstores and restaurants and movie theaters.

Bond and King, both juniors at Morehouse College, made something of an odd couple. Elegant and erudite, the son of educators, Bond had grown up in Pennsylvania attending a Quaker prep school with a mostly white student body. On the Morehouse campus he was known for his love of talking and his skill as a writer. Lonnie King, no relation to Martin Luther King, Jr., was a native Atlantan and the son of a maid. A Navy veteran with a powerful build, he starred on the Morehouse football team and displayed the physical courage and charisma of a born leader. The two men became allies.

In the summer of 1960, Bond and King distributed flyers calling on Rich's black customers to boycott the store and turn in their charge cards. "Close out your charge account with segregation, open up your account with freedom," their slogan urged. In August, King led a small group of students to a "test" sit-in at one of the store's lunch counters, which was promptly closed down in their faces. Later that same afternoon, Chief Jenkins called King and asked him to come to the police station for a meeting with Richard Rich.

The encounter went badly. Rich believed he had shown restraint. He noted that he had not ordered the students arrested, but he threatened to do so if they returned. "Well, Mr. Rich," King replied, "we *are* coming back, so you might as well put us in jail right now."

Rich fumed to his business associates that the black students were putting him in an impossible position. Even if he wanted to relax the store's racial policies, he could not afford to alienate his white customers. His greatest fear was a counter-boycott by Lester Maddox and other segregationists. He was being punished, it seemed, for having a lot of black customers.

The black students stayed away from Rich's for the next two months, not out of any sense of trepidation, but because King and Bond hoped to maximize the impact of the coming confrontation. As a measure of the rapid changes taking place in the dynamics of race relations in the city and across the country, it is noteworthy that their reason for delay was their hope of affecting the outcome of the 1960 presidential election — which, in fact, they did.

Martin Luther King, Jr., had shown little enthusiasm for joining the sit-in movement. The underlying strategy, known as "jail, not bail," called for those arrested to refuse bond and crowd the jail cells, gaining publicity while at the same time putting a strain on the legal system. King doubted his place was behind bars. But after his acquittal on the tax fraud charges in Alabama, he became the subject of an intense lobbying effort by Bond, Lonnie King, and others in SNCC. If Martin King were arrested and jailed at Rich's, the story would make headlines and ratchet up the pressure for capitulation. After several days of fruitless discussion, Lonnie King finally confronted Martin directly. "Martin, hear me out," he recalled saying. "You cannot lead this movement from the back." King reluctantly agreed to participate.

At 11 o'clock on the morning of Wednesday, October 19, 1960, hundreds of well-dressed, black college students descended on downtown Atlanta and fanned out to stage sit-ins at Rich's and seven other stores. King was part of a group that went to the sixth-floor Magnolia Room at Rich's and milled around the doorway, waiting for luncheon seating to begin. Frank Neely, the chairman of Rich's, arrived on the scene and asked them to leave. When they refused, he charged them with trespassing and had them arrested.

King declined bond and spent the night in the Fulton County jail. His incarceration had the desired effect. In the days after his arrest, black students swarmed downtown and began picketing Rich's, stepping up their calls for a boycott. White counter demonstrators, including members of the Klan, took up positions across the street. Maddox and some of his supporters formed a group called Georgians Unwilling to Surrender — GUTS — and joined the fray. Chief Jenkins had patrol cars circling Rich's every few minutes to keep the two sides apart. Few customers dared go inside the store. Newspapers and TV stations gave the standoff full coverage.

Mayor Hartsfield's worst nightmare had sprung to life. A racial conflict was taking place in Atlanta in plain view, documented for all the
world to see, giving the lie to Atlanta's carefully cultivated image. City
Hall got so many angry telegrams, Hartsfield recalled later, that he finally
called Western Union and said, "Listen, boys, bring these things over in
batches. You don't have to send every one."

The mayor spent hours on the phone, trying to round up parties who
could negotiate a settlement. But after 20 years, he could no longer judge
with certainty just who spoke for Atlanta's black leadership. Black
Atlantans themselves seemed to be confused. The old-timers — "Daddy"
King, A. T. Walden, William Holmes Borders — appointed an intermediary, Jesse Hill, a rising young executive at Atlanta Life, to talk on their
behalf with Julian Bond and Lonnie King and other student leaders.
Power was shifting, how far and fast no one could say.

On Saturday, three days after the arrest, with King still in jail and pressure mounting, Hartsfield took the expedient step of inviting every
prominent black he could think of to a meeting at City Hall. Sixty black
leaders gathered in the council chambers on the second floor, where the
mayor joined them and locked the door to keep reporters out. The deal
he proposed was disarmingly simple. If the students would agree to suspend their picketing for 30 days, he would have King and the students
released and the charges dropped. Negotiations for a permanent settlement could begin immediately. What those negotiations might accomplish was left purposely vague.

While the black leaders caucused, Hartsfield went back to his office
on the other side of City Hall. There he received a providential visit
from an old friend, Morris Abram, one of Atlanta's top lawyers, a liberal
activist with ties to Senator John F. Kennedy. Earlier that morning,
Abram told the mayor, he had received a phone call from Kennedy's top
civil rights adviser, Harris Wofford, expressing concern about the situation in Atlanta and asking what could be done to secure King's release.

Hartsfield's response, as he enjoyed recounting it, was a brainstorm of
the "Eureka!" variety. If Senator Kennedy would endorse the terms of the
mayor's proposed deal, especially the part about releasing King, Hartsfield could go back to the black leaders with his hand immeasurably
strengthened. He had Abram call Wofford back and propose that
Kennedy issue a public statement. For years afterward, Hartsfield claimed
that he recognized instantly how much Kennedy could help himself with
black voters across the nation by making such a gesture, but in truth the

mayor's concern at the time appears to have been almost entirely parochial. He had a roomful of agitated black leaders he wanted desperately to placate, and he still faced the delicate task of persuading Rich's officials and state prosecutors to drop the charges — a part of the bargain he had promised but had yet to arrange. Who won the presidential election in two weeks didn't much concern him.

In any case, Wofford turned him down, believing the risks of white backlash in the South were too great for Kennedy to intervene on King's behalf. Wofford made a half-hearted effort to reach Kennedy, who was campaigning in the Midwest, before quickly giving up. But Hartsfield, never one to surrender easily, barged ahead anyway. He went back to the council chambers and told the black leaders in vague terms that Senator Kennedy's people had called asking for King to be turned loose. The news was on the wires within the hour. Kennedy's inner circle, furious, had no choice but to issue a carefully worded statement calling for an inquiry into the situation.

There is some evidence that Hartsfield's actual goal was to get *both* presidential candidates, Richard Nixon as well as Kennedy, to press publicly for King's release. With City Hall's switchboard closed for the weekend, the mayor lent his office telephone to John Calhoun, an old-line black Republican and Nixon's top supporter in Atlanta, who called Republican campaign officials to pitch the idea. But they turned him down. Nixon, the mayor was told, "didn't want to upset the apple cart."

By Saturday evening, even without Nixon aboard, the pieces of Hartsfield's compact had fallen into place. Richard Rich and the prosecutors agreed to drop the charges, King and the students agreed to leave jail, and the black leaders agreed to suspend picketing. The Reverend Borders, in his fourth decade of negotiating with white mayors, called the day's work "the best meeting we've ever had in the city of Atlanta." Discussions were to begin the following Monday on terms for desegregating businesses in downtown Atlanta.

But Monday morning brought a stunning reversal. Oscar Mitchell, a judge in neighboring DeKalb County, issued a bench warrant for King's arrest. A month earlier, in a traffic case, Mitchell had fined King $25 for failure to obtain a Georgia driver's license. To discourage King from returning to DeKalb, Mitchell had also given him a suspended 12-month jail sentence. The judge now notified his counterparts in Fulton County that he wanted King back in his courtroom. Two detectives arrived at the Fulton jail, handcuffed King, put him in the back seat of a police car next to a huge German shepherd, and transferred him to DeKalb County.

At a hearing the next day, while King and his lawyers and family listened in disbelief, the judge ruled that King was in violation of probation and ordered him to serve four months at hard labor on a road gang. Refusing to grant an appeal bond — as state law required in misdemeanor cases — Mitchell kept King in custody. Several hours later, in the middle of the night, the judge had him driven to Reidsville, the state's maximum security prison in southeast Georgia.

The harsh, ham-fisted treatment of King sent a wave of anger and panic through the black community and triggered headlines around the country. Hartsfield was livid, worried as always about the city's reputation. "We want the world to know," he told reporters, "that Atlanta had nothing to do with this." He asked newsmen not to use an Atlanta dateline on their stories.

Oddly enough, it was Governor Vandiver, not Hartsfield, who did the most to secure King's freedom. Unlike Hartsfield, Vandiver had an urgent interest in seeing Kennedy win the presidency. Weary of the strain of holding office in Georgia, and still hogtied by his "no, not one" promise, the governor hoped to escape by landing a job in Washington with the new administration. As revulsion over the King case spread, Vandiver got an early morning call from Senator Kennedy asking him if he could pull strings and get King released. Vandiver promised to try. But it was essential, he added, for Kennedy to remain silent. Otherwise, he would alienate the state's white voters.

Two of Kennedy's aides, Wofford and Sargent Shriver, urged the senator at least to call King's wife, Coretta, with an expression of encouragement. Six months pregnant and frightened to the point of hysteria, she believed her husband might be killed in Reidsville. Moved by the Kings' plight, Kennedy placed a now-famous phone call from his hotel room in Chicago to Coretta King in Atlanta, telling her he was concerned and thinking about her, and adding, "If there is anything I can do to help, please feel free to call on me."

Meanwhile, Vandiver dispatched an intermediary to see Judge Mitchell, who agreed to release King if one of the Kennedys would provide him political cover by asking him to do so. Bobby Kennedy made the call, and the next morning Mitchell signed an order freeing King on bond. Taking no chances, King's colleagues in the Southern Christian Leadership Conference chartered a private plane, flew to Reidsville, and brought him home to a joyous reception.

Word of the Kennedy brothers' phone calls flashed immediately through Atlanta's black community. Daddy King, a lifelong Lincoln Republican, announced his conversion that very night from the pulpit of Ebenezer Baptist Church, telling the congregation he would vote for Kennedy and deliver a "suitcase" full of other black votes as well. Black newspapers trumpeted the story.

In the days ahead, Hartsfield's blithe prediction came true. Blacks in the big cities of the North went heavily for Kennedy, giving him the margin of victory in Illinois, Michigan, and other key states. In the South, no white backlash of serious proportion materialized. Kennedy carried Georgia with more than 62 percent of the vote, a better showing than his home state, Massachusetts.

King's release and the subsequent thirty-day truce in Atlanta's sit-in campaign left Hartsfield feeling almost giddy. The city's archconservative congressman, James Davis, still in office 14 years after defeating Helen Douglas Mankin, held a rally and lambasted the mayor for negotiating with the black leaders. Hartsfield responded by announcing a last-minute write-in campaign against Davis by Willie B., the Atlanta Zoo's newly arrived baby gorilla. What the city needed, Hartsfield announced, posing in the zoo's monkey house with the ape that bore his nickname, was a "laughing campaign" to break the tension. He counted it a moral victory on election day when Willie B. got several hundred votes.

The lighthearted mood proved brief. In the two weeks after the election, Hartsfield discovered that reaching a desegregation agreement with the merchants of downtown Atlanta would be far harder than he anticipated. The white businessmen all looked to Rich's to guide them, and Richard Rich, still furious over the arrests at his store and terrified of Klan reprisals, refused to budge. After years of fashioning artful compromises, the mayor sensed his magic wearing off.

In mid-November, with black and white pickets alike beginning to agitate anew, Hartsfield sent a dire letter to John Sibley. "All of these matters have now come to a point, both lunch room and school, where the power structure of this town simply must come forth and shape the future of this community," he wrote. Failure would mean severe financial loss to every business in town. "John," he warned, "the top twenty-five people of this community (the men, not the boys) have simply got to cancel a few out-of-town engagements, get together, and help me decide what to do." Making plain his urgency, he sent a carbon copy to Robert Woodruff, the most powerful man in the city.

By December, the streets of downtown Atlanta were approaching crisis again. Some chain stores, susceptible to national pressure, announced they would voluntarily desegregate. The result was picketing by Klan members who marched the sidewalks in sandwich boards blasting "the NAACP in Atlanta boycott." The Klan held a meeting in the rooftop room of the elegant Dinkler Plaza Hotel, where a speaker mocked the undercover police in attendance, calling them "pimps" and vowing big changes after the next city election. Returning to the hotel a few days later, the Klansmen threw a festive Christmas party wearing their robes and hoods and full regalia.

Things had been coming to a head for a long time, and Hartsfield began showing signs of stress and fatigue. Visitors occasionally found him napping in his office, while at other times he seemed overly energized. When a bomb went off one night at a black elementary school, he verged on despair, blaming an "ignorant rabble . . . encouraged by the silence of most of our substantial civic leaders." At 71, the mayor had mixed feelings about running for another term. Stuck for years in a loveless marriage, he wanted a divorce and planned to marry a much younger woman, Tollie Tolan, which would preclude another campaign.

At the prompting of Woodruff and Sibley, Hartsfield gave the job of negotiating the desegregation agreement to Ivan Allen, Jr., a patrician businessman just starting his term as president of the Atlanta Chamber of Commerce. With designs of his own on the mayor's office, Allen accepted the role of mediator as a kind of audition. His first challenge was to find parties willing to speak to each other. Still balking at any personal involvement, Richard Rich designated his attorney, Robert Troutman, Sr., to represent him, while refusing to accept any participation in the talks by the black student leaders or Martin Luther King, Jr. Eventually Allen invited Troutman and A. T. Walden, the venerable black lawyer known as "the Judge," to meet at his office for discussions.

One of their early sessions made a perfect metaphor for the way black and white leaders in Atlanta had grown accustomed to dealing with each other. Walden, a courtly man who drove a huge Cadillac, arrived at Allen's office and announced that he needed to use the bathroom. With a stab of embarrassment, Allen realized that the facilities in his own business, an office supply company, were segregated. He could not send Walden to the white employees' washroom without risking an incident.

Neither could he ask Walden to use the shabby lavatory reserved for blacks in the basement. Displaying a deft touch, Allen broke the impasse by showing Walden into his private bathroom.

Southern courtesy could defuse small crises, but Allen soon discovered that the larger challenge of desegregating the whole city had no such easy answer. With Troutman's blessing, he consulted the leaders of the top two dozen retail stores in town. They expressed willingness to accept token integration of some sort, if only to restore peace and reopen their cash registers. But the black leadership, Allen found, insisted on nailing down the details: "Did we mean the Negro could try on clothes in a store? Try on shoes? Go into a beauty salon? Use the restrooms and water fountains? Not have 'colored' stamped on the bills and advertising that came in the mail? Have a sandwich at the lunch counter? Use the same elevators and stand in the same lines as white customers?"

Unable to get the merchants to sign what amounted to a written contract with a list of particulars, Allen watched in exasperation as his negotiations stalled. Atlanta remained segregated.

And Vandiver remained governor. As a former adjutant general of Georgia, Vandiver figured the perfect post for him in the incoming Kennedy administration would be secretary of the Army. He had a go-between sound out Bobby Kennedy about the appointment during a visit to the Kennedy compound in Palm Beach, and the response sounded encouraging. Everyone in Georgia, it seemed, wanted to see Vandiver go to Washington. As Ralph McGill reported in a confidential letter to Kennedy, Vandiver was "a nice fellow with gentlemanly manners, but aside from a streak of stubbornness, he has not exhibited much ability."

McGill and Georgia's two U. S. senators, Richard Russell and Herman Talmadge, had a scenario worked out. They wanted Vandiver to step aside in favor of the lieutenant governor, Garland Byrd, who could oversee the desegregation of Atlanta's public schools without the handicap of the "no, not one" pledge. Byrd was the consensus choice of the state's Democratic leaders to run for governor in 1962, a crucial election because Marvin Griffin was planning to run again and bring his corruption and racist antics back to the Capitol. Beating him was essential, and facing him as an incumbent would enhance Byrd's chances.

Vandiver was so confident of his impending appointment that he leaked the news to the *Atlanta Constitution*, which proved to be a bad idea. In all likelihood, his previous public utterances on race would have disqualified him from high federal office, but as if to guarantee rejection, Vandiver went on a post-election "goodwill" tour of South America and declared with disgust upon returning that 80 percent of the people of Brazil had Negro blood — "a real example of what could happen in the event of integration in this country." With that, Vandiver's chances of conducting joint maneuvers with the Brazilian military shrank to nil. The president-elect's press secretary, Pierre Salinger, tried to warn the *Constitution* away from the story, but the newspaper went ahead and ran an eight-column, page-one headline trumpeting Vandiver's new job. The ensuing denial made Vandiver's humiliation complete.

In the first week of January 1961, McGill privately begged Bobby Kennedy to find a modest position for Vandiver to get him out of Georgia. The governor, McGill said, had become a laughingstock. Surely "something" was available in Interior or Commerce, McGill suggested hopefully. But the Kennedys, offended by the pressure and the newspaper fiasco, offered nothing.

The Georgia Legislature was about to convene, its rural members as reluctant as ever to repeal the segregation laws, presided over by a gaffe-stricken, lame-duck governor who still stood for massive resistance.

It was time for a final bit of luck.

For nearly two years, attention had been focused on the Atlanta schools. With all the commotion over the sit-ins, King's arrest, the election, and the governor's travails, very few people paid notice to a federal trial that took place in December 1960 in Athens, home of the University of Georgia.

Two black applicants, Charlayne Hunter and Hamilton Holmes, went to court attacking the welter of excuses university officials had concocted to keep them out. The two made a convincing case that the only reason they had been denied admission was segregation, pure and simple. In a ruling issued late on the afternoon of Friday, January 6, 1961, Judge William A. Bootle ordered Hunter and Holmes admitted to the school — not in six months or a year, but bright and early the next Monday morning.

The abruptness of the judge's deadline caught everyone by surprise. The university had been fending off integration for nearly eight years, ever since Horace Ward, who applied to the Law School in 1953, was suddenly and conveniently drafted into the Army. Now the regents had two days to comply. State attorneys tried desperately to appeal the ruling over the weekend and failed.

Shortly after dawn on Monday, January 9, a late-model green Plymouth pulled up to the cast-iron arch that forms the entrance to the main quadrangle at Georgia, and the two black students stepped into a 22-degree chill. Twenty-five white students who had gathered to watch their arrival greeted them with about the same amount of warmth. Across the street, a group of hard-eyed men spilled out of the Varsity restaurant and stood on the sidewalk, staring. Lending practical protection, some 50 newsmen crowded around Hunter and Holmes and followed them as they went to register.

By nine o'clock, the University of Georgia was desegregated. The General Assembly opened its 1961 session an hour later, presented with a *fait accompli*. State law required the immediate cutoff of money to any integrated school, and Vandiver, calling it "the saddest duty of my life," ordered the university closed until the law could be repealed. Members of the Legislature found themselves facing a hard choice. For all the good work of the Sibley Commission, the legislators might well have folded their arms and allowed the Atlanta public schools to remain shut. But the university was different.

As Gene Talmadge had discovered 20 years earlier, tampering with the University of Georgia was dangerous. The people of Georgia revered their school on the hill and treasured the college education that could lift them, or if not them, their children, out of agrarian poverty. In every city and small town in the state, leading citizens wore red and black, rooted for the Bulldogs on football Saturdays, and kept their diplomas framed on the wall. Support for the university — for keeping it open and functioning — went deep. If that meant accepting two black undergraduates in a student body of 7,400, many alumni said so be it.

Atlanta officials saw a chance to catch a ride on the wave of sentiment for the university. Ivan Allen quietly contacted several legislators from outside the city and asked them to be sure to include Atlanta's public schools in the repeal of the school-closing laws. Two bankers, John Sibley of Trust Company and Mills B. Lane, Jr., of Citizens & Southern, lobbied for the change indirectly, operating through their branches and affiliated banks in Rome, Columbus, Savannah, Augusta, and Athens, keeping Atlanta out of the spotlight.

While the Legislature deliberated, Judge Bootle ordered the university to reopen its doors immediately. On Wednesday, January 11, Hunter and Holmes returned to the campus. That night, after a basketball game, a rowdy crowd of Georgia students gathered in front of Hunter's dorm, Myers Hall, and began shouting epithets and insults. Someone unfurled a bed sheet that said, "Nigger Go Home." Rocks and Coke bottles were heaved through a few windows. Georgia's legendary dean of men, mountain-sized William Tate, tried to fend off the whole horde single-handedly, grabbing young men by the shirt, staring them straight in the eye, demanding, "What's your name?" and confiscating their student cards on the spot. Eventually Dean Tate found himself outnumbered, and the local police had to fire tear gas to clear the scene. Hunter and Holmes were taken away for their own safety and driven home to Atlanta.

At the governor's mansion, Vandiver played ostrich. He refused at first to accept reports of the trouble and later declined to send in a nearby contingent of state troopers to keep order. Had he acted in time, he might have prevented the riot. As it was, news cameras captured the ugly scene and transmitted it onto TV screens and front pages across the state, with a very sobering effect.

A good many white Georgians found themselves ashamed at the spectacle of the cream of the state's college elite bellowing hatred at innocent black youngsters. No one could contemplate the sight of Charlayne Hunter in tears, clutching a madonna as she left the campus, without feeling some combination of empathy and embarrassment. Judge Bootle issued another order sending Hunter and Holmes back to school, and a chastened Vandiver promised to protect them this time with all force necessary. Mocking him, wags said his new slogan ought to be, "No, not one — two!"

To his credit, the governor did not attempt to stand defiantly in the schoolhouse door. Without much encouragement from his advisers, he addressed the Legislature in a joint session and formally asked the members to revoke the school-closing laws. They complied within days. As a matter of state law, Atlanta's public schools could now be desegregated.

Older Atlantans sometimes complain that historians make them sound preoccupied with race to the exclusion of all other things. In the winter of 1961, they were.

White people's attitudes were beginning to change. A poll found that three of five white Southerners now believed their schools, restaurants and hotels eventually would be integrated. Ten percent actually favored the idea — a modest number, but up sharply from the meager one percent recorded five years earlier. "I would truly rather be pushed off the sidewalk by a few rude Negroes than have this guilt feeling," a woman wrote John Sibley. She had been moved to the point of shame during a visit to her maid's daughter's elementary school, where she listened to the little girl recite, "Let me live by the side of the road and be a friend to man."

Anticipating the desegregation of the schools in the fall, hundreds of Atlanta housewives organized themselves into a support group called Help Our Public Education — HOPE — that put out newsletters and brochures explaining the futility and high cost of resistance. A disgusted Lester Maddox sent them a Confederate $10 bill, but many others found their arguments persuasive.

Continuing his shuttle diplomacy between the white merchants and Judge Walden, Ivan Allen found that the schools were the key to reaching a compromise. If the schools would "go first" and siphon off the publicity, the businessmen said they would be willing to accept full desegregation of their stores and lunch counters 30 days afterward. When they offered to put the deal in writing, Walden accepted on behalf of the black community and announced the terms to the newspapers.

For Lonnie King and other black student leaders, the agreement brought deep frustration. After winning the battle, it seemed, they were being asked to wait six months or more for the spoils of victory. They were supposed to call off their sit-ins as a gesture of good faith when they had no guarantee that the public schools actually would be desegregated as scheduled. In an open split with their elders, some of the students threatened to continue the protests and undo the deal. Hoping to calm them down, Walden, Borders, and Daddy King announced a "clarification" meeting for the evening of March 10, 1961, at Warren Methodist Church. Two thousand people showed up in an ugly mood.

Borders spoke first, trying to reassure the assembly that the merchants would live up to their end of the bargain. Many in the audience, adults as well as students, were suspicious and brimming with contempt. Someone called Borders an "Uncle Tom" in a loud stage whisper. Daddy King, who was accustomed to complete obedience, angrily took the pulpit and tried to assert control. He defended what he called the "give and take" of the negotiations with the white merchants, saying he had been involved in such things for 30 years. "That's the problem!" a voice cried out from the balcony, and many in the crowd cheered.

A nurse, still dressed in her whites, marched up the aisle to the front of the church and berated Daddy King. "You mean I turned in my Rich's card and went without for all these months," she said, her voice rising with each word, "and now you're telling me that I should go back there again and they won't integrate the lunch counters until the fall? *No! I won't have it!*" Already restive, the congregation burst into catcalls and seemed on the verge of serious disorder.

What happened next made a vivid, indelible impression on everyone who was there that night. Martin Luther King, Jr., arrived late to find his father being jeered and heckled. Walking slowly and deliberately to the front of the church, he quieted the crowd by the sheer force of his presence. With tears in his eyes, he took his father's place in the pulpit and condemned what he called "the cancer of disunity." Praising the contributions of both sides, young and old, he gave a passionate, unscripted sermon on the need for common purpose.

For the first time, King said, black people had a signed agreement spelling out their civil rights. "And now," he said, "I find people here who are not willing to wait another four or five months, after waiting one hundred years and having nothing to show until now. If this contract is broken, it will be a disaster and a disgrace. If anyone breaks this contract, let it be the white man." His words were met by the humbled silence of assent.

Having performed the equivalent of a faith healing to save the agreement, he left as abruptly as he'd arrived.

With calm restored on the racial front, Ivan Allen was eager to raise money and begin his campaign for mayor. The hitch was that Hartsfield had yet to announce his retirement.

A perfect opportunity for the mayor to bow out gracefully came and went with the opening of a brand new, $18 million terminal at the airport. Eleven stories high, with distinctive turquoise wall panels and topped by a state-of-the-art control tower, the new facility certified Atlanta's status as one of the busiest air hubs in the nation. As laurels go, it would have made a fine one to rest on.

But the airport seemed to reawaken the politician in Hartsfield. He invited a group of state legislators for a tour and greeted them carrying a megaphone. "This is one of the world's seven biggest airports," he bragged. "It's Atlanta's, the whole Southeast's, *yours!*" He could as easily have said, "*Mine!*" A news photographer captured him leaping exuberantly in the air like a teenage boy, trying to touch his hat to the bottom of a huge mobile in the lobby.

Allen and his backers tried in not-so-subtle ways to nudge Hartsfield out the door. Mills Lane, the banker, sent out nearly 90,000 postcards that asked, "Do you think Ivan Allen, Jr., would make a good mayor?" Several thousand people responded favorably, and Lane leaked the results to the newspapers. There was more to it than just Hartsfield's age and plans to divorce and remarry. Lane and other members of the power structure believed the time had come for Atlanta to build a stadium and become a major-league city by securing a professional baseball or football franchise. But Hartsfield resisted. Indifferent to sports, his only interest was in replacing the Municipal Auditorium with a modern concert hall. He worried that a stadium would be too great a financial drain on the city's taxpayers.

His temperament was another problem. Rather than mellowing with age, he became more irascible than ever. The emerging politics of the '60s confounded him. To Hartsfield, advocates of women's rights were "civic furniture movers," while white freedom riders were "culls, misfits, and spitbacks."

For years, with blacks and well-to-do whites as his political base, Hartsfield had been able to ignore the voters in Atlanta's white, working-class neighborhoods. Now he seemed to want to goad them. "The top-club Negro votes the same ticket as the top-club white," he explained to a writer from *Holiday* magazine. "Everybody knows that except the old, rural, disgruntled type of white folks who keep mumbling about 'our Southern way of life.' We're not letting that raggedy element run our city." That had been his attitude for years, of course, but in the past he had known better than to say so out loud. Some of the mayor's oldest friends, including his main benefactor, Woodruff, dropped hints that it was time for him to head out to pasture. He tried not to listen.

By June, with the mayor's election just three months off, Allen realized that he would have to force Hartsfield into a decision. He called and made an appointment to see Hartsfield at City Hall the next afternoon. The mayor showed up in a gruff mood, nearly an hour late, and barely spoke to his visitor before stalking into his private office. After a couple of minutes, Allen followed him inside. The desk was cluttered, Allen recalled, and the windows were caked with dirt and grease, as if they hadn't been washed in 20 years. Hartsfield launched into a long, bitter tirade about the city's businessmen — how they did nothing but sip cocktails at their private clubs, leaving the city's dirty work to the mayor.

Gradually Hartsfield wound down and asked Allen what he wanted. Allen said he was prepared to raise $10,000 for Hartsfield and serve as his assistant campaign manager if he planned to run again. Hartsfield raised an eyebrow. "You must want something," he said suspiciously.

Allen admitted he did. "If you're *not* going to run," Allen said, "I'd like for you to make an announcement so that the rest of us can get in the race."

Hartsfield walked to the window and stood silently for several minutes, looking out. Allen remembered wondering if the mayor could actually see anything through all the grime. At length he turned with a weary sigh and said, "Okay."

The mayor announced his retirement at a press conference on June 7, 1961. He did not withdraw gracefully. The idea of being a lame duck chafed at him, as did the suggestion that he might be too old to run again. He challenged the reporters to a footrace around City Hall and swore he could beat all of them. He closed the session by clasping his hands over his head and bellowing, "The undefeated champ!" The words echoed in the marble hallway outside his office.

"So long, old tiger," a local columnist wrote. The newspapers brimmed with rueful reminiscences of the mayor's temper tantrums and praise for his accomplishments, just the sort of requiem he feared. "When you *say* you're through, you're through," he complained to a friend. Hartsfield had one last piece of business to attend to — the desegregation of the city's public schools — and he was determined to remain in control and bring it off properly, using all of his skills as a showman.

The plan approved by Judge Hooper called for 10 black students to integrate four white high schools when the school year began on August 30. Leaving nothing to chance, the mayor had the police chief, Herbert Jenkins, organize a screening process to help select the students from a pool of more than a hundred applicants. Black detectives were sent into dozens of homes to record the students' vital statistics — height, weight, complexion — and also their means of transportation, the layout of their houses, their parents' jobs, even their parents' personalities.

The students were questioned closely about how they would respond to violence. A detective's report on one 15-year-old boy noted that "he does not plan to return any insults, engage in any conversation or return any blows if attacked. Asked what he would do if someone spat in his face . . . he said that he would wipe it off and smile." The boy's main concern was what he should do if someone tried to stab him with a knife.

Once the 10 were picked, the police became their protectors. Kathryn Johnson, an Associated Press reporter who tried to interview them, was subjected to a background investigation. "She checks out all right," Detective J. D. Hudson reported to Chief Jenkins. When a Klan flyer listing the children's addresses was intercepted, their homes were placed under police watch. Officers attended seminars on race relations, and several were dispatched to cities that had gone through school desegregation to learn from their experiences.

The mayor stayed in close touch with Burke Marshall, President Kennedy's deputy attorney general for civil rights, urging him confidentially to keep Governor Vandiver from deploying the National Guard, since "we are very much afraid that the State officials secretly hope the situation will get bad enough to authorize them to move in over the Atlanta police." The mayor also asked Marshall's help in keeping the national media from going to the schools.

Hartsfield's strategy, a refinement of past practice, was to move heaven and earth to prevent violence, and then to make sure that if it happened, the media were kept as far away as possible. In mid-August, the city sent a letter to the parents of all public school students warning that "spectators, sightseers and loiterers" would not be permitted to gather near the schools. Reporters would be allowed to observe the schools from across the street but could not go inside. The mayor set up a press center at City Hall and had a special telephone hookup installed so the principals could be interviewed at long range.

The day before school started, Jenkins put the whole police force, from the K-9 corps to the helicopter squad, through a dry run. The daily report listed several white "racists and agitators" who should be tailed. The city's municipal judges arranged an extra shift to accommodate any emergency cases. That night, Jenkins assigned a squad to each school to guard against the planting of bombs, warning sternly that if the schools were hit, "the patrolmen better get blown up with them."

By the morning of August 30, every conceivable preparation had been made. A team of four patrolmen, a policewoman, a photographer, and a deputy chief went to each school. Paddy wagons were parked nearby. An anti-riot car stood by. At 7:30, as the black students left their homes, nearly 300 members of the local and national media were herded into their makeshift headquarters in the council chambers on the second floor of City Hall. A civic group greeted them and handed out booklets with welcoming messages, phone numbers, background information, even a copy of Sigma Delta Chi's code of journalistic ethics. Free coffee, Cokes, and sandwiches were served.

Out on the streets, the police arrested anyone who looked funny. A man wearing the emblem of the American Nazi Party walked up to an officer at one of the schools and asked politely if he could picket. He was taken into custody. So were two suspicious men at Northside High, who turned out to be FBI undercover agents. The question of civil liberties did not bother Hartsfield in the least. "A mob sizes you up," he explained. "They can tell when the law-enforcement officers have their hearts in it. When racists come in *this* town, they know they're going to get their heads knocked together." In all, only five arrests were necessary, so cowed were the forces of resistance.

The schools were desegregated without incident. At four o'clock in the afternoon, with the children safely back home, the mayor gave a tour of the city in air-conditioned buses to members of the press who had finished filing their stories. A later generation of journalists might not have been so compliant, but many of the reporters on the scene shared the mayor's feeling of pride in the successful outcome. The *New York Times* commended Atlanta for its "display of sanity and good sense," and for demonstrating a "new and shining example" other cities could follow. President Kennedy held a press conference to extend his congratulations.

Hartsfield's crowning touch went unremarked at the time. After the bus tour, he invited the press to join him for a cocktail reception at the Biltmore Hotel, one of the city's premiere gathering spots. A few of the visiting journalists were black, and by their presence, they unknowingly integrated an Atlanta public accommodation for the first time.

CHAPTER 6

ATLANTA, U.S.A.

To appreciate Ivan Allen's personality, one had to hear his rattlesnake story.

The encounter took place on a plantation in southwest Georgia, where the ruling elite of Atlanta liked to gather on winter weekends to hunt quail, dove, and wild turkey. On mild days in that part of the world, snakes frequently come out of their holes and curl up on the ground in warm pools of sunlight. Men, dogs, and horses have to be very careful not to step on rattlers dozing on beds of wire grass between the pine stands.

One day Allen was hunting quail with a female friend when they happened on three big snakes right at their feet, coiled and beginning to rattle loudly, ready to strike. Allen stopped in his tracks, calmly loaded his shotgun and fired both barrels in quick succession, killing two of the snakes. With the third snake still menacing them, he reached back with one hand and whispered to the frightened woman, "Give me two more shells." He reloaded and was just taking aim when a single quail broke cover and fluttered toward the horizon. He whipped the gun around, hit the quail, then turned back and killed the third rattler.

Allen, in a word, was a hunter. Unlike Bill Hartsfield, a fighter who lost his temper and bickered with friend and enemy alike, Allen tended to stay cool under trying circumstances. The Atlanta mayor's race of 1961 gave him a chance to bag a real trophy — Lester Maddox — and he did so with a marksman's bold instinct. At the first debate, while the other candidates held back cautiously, Allen deliberately assailed Maddox, calling him an extremist and accusing him of wanting to defy the courts and turn Atlanta into another Little Rock. Overnight, the campaign turned into a two-man contest, Allen against Maddox, the rest of the field all but forgotten.

At the age of 50, with a thatch of gray-white hair and a trim, athletic build, Allen looked like an English peer and carried himself with the breezy self-assurance of the well-born. His father, Ivan Sr., was the founder of an office supply company that gave the family wealth, and young Ivan made a good marriage to Louise Richardson, daughter of one of Atlanta's most prominent families. "I inherited money, I married money, and I made money," he often joked, displaying such good-natured pleasure in his circumstances that most people liked him anyway.

In 1958, considering a run for governor of Georgia, Allen had portrayed himself as a believer in segregation. Among other things, he advocated sending black Georgians back to Africa or, failing that, dividing the state's counties into all-white or all-black homelands. Three years later, after mediating the sit-in dispute, he had moved to the left and called himself a moderate. It was a measure of the black community's fear of Maddox that they accepted Allen's conversion, forgave his sins, and delivered him nearly unanimous support. With $175,000 in contributions from banker Mills Lane and others in the power structure fueling his effort, Allen whipped Maddox in a runoff by a two-to-one margin.

Maddox did not accept his loss with much grace. On election night, he and Allen made the traditional visit to the newsroom of the *Atlanta Constitution*, where they encountered Martin Luther King, Jr. As King shook hands with Allen and congratulated him warmly on his victory, an observer noted, Maddox "danced up and down on his toes, in a highly excited state and squealed, 'Lookee! Lookee! He goin' to *kiss* him!'"

The new mayor took office brimming with energy, ready to harvest the rewards that seemed certain to come Atlanta's way for its achievements in race relations. At his inaugural — which was delayed five minutes when Hartsfield showed up late for a final time — Allen dazzled the audience by calling for an $80 million bond issue, a highly ambitious program to build new schools, roads, sewers, rapid transit, a civic center, and a fine arts complex. He would need the voters' approval, but that appeared a sure thing in the flush of good feeling.

Signs of progress abounded. A non-stop jet from Los Angeles landed at the new airport, marking the debut of transcontinental flights. A bold young architect and developer named John Portman began the transformation of downtown Peachtree Street with a sleek, modern, 23-story merchandise mart that towered over the red brick office buildings and storefronts nearby. The Chamber of Commerce launched *Atlanta* magazine, a slick, well-written monthly whose inaugural editorial bragged that Atlanta, in effect, had "seceded from the Confederacy. . . ."

"This is some city," the Detroit *Free Press* gushed, "a real good one, throbbing with activity, on the make for the next main chance, the 'sleepy sand' of yesterday rubbed out of its eyes, southern in location, proud of its past — but national rather than regional in its outlook and motivations." When a story broke that Atlanta was third on the Kremlin's list of targets in the event of nuclear war (after Washington and New York), the news provoked civic pride, not panic.

Caught up in the excitement of the times, Atlantans embraced any and all superlatives they could muster. A study found that on weekdays between the hours of 11:30 a.m. and 1:30 p.m., the Atlanta Airport was the busiest in the world — a narrow distinction, perhaps, but for a city in the American Deep South to be first in the world in *anything* created a genuine feeling of accomplishment.

Even in the category of bad taste, Atlanta reached new heights (or depths). The Teamsters opened a motel on Peachtree called the Cabana, featuring a garden with reflecting pools and marble goddesses, central Muzak, a swimming pool with subsurface lights, and guest rooms furnished in Italian provincial and Oriental Mandarin. The lobby, decorated in gold, white, and blue, offered seating on marshmallowy, horseshoe-shaped sofas under wall murals depicting the birth of Venus. An underground passage led past a gypsy palmist and a knight's suit of armor to a plush restaurant, the King's Inn. The doorman was a dwarf dressed in a gold-braided coat, red pantaloons, and Hessian boots.

After the high drama of the public schools, the next step in the process of desegregation came off smoothly. Following the pattern of the retail stores, the city's theater owners agreed to allow open seating for blacks, provided the Fox Theatre went first and integrated its audiences when the Metropolitan Opera visited in the spring. As always, discretion was vital. According to the confidential minutes of one of the negotiating sessions, "The theater owners asked that the Negro community, as far as possible, try to prevent a large number [from] embarrassing any one theater during this beginning period." The Negro community, wearily accustomed to such concerns, agreed.

In April 1962, the U.S. Supreme Court handed down its "one man, one vote" decision, ruling that state legislatures could not be unfairly apportioned. Though it resulted from a Tennessee case, *Baker v. Carr*,

the order plainly doomed the grotesquely unbalanced county-unit system in Georgia. An hour and 17 minutes after it was handed down,
Hartsfield and two other plaintiffs raced to the federal courthouse and
filed suit seeking to have the order extended to Georgia. Not only
would Atlanta gain proper representation in the General Assembly,
the governor would be elected by popular vote — throwing the re-
election hopes of Marvin Griffin into serious doubt. Instead of a raging segregationist, the state might elect a progressive, the first since
Ellis Arnall in the 1940s.

In this climate of exuberance and promise, several of the men in the
power structure began to think seriously about reaching the next rung.
Atlanta had money, a growing populace, a strong economy, and a gilt-
edged image, but to become a great city, it would have to add cultural
amenities. Before Atlanta could enter the top echelon of American
cities, it needed a major league sports franchise. Everyone loved the
Crackers, the AA baseball team that played in cozy Ponce de Leon Park
with its grand magnolia tree in deep center field. But the Crackers were
literally minor league, members of the Southern Association, playing
against the Birmingham Barons and other regional teams. Atlantans
wanted to play in the World Series.

The Municipal Auditorium, with its venerable aroma, remained the
lone concert and convention venue in town, seating only 5,000 guests.
Both a civic center and coliseum would be needed to replace it. And the
High Museum continued to be plagued by money woes, especially its
affiliated Atlanta Art Institute. According to one internal audit, the
school had not operated in the black since just after World War II, when
veterans attending on the GI Bill were charged double tuition. The
High's exhibitions in recent years had been less than stellar: "Timeless
Wedgwood in Today's Settings."

Though all these shortcomings required attention, the city's business
leaders found themselves unable to agree on a list of priorities. In the privacy of the boardrooms of Citizens & Southern Bank, the Coca-Cola
Company, and other major institutions, a series of conflicts began to
break out, with the future of Atlanta's cultural flowering in the balance.

As is always the case, the problem centered on strong personalities in
pursuit of different goals. Mills Lane, the head of C&S Bank, an effer-
vescent soul whose office door had a brass plaque reading "It's a Wonderful World," wanted most of all to build a new stadium for major league
sports. In keeping with his aspirations, he often wore lace-up sneakers to

work. But Coca-Cola's Robert Woodruff balked. During the Depression, Woodruff had bailed out the Crackers, in effect buying the team, and the experience left him with little appetite for involvement in professional sports. His lawyer, Hughes Spalding, who managed the team for a brief spell, thought it was a smart move when Woodruff sold out in 1949. "It is just a matter of time," Spalding predicted, gazing into the wrong side of the crystal ball, "before the major leagues will lose their glamour and won't have the money to subsidize the minor leagues. And when that happens, baseball will go the way of bustles. . . ."

Instead of a stadium, Woodruff favored a center for the performing arts. At age 72, Woodruff remained in absolute control of the Coca-Cola Company and was still the town's leading citizen, utterly accustomed to having his way. He hired a retired educator, Philip Weltner, to design the arts complex, and Weltner quickly discovered that he was working for a demanding master. Those who envisioned philanthropists as kindly, white-haired, malleable altruists had never spent time with Woodruff, inhaling the fumes from his cigar and listening to him bark orders in a gruff mumble.

The immediate challenge, Weltner found, was to keep from passing out at lunch. Woodruff expected his guests to join him in a round of martinis before eating and refused to take no for an answer, even from "the professor." Eventually Weltner persuaded the staff in Woodruff's private dining room to pour him fake martinis, using water instead of gin, so he could keep a clear head.

Weltner's first plan, calling for a music hall and theater, was rejected out of hand. Woodruff wanted something much grander and also insisted that it be self-supporting. Weltner came back with a fantasy he called the "Bois d'Atlante," a grandiose design to transform Piedmont Park, the city's central commons, into the equivalent of Copenhagen's Tivoli Gardens. In Weltner's expanded blueprint, there would be a symphony hall, a pair of theaters, and an exhibit pavilion, surrounded by fountains, formal gardens, outdoor cafes, and children's playgrounds. In the second phase, Weltner imagined building a funicular, crystal palace, planetarium, a headquarters for the Atlanta Historical Society, and a library for the fine arts. It would become a national tourist attraction, he assured Woodruff, that would "keep the turnstiles spinning."

Satisfied with the revision, Woodruff drove out to Ivan Allen's house and offered to give the city $4 million to pay for the project. The only conditions were that the city match the gift by raising $2.5 million of its own in the upcoming bond issue and that Woodruff's participation be kept a strict secret. Accepting the terms, Allen helped brief the editors of the *Journal* and *Constitution*, who agreed to keep the publicity-shy Woodruff's name out of the newspapers. To guard against disclosure of his role, Woodruff instructed Weltner to "start a groundswell of public demand" for the arts center, and in due course a group of ballerinas arrived at City Hall carrying peach baskets filled with petitions from citizens supporting the project.

In theory, no one should have objected to the Bois d'Atlante (except, perhaps, for its name), but privately a number of people were grousing. Stadium advocates wondered how long they would have to wait to get public or private financing for their venture. And to members of the Atlanta Art Association, which ran the High Museum and the art school, Woodruff's plan looked like a thinly camouflaged campaign to eclipse them by building a new, competing museum. The inclusion of a "library of fine arts," whatever that might be, made them suspicious.

Within the Art Association, meanwhile, members had been squabbling for years over the future of the school, with one faction determined to shut it down and another resolved to give it a bigger building and an adequate endowment. In the spring of 1962, an outside consultant submitted a highly critical report, saying the museum and the school were working at cross purposes, undermining each other financially and "floundering in a kind of vacuum of direction."

Among those eager to close the school and redirect its resources to the High Museum was Ivan Allen, Sr., the mayor's father. A former state senator and longtime civic booster, originator of the famous "Forward Atlanta" promotional campaign of the 1920s, Allen believed the association "should conduct a museum and a museum only. We are too poor to go out in other fields." According to the outside report, the High's new building, completed just seven years earlier, was woefully inadequate and its collection unimpressive.

But the art school had a tenacious champion in Jimmy Carmichael, the one-time candidate for governor against Gene Talmadge. Carmichael was now president of Scripto, the giant pen and pencil manufacturer, and chairman of the Art Association. Rallying support from his fellow trustees, he outflanked Ivan Allen, Sr., (who accused him of behaving like "a czar") and got a green light to proceed with fundraising for a new building for the art school. For good measure, he also gained permission to recruit a full-time professional curator for the High.

In effect, Carmichael sent a signal that the Art Association did not intend to sit by idly while Woodruff and Weltner built a newer, grander cultural center halfway across town. The High and the art school, he indicated, would compete with the "Bois" for money and civic support.

As this intramural tension simmered, many association members turned their thoughts to a happier prospect and set off on a 25-day trip to Europe to see the masterworks of the continent's great museums. After a successful tour, the expedition ended in disaster. The return flight, a Boeing 707 chartered from Air France, crashed during an aborted take-off from Orly field in Paris, killing everyone on board save two flight attendants. In all, 106 members of the association perished on Sunday, June 3, 1962, wiping out the cream of Atlanta's art community.

When he heard the news of the crash, Mayor Allen raced to City Hall, still wearing the khaki work clothes from his farm outside the city. His grief was severe and also intensely personal. "This was my generation," he said. "So many of my friends." One of the victims, Nancy Pegram Frederick, had been his first serious date. "I remember riding a red bicycle over to her house when I was 14," the mayor recalled, stricken. All cities are alike when it comes to high society — an intimate coterie of close friends who see each other over and over again at the same balls, churches, and clubs — but Atlanta's elite was smaller than most and its loss more devastating.

Heeding an instinct to try to help somehow, Allen flew to Paris to identify the dead, but he found they were burned beyond recognition. He went to look at the wreckage and, as *Newsweek* reported, discovered a field strewn with "guidebooks, billfolds, travelers' checks, souvenir ashtrays, menus, gold slippers, blackened opera glasses, charred cameras" — the belongings of his friends. He picked up a vacation brochure that said, "Your trip will be carefree and unforgettable." It crumbled in his hand.

The immensity of the tragedy is remembered with great pain in Atlanta to this day. Over the years, it has inspired several heroic acts of philanthropy, insuring that the fine arts would be available to later generations. At the time, though, it worsened the friction between the remaining leaders of the Art Association and the backers of Woodruff's colossal project for Piedmont Park.

On the day after the crash, the association chairman, Carmichael, called an emergency meeting of the surviving trustees and vowed to press ahead with plans for the new school. He stressed the importance of treating the project as a memorial to the victims, who, after all, had been the heart and soul of the association's membership. Specifically, Carmichael said he was worried that a public outpouring of sentiment — and contributions — might be misdirected toward the Piedmont Park project. He wanted the High Museum and the art school to benefit, not a rival venture only recently conceived by others. The minutes of a trustees' meeting quote Carmichael as saying Piedmont Park "is in no way to be confused with the memorial we will build."

Had Atlanta's voters approved the bond issue, as expected, Carmichael's fiercely protective attitude might have remained a small footnote in the history of the arts in Atlanta. But a second misfortune was on the way, a political setback that caught everyone by surprise. Part of the problem was Woodruff's insistence on anonymity. His shadowy $4 million grant, the city's segregationists began whispering, was actually part of a scheme to integrate Piedmont Park. One rumor had it that a foundation started by Alonzo Herndon, the founder of Atlanta Life, the city's premier black-owned business, was the true donor.

Many elections in the past had been won without the "redneck element," as Ivan Allen called them, but in the campaign for the bond issue the black community was lost as well. Better able than their white counterparts to interpret the actual plans for Piedmont Park, many black voters saw the Bois d'Atlante as an expensive piece of confection intended for the exclusive enjoyment of the white fingerbowl crowd. On August 2, 1962, the entire $80 million bond issue failed, and the Piedmont Park portion took the worst drubbing of all, losing by a two-to-one margin.

Mayor Allen blamed himself for failing to campaign hard enough. It was true that he suffered from overconfidence after the relative ease of his own victory in the mayor's race, but in hindsight, the powerful combination of factors at work — black mistrust, the racism of poor whites and the grief and distraction of rich whites — made the outcome easier to understand. Still, Atlanta's bubbling self-esteem absorbed a heavy blow. Woodruff, by most accounts, greeted the defeat in an icy rage, mystified and offended by the outcome. For a time, it seemed he might be on the verge of abandoning the arts project entirely.

"I hate to quit," Weltner argued in a condolence note to him. "It may add to the grave danger all of us are in of finding our town drift into the hands of the ill-tempered race mongers and blackguards." Before long, Woodruff regained his patience and agreed to try again, though his options now appeared limited and far less certain of success.

In the weeks after the loss of the bond issue, Weltner began, as he put it, "to mozie [sic] around here and yonder, just in case," looking for a new site for the Bois d'Atlante. The mayor intended to try a second, more modest bond issue in 1963, omitting Piedmont Park. Searching for an alternate spot, Weltner was drawn to a large tract on Washington Street, just recently cleared of slum housing through the Urban Renewal program. Near the state Capitol and downtown business district, with 32 lanes of expressway immediately adjacent, the land presented possibilities that were nothing short of "brilliant," Weltner reported to Woodruff.

The more he thought about it, the more Weltner came to believe the Washington Street tract was perfect for the fine arts complex. He was not, however, the only one with an eye on it. The stadium crowd liked it, too. The city's benefactors were about to play a game of musical chairs.

By the middle part of 1962, Marvin Griffin's campaign for governor was in full swing. A master of the old school of politics, he staged giant barbecues around rural Georgia that attracted voters by the thousands. He always made sure to speak before the food was served, so no one would be tempted to wander away with a full stomach and miss the message.

The state's Democratic leadership had tried in vain to get Griffin indicted for the crimes of his first term, only to watch in amazement as he appeared before a grand jury in Atlanta and sweet-talked its members into returning a no-bill. He bragged that he had received a "clean sheet," when in fact he had charmed and wriggled his way out of serious trouble.

Griffin's lone issue was race. Were he governor again, he vowed, he would put Martin Luther King, Jr., back in jail, in a cell so remote "they'll have to shoot peas to feed him." As for civil rights activists generally, Griffin said, "There ain't but one thing to do and that is cut down a blackjack sapling and brain 'em and nip 'em in the bud." The Klan, in the midst of a spurt of renewed activity that included a cross-burning atop Stone Mountain, publicly endorsed him. Calvin Craig, the grand dragon of the Klan faction in Atlanta, arranged use of the Berrien County courthouse in south Georgia one night to show a pro-KKK film and speak on Griffin's behalf.

Having survived one Griffin administration, Atlanta's business leaders roused themselves to prevent a second. When Garland Byrd, the lieutenant governor, suffered a mild heart attack and withdrew from the race, the power structure united behind a handsome, hard-charging state sen- ator from Augusta named Carl Sanders, who was pro-business and, by the standards of the day, a pragmatist on race. "I'm a segregationist but not a damned fool," he announced, making a distinction every Georgian could understand. With the help of Lane and Woodruff and other "Big Mules" in Atlanta, Sanders raised a war chest of $750,000, more than adequate to cure his lack of name recognition.

As a practical matter, Griffin's candidacy was doomed the minute the federal courts extended the "one man, one vote" doctrine to Georgia. Griffin might have been able to carry (or fix) enough tiny counties to win under the state's old, eccentric form of electoral college, but the pop- ular vote now controlled the outcome, and Sanders won by more than 100,000 votes. In a memorable piece of political analysis, Griffin gamely accepted the outcome by saying of his fellow Georgians, "They ate my barbecue, but they didn't vote for me."

In Atlanta's Fifth Congressional District, the demise of the county- unit system put an end to the career of James C. Davis, the ardent segre- gationist who had beaten Helen Douglas Mankin in the ugly election of 1946. Fittingly, the victor was Philip Weltner's son, Charles, a liberal lawyer whose views on race would be considered enlightened in any era. Members of the state Senate, in a remarkable act of capitulation, accepted the court's guidance and redrew their own district lines to establish fair apportionment. In the ensuing special election, voters in Atlanta elect- ed Leroy Johnson to the state Senate, making him the first black to gain a seat in the Legislature since Reconstruction.

Unhappily, though, just at a time when the state finally seemed to be progressing, the city of Atlanta developed a few cracks in its shiny facade. Not only was the future of the arts in doubt, but in December 1962, Mayor Allen made the worst misstep of his political career. Hop- ing to discourage an outbreak of blockbusting in a pair of white subdivi- sions in southwest Atlanta, he had city workers erect a barricade across Peyton Road, shutting off access from a nearby black neighborhood. A large sign appeared overnight, announcing, "Road Closed." As if to stress its finality, the notice was fixed to a pair of sturdy two-by-twelve- foot wooden rails painted with black and white stripes and bolted firmly to an I-beam sunk deep in the ground. Critics immediately dubbed it "Atlanta's Berlin Wall."

Like Hartsfield before him, Allen had felt a legitimate concern for white homeowners scared of losing their equity as neighbors panicked and sold out. But lacking his predecessor's finesse, he made Atlanta look like a South African city engaged in the practice of apartheid. "Never make a mistake they can take a picture of," Hartsfield liked to say, and he tartly repeated the adage when reporters asked him for a comment. A cartoon in the *Atlanta Journal* depicted Allen as a trampoline, with various political enemies bouncing up and down on his back. "Mighty good way to keep in the public eye," said the caption. Reports in the national media were withering, as was the sense of betrayal in Atlanta's black community. The Reverend Sam Williams, one of Allen's staunchest supporters, said to him in sorrow, "I don't see how any decent white man can do what you have done."

Allen's protests, that he meant only to dampen the panic in Peyton Forest and that he intended the barricade to be temporary, failed to gain him much sympathy. He compounded his error by arguing that other roads in Atlanta had been closed for similar reasons, which led to further news stories and photographs. The editors of *Town & Country*, planning a spread called "The Miracle in Atlanta," very nearly killed the feature before opting for the more tasteful solution of ignoring the wall controversy entirely. At length the courts declared the barrier illegal, and Allen admitted later that he felt relief when it came down.

As the embarrassment of the wall waned, the city stubbed its toe again when the trustees of an exclusive Episcopal academy, the Lovett School, denied admission to five-year-old Martin Luther King, III, because of his color. The *Constitution*'s Ralph McGill made a point of resigning from the Cathedral of Saint Philip, the seat of the Episcopal diocese, in protest.

In the spring of 1963, the city integrated its municipal swimming pools, and in response huge numbers of whites withdrew and began installing private pools in their backyards. So many shoddy operators came along fleecing customers that Atlanta's legitimate pool builders had to create an organization called the Greater Atlanta Swimming Pool Association — GASPA — to clean up the business.

Bad as the publicity got, however, Atlantans could always count on their neighbor to the west, Birmingham, to provide a worse example. In the South during the 1960s, racial enlightenment was very much a relative question. Atlanta might slip from time to time, might move slowly and grudgingly, might offer a juicy target for liberals with a nose for hypocrisy — but then there was Birmingham, serving as Exhibit A for anyone who cared to watch raw, unapologetic racism carried out at the express direction of the governing authorities, namely the city's infamous public safety commissioner, Eugene "Bull" Connor.

Facing various court orders to desegregate its public facilities, Birmingham had closed its parks, pools, and municipal auditorium and had even stopped playing minor league baseball. In May 1963, Connor used police dogs and fire hoses — high-pressure hoses powerful enough to strip the bark from a tree at a hundred feet — to break up a "children's crusade" of high school students trying to march on City Hall. The resulting mayhem revolted the nation.

The differences between Atlanta and Birmingham were subtle but important. In Atlanta, thanks to Hartsfield's expansion drive, many wealthy whites lived inside the city limits and were forced to deal with racial issues if they hoped to preserve their property values. Birmingham's white elite, on the other hand, lived "over the mountain" in separate suburbs — Homewood, Mountain Brook, and Vestavia Hills — where it was easier to ignore the fate of the central business district. "Too late," a rueful Birmingham native admitted in *Look* magazine, "our 'nice people' learned that the whirlwinds of race hatred do not stop at suburban boundaries."

Atlanta's businesses, typified by Coca-Cola, tended to be home-grown and civic-minded, while Birmingham's steel mills were run by absentee owners slow to recognize their obligations. "The trouble with Birmingham is, the people who own it and run it don't live in it," one saying went. Arthur Weibel, president of the U.S. Steel subsidiary in Birmingham, counted himself an ally of Bull Connor and resisted entreaties by the Kennedy administration to intervene and force compromise.

In one sense, white moderates in Birmingham deserved greater credit than their Atlanta counterparts, since they contended with far greater resistance, but that was just another way of saying they found themselves outnumbered. Chuck Morgan, a white liberal who sat in on an early negotiating session between black leaders and white merchants in Birmingham, recalled that one of the white leaders opened his remarks by saying, "Tell me, what is it you niggers want?"

"Well, one thing," Morgan remembered answering, "probably they don't want to be called niggers."

Atlanta was blessed with a black middle class and a substantial pool of smart, talented black students at the six black colleges of the Atlanta University Center. Atlanta's sit-ins were orchestrated by Julian Bond and other savvy tacticians, who knew when to advance and when to retreat.

A great irony of Birmingham was that its lone black institution, Miles College, could not provide enough bodies to pursue the "jail, not bail" strategy meant to overcrowd the local jail cells and put pressure on law enforcement authorities. Protest organizers were forced to enlist elementary and high school kids in the cause, with the result that news footage showed the German shepherds and fire hoses being turned on children, not young adults.

At the very moment scenes from Birmingham were transfixing a national television audience (and setting the stage for passage of the Civil Rights Act of 1964), Atlanta's elders were taking steps to repair the damage done by Mayor Allen's wall. John Sibley and his bank, Trust Company, formed an investment group called Atlanta Civic Enterprises that quietly pumped $1 million in loans into a program to develop new housing for blacks. T. M. Alexander, the prominent black businessman, used the money to build two subdivisions and an apartment complex, paying back every dime with interest. And white investors helped "Chief" Aiken, the black builder, stay afloat after he overextended himself developing the luxurious Waluhaje apartment complex (whose vaguely Indian-sounding name actually derived from the first two letters of his family's first names: Walter, Lucy, Hazel, and Jefferson).

Other advances came in fits and starts. Mayor Allen personally integrated the City Hall cafeteria when he sat down at a table there with a black lawyer, Pruden Herndon, and ordered a Coke. The Chamber of Commerce was desegregated by accident, when a secretary routinely sent a membership application to a new business, the H. J. Russell Plastering Company, without knowing that its owner, Herman J. Russell, was a black man. When he sent in his dues, the chamber leadership accepted him rather than provoke an incident.

The Commerce Club was trickier. Built by Mills Lane atop a new, multi-story parking garage, the Commerce Club was an exclusive institution whose by-laws specifically prohibited black membership or even black guests. Early in 1963, Leroy Johnson, the newly inaugurated state senator, arrived for a luncheon honoring members of the Legislature, and watched in fury as a manager made a show of removing the knife, fork, spoon, water glass, plate, coffee cup, and saucer from his place at the table. Some time later, Ivan Allen convened a meeting of the club's board of directors and offered a motion that blacks be permitted as guests. In the ensuing silence, no one seconded him, until Woodruff leaned forward and whispered firmly, "Ivan, you're absolutely right." Such was

Woodruff's influence that the motion then passed unanimously.

During this period, in spite of the Peyton Road wall and other occasional blunders, Atlanta's national reputation continued to burn brightly. As if awarding a gold star, the *Saturday Evening Post* ran a feature whose headline, "Progress Goes Marching Through Georgia — Retreat of the Rednecks," nicely summed up the prevailing view. McGill had a pair of off-the-record meetings with President Kennedy at the White House in which the tables were turned and the President asked the questions. How, Kennedy wanted to know, had Atlanta managed change when so many other Southern cities behaved like Birmingham? Could Atlanta's example be applied elsewhere? "It couldn't," McGill answered. "Here you have the newspapers, and you have a mayor. You have a business community that has wanted to go along even though they might not all have liked it. But in these other communities, you had the opposite."

The newspapers, the morning *Constitution* and afternoon *Journal*, reflected the views of their late owner, James M. Cox, Sr., who died in 1957. The one-time Democratic presidential nominee was an ardent capitalist with an eye for profits, an unabashed booster of Atlanta, and also a raging liberal on social policy. Many observers have professed puzzlement at the newspapers' coverage and positions over the years, but in truth a long succession of editors and publishers, including McGill, simply carried out the Cox family's philosophy: Make money, support the Chamber of Commerce, vote Democratic, and urge a progressive approach to race.

During the sit-in protests at Rich's, rumors abounded that Robert Troutman, Sr., the store's lawyer, had threatened to pull his client's lucrative advertising if the *Constitution* and *Journal* failed to tone down their coverage. In fact, no such threat was leveled. The president of the newspapers, Jack Tarver, a hard-edged man who prided himself on "steadying the soapbox" for McGill, recalled many years later that it was John Sibley who approached him with a request — not a demand — that the Rich's reports be taken off the front page. Tarver declined. His lone concession was to kill a story about the rebellious daughter of a Rich's executive who participated in the protests. Putting her name in the paper, Tarver felt, would only have encouraged her and embarrassed her father.

As McGill tried to explain to Kennedy, the Atlanta newspapers walked a fine line. Episodes in the civil rights struggle were reported, usually in detail, but with restraint. The papers did not wish to whip up either side with lurid headlines or sensational writing. Nor did the papers like to spend money: When the Birmingham riots erupted, Tarver failed to send reporters to cover the story first-hand. He was accused of trying to play down the bad news from next door, when in truth he just wanted to spare the expense.

McGill saw himself as an insider and political player, a role most editors shun today. At one of his White House meetings with Kennedy, on a spring evening in March 1963, the President rocked back and forth in his famous chair, wearing a perplexed look, trying to get McGill to explain Georgia Senator Richard Russell's adamant opposition to civil rights. Kennedy seemed genuinely concerned about Russell, worried that the lifelong bachelor was "becoming lonely" and withdrawn, possibly ill. McGill answered that the administration might have more luck with Georgia's other senator, Herman Talmadge, whose harsh rhetoric concealed a more pragmatic approach to racial matters.

If, as seems likely, Kennedy was appealing to McGill's vanity, trying to enlist him in the campaign to break Russell's filibuster and pass the pending Civil Rights bill, the ploy failed. McGill had come a long way in his thinking, but he balked at the bill's public accommodations provision, which would force the owners of private hotels and restaurants to open their doors to black customers. Such coercion, McGill believed, violated the tenets of free enterprise. Kennedy could not budge McGill, nor could he get Talmadge or any other Georgian in Congress — not even the liberal Charles Weltner — to support the bill.

Several weeks later, still in sore need of a Southern ally, Kennedy phoned Mayor Allen at City Hall and asked him to come to Washington to testify in favor of the bill before a Senate committee. Allen's initial response was that doing so would cost him re-election and end his political career. White voters constituted a majority in Atlanta, and they appeared united and adamant in opposition to the bill. No less a pragmatist than John Sibley, who believed in obeying the federal courts and in raising the economic status of blacks, expressed disgust with the idea of stripping private businessmen of the right to pick and choose their clientele.

There were two practical reasons for Allen to consider accepting the summons to Washington. Supporting the Civil Rights bill would repair his frayed relations with Atlanta's black voters, who were still smoldering over the Peyton Road fiasco. And on a far less obvious note, it happened that some of the city's hotel and restaurant owners actually favored the bill, at least in private, since it would impose a settlement on them and thus remove their establishments from the continuing crossfire of black and white protest.

Still, the mayor had ample cause to fear the consequences of going to testify. He talked it over with his wife, Louise, who encouraged him to follow his conscience. In his year and a half in office, bombarded almost daily with disputes about the terms and pace of desegregation, Allen had concluded that change could never succeed on a voluntary basis. Some of Atlanta's restaurants had agreed to desegregate, only to re-segregate soon afterward through rules that limited the number of blacks they would serve or restricted black customers to certain days of the week. Only five hotels in the city freely accepted black guests. If supposedly enlightened Atlanta was having such difficulty, Allen recognized, it would be an eternity before the rest of the South accepted integration.

Allen prepared a statement to read to the Senate committee and took it by Robert Woodruff's office for approval. Twenty-two years Woodruff's junior, Allen regarded the Coca-Cola tycoon as a sort of oracle. Like many Atlantans, Allen had grown up with a keen appreciation of Woodruff's willingness to use the wealth and clout of the Coca-Cola Company on behalf of the city and region. He valued Woodruff's advice, and of course he also knew there would be some political protection in gaining his blessing. "You're in a dilemma, and I know it's a very unpopular thing to do," Woodruff counseled him, "but you've made up your mind, and you're probably right about it, and I think you should go."

On July 26, 1963, Allen became the only elected official in the South to endorse the Civil Rights bill. He went to Washington, read his statement, withstood a thorough, hostile grilling from Senator Strom Thurmond of South Carolina, and returned home to a cold shoulder from all of his friends.

———————

At the same time he sought Woodruff's counsel on the Civil Rights bill, Allen asked for another favor. He wanted Woodruff to buy the land for a major league sports stadium and give it to the city as a gift.

The idea of building a stadium had been floating around for several years without taking finite shape. Then, in the spring of 1963, Charles O. Finley came to town looking for a new home for his baseball team, the Kansas City Athletics of the American League. Finley spent a day with

Furman Bisher, the sports editor of the *Atlanta Journal*, looking at possible sites. Bisher, an ardent proponent of bringing major league sports to Atlanta, took Finley to the James L. Key golf course and Lakewood Park, both of which left him cold, and then swung by the tract of Urban Renewal land that had caught Philip Weltner's eye. It caught Finley's as well. Sitting at the juncture of three interstate highways, I-20, I-75 and I-85, the site promised easy accessibility to people from all of north Georgia, even from nearby parts of Alabama, Tennessee and the Carolinas.

With the characteristic impulsiveness that made him a legend in baseball circles, Finley announced to Bisher and Mayor Allen that if the city would build a suitable stadium, he would move his franchise to Atlanta immediately. If possible, he said, he would like to make the switch in time for Opening Day, 1964, just a year away. Allen quickly agreed. As he put it later, "We offered [Finley] a stadium not yet designed, to be built with money we didn't yet have, on land we didn't yet own."

Allen prepared a confidential document for Woodruff spelling out the terms of the deal. The city and Fulton County could create an authority and issue revenue bonds to pay for the stadium over the long term, but there was an immediate need to acquire the land and get the architects busy on plans for design and construction. "To accomplish this," Allen urged, "I must have your full support and cooperation." Not only did he want Woodruff to pay for the land, Allen also asked him to underwrite the stadium's initial financing.

Woodruff, still cool to the idea of professional sports, turned him down. A little shaken, Allen made his next stop the office of Mills Lane, the head of C&S Bank. What he lacked in the way of personal wealth, Lane more than offset with sunny confidence and a willingness to risk his depositors' money. "How bad do you want this?" Lane asked. "Bad," Allen replied. In that case, Lane said, he would build it. Operating on a handshake and $700,000 in unsecured loans, Lane took an option on the building site and hired a pair of architectural firms to begin designing the stadium.

The decision to press ahead was acceptable to Woodruff, but the same could not be said of Philip Weltner, his philanthropic adviser. Weltner had been counting on the stadium land for his fine arts complex, he complained to Woodruff, and now it was being "jerked out from under us." For the second time in as many years, Weltner's dream, the Bois d'Atlante, found itself homeless.

With mounting frustration, Weltner turned his aim toward the area around the High Museum on Peachtree Street, the same place Jimmy Carmichael intended to build a new home for the Atlanta Art Institute as a memorial to the victims of the Orly crash. A collision of interests was inevitable, and it erupted when Weltner went to see Carmichael to suggest that he defer his plan in favor of the larger arts center. "Jimmy is dead set to do his art school and is stone deaf to a total perspective embracing all the arts," Weltner reported to Woodruff. "I cannot handle Jimmy. You can."

The exact timing and circumstances of the birth of Atlanta's Memorial Arts Center, long a mystery to the city's cultural patrons, can be traced to Weltner's plea to Woodruff for help. On Friday, June 21, 1963, according to Woodruff's private papers, he summoned Carmichael to lunch in his dining room on the fourth floor of Coca-Cola's headquarters. With single-minded firmness, Woodruff explained that he wished to acquire land around the High Museum for a performing arts center — specifically a repertory theater and a home for the Atlanta Symphony. Carmichael could have his art school as part of the complex, but its role would have to be subordinated to the greater project.

Carmichael did not give in easily. The school, he argued, was "a basic need" if Atlanta hoped to become a regional capital for the arts, as it already was in medicine and business. His first interest, he told Woodruff, "is always on the side of trying to assist in any cause in which you are even remotely interested." But in a politely worded ultimatum, he gave Woodruff a deadline. Unless Woodruff assembled the necessary land and got the project underway within two weeks, Carmichael would resume his independent campaign for the school.

Weltner, whose relationship with Carmichael had soured beyond retrieval, was not asked to attend the lunch. When he heard about it later, he was deeply upset, thinking Woodruff had made too many concessions. Weltner wanted to scrap the art school entirely, considering it "ill-advised" and doomed to remain inferior to programs offered at some of the area's colleges. And the idea of a deadline irritated and offended him. "This is a tall order," he protested to Woodruff, "and cannot be performed with a stop watch in hand."

But Weltner's fears were misplaced. As strong-willed as he was, Carmichael found himself outmatched by Woodruff. Within days, Woodruff had enlisted a team of dutiful allies, including real estate executive John O. Chiles, who got to work assembling the desired land around the museum. Richard Rich, the retail baron, agreed to help lead

a fundraising drive for the Art Association, but only if the money went
to build the sort of combined facility Woodruff had in mind.

In the end, as always, Woodruff's wealth tipped the balance. He still
had $4 million to contribute to the cause, and no one, Carmichael
included, could afford to be the nay-sayer who killed the gift. If anything,
Carmichael was fortunate that Woodruff agreed to keep the school at all.
At the Art Association's next monthly meeting, in July 1963,
Carmichael embraced the idea of a complex for the visual and performing arts, and accordingly proposed changing the organization's name to
the Atlanta Arts Alliance. The trustees of the new entity represented the
elite of the business community.

The stadium deal, meanwhile, ran into a snag. Unable to lure
Woodruff aboard, Mayor Allen and Mills Lane recruited Arthur Montgomery, head of the independent Coca-Cola bottling company in
Atlanta, to serve as chairman of the stadium authority. Montgomery and
Allen led a large contingent of baseball boosters to Cleveland for the July
1963 All-Star game, where they received a startling piece of news from
Joe Cronin, president of the American League. Charlie Finley could not
get permission from his fellow owners to move the team to Atlanta. The
stadium would not have a tenant.

Shifting gears, Montgomery immediately began sounding out owners
in the National League about the idea of coming south. Within a day, he
had arranged lunch with the major stockholders of the Milwaukee
Braves, who were suffering a run of poor attendance and looking for a
new home. The Braves' owners expressed a keen interest in switching the
franchise to Atlanta, but they had a contract with the city of Milwaukee.
They felt confident they could negotiate a release, but in the meantime
they could not make a formal, legally binding commitment to move.

Mills Lane wanted to build the stadium anyway. In September 1963,
he and Montgomery made a final appeal to Woodruff to shoulder the
financial responsibility, and Woodruff declined again. When he "did not
tell us what we wanted to hear," Lane committed the bank's money to
the project and gave it a green light.

The mayor warned Lane that he was taking a dangerous step.

"You go back over to City Hall and run the city's business," Lane
replied, "and let me run this show."

If it was possible for a city to reflect the personality of its business leadership, the Atlanta of 1963 could only be described as cocky.

Some of the decisions made in that year had serious, lasting repercussions, none so much as the placement of the stadium. The land that so many white Atlantans coveted for civic projects had once been an upscale neighborhood full of Victorian houses. Later it had degenerated into cheap apartments and eventually into a slum that fell to the bulldozers of the Urban Renewal program. The displaced were black families, who became the forgotten people of the booming 1960s. It simply never occurred to the mayor or his friends in the white power structure that such prime acreage ought to be restored to black ownership. The stadium was built on 62 acres of land acquired from the Atlanta Housing Authority, and one of its legacies was a belief among many black Atlantans that they had been deliberately uprooted from their homes in the name of progress.

At the same time the stadium and arts center were being launched, Atlanta voters approved a scaled-back bond referendum that allocated $9 million for a new civic center to replace the decaying Municipal Auditorium. The site chosen for the new facility was in Buttermilk Bottom, another black neighborhood cleared through Urban Renewal. Coupled with the condemnation of black housing in the path of the interstate highways, the pattern of dislocation of black families triggered deep resentments that survive to this day.

Yet even as some older black neighborhoods disappeared, the black population in the city continued to rise, padded by new arrivals eager to find jobs and join the middle class. Every advance in civil rights brought new black residents to town and sent increasing numbers of whites fleeing to the suburbs. Blacks swelled from 31 percent of Atlanta's population in 1950 to 36 percent in 1960, and the rate of growth accelerated in the early years of the new decade.

To Bill Hartsfield, settling uneasily into retirement and keeping a skeptical eye on his successor, the situation was alarming. Unless some unknown factor intervened, Atlanta was headed for a black majority, and that majority, Hartsfield believed, would seize political power and try to settle old scores. In Hartsfield's jaundiced view, the worst elements of the black community — those with the least education and the greatest sense of anger and impatience — would be the victors seeking the spoils.

As if to confirm Hartsfield's worst fears, the sit-in movement entered a new, ugly phase when a militant element led by James Forman took control of the Student Nonviolent Coordinating Committee. In January

1964, Mayor Allen announced that the major hotels and most restaurants in Atlanta had agreed to full and complete desegregation and would no longer try to discourage black patronage. Instead of welcoming the development, black protesters targeted the few holdout establishments for direct confrontation.

On the morning of Saturday, January 25, 1964, a large contingent of SNCC demonstrators entered Leb's, a working-class restaurant in downtown Atlanta whose owner, immigrant Charles Lebedin, had made a show of evicting black customers, occasionally by force, since the beginning of the sit-in movement. The black group claimed chairs at every table in the place and sat back awaiting service. Lebedin, short, stocky, and red-faced with anger, shouted at them to leave. When they refused, he asked police lieutenant Howard Baugh, a seasoned, street-wise black officer, to arrest them. Baugh declined.

The law applicable to such a stalemate was dangerously murky. The U.S. Supreme Court had ruled that black customers could not be arrested merely for entering an establishment and asking to be served. But Congress, still hung up by the Senate filibuster, had yet to pass the Civil Rights bill requiring proprietors to provide service on demand. In principle, the blacks could sit at Leb's as long as they wanted, and Leb could fold his arms and ignore them as long as *he* wanted. Only no one had that much patience.

Shortly after taking their seats, some of the protesters began nibbling on the pickles and crackers on the tables. Lebedin rushed at them demanding 25 cents apiece to pay for the food. Lieutenant Baugh, sensitive to the legal niceties at work, asked Lebedin, "Do I understand you to be serving these people?" Seeing the trap, Lebedin quickly rejected payment and, instead, snatched up all of the remaining condiments on the tables. Then he retreated behind the counter, locked his restrooms, and began a war of attrition. In the hours after the media left, Lebedin complained later, the protesters damaged his furniture and equipment, and some of them urinated on his floor.

Outside Leb's, word of the standoff spread quickly. A group of about 20 robed Klansmen had spent much of the day across the street and up the next block at the Dinkler Plaza Hotel, protesting the management's acceptance of Mayor Allen's desegregation agreement. "Don't trade here," urged a placard carried by one of the Klan members. "Owners of this business surrendered to the race mixers." Toward dusk, the Klan leader, Calvin Craig, began marching his people around the block in front of Leb's, picking up white supporters as he went.

Black demonstrators gathered outside Leb's, too, creating what one policeman called the most volatile mix yet in Atlanta's long experiment with racial chemistry. At the rudimentary level of street protest, those on opposite sides of the racial divide had begun to adopt each others' tactics. Craig was a modern Klansman, if such a thing is possible — an amiable fellow with an open, slightly doughy face, who actually wanted to be liked and seemed stung when people shunned him. A dry cleaner by day and a grand dragon by night, Craig drove a blue Ford Falcon, talked lovingly about his wife and daughter, and tried to cultivate friendships with the journalists who covered him. One reporter, struck by Craig's lack of redneck speech, said he was a "nice guy" who "sounded like my next door neighbor calling up to borrow the lawn mower."

As part of the overall tidal flow of the period, the main branch of the Klan had moved its headquarters out of Atlanta to Tuscaloosa, Alabama, where Robert Shelton led the most menacing of the KKK's various splinter groups. Craig's chapter in Atlanta had renounced violence and was relying instead on improved public relations. Among other things, Craig had organized a "Klonvocation" the previous summer that turned out to be little more than a family-style picnic for racists.

The blacks on the sidewalk outside Leb's, meanwhile, were far from passive. Having the Klan outnumbered, they began mocking and taunting their old tormentors. Just after sunset, one SNCC member pulled a white sheet over his head and yelled, "Hey! The Klan's integrated!" Other black demonstrators marched alongside the Klan members, calling out a cadence like drill instructors. Then the blacks began singing, "The old K-K, she ain't what she used to be, ain't what she used to be" — possibly the oddest adaptation of "The Old Gray Mare" ever performed. One of the blacks boldly lifted the hem of a Klansman's robe and pointed at his scuffed shoes, laughing. Dick Gregory, the comedian and activist, pulled the hood off another Klansman and asked, "Is dat you, Lawd?"

As night fell, Craig's following grew to about 80 people, confronted by more than 100 blacks, with both factions trying to occupy the same stretch of sidewalk. Jeers were thrown, then some elbows, but Craig entreated his people not to strike back. They had to be non-violent, he admonished them, "just like the niggers." The Atlanta police broke up a few incipient fist fights before they got out of hand. Order held.

The next morning, a Sunday, black demonstrators entered the Downtown Motel, where Lebedin ran another restaurant, and sprawled on the floor, singing. Other blacks returned to his main business and set up picket lines on the sidewalk. Police made arrests at both sites on charges of incitement to riot. Craig, having gained points for the Klan by his restraint the night before, kept his group away. For the first time, blacks seemed to be in danger of losing the moral high ground, or at least the battle for TV news footage helpful to their cause. White backlash, ordinarily confined to the ranks of the segregationists, threatened to spread. Mayor Allen vowed to apply "the full protection of the law" to all citizens, the first time in recent memory that phrase had been used to refer to whites.

On Sunday afternoon, trying to revive the kind of deal that had worked several times in the past, Police Chief Herbert Jenkins arranged to release the arrested black protesters, provided they would obey the law and heed the orders of his officers during picketing. Reneging on the agreement, a group of blacks gathered in front of Leb's later in the day and tried four times to charge the front door and force their way in. A line of black police blocked them and made arrests. Several protesters resisted. At the city jail, a black trusty had his leg broken in three places when he was kicked by a struggling detainee.

As the scene in front of Leb's unfolded, A. T. Walden, the black elder statesman, now 78 years old, had a bitter argument with James Forman of SNCC. Walden begged him to stop the protests and accept the mayor's proposal of a 30-day moratorium. Forman refused.

On Monday, the police seized control of the sidewalk in front of Leb's, in effect closing the restaurant. Lebedin came charging out the door in a frenzy — "jowls quivering, eyes bulging," according to one account — and shouted, "Bastards! What's happened to capitalism? They're closing a man's business. What is this, Russia?" He was jeered in turn by blacks who had gathered to watch, many of them furious that they were now being treated, in effect, as the bad guys.

The worst of it occurred on Monday night, January 27, 1964. The police began arresting protesters again, and many of those taken into custody reacted violently. They rocked the paddy wagon and pounded and hammered the sides as they were driven off. When they were booked at the jail, many of them gave false names. Few turned out to be students. Later, in their cells, they heaved their beds against the bars and created a loud ruckus.

As racial incidents go, the long weekend of disorder at Leb's barely scratched national awareness. The Atlanta bureau of the Associated

Press sent out an analysis saying the city's reputation as "a model in racial progress" had been tarnished, but that was hardly the case — not with so many genuine horrors taking place elsewhere: Medgar Evers dead in Mississippi and four black children killed in a church bombing in Birmingham in recent months. Instead, the real significance of Leb's was the sharp erosion of goodwill toward civil rights that it provoked locally among Atlanta's whites. The leaders of SNCC, according to the *Constitution*, had "fouled the nest of equal rights." The *Journal* lumped the black protesters in with the Klan as "wrong-headed zealots."

The core theory of Atlanta's progressive leaders, that desegregation could be gradual and cosmetic, involving only token participation by the elite of the black community, lay shattered. Hartsfield and Sibley, among others, had preached the gospel of gradualism for nearly 10 years, and now it appeared that Atlanta's black community would not be content to send small numbers of its best and brightest into white institutions, but would insist on full, complete, and immediate integration instead.

The impact of this revelation among members of the white power structure can hardly be overstated. Just two years earlier, Hartsfield had written a friend in Birmingham urging him to "get realistic about the race question. [You] will never be bothered with more than a small number and they will be fairly well educated, literate, wearing good clothes, etc." Sibley had traversed Georgia selling a painless scenario in which Atlanta's public school officials would screen worthy black children and allow a select few to attend white schools at their parents' expense. Now the NAACP was suing to expand and hasten the process. Both men were badly shaken by the turn of events, Sibley so much that he wrote Senator Russell encouraging him to continue his filibuster against the Civil Rights bill, which he called "a step toward a police state."

In many ways, Leb's marked the moment when the curtain began dropping on the era of white paternalism in Atlanta. Leaders of the black community deplored the excesses of the incident, naturally. But they could do nothing to stem the deep yearning of their people for full civil rights. Judge Walden saved face by retiring as co-chairman of the Negro Summit Leadership Conference before the younger members could oust him. Martin Luther King, Jr., endorsed the leadership of SNCC. As in all social upheaval, the pace of change quickened.

"The danger flags are flying," Hartsfield wrote Sibley in a private note. Atlanta had to annex the white, well-to-do suburbs of Sandy Springs to the north and Druid Hills to the east, Hartsfield argued, "or we are gone in a few years." Maintaining a white majority was imperative, he believed, in the face of rising black activism.

Under similar circumstances elsewhere, white businessmen were beginning to snap their briefcases shut and abandon downtown business districts for the relative peace and calm of the suburbs. Not so in Atlanta. For two decades, all efforts had been directed toward building up the city proper — not "greater" Atlanta, or "metro" Atlanta, but Atlanta, period. Success was too fresh to allow a sudden shift of strategy.

In part, it was a question of psychology. As Jack Spalding, the editor of the *Journal*, explained in an insightful article, the long-standing goal of the city fathers had been to strip the "Ga." from Atlanta's dateline. "Atlanta, *Ga.*, had an auditorium . . . good for ice shows, wrestling, and little else," he wrote. Atlanta, *U.S.A.*, on the other hand, offered jets and interstates, and would serve "as a national city, not a provincial capital." The downtown skyline was a source of pride to Atlantans, who reveled in the tall new buildings shooting up along Peachtree Street. A local theater troupe dedicated a song to the flurry of construction: "They're tearin' up Peachtree, again!" Almost any sign of modernization, including the opening of a Playboy Club at the Dinkler Plaza, was counted as a positive development. New parking lots and garages dotted the streets of the central city, evidence of the downtown boom.

Cold, hard cash became part of the equation, too. By Hartsfield's calculation, the value of real property inside the city limits had risen to $1 billion — more than all of the surrounding counties combined. When Ben Massell, the largest individual landowner in Atlanta, was shown a set of plans for a perimeter highway around Atlanta, he exclaimed, "Like the Chicago loop! Everything on the inside, chicken salad! Everything on the outside, chicken shit!" Fleeing to the suburbs would mean abandoning the city's wealth. Executives of the *Journal* and *Constitution* briefly considered moving their operations from Marietta Street, but were pressured by their biggest retail advertisers, Rich's, Davison's, and Sears, into staying downtown.

Atlanta's growth had been driven in considerable measure by good race relations. The question now, in the minds of Hartsfield and Sibley and other white leaders, was whether the city could survive a period of racial turmoil. They thought it could. It had to. They had no intention of leaving.

A few weeks after the Leb's episode, Woodruff renewed his $4 million

pledge for the arts center. Work on the stadium began in the spring of
1964 on a crash schedule calling for completion in a scant 51 weeks. The
owners of the Braves planned to open the next baseball season in
Atlanta, and Mayor Allen agreed to pay the contractors a $700,000 pre-
mium to finish the new facility in time. Watching the beams go up, he
got the feeling that "we had broken away from the old small-town attitudes and were moving up a notch to join the very biggest cities in the
United States."

As ever, the airport cemented Atlanta's position. Delta Air Lines
had become the nation's fifth largest carrier and also the most profitable, thanks to its irrepressible president, C. E. (for Collett Everman)
Woolman. An old crop-duster with "a touch of cactus in his voice,"
Woolman saved money by refusing to carpet Delta's offices and by
keeping executive salaries low, including his own. He brought his lunch
to work in a paper bag. At age 74, after running the business for 38
years, he still kept his phone number listed so passengers could call him
at home. One night he stayed up late, personally helping a man track
down a lost piece of luggage.

Woolman's greatest joy was getting the better of Eastern Airlines, his
rival for dominance of the Atlanta market. He took a gamble in the
1950s and invested in jetliners, skipping the prop-jet era. When Eastern
had mechanical troubles with its Electras, Delta raced ahead in total
boardings using DC-8s. Legendary for his hustle, Woolman hired "girl
specialists" to call mostly male convention organizers around the country and sell them round-trip packages for meetings in Atlanta. His per-
sistent lobbying led federal regulators to grant Delta routes to Los Angeles and San Francisco, opening up non-stop travel between the South
and the West Coast.

As much as anyone, Woolman could take credit for Atlanta's status
as a national city. It seemed fitting, therefore, when Delta became the
litmus test for the next step in municipal ambition, the right to be
called "international." The first recorded use of the phrase came in
Atlanta magazine in the summer of 1964, in an article extolling the new
stadium. Major league sports, the writer said, would "complete the
transformation of Atlanta from a semi-Southern to a full-fledged
national and international city."

The same issue contained a full-page Delta ad touting a new way for
Atlantans to get to Europe. Passengers could board a Pan Am Clipper
manned by a Delta crew for a flight from Atlanta to Washington, and

from there a Pan Am crew would take over and fly the plane to London or Paris. It *sounded* like world travel. But what the ad really meant, strictly speaking, was that Atlanta did not yet have any international flights.

And until it did, the label "international" would be woefully premature.

CHAPTER 7

President Johnson signed the Civil Rights Act into law on July 2, 1964.

The next day, a car pulled up to the Pickrick, Lester Maddox's restaurant, with three black men inside. As one of them got out, Maddox came rushing toward him with a pistol in his hand, shouting, "Get out of here! And don't ever come back!" Maddox's son, Lester Jr., accosted the man, the Reverend Albert Dunn, with a pick handle. As the crowd in the parking lot jeered and beat on the rooftop of the car, Dunn got back in and the men drove away. An Associated Press photographer captured the scene and transmitted it to newspapers across the country.

The period of racial turbulence that Atlanta's white business leaders feared and anticipated had arrived. When it ended, two years later, Maddox was the governor of Georgia, and by that lone standard the city could be said to have failed its test. Yet the mid-'60s actually propelled Atlanta to the new, higher level its civic boosters craved. Depending on one's point of view, it could be argued that progress came in spite of Maddox — or even because of him.

Watching the dramatic encounter at the Pickrick, many people saw Maddox as the winner. The black men were chased off, after all, and the restaurant remained segregated, at least in the short term. An observer described the victors as "Maddox's friends in torn sweat shirts and Bermuda shorts, gas-station attendants in sockless tennis shoes, frowsy Southern white girls licking Eskimo Pies, and Maddox's own Negro kitchen help."

Within 72 hours, however, Maddox found himself snarled in the criminal justice system, accused of a firearms violation in the local courts and

subjected to the scrutiny of federal marshals enforcing the Civil Rights
Act. Maddox spent his time shuttling back and forth between court-
rooms in the ensuing weeks, until at last he confronted a hard choice
from a federal judge: serve black customers or close his doors. He chose
the latter, making himself a martyr to some and an example to others.
Either way, he proved that the new law had teeth.

Most white Southerners responded to the Civil Rights Act with furious contempt, as evidenced by the collapse of Lyndon Johnson's political
fortunes in the region. The "Solid South," so nicknamed because it had
voted Democratic since the aftermath of the Civil War (and especially
during the New Deal era), suddenly cracked. Ralph McGill of the Constitution, who consulted privately with Johnson as he had with John
Kennedy, warned the president that white voters in Georgia were in "an
ugly mood." Johnson's running mate, Hubert Humphrey, got first-hand
confirmation when he was booed lustily while campaigning in Moultrie,
a small town in south Georgia. Republican Barry Goldwater won the
state easily in the fall election.

Given the temper of the times, a substantial danger existed that white
backlash would overtake even the most progressive of Atlanta's business
leaders. Coca-Cola's Robert Woodruff, for one, groused to friends about
the "outside agitators" and "beatnik-types" who were coming to the Deep
South to register black voters and push economic reforms. In turn, some
of Woodruff's associates criticized his close relationship with McGill,
Mayor Ivan Allen, and other liberals. Many of Atlanta's "Big Mules"
made it clear they thought civil rights had gone way too far.

The valuable service Maddox provided was to draw attention away
from the growing surliness of Atlanta's mainstream whites. For years,
Atlanta had benefited from the sharp contrast it drew with other Southern cities and with the rest of Georgia. In the '60s, as that distinction
threatened to evaporate, Maddox gave Atlanta a chance to live up to its
image. So long as the leaders of Atlanta's power structure considered
Maddox an enemy and treated him accordingly, they would continue to
appear more liberal than they really were. Maddox was not some hooded,
anonymous night rider from the boondocks, but a well-known native
Atlantan, a practicing politician who placed his beliefs on the ballot. He
made a perfect foil, the embodiment of the ugliest form of white resistance. Fighting him meant scourging the dark side of Atlanta's soul.

In the fall of 1964, Martin Luther King, Jr., won the Nobel Peace
Prize, an honor that capped his rise to international prominence and

enhanced his moral standing. The award left many white Atlantans unimpressed. In addition to their frustration with the direction of the civil rights movement generally, they were angry with King for lending his support to a strike at Scripto, the pen and pencil manufacturer, where black workers recently had begun picketing for equal pay. In Atlanta's boardrooms, King's new interest in economic justice was an unwelcome, disquieting development.

For others, though, the Peace Prize triggered a burst of civic pride. Former Mayor Bill Hartsfield likened the situation to the Grand Slam of golf won by Atlanta's great amateur champion Bobby Jones in 1930, when the whole town turned out for a parade. Much as he brooded over Atlanta's future, Hartsfield still believed in the importance of protocol, which dictated recognition of King's achievement. The city might not yet be "international," but one of its citizens was.

With the encouragement of Hartsfield and Mayor Allen, four of the city's top leaders — McGill, Dr. Benjamin Mays of Morehouse College, Archbishop Paul Hallinan of the Catholic Church, and Rabbi Jacob Rothschild of the Temple — organized a biracial dinner in honor of King and invited hundreds of the city's top businessmen to attend.

At first, no one responded. Feeling against King ran high, and the idea of a fully integrated social event was still too novel for most whites to feel comfortable. Many white businessmen feared the threat of counter-protests if they participated. Maddox had replaced his old organization, Georgians Unwilling to Surrender (GUTS), with a new outfit, the People's Association for Selective Shopping (PASS), whose mission was to boycott integrated businesses. He warned proprietors that there should be "no weakening on the resistance you offer to the agitators."

By mid-December a full-blown fiasco was in the making. The dinner was scheduled for January 27, 1965, at the Dinkler Plaza Hotel, and only a handful of whites had accepted. At one point, McGill grew so discouraged he considered calling the event off. Finally Ivan Allen went to see Woodruff at his plantation in south Georgia to explain that the city stood on the verge of a major embarrassment.

As he had many times before, Woodruff set aside his personal feelings and agreed that Atlanta should respond appropriately. He instructed Coca-Cola's president, Paul Austin, to assemble the business leadership and tell them to start buying tickets. In a perfect expression of the social etiquette of the day, Austin convened a meeting of top white laywers, bankers, and businessmen at the Piedmont Driving Club, the most exclusive enclave in town, where he sternly informed them that Woodruff expected them to attend the biracial dinner.

Even then, ticket orders remained sluggish. It took an almost unbelievable accident of circumstances to make the dinner a success, one that has since become part of Atlanta's folklore. Austin's campaign angered some of the hard-liners in the business community, including a white banker who began making calls of his own, disparaging King in the crudest terms and urging a boycott of the dinner. One of the men he phoned, Lou Oliver of Sears, Roebuck, objected to his language and complained about it to his secretary, who in turn mentioned the incident to a stringer for the *New York Times*.

In an article headlined "Banquet to Honor Dr. King Sets Off Quiet Dispute Here," the *Times* broke the story of the discord over the dinner, including the activities of the unnamed banker. As it happened, Mills Lane of Citizens & Southern Bank was negotiating a $20 million loan with the government of Haiti at the time, and representatives of President-for-Life François "Papa Doc" Duvalier called Atlanta inquiring if Lane were the banker in question. If so, they said, the deal with C&S was off. Lane swore he was not the culprit, and to reassure Duvalier he arranged to buy a block of tickets to the King dinner.

Other white leaders, on improved behavior with the national press watching, recognized the importance of supporting the dinner and began ordering tickets, too, until more than a thousand were sold at $6.50 apiece.

One final hazard remained. A few weeks earlier, exposing a breach long in the making, FBI Director J. Edgar Hoover had launched a fierce public attack on King, labeling him the "most notorious liar" in America. On the eve of the dinner, Hoover's deputies began contacting newsmen in Atlanta, peddling tips that King had been involved in extramarital affairs. Adhering to the statelier privacy standards of the era, the local newspapers refused to touch the material.

On the night of the dinner, nearly 1,500 guests jammed the Dinkler ballroom, more than half of them white. Gracious gestures abounded. Jimmy Carmichael, who had settled the bitter strike with his Scripto workers just a few days before Christmas, came to the dinner and sat at the head table with King. Archbishop Hallinan, gravely ill, insisted on coming to the ballroom straight from the hospital. King arrived late and apologized to Mayor Allen, saying with a smile that he was operating on "CPT" — Colored People's Time. "It always takes us longer to get where we're going," he explained. Allen watched in amusement as King's young children scampered around under the table.

Outside the Dinkler, Police Chief Herbert Jenkins deployed several hundred uniformed and undercover officers to squelch any trouble before it could get started. Despite a wave of threats, few protesters dared to show up. The only fuss came when Charlie Lebedin emerged from his restaurant across the street and stood on the sidewalk yelling, "Peace? Peace? A lot of baloney!" A white patrolman took him by the arm and led him away, saying gently, "Charlie, be careful. Don't get in trouble."

In the ballroom, Rabbi Rothschild presented King with a Steuben bowl inscribed with a dogwood blossom, the city's symbol. King spoke for about 45 minutes, evoking a "white South" full of "millions of people of goodwill, whose voices are yet unheard, whose course is yet unclear, and whose courageous acts are yet unseen." Afterward, members of the audience, black and white, stood together and sang "We Shall Overcome."

The evening marked a high point of racial harmony in Atlanta's history. As always, the lure of civic reward was at work. With the ceremony broadcast live over the 240 stations of the ABC radio network, and with dozens of members of the national media on hand to record events, Atlantans of both races understood the stakes. Yet much of the feeling was entirely genuine. People stood and talked for an hour after the dinner ended, waiting to shake hands with King, and one of the organizers noticed later with immense satisfaction that all of the programs had been gathered up and taken home as souvenirs.

"I must confess," King wrote Hartsfield afterward, "that few events have warmed my heart as did this occasion."

In the same month in the same city, with far less notice, a school changed color overnight. Kirkwood Elementary School, in the heart of a transitional neighborhood, was operating with a dwindling enrollment of 470 white children, while two nearby black schools suffered serious overcrowding. The situation prompted black parents to press the school board to integrate Kirkwood.

Under Atlanta's unique school desegregation plan, the original idea had been to integrate "downward" at the rate of one new grade per year, starting with high school seniors, so that it would take twelve years to reach the first grade. The point was to allow the white children already in the system to finish school without having to attend classes with blacks. Not surprisingly, the black community began agitating almost immediately for a faster, fairer pace.

At Kirkwood, with empty classrooms inside and picketing black parents outside, the need to accommodate black youngsters became too strong to ignore. On the last Friday of January 1965, the school board announced that blacks could begin attending classes the following Monday.

During the weekend, all but seven of Kirkwood's white pupils abruptly transferred to other schools. Five hundred black children arrived on Monday morning and found they had the place almost completely to themselves.

The warning uttered five years earlier by Roy Harris, the fiery white supremacist, turned out to be true. The desegregation of Atlanta's public schools would be more extensive — and more difficult — than John Sibley had suggested during his famous hearings. In the spring of 1965, responding to an NAACP lawsuit, federal Judge Frank Hooper ordered the schedule of integration speeded up to two grades a year. By summer, seeing the futility of further resistance, the school board voted to allow the immediate desegregation of all grades.

Since the plan provided no system-wide busing, the actual integration of individual schools commenced at a relatively slow pace. Black parents now could send their children to any school they wished, but only if they paid the cost of transportation out of their own pockets. As a result, most schools continued to reflect the racial composition of their neighborhoods, which in turn remained mostly segregated. But where blacks and whites were sent to the same school, it seemed plain that whites would flee.

The lesson of Kirkwood drew little attention at the time, partly because it was an isolated instance, and mostly because few Atlantans, black or white, cared to dwell on what might happen to the schools in the years to come.

The King dinner made it easier to think that race relations would continue to improve. So did the opening of the stadium. On a balmy, 74-degree night in April 1965, the Braves inaugurated the new facility with an exhibition game against the Detroit Tigers, winning 6-3 in front of 37,000 paying customers. Observers noted that all vestiges of segregation were gone. The restrooms were marked "Braves" and "Squaws," not "White" and "Colored." The ushers and usherettes, decked out in red-and-white-striped top hats, were fully integrated. So were the players and the crowd.

As a technical matter, the game did not mark the advent of major league sports in Atlanta. Officials in Milwaukee sued to keep the Braves, and much to Mayor Allen's embarrassment, the courts ordered the team to play one final season there. After a series of three exhibition games, the Braves packed up and left. But the certainty that big league baseball was coming to Atlanta for good the following year more than made up for the temporary disappointment.

The stadium proved to be exactly the magnet Allen and others predicted. The American Football League offered Atlanta a franchise for an expansion team, which spurred Pete Rozelle of the older, better-established National Football League to quit stalling and grant the city an NFL franchise. Governor Carl Sanders persuaded a friend, insurance magnate Rankin Smith, to pony up $8.5 million and become the owner of the new team. The Falcons were scheduled to begin play in the fall of 1966.

As a further rite of passage, the Beatles played in the stadium during their American concert tour in the summer of 1965 and drew a large crowd.

Some of the mayor's critics nicknamed the stadium "Allen's Coffin" because of the delay in getting baseball (and because he gave the Braves a very generous deal with the taxpayers' money), but the fact was that most Atlantans took great satisfaction in their new status symbol. Mayor Hartsfield had never enjoyed going to Ponce de Leon Park to watch the Crackers play because the working-class white men in the stands often booed him. Those same fans applauded Allen and helped re-elect him to a second term in a landslide.

By almost any standard, 1965 was a banner year for Atlanta. Unemployment fell to two percent. The number of hotel rooms doubled. Retail sales jumped. Twenty new office buildings sprang up. The phone book got so big, the Yellow Pages had to be spun off into a separate volume.

Almost everyone behaved like a booster. "We're building, as you know, a new South, a greater South," Dr. King told an audience in Philadelphia, sharing a stage with McGill. "And in a real sense, Atlanta is one of the brightest and most promising spots of that new South."

Some civil rights issues were easy to understand. Xernona Clayton picked up a copy of the combined Sunday edition of the *Journal-Constitution* one morning, turned to the bridal pages, and saw that every face was white. She called her friend Ralph McGill, who was always bragging about Atlanta's progress in race relations, and asked in a sweet voice, "Do black girls get married here?"

Clayton, a petite black woman with a warm manner and disarming smile, moved to Atlanta in 1965. She was widowed soon afterward and busied herself trying to build bridges between blacks and whites. McGill took an immediate liking to her and often asked her to speak to white groups. He thought she had a knack of expressing forceful ideas without putting people off.

Her question about the bridal photographs stung McGill. He had the newspaper's society editor call Clayton the next day with information about placing wedding announcements and pictures, and soon the pages were integrated. The same ideal of rudimentary fairness lay behind a far more significant milestone, the passage of the federal Voting Rights Act of 1965, meant to guarantee blacks access to the ballot.

Other matters were more complicated. Dozens of voices now competed to be heard, as Atlanta's black leadership, never quite so monolithic as white Atlantans liked to think, split increasingly into factions. King's organization, the Southern Christian Leadership Conference, faced mounting criticism and dissent from other black groups, notably the Student Nonviolent Coordinating Committee, whose young members had grown increasingly strident. And SNCC, in turn, confronted a serious internal rupture over the militancy of its tactics. Along with their attacks on poverty, black leaders began speaking out against the war in Vietnam, mixing civil rights into the stew of other burdensome disputes of the era.

In January of 1966, Julian Bond arrived at the Georgia Capitol to take his place in the General Assembly, one of several blacks who won election after the state House was reapportioned to give urban areas fair representation. Bond championed SNCC's position that young men should avoid the draft, which brought him into conflict with his rural, white colleagues. They voted to deny him his seat, setting off charges of racism and the inevitable federal lawsuit.

What the legislators failed to recognize was that Bond, while still youthful and impetuous, actually represented the moderate faction of SNCC. In May 1966, after a tense confrontation, 24-year-old Stokely Carmichael seized the leadership of SNCC away from John Lewis, a dedicated practitioner of nonviolence and a survivor of the bloody clash at the Edmund Pettus Bridge in Selma, Alabama. A man of very different thinking, Carmichael added the cry "Black Power!" to the nation's vocabulary, frightening whites in a whole new way. His hostility toward "whitey" was open and virulent. "When I see a Tarzan movie," he told a black college audience, "I want the chief to kill him and send him back to Europe." He announced that SNCC would no longer welcome white supporters.

The vague, gauzy goodwill of 1965 evaporated quickly under the strains of the new year. McGill passed along a confidential tip to the FBI that radical whites working for VISTA — Volunteers in Service to America, the domestic arm of the Peace Corps — were providing wine and marijuana to blacks in Vine City, one of Atlanta's poorest neighborhoods. Some of the white women from VISTA, McGill said, were sleeping with the local black men. And some of the blacks, he warned, "have been coached in how to turn over automobiles." Had it been written by Calvin Craig, the local Klan leader, McGill's memo to the bureau could not have sounded more like the work of a fevered racist.

The rumors of radical racial upheaval that swirled around Atlanta in 1966 triggered a fierce reaction among whites. One of Hartsfield's long-cherished dreams died when voters in Sandy Springs, an unincorporated white enclave just north of Atlanta, refused by a three-to-one margin to become part of the city. Blacks grew to 44 percent of Atlanta's population and seemed certain to reach a majority within a few years. Even the most liberal of white leaders, among them M. M. "Muggsy" Smith, worried openly that blacks would inflict punishing taxes on the new white minority.

With his restaurant closed, Lester Maddox placed a coffin in front of the entrance (mourning the death of "freedom, liberty, and independence") and began a campaign for governor. After losing two elections for mayor of Atlanta and failing a third time as a candidate in the lieutenant governor's race of 1962, Maddox appeared to many political observers to be a perennial also-ran. A poll taken early in 1966 showed that he trailed all other serious contenders. But by summer his stock had risen.

With few aides and almost no budget, Maddox drove his big, white Pontiac station wagon back and forth across the state until he'd worn out three sets of tires, speaking in countless small towns, shaking hands in courthouse squares, and tacking up thousands of signs along the roadside that proclaimed "Maddox Country." The two words successfully conveyed his entire message. One day he jotted his notes for a speech on the back of a sign, which he then inadvertently nailed to a tree 25 miles from his destination. It scarcely mattered. Few voters cared what he had to say, only what he stood for.

Maddox's main opposition in the Democratic primary came from Ellis Arnall, the former governor whose progressive administration in the 1940s had earned him national accolades and a liberal reputation. The wild card in the race was Jimmy Carter, a little-known state senator from south Georgia whose energetic campaigning and progressive stance lifted him within striking distance of the leaders. Polling was notoriously unreliable in the contest, since respondents tended not to admit their support for Maddox, but it appeared Arnall and Carter might finish one-two and face each other in a runoff. The winner would then take on Republican Howard "Bo" Callaway, a freshman congressman from southwest Georgia, in the November general election.

As far as the state's image-makers were concerned, anyone besides Maddox would do nicely as governor. The state Department of Industry and Trade placed a paid advertising section in the New York Times touting Georgia as the "Pace-setter of the New South," with the predictable attributes of a good climate, robust economy, abundant resources — and also an "intelligent government, stable but progressive, respectful of law, resisting extremes. . . ." The copywriter might as well have added, "Not Lester Maddox." But events dictated otherwise.

On September 6, 1966, a week before the Democratic primary, an Atlanta policeman shot and wounded an auto theft suspect during a chase through Summerhill, the sprawling black slum next to the new stadium. Within an hour Stokely Carmichael had a Dodge van weaving through the streets with a loudspeaker on top blaring, "Black Power!" Crowds gathered in the summer heat, and some of the men threw bricks and bottles at the handful of police on the scene.

At City Hall, Mayor Allen was told about the disturbance by his police aide, Captain George Royal. "I'm going down there," Allen announced. He and Royal set off by car and arrived a few minutes later to find several hundred people milling around. Some cars had been overturned and burned, and the streets glittered with shards of broken glass. Accompanied by Royal and a lone, uniformed officer, Allen began walking along Capitol Avenue in his shirtsleeves, moving among people and telling them, "Everybody, go to your homes. Let's go home. Come on, let's go home." He realized, he said later, that he might have been killed at any moment.

The mayor's act of courage worked for a while. But at dusk, as he climbed on top of a police car and tried to speak to the remaining crowd through a bullhorn, a brick flew by his ear. There was jeering and jostling, and he was pitched to the ground. Allen handed the megaphone to a young black man standing nearby, thinking the fellow meant to try to calm the crowd. Instead, the young man spat out a stream of invective. "Atlanta's a cracker town," he shouted. "It's no different from Watts. The mayor walks around on plush carpet and wears $500 suits and eats big steaks, while we eat pig foots and chitlins!" Soon the police were firing tear gas.

By the time the Summerhill riot ended, 16 people had been injured and 75 arrested. While minor in comparison with some other disturbances of the time, its reverberations were enormous. White response was immediate and hot. "Kill four hundred right away and stop this thing," Richard Courts, a crusty businessman, advised the mayor. "I told him he was a fool to go out on top of his car," Courts recounted later. "Tour the place in an armored car, yes, but suppose he were knifed? I'd rather see hundreds in the Grady Hospital."

Others whites shared Courts's anger, if not his violent candor. On primary night, Arnall finished first as expected, but with a surprisingly meager 29 percent of the vote. Maddox captured second place, just ahead of Carter, and gained a spot in the runoff. Two weeks later, thousands of opportunistic Republicans crossed party lines and voted for Maddox, thinking he would make a soft mark for their man, Callaway, in the general election. In the relative blink of an eye, Maddox was the Democratic nominee for governor.

The sobering effect of Maddox's rise was almost as sharp and sudden as the white backlash that helped fuel it. Mayor Allen erupted the morning after the runoff and denounced Maddox as "totally unqualified," his nomination the result of "the combined forces of ignorance, prejudice, reactionism, and the duplicity of many Republican voters. . . . The seal of the great state of Georgia lies tarnished." One of Allen's friends told the New York Times, "If you think that was a strong statement, you should have seen what he was going to say before we toned him down."

The mayor did not reflect on the role his new stadium might have played in triggering the unrest in Summerhill. Sixty-two acres of slums had been cleared, as the Urban Renewal program envisioned. But instead of building new housing, the city had given itself a shiny gift. Many of the black families displaced from the stadium site had wandered into even more cramped conditions next door in Summerhill, where some 10,000 people were packed into an area of about 350 acres. Stokely Carmichael had found an audience primed for trouble. Without much of a stretch, it could be said that "progress" had toppled a row of dominoes: First came slum clearance, followed by the stadium, overcrowding, black rage, riot, white backlash, Maddox.

There were other repercussions. Charles Weltner, the liberal congressman from Atlanta, announced that he would withdraw as a candidate for re-election rather than pledge loyalty to a Democratic ticket headed by Maddox. Alarmed, Woodruff sent Coca-Cola's top lobbyist, Ovid Davis, to persuade Weltner to change his mind. Davis spent an entire Saturday afternoon explaining to the young politician how important he was to the city's future (and how much money the power structure had invested in him). The next morning in church, Davis could tell by Weltner's haggard look that he had been up all night struggling with his conscience. He still intended to quit.

McGill felt wretched. "Things here in Georgia are bad," he wrote President Johnson, giving him a confidential briefing. Maddox was a "psycho," in McGill's unvarnished wording, and the thought of him as governor "is something that makes you draw back in disbelief that such a thing could be possible. The very worst old ones in the state are attached to him like leeches — Marvin Griffin, Roy Harris, and that crowd — but maybe Georgia deserves it. It is really an appalling situation."

The obvious solution of electing Bo Callaway instead of Maddox in the November general election proved to be a difficult challenge. As McGill explained to the President, Callaway was "an arrogant young man of great wealth who has never asked or taken advice. His banker and lawyer friends here are all in much distress because he will not listen to anyone." The handsome, polished scion of a textile manufacturing dynasty, Callaway had aligned himself with Goldwater in 1964, becoming the first Republican to represent Georgia in Congress since Reconstruction. He enjoyed the backing of Atlanta's business elite, led by Woodruff, who pledged to raise $100,000 in contributions for him. But he squandered his advantages.

Callaway lacked the common touch. Bad as he was at remembering names, Maddox liked to meet people and grip their hands. He had a politician's natural knack for working a crowd. He would press the flesh, literally, by squeezing people on the arm or shoulder as they talked. He delighted in greeting Mills Lane, his lone supporter in the Atlanta power structure, by chirping, "Hello, fat cat!" Callaway came off as stiff and aloof by comparison. Asked about Weltner's withdrawal, Callaway replied in a chilly turn of phrase that he was "amused," a response that did little to attract support from principled Democrats ready to abandon their party's nominee.

Maddox did a clever job of turning Callaway's wealth and connections against him. At one point, after Callaway paid a modest $6,000 fee for a two-page ad in the regional edition of *Life* magazine, Maddox accused him of spending millions on a slick "national" ad. On the stump, Maddox portrayed himself as a champion of ordinary Georgians, promising to hold a "Little People's Day" every other week in the governor's office, while hammering away at Callaway as "a puppet of the czars of politics and finance."

Viewing a win by Maddox as "absolutely incompatible" with Coca-Cola's business interests, lobbyist Davis went to work behind the scenes on Callaway's behalf. Among other things, he gave reporters the tip that Maddox had sold his restaurant site to Georgia Tech for $290,000, a generous amount that undercut Maddox's image as a martyr. Less successfully, Davis set up meetings for Callaway with Atlanta's black leadership, who viewed the Republican as only marginally more enlightened than Maddox.

The litany of Callaway's sins was lengthy, but in the final analysis he simply failed to appeal to black voters and liberal Democrats, who launched a write-in campaign for Arnall instead. Callaway finished first on election day, a few thousand votes ahead of Maddox, but fell short of the 50-percent majority required by Georgia law. In a reprise of the "two governors" debacle of 1946, members of the General Assembly would have to pick between Callaway and Maddox. With Democrats in firm control, Maddox would be the likely winner.

Cries of aversion flowed from every corner. As the *New York Times* explained, the outcome marked "a triumph of small-town, segregationist resentments against what Maddox has called 'the kings, the king-makers and the Wall Street crowd.'"

"Georgia was a most progressive Southern state," Barry Goldwater lamented in an interview on CBS television, "and all of a sudden they have a fellow that belongs back in the Stone Age, and I think if the Legislature of Georgia were really true to their state's reputation, they'd see that Maddox went back to serving hot dogs. . . ."

"It was fried chicken," Walter Cronkite corrected him.

"Fried chicken, is that right?" Goldwater said. "And baseball bats."
In the final weeks of 1966, Callaway and his boardroom backers filed suit seeking to arrange a one-on-one runoff with Maddox. But the U.S. Supreme Court upheld the legislators' right to choose the new governor, and on January 10, 1967, meeting in joint session, they chose Maddox.

In the 1950s, John Portman once observed, outsiders built Atlanta's buildings. By the 1960s, Atlantans were doing the job themselves, Portman foremost among their number. His Merchandise Mart was the first of five towering skyscrapers that transformed a two-block stretch of downtown Peachtree Street into an urban canyon worthy of Manhattan.

Portman himself was a distinctive feature of the cityscape, a dandy dresser with a remarkable crown of meticulously coifed hair artfully arranged to hide his baldness. But what truly set Portman apart was his unorthodox approach to design. His blueprint for the Regency-Hyatt House, the first new hotel in Atlanta since 1924, turned the theory of hotel planning inside-out and became the prototype for a whole new school of architecture. Instead of rooms that opened onto narrow, closed corridors, Portman created a giant, dazzling indoor atrium with the rooms on balconies that overlooked the lobby and cafe below. Glass elevators slid up and down exposed shafts like rides in an amusement park.

A student of urban psychology, Portman designed the hotel and other buildings in his Peachtree Center complex as a self-contained environment where, as he put it, people could work, live, play, shop, worship, and die — all without going outside. After calculating that the average man or woman was willing to walk for a maximum of exactly 7.5 minutes rather than take a taxi or bus, Portman laid out his complex so that pedestrians could reach each unit from the others quickly and easily. Two of the center's buildings, the Atlanta Gas Light Tower and the Merchandise Mart, were connected by a narrow, 80-foot catwalk 22 stories above the street. (Not many people actually braved the catwalk, but the dizzying sight of it from street level reinforced the message Portman wanted to deliver.)

Portman gave the Atlanta skyline of the '60s its signature silhouette, the Polaris Lounge, a revolving bar atop the Regency-Hyatt that was shaped like a flying saucer and enclosed in dark blue glass. And he opened the city's first fine restaurant, the Midnight Sun, with a sophisti-cated menu and intimate, Danish-modern decor. One of his influences, Portman said, was the Tivoli Gardens in Copenhagen, where visitors could sit and watch strollers pass by without being noticed. "People enjoy seeing without being seen," he explained. "There is a little Peep-ing Tom in all of us." Thus did the ghost of Philip Weltner's dream, the Bois d'Atlante, come back to life in the form of a slightly voyeuristic commercial development in the heart of downtown.

In time, critics would attack Portman's work as a return to the concept of the medieval castle, in which the privileged few lived safe lives, tucked away behind high walls meant to keep out the unwashed hordes. Look-ing at his later projects in Detroit, Los Angeles, and other cities, liberals complained that the ambiance of Portman's architecture discouraged street traffic — black people — from wandering inside and mingling with the predominantly white, well-to-do residents and guests. Conservatives said that was precisely the point. But such arguments were unheard in Atlanta in the mid-'60s. Portman was hailed as a hero for breathing fresh energy into the downtown streets at a time when central cities elsewhere were being deserted.

Portman viewed the downtown area as the "strong, vibrant core" that gave Atlanta its personality, and others agreed. Most of the city's major companies built expensive new headquarters in the 1960s, digging their roots into the soil of the central business district. Like little boys mea-suring their heights back to back, grown men took immense pride in the competition for the tallest building, a prize won by the First National Bank of Atlanta with a 41-story tower at Five Points, next to the Zero Mile post where Atlanta was founded.

In some cities, an observer noted, real estate developers were regarded with distaste as members of the "shiny-suit crowd," but Atlantans for the most part appreciated and admired their builders. With little in the way of grand old architecture to protect, the city was slow to embrace the idea of preservation. Indeed, since the past was something to escape, in many respects, each new steel-and-glass tower took its place as a mark of civic accomplishment.

One deal in particular seemed to exemplify the city's mood and way of doing business. After the turn of the century, a layer of viaducts had been built over the railroad tracks in the center of town, in effect raising the street level one full story over several square blocks. At the southwest edge of this elevated platform, along Spring Street, there was a drop-off to an open gulch, overgrown with grass and cross-stitched with rail lines, more than 20 feet below. In 1956, Robert Troutman, Jr., talked the Georgia Legislature into granting him the air rights above the 12-acre tract.

The only condition was that Troutman, a lawyer turned wheeler-dealer, had to complete at least $5 million of construction on the site within ten years or lose the lease. In October 1966, with the clock ticking, he had yet to find backers or pour an ounce of concrete. In desperation, Troutman turned to Tom Cousins, a home-builder just beginning to expand into larger commercial ventures.

Handsome, square-jawed, and soft-spoken, as conventional in appearance as his rival Portman was flamboyant, Cousins had begun his career in 1958 with a $13,000 investment in pre-fabricated houses. His first offering nearly ended in disaster when he built a model unit and arranged an open house for prospective buyers, only to watch in dismay as the heavens burst into a soaking, daylong downpour. Instead of admitting defeat, he bought time on a radio station and ran an ad every hour promising umbrellas, soft drinks, and snacks for anyone who braved the weather. By the end of the day he'd written orders for a hundred homes. His business flourished.

The problem with the railroad gulch was figuring out what, exactly, to build over it. Most of the new development in the city, typified by Portman's, was going up along the north-south corridor of Peachtree Street. Troutman's site was four blocks west of the city's epicenter, just a little too far off the beaten path for comfort. Beyond it lay black neighborhoods and a light industrial district. No lender wanted to risk millions on a marginal area.

In Cousins' view, the vital thing was to keep the lease alive by meeting the deadline. To do so, he erected giant columns of steel and concrete, 23 feet tall, clearing the airspace beneath, and then covered them with huge slabs of concrete that he turned into a parking deck. With his own form of vision, very different from Portman's, Cousins recognized that a simple, stodgy parking operation was the key to safeguarding his options for the future. The facility cost the minimum $5 million and gained Cousins the air rights he coveted. Those who bothered to check the quality of construction could see that his columns and concrete surfacing were built sturdily enough to support major projects to come.

Thirty years later, people were still parking at the Decks, which gave them easy access to the Omni, CNN Center, the World Congress Center, and the Georgia Dome — all of the nearby landmarks that eventually sprang from Cousins' gambit.

One began to sense that Atlanta had reached the point where no single misstep, be it a riot or a slapstick governor, could undo the march forward.

For obvious reasons, the prospect of Maddox as governor scared black Georgians to the bone. The pistol-toting former owner of the Pickrick now would have charge of the Georgia National Guard. But on the day of his inaugural in January 1967, with the temperature down to freezing and a harsh wind howling, Maddox surprised his listeners by denouncing violence and extremism and vowing to uphold the authority of the federal government.

Unlike many politicians who merely mouthed the words, Maddox was a genuine populist, a champion of ordinary people caught in the gears of the system. His loathing for civil rights was balanced by a sympathy for individual black men and women who suffered unfairly at the hands of white authorities. Early in Maddox's administration, a black inmate at a county work camp drowned in a pond while retrieving ducks shot by a guard. When the warden claimed that the convict had been swimming in the icy waters voluntarily, Maddox answered with open contempt, "You tell me the number of people who believe that, and I'll tell you the number of fools in Georgia." He instituted a program of prison reform.

Maddox agreed to meet with a group of black leaders, who urged him to support their agenda for social and political change. "How many of you voted for me?" he asked. No one spoke up. He asked how many of them had supported the outgoing governor, Carl Sanders, and all of them said they had. "Well," Maddox replied, "I'll do as much for you as he did." Many years later, Maddox recalled with a guffaw that "Daddy" King shot back, "We hope you'll do more than that!"

Making good on a campaign promise, Maddox instituted "Little People's Day" at the Capitol every other Wednesday and opened the Governor's Mansion to black and white visitors alike. He appointed blacks to local draft boards and the State Patrol, and named a liberal, Bill Burson, as head of the state welfare department. "It wouldn't do to have a hard-core right-winger in that job," Maddox explained. "You're dealing with the hungry and the poor every day." He even supported legislation aimed at preventing cross-burnings by the Klan, a stance that brought him a public rebuke from Klan leader Calvin Craig.

Though the media quickly proclaimed a "new" Maddox, his core beliefs had not changed. When it came to integration, Maddox advised whites to "flatten the tires" of the school buses rather than comply. He lowered the flags at the Capitol in response to a Supreme Court ruling expanding civil rights. The point was what Maddox did *not* do. He did not stand in schoolhouse doors or encourage violent resistance or otherwise fulfill the worst fears of his detractors. When Atlanta experienced another small riot in the summer of 1967, a repeat of the Summerhill fracas a year earlier, Maddox accepted Mayor Allen's plea to let the Atlanta police handle the trouble without calling out the National Guard. Six months into his administration, the Associated Press marveled that Maddox "has not tried to turn back the clock."

Before long, reassured that they had been spared the presence of another George Wallace, liberal Georgians could relax and enjoy the relative luxury of worrying about Maddox's fondness for riding his bicycle backwards on the Capitol lawn and otherwise compromising the dignity of his office. Much as they fretted about his handling of race relations, the truth was that Atlanta's elite had an almost equal concern about Maddox's breeding and comportment, how his bumpkin attitudes and antics might reflect on a city eager to showcase itself on the international stage.

As restrained as he proved to be on matters of race, Maddox remained an all-out crusader on other social issues of the day, notably the sins of the big city and its fleshpots. For years, Atlanta police had ignored a state law that required bars to close at midnight Saturday. Maddox, an ardent teetotaler, demanded a crackdown and got results. New Year's Eve of 1967 fell on a Sunday, and every saloon in town had to stay shut.

The governor refused to consider the damage he might be doing to Atlanta's convention business. "People in conventions are not out drinking on Sunday and cutting up," he told a radio audience, displaying an imperfect understanding of the habits of many of Atlanta's visitors. The complaints, he added, must be coming from "some of our beatniks, some of our long-haired, short-skirted people that don't have anything else to do on Sunday morning."

Nothing horrified Maddox more than the hippies who began congregating in "the Strip," a stretch of Peachtree Street between 10th and 14th streets in Atlanta's slightly bohemian Midtown neighborhood. Maddox's mother, Flonnie, saw the arrival of the flower children, along with the government's effort to place a man on the Moon, as portents that signaled the impending arrival of the Millenium. Her son thought the city had come under siege by "bums, criminals, anarchists, and drug addicts."

In Atlanta, the Age of Aquarius began with the opening of a coffee house called the Catacombs in 1966. In the early going, at least, the young people who gathered there seemed much like their generational counterparts elsewhere — dreamy, pacifistic, fond of marijuana, alienated from mainstream culture and values. They founded the inevitable underground newspaper, the *Great Speckled Bird*, whose first edition announced, "Chirp, we're here." The editor, Tom Coffin, explained in a front-page article that "people, especially the young, are now tired of the pap-feeding, the absurd sloganeering, the lies, the bullshit. With the discovery that our plastic civilization is hollow and void, these the 'turned on' seek meaning. Through involvement. Political activism. Art. Drugs. . . ."

By the standards of the era, the *Bird* was fairly tame, yet it introduced a new wrinkle into Atlanta's social fabric. For the first time, a public organ — albeit a counterculture weekly — began questioning the city's boosterism. For a full generation, ever since the postwar years, the desirability of untrammeled growth had been accepted as a given. Now a dissenting view could be heard. "Taken as a whole," one young writer proclaimed, "the city's defects — its moral and cultural pretensions, its glad-handing commercialism and Babbittry, its cynicism toward the arts, its suburban spread, its flatulent middle class, its leaders' failure to lead — far outweigh its virtues."

Old-timers could hardly fathom the attacks. Hartsfield went through the first issue of the *Bird* with a pencil underlining every dirty word, appalled at the lack of decorum. He had made a career of fighting the Klan, he wrote a friend later, "but now that the liberals are in command, having thoroughly infiltrated colleges, the news media and the government services, I find them far more bigoted and intolerant than the old Southern racists. . . ." McGill saw himself rudely denounced as "an exponent of U.S. Imperialism and deception, of pronounced self-righteousness and senility."

The harsh judgments of the New Left eventually found their way into mainstream journalism. As a *Newsweek* reporter put it, Atlanta gained a reputation as "the kind of town in which it would be unthinkable not to fill its United Appeal goal." The work of the Chamber of Commerce, once embraced without question, took on a slightly grubby aspect. Some cynics went so far as to condemn Atlanta's record on civil rights as purely profit-driven — "the triumph of Babbittry over bigotry."

For a time, as Maddox and the *Bird* editors traded insults, it was possible to believe that the turmoil of the civil rights era had faded and that race had taken a back seat to the larger political and social discord that swept the country. Some of Atlanta's racial battlegrounds seemed spent and exhausted. The yellow brick warehouse that served as headquarters of SNCC was closed much of the time, its telephones silenced by unpaid bills and its leaders ostracized for their violent rhetoric. In the words of the *National Observer*, the organization was "broke, demoralized, barely functioning." Stokely Carmichael returned from a tour of the Third World, where he had hoped to find allies and contributions, complaining that many African leaders "were more interested in big cars than in making revolution."

The Klan was scarcely better off. According to Calvin Craig's private papers, attendance at meetings fell off because an unnamed "E.C." — exalted cyclops — had begun charging members for the food he brought and for other "services rendered." At one point the state office was down to its last 75 postage stamps, and Klan leaders had to pay for mailings out of their own pockets. In 1965, Craig had refused to turn over Klan records to the House Un-American Activities Committee, and as a result he was forced to plead guilty to a charge of contempt of Congress and pay a $1,000 fine. After that, his enthusiasm for the cause seemed to wane.

The city of Atlanta had passed many racial tests over the years, and it appeared that surviving Lester Maddox's governorship could safely be added to the list. But then an assassin's bullet claimed the life of Martin Luther King, Jr.

King's death brought out the worst in Maddox. Just past the midpoint of his term, having surprised everyone with his restraint, Maddox reacted to the tragedy in Memphis in a near panic. He holed up at the Mansion as if awaiting the start of a race war.

Most other officials, led by Mayor Allen, moved with a seasoned instinct to minimize the chances of serious disruption in King's hometown. When he saw the news of the shooting on television, Allen drove directly to King's home to lend what comfort he could to Coretta King. As if reading his mind, Allen noted later, his senior police aides met him there and began setting up a protective cordon for the family.

In Washington, Robert Woodruff and former Governor Sanders were at the White House having cocktails with President Johnson when the first reports came in. Later that night, after King's death was confirmed, Woodruff put in a call to Allen. "Ivan," he warned, "the minute they bring King's body back tomorrow — between then and the time of the funeral — Atlanta, Georgia, is going to be the center of the universe. I want you to do whatever is right and necessary, and whatever the city can't pay for will be taken care of. Just do it right." A similar blank check was offered by Harry Belafonte, the black entertainer and activist.

Other cities witnessed outbursts of violence, but not Atlanta. On Friday, April 5, 1968, the day after King died, several thousand black students from the six schools of the Atlanta University Center held a somber, entirely peaceful march with the blessing of their school presidents and the mayor. Ralph David Abernathy, Jr., and other officials of King's organization, the Southern Christian Leadership Conference, went about the solemn task of arranging their fallen leader's funeral, scheduled for the following Tuesday. Benjamin Mays prepared the eulogy, feeling, he said, as if his own son had died.

Everyone was determined to behave with composure, it seemed, except the governor. On the day before the funeral, Maddox arrived at the state Capitol and flew into a rage when he saw that the state and national flags had been lowered to half-staff. It made him "sick at the stomach," he said, to see King honored that way. Maddox called Secretary of State Ben Fortson, who managed the Capitol grounds, and demanded that the flags be raised or else removed entirely. Fortson replied that the flags had been positioned by order of President Johnson and would remain where they were unless Maddox issued and signed an executive order to the contrary.

Maddox stalked out of his office onto the Capitol grounds, bent on raising the flags by himself, only to see that several local TV crews were on hand with their cameras trained on him. After a minute of fidgety indecision, he turned abruptly and went back inside, leaving the flags alone.

By the eve of the funeral, tens of thousands of mourners had begun descending on Atlanta. Eastern Airlines set a one-day record for charter flights. Greyhound buses were pouring in, 40 from New York City alone. A contingent of dignitaries led by Vice President Humphrey and Jacqueline Kennedy was due. Concerned about public safety, the mayor

issued an order shutting off liquor sales after six o'clock Monday evening.
Police went on 12-hour shifts, FBI and Secret Service agents spread out
around the city, and 1,400 black collegians were given assignments as
special marshals.

A certain degree of edginess was understandable, but Maddox went
haywire. He announced that the Capitol would be open for business during the funeral, even though the cortege was scheduled to pass by directly
outside. On the morning of the event, he deployed 160 riot-helmeted
state troopers inside the building and gave orders that if any mourners
broke ranks and stepped on the Capitol lawn, the doors were to be
locked. Then, he said, if anyone tried to enter the building, the troopers
were authorized to shoot to kill. "Shoot them down and stack them up,"
were his exact words. He tried to call out 6,000 members of the National
Guard, but Chief Jenkins talked him out of it.

Had there been any violence on the part of the marchers, history
might not judge Maddox so harshly. As it was, 200,000 mourners walked
peacefully through downtown Atlanta in slow cadence, following the
mule-drawn wagon that carried King's body from his family's church,
Ebenezer Baptist, to Morehouse College. In spite of a hot sun and tem-
peratures that quickly shot into the 80s, not a single incident was
recorded. Maddox and his phalanx watched the procession from inside
the Capitol, cowering behind drawn curtains.

"I remember glancing toward the Capitol," the mayor wrote later in
his memoirs, "and thanking God that I was on the side I was on, instead
of on the side of the racists who have plagued Georgia and the rest of the
South for more than one hundred years."

Maddox's reputation never recovered. His chance to be remembered
as a colorful character with a kind heart disappeared forever. He ran for
president in the summer of 1968 and was treated as a laughingstock. By
autumn, a cruel satire called "Red, White and Maddox" was playing in
Atlanta and headed for Broadway, dooming the governor to a life of
ridicule. For the next quarter-century, he would protest that he had done
more for black Georgians than any of his so-called "moderate" counterparts — a claim with an element of truth — but there was no getting
over the ugliness of his display on April 9, 1968.

For the city of Atlanta, King's funeral closed a chapter. The Atlanta
"story," as it came to be known, was fixed in place. For 14 years, ever
since the *Brown* decision, Atlanta's white power structure had been
watched closely and judged on its handling of racial matters. Time and

again, the white leaders had risen to the occasion, giving paternalism a good name while giving the city a gleaming national image.

Now the moment was approaching when blacks would insist on filling those leadership roles themselves. Blacks had benefited in many ways from the benign rule of the business community, not least by having a buffer that protected them from the hard-line segregationists who held sway in the state Legislature. The flow of revenue from Atlanta's economic boom had swirled through the ranks of black workers as well as white.

But the plain fact was that blacks had been given no place at the boardroom table. Vernon Jordan, who went on to become president of the National Urban League and a close friend and adviser to President Bill Clinton, recalled drily, "My only contact with Robert Woodruff was when I was a waiter at the Capital City Club. I was not exactly sitting down and having tea with him, or drinks, or playing gin rummy." The Coca-Cola Company's board of directors was all white, and would remain so until 1974 (when Paul Austin wrote Woodruff a confidential memo urging the selection of "a quiet-spoken, modest-mannered" candidate to break the color line).

The one place blacks exercised power was at the ballot box. At a time when blacks elsewhere in the South were just beginning to escape the poll taxes, literacy tests, and incidents of sheer physical intimidation that had kept them from voting, black Atlantans could look back on more than 20 years of political involvement. In effect, the white power structure had nominated candidates for mayor, and black voters had given their approval. Both Hartsfield and Allen had survived elections in which they lost the white vote while piling up huge margins in the black community.

Now, however, that pattern was about to be broken. It started in the fall of 1968, when Allen and Richard Rich, the civic-minded chairman of Rich's department store, led the drive for passage of a $377 million bond issue for a rapid transit system. Black voters were assured that MARTA — the Metropolitan Atlanta Rapid Transit Authority — would operate mostly for their benefit, giving them access to jobs in the spreading suburbs outside the center city. But black leaders had little say in the planning for MARTA, and some of them dismissed the whole project as a boondoggle meant to shuttle customers downtown to Rich's. The referendum failed, leaving Richard Rich embittered.

The gulf in perceptions that divided black and white Atlantans grew wider. Jim Townsend, the popular editor of *Atlanta* magazine, proclaimed the '60s "Atlanta's decade," and from a white perspective it certainly seemed so. New facilities popped up like dandelions. The Civic Center opened, along with the Memorial Arts Center and the 270-acre amusement park Six Flags Over Georgia. Tom Cousins and Carl Sanders bought the St. Louis Hawks and brought the franchise to Atlanta, adding professional basketball as the city's third major league sport. The Braves won the division title in the National League West in 1969, giving Atlanta a taste of champagne before the New York Mets captured the pennant in a playoff sweep.

Travelers who had grown accustomed to changing planes in Atlanta began staying over a few days on tours. Recognizing the city's growing attraction as a convention mecca, the Marriott chain built a 500-room motel in downtown Atlanta and quickly enlarged it by adding another 300 rooms, a 500-space parking garage, a 24-hour restaurant, and a cocktail lounge. The city moved to seventh place — behind New York, Washington, Miami, Chicago, San Francisco, and Atlantic City — in the number of convention-goers it drew annually.

From 1961 to 1969, according to one report, the metropolitan area added 160,000 jobs, a 43 percent increase, the highest rate of growth in the country.

A handful of black businesses shared in the gold rush. The city's preeminent black bank, Citizens Trust, prepared to move into a new, 11-story headquarters. Showing the site to a visitor, Warren Cochrane, the head of the Butler Street YMCA, pointed out proudly that it was no "pygmy building" of five or six stories, but a genuine financial tower. Across town, the Paschal brothers, James and Robert, expanded their famous restaurant by adding a 120-room motel. Their nightclub, La Carrousel, attracted the likes of Aretha Franklin, Ramsey Lewis, Lou Rawls, Dizzy Gillespie, and Cannonball Adderly as headliners.

But for thousands of ordinary black citizens, Atlanta's surge was something happening at a distance. By one calculation, some 75,000 black Atlantans had been swept out of their homes during the ten-year period that ended in 1968, while only 5,000 new units of public housing were built in replacement. John Sibley, the white banker, orchestrated a campaign to encourage black housing outside the city limits — "in order," he said, "to lessen the [black] population within the inner city" — only to founder against high land prices and resistance from white suburbanites. With nowhere else to go, black Atlantans jammed Vine City, Summerhill, and other established neighborhoods.

The public schools witnessed the swiftest and most dramatic change in Atlanta's demographics. At the start of the school year in 1967, blacks jumped from 45 percent of the student population to 57 percent. An increase in the raw numbers of black students was part of the reason, but the "melancholy truth," an *Atlanta Constitution* columnist noted, was that whites were beginning to flee the schools in droves in the face of integration. A later study of the '60s concluded that some 60,000 whites moved out of the city during the decade, while 70,000 blacks moved in, pushing blacks to the brink of an outright majority.

Understandably, blacks yearned to take a greater hand in governing themselves. Only one black, Q. V. Williamson, served on the 16-member Board of Aldermen. None of the city's departments was headed by a black. And while Chief Jenkins was still respected by most blacks for his enlightened approach to law enforcement, complaints of police brutality were periodically brought against his men. In the summer of 1969, a black officer described in tears how several of his white counterparts had beaten two black prisoners at the city jail.

With Mayor Allen planning to retire after two terms, the election of 1969 loomed as a severe test of the union of interests that had bound the white power structure with the masses of black voters. Given the circumstances, finding a candidate who could carry the business community's coat of arms and still appeal to black voters promised to be a difficult task.

For years, Woodruff's friend and lawyer, Hughes Spalding, had been urging him to recruit and prepare a new generation of leaders to take over at the Coca-Cola Company, Trust Company Bank, and other key institutions, including City Hall. But Woodruff dragged his feet. "It's getting a little late," Spalding warned with his customary flourish. "The sun has passed its zenith, soon there will be twilight, and we have no Joshua." Still Woodruff dawdled, unwilling to cede power.

By 1969, the pride of old lions who ran Atlanta was thinning. Spalding died in that year, as did McGill. Mills Lane, preparing for retirement, warned that the city's single greatest problem was a lack of strong leaders aged 40 to 50. Woodruff was approaching his eightieth birthday and had fallen out of touch with the younger men rising in Atlanta's business and political circles. Without giving the matter much thought, the business elite threw their support in the 1969 mayor's race to Rodney Cook, an amiable state representative who suffered a fatal flaw: He was a Republican. In spite of his progressive record, Cook's membership in the GOP made him unacceptable to black voters, and the election was thrown up for grabs.

The black leadership, too, was in transition between generations. The old Atlanta Negro Voters League run by A. T. Walden and John Wesley Dobbs had disbanded. A new group began meeting at Paschal's restaurant over iced tea and fried chicken, hoping to unify and deliver the black vote. They called themselves "Black Young Men on the Go," a mocking reference to their white counterparts at the Chamber of Commerce. Among the leaders was Jesse Hill, who took charge of Atlanta Life after founder Alonzo Herndon's son and sole heir, Norris, turned out to be a reclusive, homosexual alcoholic. Others in the vanguard included John Cox, a sharp-eyed lobbyist with Delta Air Lines, builder Herman Russell, and Lonnie King, the former sit-in leader who now headed the Atlanta office of the NAACP. And there were many others — churchmen, civil rights leaders, businessmen, lawyers, and public officials — who reflected the varied interests that emerged as the black community grew and matured.

On some issues the group found easy accord. Benjamin Mays had recently retired after 27 years as president of Morehouse College, and the Black Young Men agreed unanimously to support him in a bid for a seat on the Atlanta Board of Education. When an ambitious young minister, Cameron Jackson, dared to run against Dr. Mays, the group made a few phone calls and arranged to have Jackson's bishop transfer him out of town.

On the paramount question of the day, however, the black leaders disagreed. One of their number, an educator named Horace Tate, announced he was running for mayor. The others doubted he could win, since whites still constituted a majority of registered voters. Spurning Tate, most of the black leadership turned instead to the city's vice mayor, Sam Massell, who seemed a logical compromise. Jewish, unabashedly liberal, a friend of organized labor, Massell had such a perfect profile as a transitional figure that he might have come from central casting. He ran on a promise to accelerate progress for blacks and to devote less energy to "glamorous" civic projects.

In the primary, Massell and Cook finished first and second, as expected, and entered a runoff contest that threatened to divide Atlantans as never before.

Though Massell had served under Ivan Allen for eight years, the two men were not at all close. Not surprisingly, in a city whose top social clubs still barred Jews as members, Massell believed that anti-Semitism was the reason the power structure had ignored him in favor of Rodney

A reluctant Mayor Hartsfield (*above*) declared his retirement in 1961 after a quarter century at City Hall. Ivan Allen, Jr., (*below, left*) replaced Hartsfield after beating segregationist restaurant owner Lester Maddox at the polls.

Black leader A. T. Walden (*right*) helped negotiate the desegregation of Atlanta's retail stores, lunch counters, and theaters, much to the disgust of the Klan's Grand Dragon, Calvin Craig (*below, left*), shown here in his official green satin robe.

33

34

36

35

Left: Former governor Marvin Griffin and his wife were all smiles after a grand jury declined to indict him for corruption. But he lost his comeback bid in the 1962 governor's race to Carl Sanders, (*above left,* with Hubert Humphrey). Sanders was a moderate who called himself "a segregationist but not a damn fool."

37

38

Above: When Albert Dunn (*left*) tested the Civil Rights Act of 1963 by trying to enter the Pickrick restaurant, he was chased away by owner Lester Maddox (*right*) and his son, Lester Jr. Note the pistol in Maddox's hand.

Right: The desegregation of Leb's and other Atlanta lunch counters stirred picketing by the Klan.

39

Above: Coca-Cola magnate Robert Woodruff (*left*) backed the moderate racial policies of mayors William Hartsfield (*center*) and Ivan Allen, Jr.

Below: Allen sat next to Coretta Scott King at a dinner honoring her husband, Dr. Martin Luther King, Jr., (*center, leaning forward*) after he won the Nobel Peace Prize.

40

Atlantans loved their minor league baseball team, the Crackers. Here the players were posing for a photographer who promised to shoot their pictures from the waist up.

Flamboyant banker Mills B. Lane, shown polishing one of his fleet of antique cars, wanted the city to join the Major Leagues. He led the effort for a new stadium (*below*), built in a scant 51 weeks on slum land cleared through the Urban Renewal program.

45

46

The arrest of an auto theft suspect (*above*) in over-crowded Summerhill, the neighborhood next to the new stadium, triggered a riot (*below*) in September 1966.

White backlash led to the election of Lester Maddox as governor. Though he horrified proper Atlantans by riding his bicycle backwards, not even Maddox could hold back the rapid progress of the city's growth. *See next page.*

Below: A mule team pulled the coffin of Martin Luther King, Jr., through Atlanta after his funeral in 1968.

Facing: A mix of ordinary citizens (*above*) and VIPs (*below*), including Richard Nixon and Wilt Chamberlain, turned out to mourn.

Architect John Portman (*left*) revolutionized hotel design with the Regency-Hyatt House and gave the city a new silhouette (*right*) topped by the flying saucer-shaped Polaris Lounge.

54

Above: Portman's great rival, developer Tom Cousins, dreamed for years of creating a giant retail and office complex called Omnisouth on the southern fringe of downtown Atlanta.

Right: In Atlanta's go-go '60s, Mayor Allen collected the commemorative shovels from dozens of groundbreaking ceremonies.

55

Cook. For his part, Allen hotly denied the accusation, and it was true that he and Woodruff and others in their circle had long maintained cordial relations with Atlanta's well-established Jewish community.

The issue might not have arisen publicly, except for a scandal that erupted in the final days of the campaign. Massell requested the assignment of a police captain, H. L. "Buddy" Whalen, to provide him personal protection. Whalen soon began dropping by Atlanta's nightclubs in the company of Massell's brother, Howard, who busied himself soliciting campaign contributions from the owners and managers. The *Atlanta Constitution* broke the story less than a week before the election, giving the plain impression that some sort of shakedown operation was taking place.

For those who knew Sam Massell, the accusation of strong-arm tactics seemed wildly improbable. A short, soft-spoken man with a bad lisp — he called his opponent "Wodney" Cook — Massell struck most observers as earnest and reform-minded. One reporter described him as having "the look of a man who has just failed to catch on to a joke." Even if his brother had behaved inappropriately, Massell's defenders argued, the affair was hardly serious enough to alter the outcome of the election. Massell admitted "bad judgment," nothing more.

Mayor Allen saw things differently. On the afternoon of Sunday, October 19, 1969, less than 48 hours before the polls were to open, Allen called a press conference at City Hall and urged Massell to withdraw from the race, saying he had "badly misused his position." As the mayor spoke, Massell and Cook were a few blocks away in the studios of WSB-TV, holding a final debate on live television. When the moderator told him about Allen's statement and asked for a response, Massell replied tightly, "No, I shall not withdraw." Off-camera, Massell's wife, Doris, hissed audibly, "Anti-Semitic WASPs!"

The next day, Massell hammered the point home. Allen and his friends, he said, "are the same men that don't want me to sit in their clubs. I don't know any other way to put it." The backlash against Allen cemented Massell's victory. Atlanta's Jewish voters were energized to defend one of their own, and the black community hastened to his side as well. Two of the city's most respected black figures, "Daddy" King and Benjamin Mays, went to City Hall to lend Massell public support.

Election night at Massell's headquarters in the Dinkler Plaza Hotel, according to a *Newsweek* reporter, resembled a scene from Andrew Jackson's populist victory in 1832, with celebrants of all stripes jamming the ballroom. When the ballots were counted, Massell got slightly more than a quarter of the white vote and an estimated 93 percent of the black vote, good for 55 percent overall. Across town, a Republican strategist muttered, "Sam's brother lost it for him on Friday, and then Ivan won it back for him on Sunday."

Allen, the hunter, had misfired. By investing his personal prestige in the outcome, he had elevated the stakes beyond the head-to-head contest between Massell and Cook into a referendum on the power structure's stewardship of the city. And he had lost. Allen retired as a highly respected figure, but he took the political influence of the business elite into retirement with him. The boardroom patricians never won another election.

CHAPTER 8

TOO YOUNG TO DIE

People who visited Atlanta in the early 1970s occasionally wondered aloud if a municipal ordinance had been enacted banning the elderly from appearing in public. An atmosphere of youthful revelry gripped the town, from the hippies and bikers who gathered in Piedmont Park to the burgeoning gay community centered along Cheshire Bridge Road. "Singles" apartment complexes flourished on the banks of the Chattahoochee River, full of stewardesses. Beneath the viaducts of the central business district, a gaslit warren of restaurants and nightclubs called Underground Atlanta rollicked in its heyday.

The median age in Atlanta was 26, according to one report, and at times it seemed all of the young were in the streets at once, partying. After two full decades covering tense civil rights maneuvers, reporters for the various national media switched their focus to the "scene" in Atlanta. Women, "mostly in miniskirts," outnumbered men five to one in Atlanta, according to the New York *Sunday News*, whose correspondent sounded like an anthropologist discovering a lost paradise. "Atlanta is the sauciest, swingingest city in America today," the *National Observer* reported breathlessly, with "more grooving guys, girls and grass per apartment than Los Angeles, San Francisco, Chicago or perhaps even New York." *Esquire* devoted a whole article to the city's restaurants, a topic that could have been exhausted in a single paragraph just a few years earlier.

With his term as governor drawing to a close, Lester Maddox did the city an uncharacteristic favor. Much to their chagrin, the owners of Underground Atlanta discovered that they might be in violation of a state law forbidding the sale of liquor within 200 feet of a school or church. Their complex, modeled on the French Quarter in New Orleans, was chock-a-block with bars, pubs, and nightclubs. Directly overhead, on the viaduct that covered the old railroad warehouse district, stood Georgia State University and the Shrine of the Immaculate Conception. A serious question arose about Underground's legal right to operate.

Acting with the governor's tacit approval, state revenue commissioner Peyton Hawes, Sr., issued a ruling that saved the day. For purposes of enforcing the state liquor law, Hawes decreed, distances would not be measured in a straight line but by "the nearest traveled road," which in the case of Underground meant the winding pedestrian staircases that meandered up to the level above — a route that was paced off at slightly more than 200 feet. The party went on.

The city's new mayor, Sam Massell, made a concerted effort to heal the ugly divisions of the recent election. On vacation in Acapulco, he bought tie clasps that showed tiny doves carrying olive branches and sent them to the men he believed had tried to wreck his campaign in its final days. Early in his administration, he broke a strike by the city's garbage collectors, winning the respect of the business leadership. And he had the police crack down on drug use among the hippies and bikers, further toughening his image.

Above all, Massell faced the challenge of presiding over an economic boom that showed no signs of letting up. The city was like a teenager who gradually outgrew the clothes of childhood and got a new wardrobe, only to experience a sudden, secondary growth spurt that necessitated *another* complete change. The new airport terminal, finished in 1961, handled 3.5 million passengers its first year; by 1970, traffic had quadrupled to more than 14 million passengers and talk had begun of building a second airport. The new Civic Center had opened in the fall of 1967 and already seemed tight-fitting. Its auditorium seated only 4,600 people, adequate for the symphony and opera but too small for major concerts.

Before buying the Hawks, developer Tom Cousins had asked Ivan Allen, Jr., if the city would build a coliseum to provide the team a home. "Oh, no," Allen answered, shaking his head. "I almost had a stadium without a tenant. Get your franchise first." Cousins had done so, and for two seasons the basketball team played in Georgia Tech's smallish arena. Once Massell took office, he and Cousins quickly reached agreement on construction of a new facility the size of Madison Square Garden, with the tenant, not the taxpayers, obligated to pay off the bonds. As Massell delighted in pointing out, it was a better deal than Allen made in financing the stadium.

Cousins could afford to be generous. The new coliseum, called the Omni, was his key to unlocking the vast potential of the air rights he controlled above the railroad gulch in downtown Atlanta. With Atlanta's social life growing by leaps and bounds, Cousins had in mind creating a new heart of the city, a maze of public and private facilities that would attract hordes of locals and out-of-towners alike. His plans were so ambitious they brought him into conflict with the other great developer of the era, John Portman, triggering a tug of war over Atlanta's center of gravity that continues to this day.

As the reigning architect and builder of the '60s, Portman had turned upper Peachtree Street into a small mountain range of modern, high-rise buildings, giving his section of Atlanta the look of a contemporary big city. Understandably, he hoped to protect the primacy of his Peachtree Center complex — he called it his "private urban renewal program" — and he took a dim view of Cousins' flanking maneuvers a mile or so to the south along the lower edge of the downtown area.

The focus of their budding rivalry was the prospect of a giant exhibition hall, to be built by the state, that would place Atlanta on an equal footing with New York and Chicago in competing for the top national conventions. In the past year, Atlanta had played host to 45,000 Jehovah's Witnesses and 60,000 American Legionnaires. But to reach the next level, the city would have to offer a hall big enough to accommodate the major trade shows that required hundreds of thousands of square feet of floor space. As a gauge of the size of the project, known as the World Congress Center, it carried a price tag of $35 million — the cost of the airport terminal and stadium combined. Its site, in all likelihood, would become the city's new ground zero.

Until he bought the Hawks and got the green light for the coliseum, Cousins brought very little to the table in lobbying for placement of the exhibition hall. He had secured the air rights over 12 acres of weed-choked railroad tracks, but all he'd built there was a parking deck. Now, with a 15,000-seat coliseum on the way, he suddenly became an important player. He offered to give the state six acres of adjacent land for the Congress Center, and his offer was taken seriously.

Portman had trouble believing that an upstart like Cousins meant to shoulder him aside. He referred to Cousins' site dismissively as "over there in the hole." Portman thought the exhibition hall should be built

on the northern edge of downtown next to the Civic Center, to comple-
ment the smaller facility and give it enhanced appeal. That the Civic
Center also happened to be near Portman's Peachtree Street empire
seemed to be a part of the equation.

The two men launched an intense, behind-the-scenes battle whose
significance was hard to exaggerate. Not only was the future shape of
downtown Atlanta at stake, so was the relationship between the city and
the state. After years of open antagonism, leaders in the General Assembly had begun to see Atlanta in a new light as an economic winch that
could haul the rest of Georgia out of its residual poverty. The Congress
Center became a pet project of a colorful lawmaker named James H.
"Sloppy" Floyd (so nicknamed for fumbling a football in high school),
the chairman of the House Appropriations Committee, who earmarked
$175,000 for preliminary planning. Another state official, auditor Ernest
Davis, took charge of the site selection committee and began the ticklish
process of choosing between Cousins and Portman.

Before any further steps could be taken, the state's voters confronted
the task of picking a successor to Maddox. The new spirit of cooperation
between state and city would not survive unless the next governor
embraced it, and that question came into doubt as the campaign
unfolded. The front-runner, former Governor Carl Sanders, offered a
progressive record and ran as a friend of Atlanta. But he proved unex-
pectedly vulnerable to an attack from the right.

The campaign Jimmy Carter waged in the summer of 1970 has been
remembered ever since as a dark spot on his career. After running and
losing four years earlier as a moderate, Carter switched gears entirely and
positioned himself as Maddox's heir. If elected, Carter promised, he
would continue Maddox's practice of holding "Little People's Day." And
he would invite Alabama Governor George Wallace to visit Georgia,
something Sanders had pointedly declined to do. Among other excesses,
Carter called himself "basically a redneck," made a campaign appearance
at a segregated academy, and accepted endorsements from Roy Harris
and Marvin Griffin, the most notorious pair of political throwbacks in
the state. The lowest moment, witnessed by the *Constitution*'s political
editor, Bill Shipp, came when one of Carter's aides stopped by a Ku Klux
Klan rally and distributed copies of a photograph that showed Sanders
being doused with champagne by a black player on the Hawks basketball
team.

Distasteful as it was, Carter's campaign made good sense politically.

With racial resentments still burning across Georgia, Maddox remained immensely popular, enjoying an approval rating of 62 percent in one poll. Barred by state law from seeking a second consecutive term, Maddox ran for lieutenant governor instead, and Carter played up to his followers by saying he was "proud to be on the ticket."

What bothered the leaders of the business community in Atlanta was not so much Carter's pandering, which they could understand, as the accompanying tone of hostility toward the city itself. One of Carter's TV ads focused on a heavy wooden portal as an announcer intoned, "This is the door to an exclusive country club, where the big-money boys play cards, drink cocktails, and raise money for their candidate — Carl Sanders. People like *us* aren't invited. We're busy working for a living. That's why our votes are going for Jimmy Carter." With devastating effect, Carter's people hung the nickname "Cufflinks Carl" on Sanders, suggesting that he had enriched himself in office doing favors for big businesses in Atlanta.

Since they did, in fact, play cards, drink cocktails, and support Sanders, many of the city's top men feared the consequences when Carter claimed victory. For all they knew, he might cancel the Congress Center and several other vital projects as well. But much to everyone's surprise, Carter took office vowing to be a "New South" governor dedicated to progress. In his inaugural, he uttered the now-famous line, "I say to you quite frankly that the time for racial discrimination is over," leaving many of the people who had voted for him flabbergasted. Before long he was on the cover of *Time*.

With Carter's support, the General Assembly approved a one-cent local sales tax and set up another referendum on MARTA, the subway and rail system that promised to make Atlanta the first city in the South with rapid transit. Rural lawmakers helped provide the margin of passage. On the last day of the session, marking the new spirit of cooperation, Mayor Massell called a press conference on the lawn at City Hall and unveiled a sign that said, "Thank You Georgia Legislators." Symbolizing the end of old antagonisms, he buried a small hatchet in the ground.

The issue of a site for the Congress Center continued to simmer. In the early going, the odds favored Portman over Cousins. By far the better-established man, Portman could sit in his penthouse office, sweep an arm across a panorama of several blocks of downtown Atlanta, and point out the evidence of his success as an urban designer. *Business Week* called him the leading architect and developer in the nation. He did not think he had much to prove to anyone, which turned out to be his undoing. Portman treated the members of the selection committee as if they were unlettered dolts. "The burden of what he said," a participant in one meeting recalled, "was that any damn fool could see that the Civic Center site was the best, and if you couldn't see that without a whole lot of thought and explanation, then you really didn't have sense enough to be talked to by an intelligent man."

Not long afterward, the committee picked Cousins' site for the Congress Center. His aw-shucks demeanor helped his cause, as did his offer of free land for the state (and his use of Carl Sanders as a lobbyist). Mostly he succeeded because he spun a convincing argument that the center would trigger development across the entire southern tier of downtown, from the railroad gulch past Rich's department store and Underground Atlanta to the Capitol itself. The deal hit a final snag when Governor Carter tried to steer the project to another developer, the son-in-law of a political supporter, who claimed he could build the center with private funds. But when that prospect fell through, Carter relented and Cousins broke ground.

Built as planned (and later doubled in size so that it offered floor space equal to 108 football fields), the Congress Center cemented Atlanta's place as one of the country's premier convention destinations. Hospitality became downtown Atlanta's leading industry. And Cousins gained the opportunity to begin building an urban empire of his own.

Not one to sit around licking his wounds, Portman got to work erecting the tallest building in the South, a cylindrical, 70-story hotel whose shape dominated Atlanta's skyline and seemed to be making a statement.

———————

The awakening of political hunger in Atlanta's black community could be traced to a single individual, Maynard Holbrook Jackson, Jr., and the quixotic campaign he ran for the U.S. Senate in 1968.

The incumbent, Herman Talmadge, then at the height of his power and influence, was seeking a third term. No one in Georgia could have beaten him, let alone a light-skinned, soft-haired, hazel-eyed, 30-year-old black man. A grandson of John Wesley Dobbs, the legendary Republican leader who wrote the "ticket" for black voters in the '40s and '50s, and the nephew of the celebrated opera singer Mattiwilda Dobbs, Jackson belonged to Atlanta's black aristocracy. He had finished high school at 14, graduated from Morehouse College with honors at 18, and then earned a law degree. His most successful year had come when he made $30,000 selling encyclopedias door to door.

Without bothering to ask the blessings of any of the city's established black leaders, Jackson borrowed the $3,000 for his qualifying fee and plunked it down 30 minutes before the deadline, springing a surprise on everyone. "Negro Attorney to Face Talmadge," said the headline in the *Atlanta Constitution*, as if reporting a human sacrifice.

Doomed to defeat, Jackson made quite an impression anyway, not least because he stood six-foot-three and weighed nearly 300 pounds. His most striking feature was his voice, a velvety, mellifluous instrument that he used to preach, cajole, and occasionally to intimidate, usually in words of many syllables. His favorite term was "jejune," a criticism he applied to people, things, and ideas he found insubstantial. He liked to draw out the pronunciation, so that it echoed: "Juh-jooooon." His politics blended elegance with populism. He favored gray, pinstripe suits and zip-up, ankle-length alligator boots. "We reject the vapid, jejune trappings of middle-classness," he once explained. "Just because I wear a white handkerchief in my breast pocket doesn't mean that's all I care about."

Many voters had trouble figuring out exactly what to make of Jackson. In some parts of rural Georgia, it was said, country whites assumed he was Greek. To ensure that blacks did not make the same mistake, one of his volunteers revealed later, a photograph of Jackson mailed to black households around the state was deliberately altered to darken his skin color. In Atlanta, Jackson quickly captured the fancy of liberals, die-hard Talmadge haters, and large numbers of ordinary blacks who were tickled to see one of their own take on an incumbent who stood for segregation. The editors of the *Constitution* almost endorsed Jackson before deciding their support probably would cost him votes.

Talmadge, no fool, softened his position on race, but even so, Jackson ended up carrying the city of Atlanta by 6,000 votes. Though he lost the statewide Democratic primary in a landslide, the Senate race made Jackson an overnight sensation in city politics.

Just months afterward, well in advance of the 1969 city elections, Jackson announced that he would be a candidate for vice mayor. Some of Atlanta's black elders called a special meeting. "Who'd he *check* with?" one of them asked, showing annoyance. Jesse Hill, Herman Russell, Lonnie King, and others had decided not to recruit a black candidate for mayor or vice mayor, but to concentrate instead on electing blacks to the Board of Aldermen and Board of Education. Jackson frustrated their plans without the courtesy of a phone call.

And he won. Despite the chilly reception he got from the top black leaders, Jackson took 98 percent of the city's black vote in the contest for vice mayor and defeated a white opponent without a runoff. The whole premise of Massell's victory — that it was too soon to elect a black mayor — lay exposed as a fallacy by Jackson's showing. Massell took office knowing he was headed for a showdown in four years, when Jackson would challenge him for the top spot.

Friction between the new mayor and vice mayor began almost from day one. When Massell fired the striking garbage workers, many of them black, Jackson joined their picket line. When complaints of police brutality arose, Jackson lent a sympathetic ear. Massell's attempts to please the white business leadership tended to distance him from his poor black constituents, which worked to Jackson's advantage. There was no specific gripe against Massell, just the feeling among many blacks that a black mayor would better serve their needs. As one black leader put it, Massell was a good mayor — a good *one-term* mayor.

In the summer of 1971, midway through his second year in office, Massell found himself trying to serve two masters. Determined to revive the rapid transit project, Massell faced a business community and a black community that had fundamentally different visions of the way the system should be built. In the city's boardrooms, MARTA was seen as the final ingredient in the recipe for becoming a national city. With a subway system, Atlanta would finally stand apart from the rest of the South and take its place as a genuine metropolis. Like the stadium, Congress Center, airport, and expressways, rapid transit was a down payment on further economic development.

For most blacks, though, rapid transit promised an affordable way to get to work, nothing more or less. The fate of MARTA was to be decided by a referendum in the fall. Black voters had proven three years earlier that they could defeat MARTA, and this time their leaders vowed to be heard. At the insistence of the black leadership, including the vice mayor, the fare was pegged at 15 cents and guaranteed for seven years, a substantial reduction from the 40 cents riders had to pay for the bus. Other concessions were made as well, including a promise that a rail spur would be built from Perry Homes, a housing project on the west side of town, to the main line. It was meant to relieve maids of the need to switch buses to get to their jobs in the rich, white enclave of Buckhead to the north.

In the months leading up to the vote on MARTA, black leaders issued a list of "concerns," 26 in all, that had to be met to secure black support at the polls. With growing frustration, Massell warned that the demands were threatening to spark a white backlash that might doom the project. The city stood to reap more than $1 billion in federal construction funds if MARTA were approved, Massell argued, and that money would provide jobs in the black community for decades to come. Jeopardizing such a windfall over petty issues was stupid, Massell believed. He decided to say so to the city's black leaders, face-to-face.

On October 6, 1971, a month before the referendum, Massell spoke at the Hungry Club, the weekly lunch at the Butler Street YMCA that still served as the principal forum when blacks and whites had serious political business to transact. With a live TV audience watching, the mayor lit into the black leadership for making too many demands. Rapid transit, he told them, was too important to risk losing. In a fateful choice of words, he urged them to "think white." The phrase was greeted with a few gasps and then an icy silence. A handful of members of the audience stood up, turned their backs, and walked out.

Some good came of the speech. Worried about fraying relations, leaders of both races agreed to set up a private, biracial association, the Action Forum, that would meet once a month on Saturday mornings to air grievances before they burst into public conflict. And MARTA was approved at the polls. In the days before the balloting, Massell campaigned from a helicopter above the crowded Downtown Connector, urging commuters through a bullhorn to "do something about this traffic!" With overwhelming support from black voters, the referendum passed in Fulton and DeKalb counties, giving Massell the greatest victory of his political career.

But his appearance at the Hungry Club marked the beginning of the end of Massell's chances for re-election. The numbers were against him, as the city's population continued to edge toward a black majority. Several attempts to reverse the tide failed. A group in the Legislature tried to consolidate the city with the rest of Fulton County, but the newspapers gave the measure a damaging nickname — the "Abolish Atlanta bill" — that contributed to its narrow defeat. Lieutenant Governor Maddox, as presiding officer of the state Senate, single-handedly killed another measure that would have annexed some 55,000 white voters from the northern suburbs.

White flight continued. By the start of the school year in the late summer of 1971, the city schools were 73 percent black. And they remained segregated. Every attempt at integrating individual schools resulted in the swift exodus of white pupils. "I don't know what you can do to keep white folks from being scared if you move into their neighborhood," sighed Benjamin Mays, the president of the school board.

The plaintiffs in Atlanta's long-standing school desegregation suit despaired of integrating the system and eventually gave up. In October 1972, Lonnie King, president of the Atlanta branch of the NAACP, spent a week behind closed doors with members of the school board negotiating a compromise settlement. In exchange for a black superintendent and a guarantee that blacks would get half the top administrative jobs in the system, King abandoned the goal of extensive busing. In fact, the plan he accepted called for busing only 2,765 of the system's 95,000 pupils. Most of the city's black children would remain in all-black schools.

The agreement came under withering fire from liberals and black leaders outside the city, who considered it a sellout. Lawyers from the NAACP's Legal Defense Fund in New York, who had been pursuing the suit in court for 15 years, were appalled and tried unsuccessfully to have the settlement overturned. The New York Times called the dispute a "falling out among friends," but there was nothing friendly about the outcome. The NAACP's national office ousted King as head of its Atlanta branch and suspended several members, including Maynard Jackson, who took his side.

Atlanta's black leaders found themselves drawn together by the controversy. Sounding remarkably like their white counterparts of the previous generation, they protested that liberals from the North did not understand how Atlanta operated. "The people in New York think all the brains are up there," King complained, "and that we're all stupid down here." He argued that at 27 percent and tumbling, the white population in the schools was simply too small for busing to work. Most black parents, he added, disliked the idea of sending their children on long bus rides anyway. Critics responded that King had created a jobs program for black educators at the expense of black children.

The debate ultimately proved moot, as whites continued withdrawing their children from the system. Just two years after the compromise took effect, the school population was down to 85,000 children, 84 percent of them black. "They're fighting over a dead body," one observer noted sadly. "There ain't no school system to integrate."

The one indisputable result of the affair was a fresh sense of determination on the part of the city's black leaders to seize control of their own destiny. Had there been any doubt before, they now openly embraced the goal of electing a black mayor in 1973. The only question was who would gain their backing. Maynard Jackson made it plain that he intended to run, as did state Senator Leroy Johnson, the man who had broken the color line in the Legislature.

After a decade operating as a canny insider, Johnson had earned the respect of his white colleagues. He seemed a more conventional choice than the exuberant Jackson, and in the early going the city's two leading black businessmen, Jesse Hill and Herman Russell, leaned strongly toward supporting him. Worried, Jackson's friends commissioned a poll by Pat Caddell that showed him taking 85 percent of the black vote against Johnson. Jackson's top strategist, David Franklin, showed the results to Hill and others in the black leadership. "Jesse and them would start arguing with the poll," Franklin recalled, "[and] I'd say, 'Man, I don't know who you been dealing with, but I've got a pro, the best, the pollster's pollster.'"

According to Caddell, black voters admired Johnson for the most part but also expressed qualms about his reputation as a wheeler-dealer. Johnson had promoted Muhammad Ali's comeback boxing match against Jerry Quarry in Atlanta in the fall of 1970, a splashy event that made Johnson seem, in the words of one analyst, "too much a hustler." The *New York Times* called him a "black Machiavelli."

Before long, Hill and Russell joined Maynard Jackson's cause. They helped raise $325,000 for him and, just as important, pitched his candidacy to the other members of the Action Forum, the biracial group that had been formed in the wake of Massell's impolitic speech at the Hungry Club. Thus was born one of Atlanta's most enduring legends — the so-called "Power Structure Deal," in which the white business elite, never enamored of Massell to begin with, spurned him in favor of Jackson, in return for a promise from the black leaders that they would support a white candidate as his unofficial running mate.

For two decades, various participants have vehemently denied making such an explicit compact, but in fact something very close to it happened. Unified behind Jackson, the black leaders took advantage of the

Action Forum's Saturday morning meetings to urge their white associates to jump on the bandwagon. In the early going, the whites balked. But polls of their own eventually persuaded them of Jackson's inevitability, and they proposed an accommodation. The next mayor would take office under a new city charter that replaced the old Board of Aldermen with a City Council and changed the title of vice mayor to president of the council. In the interests of biracial harmony and Atlanta's image, some of the whites argued, it would be good if the new council president were white. The candidate they had in mind was an alderman named Wade Mitchell, a Trust Company Bank executive and former football star from Georgia Tech. The blacks agreed to support him.

In theory, the deal seemed harmless enough. The spate of recent skirmishes and controversies in the city had yielded an unexpected, positive by-product. Race relations were actually in fairly good overall repair. Though the process had been rough, whites were optimistic that the Congress Center and MARTA would fuel continued prosperity in the downtown area, no matter which race was in charge of City Hall. And blacks, despite their impatience on a number of fronts, recognized a vital interest in preserving and enhancing the city's tax base. That meant keeping white flight from turning into a stampede.

In effect, the races had begun to act like rival political parties, pursuing different agendas but willing to cross party lines occasionally on issues of importance. With the city's electorate divided almost equally between black and white, a candidate who could attract even modest crossover support from voters of the opposite race had an excellent chance of winning. A good example occurred in the congressional elections of 1972. A black minister, Andrew Young, captured Atlanta's Fifth District seat, even though the electorate (which included several suburbs) was 62 percent white. As one of Dr. King's top lieutenants, Young had long served as a sort of ambassador to the white community, and he was able to draw enough votes from white liberals to defeat an incumbent white Republican.

The mathematics that served Sam Massell in 1969 — overwhelming support from blacks and modest backing from white liberals — now threatened to turn against him. Black voters meant to switch to Maynard Jackson in 1973. If Jackson could also attract a handful of white votes, which seemed entirely likely, he would win. In joining forces with him, the leaders of the white power structure were bowing to the inevitable, hoping to pick up a favor or two along the way. If the "black" party was going to capture the mayor's office, then perhaps the "white" party could fill the number-two spot.

Already handicapped by mass defections, Massell further damaged his chances with a lapse in judgment on a crucial personnel decision. Police Chief Herbert Jenkins announced his retirement, and Massell listened to advice from his brother, Howard, in picking a successor. The mayor had steered skillfully through quite a number of tricky situations, but his own brother seemed to have a mandate to embarrass and confound him. The two men barely appeared related. Howard, in the parlance of the era, was a swinger. A wealthy bachelor, he frequented the nightclub scene and lived in a well-appointed pad with a mirrored ceiling in the bedroom. A photograph from the period shows him with slicked hair and mutton-chops, wearing a dark shirt, a black-and-white tie and a jacket with horizontal, candy-color stripes.

Howard Massell's choice for chief, John Inman, had been an Atlanta policeman for 22 years, but only belatedly earned his sergeant's stripes in 1966. Known within the department as a hard worker and dogged investigator, he remained untested as a leader. When the mayor announced Inman's appointment, City Hall buzzed with speculation and criticism. The first hint of trouble came a few months afterward, in the fall of 1972, when Sam Massell went on television and stunned viewers by declaring that "gangsters" from Chicago had gotten close to his brother and were attempting to move into Atlanta "with a great deal of money, a lot of brain power, and plenty of muscle."

The mobsters in question turned out to be two brothers named Burton and Robert Wolcoff, who had opened a vending machine business in Atlanta. The mayor ordered Chief Inman to run them out of town, though it was not clear that they had committed any crime. Howard Massell defended the Wolcoffs, saying they planned to "go straight." Inman, caught in the middle, publicly declared his independence from Howard Massell and soon found himself estranged from both Massell brothers. One day the mayor summoned Inman to City Hall and gave him a severe tongue-lashing, conveniently overheard by a reporter from the *Constitution*. "If you can't run the police department any better," Massell shouted, "we've got to have a change!" Though the seriousness of the whole affair was hard to gauge, it left the mayor's dignity badly bruised.

Inman's difficulties were compounded by a steadily worsening relationship with the black community. With much fanfare, he announced an investigation of a popular black alderman on corruption charges, only to have the district attorney dismiss the case as groundless. Within the department, the chief allied himself with a predominantly white police union, alienating many of his black officers. By the time Massell and Jackson squared off in the mayor's race of 1973, many in the black community considered Inman a racist and were calling for his ouster. The mayor came within an eyelash of firing Inman, then backed off and decided to keep him in office.

Given Massell's rapidly ebbing fortunes, members of the white power structure counted themselves lucky to have signed on with Jackson. Some, including the immediate past president of the Chamber of Commerce, builder Larry Gellerstedt, did so reluctantly. Others, led by John Portman, embraced Jackson with enthusiasm. Either way, the white leadership got on board, asking only that Jackson and his crowd support their choice for council president in return.

Wade Mitchell was a perfectly decent man with little political experience and virtually no public following. His candidacy for council president depended on the Action Forum delivering the vote for him, and that proved to be a tall order. Another white candidate, a liberal alderman named Wyche Fowler, jumped into the race, as did Hosea Williams, the firebrand black activist. Poor Mitchell found himself squeezed out. Even though he was endorsed on the black "ticket," he finished in third place, out of the runoff.

The results of the primary brought home some hard truths to the elite that had run the city for so many years. Black leaders could no longer compel black voters to vote for a white man against a black man. And the white power structure learned that it could not deliver the white vote at all, not even to a white candidate. "The 'machine' may appear sound," an observer noted tartly, "until someone lifts the hood and exposes the squirrels on the drum inside."

In the mayoral contest, Jackson got 47 percent of the vote, very nearly winning the election with an outright majority. Massell trailed distantly, with only 20 percent, and confronted the dismal prospect of a runoff election he was certain to lose. The next two weeks marked the low point of Massell's public life. Desperate, he ran a two-page ad in the *Constitution* that showed a stark, grainy photograph of a rubble-strewn sidewalk and a burned-out business, dimmed by a dark shadow. "Atlanta's Too Young to Die," proclaimed the lurid headline. Blacks and whites alike were shocked. Hal Gulliver, a *Constitution* columnist, answered the ad with a stinging headline of his own — "Sam's Issue: Niggers."

Change had come to Atlanta in dozens of guises over the years, never quite so rudely. There was, however, a reassuring outcome. Jackson won the runoff with ease, taking nearly a quarter of the white vote. The council president's race had a mirror-image outcome. Fowler, a white intellectual with a sharp wit, gained 30 percent of the black vote in beating "Hosie" Williams, whose fiery oratory and frequent street demonstrations badly frightened the white community. Black voters seemed to recognize the danger of supporting a radical black candidate, and Williams, who had not expected to do very well in the first place, accepted the result with good cheer. He began his concession speech on election night by saying, "If anybody has any use for some coats and ties . . ." He was drowned out by laughter. After spending the past few weeks in conventional attire, he planned to put on his dashiki and get back to the protest movement.

Jackson won precisely because he did not emerge from the ranks of black activists. He understood quite well the anxieties of the white community. According to David Franklin, his campaign manager, he deliberately pursued a law-and-order theme meant to be reassuring to white voters. "Jackson: Crime Is His Issue," said the headline over a profile in the *Constitution*. He managed to connect with the deepest feelings of black voters without engaging in the politics of anger. He dismissed Massell's attack as an act of "desperation" and praised the city for emerging with its image and reputation intact.

At Jackson's inaugural in January 1974, the elite of the black community turned out, dressed to the nines, many of the women in fur coats, and filled the 4,600 seats of the Civic Center. Robert Shaw conducted as the Atlanta Symphony Orchestra played the final movement of Beethoven's Ninth, and Jackson's aunt, Mattiwilda Dobbs, sang a French aria and a Negro spiritual. The program began and ended on schedule, not at the old-fashioned, leisurely pace of "Colored People's Time." In the words of one journalist, it was "an eminently middle-class affair."

The city Jackson inherited appeared as full of promise as ever. Several publications took note of the relative wealth of Atlanta's black community and proclaimed a "black mecca," personified by the new mayor. Whatever fears whites might harbor about the new order, they had to admit that black Atlantans, many thousands of them, were also citizens of means with a stake in Atlanta's future. Jackson's press secretary, Pearl

Cleage, made the point in a nice, backhanded way, saying, "This is the only city I know where when things go wrong, black people say 'oh my God' just like the Chamber does." The *Saturday Evening Post* called Atlanta "manageable, many-sided, magnificent."

At age 35, the new mayor took office brimming with energy, determined to have fun and shake things up. A preacher's son, he could summon up the oratory of the pulpit when it suited him, but more often he wore the mantle of lawyer and spoke as an advocate in the lofty tones of the courtroom. Challenged with a tough question at an early press conference, he shot back, "I find such assertions to be specious, illogical, vapid, inane — and juh-jooooon." He loved words. One night at a Richard Pryor concert, a reporter spotted Jackson during intermission and asked what he thought of the performer. "Scatological," Jackson answered, "but a comic genius." When Henry Aaron, the great star of the Atlanta Braves, hit his 715th home run at Atlanta Stadium in the spring of 1974, eclipsing Babe Ruth's record after a long chase, Jackson told reporters at the park, "I prayed for it. I felt it coming. I rode with it. I exulted in it. I listened to myself screaming, whistling, waving my arms, and bathing joyfully in Hank's special time of glory." Aaron himself was more succinct. "Just wanted to get it over with," he said.

Jackson reveled in the trappings of his new job, including the Lincoln limousine with the crane-necked reading light that bore him around the city. And he had high ambitions. He wanted to create a "people's administration," as he put it in his inaugural address, "that will afford even the poorest and most destitute person an alternative to agony." But Jackson's political honeymoon ended abruptly, thanks to police politics. Though he had avoided any direct threats during the campaign, everyone in town expected Jackson to remove Chief Inman, whose relationship with the black community had hit rock bottom. Inman had an eight-year contract that insulated him from an outright sacking, but the new city charter gave the mayor and council an opportunity to create a Department of Public Safety with a commissioner — known as the "superchief" — who would outrank Inman and strip him of authority.

Seeing what was coming, Inman filed suit trying to block the creation of the new department. Jackson, furious at what he considered an act of insubordination, responded by firing Inman and giving his job to a white captain named Clint Chafin, a respected veteran of the department. With the mayor's legal right to dismiss him at issue, Inman refused to vacate his office.

The firing took place on the afternoon of Friday, May 3, 1974. Bright and early the next Monday morning, Chafin arrived at the police station on Decatur Street, where he found Inman's blue sedan already parked in the spot reserved for the chief. When he went up to the chief's suite, Chafin discovered Inman occupying the inner office, protected by seven heavily armed members of the police SWAT team. Inman accompanied the SWAT squad into the outer office and confronted Chafin. "You have no authority to give orders," Inman rasped at Chafin. "I am still in command. You are suspended immediately."

Chafin held his ground. With about two dozen uniformed officers arrayed behind him, he told Inman, "You don't have the authority to suspend me. The mayor has suspended *you*." At this point, the faces of the officers on both sides grew tight and drawn. Newsmen and camera crews, observing the showdown from behind a waist-high wooden railing just a few feet away, backed up slightly. Chafin ordered the SWAT team to leave. Inman ordered them to stay. "Please, sir," the team's leader, Lieutenant Emery Sikes, begged Chafin. "I am being ordered by two different chiefs. I can't take orders from two chiefs. My job is at stake. Seventeen and a half years on the force . . ." Hands remained on weapons.

The mayor's top police aide, a captain named Eldrin Bell, slipped down a corridor and found a telephone. He tracked Jackson to the dentist's office and told him what was unfolding. "Oh, no!" Jackson said. "And," Bell added, "it's happening in front of the press."

"Oh, *shit!*" Jackson said.

Everyone who was there at police headquarters that morning remembers experiencing a sick, fearful feeling that shots might actually be exchanged between the armed followers of the rival claimants. Not since the "two governors" controversy of 1947 had a comparable threat of violence enveloped men charged with maintaining the peace. Fortunately, Lieutenant Sikes kept a clear head. Caught between two chiefs, he defused the situation before it got further out of hand. "I'm moving my men out of here," he said at last. The two chiefs could sort it out themselves.

Chafin, believing he had the upper hand, suspended Inman and everyone in his coterie. But later that afternoon, in neighboring DeKalb County, a judge restored Inman to command, throwing the situation back into complete turmoil. Until the matter could be adjudicated, it seemed, the mayor of Atlanta would have no authority over the city's chief of police. Deeply concerned, Jackson called on Governor Carter for help. But with the matter in the courts, Carter declined to intervene. Jackson, reduced to name-calling, denounced Inman as lawless.

As the mess at City Hall unfolded, the business community generally sided with Jackson. They had little sympathy for Inman, while Chafin, as a protégé of former Chief Jenkins, was more than acceptable to them as a replacement. And common sense seemed to warrant giving the new mayor a chance to install his own team. The *Constitution* deplored Inman's behavior and called on him to resign. A group of businessmen talked about buying out the chief's contract, as if he were an unpopular football coach.

The affair might have sorted itself out in due course, except that the chairman of the Atlanta Crime Commission, a conservative white businessman named Dillard Munford, issued a glowing public endorsement of Inman. Had he been a little more experienced, Jackson might have recognized and dismissed Munford's gesture as a minor annoyance. As head of the Majik Market chain of convenience stores, Munford had an understandable interest in police protection and was close to many individual officers, Inman among them. A blustery sort, he did not speak for the white power structure.

Instead of ignoring it, however, Jackson misinterpreted Munford's statement as evidence that the white community was out to get him. The mayor gave a vivid, stunning speech warning of a "plot" to topple city government, hatched by racist whites bent on destroying Atlanta's first black administration. The point of the speech, Jackson's aides explained later, was to rouse the black community to protect their gains. Unhappily, the speech also convinced many in the white community that the new mayor had come unglued.

After Jackson's speech, his relationship with the white business community eroded quickly. Suspicions mounted on both sides of the racial divide. Inman was found to have planted a police spy at the *Atlanta Voice*, the black daily newspaper, which fueled the sense of conspiracy. Whites were offended in turn when Jackson tried to sidestep the city attorney, a highly respected white man, in favor of an outside counsel. In a bizarre development that had both sides scratching their heads, Inman's landlord, a wealthy pesticide heir named Billy Orkin, was indicted on charges of trying to hire a hit man to exterminate his estranged wife, a sideshow that had nothing to do with Inman but added considerably to the confusion.

By the first week of summer in 1974, as the issue of who commanded the Atlanta Police Department entered its fourth month, tempers were wearing thin. One Saturday a 17-year-old black youth, Brandon Gibson, was shot and killed by the police while resisting arrest for a parole violation. Though all of the officers involved in the incident were black, the black community erupted in angry protest. Hosea Williams announced that he planned to lead a mock funeral procession into the heart of the city. The governor, the mayor, and the boy's parents all asked Williams to cancel the demonstration, and City Hall refused to give him a permit. But he insisted on proceeding. Riding a hand-drawn mule wagon, Williams led a group of about 250 marchers to the corner of Courtland Street and Auburn Avenue, where mounted police and members of the SWAT team awaited them.

The ensuing fracas made vivid television footage. Pulled from the wagon and arrested, Williams broke into tears and began cursing the police. Mounted officers rode into the crowd, swinging clubs. Marchers fell underfoot. Reporters spotted a young white officer reaching for his service revolver and being restrained by other officers. No one was seriously injured, but the plain impression was that Atlanta had slipped back into the dark days of the civil rights era. Jackson, who was out of town attending a National Mayors Conference, hurried home and condemned Inman and his top officers for "overreaction" in their handling of the episode.

As if admitting that the impasse had gone on too long, the Georgia Supreme Court ruled a week later that the mayor and council could go ahead with the appointment of a superchief over Inman. At last the crisis appeared to be ending. Amid considerable fanfare, Jackson announced a national search for a prominent law enforcement expert to fill the job. Business leaders volunteered to help scout for a blue-chip administrator and conducted interviews of several top candidates.

After a month looking high and low for the ideal selection, Jackson stunned Atlantans black and white by announcing a surprise choice. A. Reginald Eaves, a friend and former classmate from Morehouse who had virtually no experience whatsoever in law enforcement, but who had been serving as one of Jackson's closest political advisers, would be the new superchief. In a word, Jackson picked a crony, opting for loyalty over qualification.

With the selection of Eaves, the mayor effectively snuffed whatever goodwill remained toward him in the business community. "The Eaves appointment," the Constitution complained, "simply is wrong." In the city's boardrooms, executives concluded that Jackson meant to run the city in defiance of the old power structure. Harold Brockey, the chairman of Rich's and head of a downtown lobbying group called Central Atlanta Progress, wrote a tough-minded letter to Jackson with a list of complaints, including a "perceived attitude of the mayor as anti-white." Released publicly, the letter triggered headlines around the country and even overseas.

Jackson's relationship with the Coca-Cola Company became especially brittle. Just three years earlier, the company's gray eminence, Robert Woodruff, had given the city $10 million to pay for a two-acre park in the middle of downtown Atlanta, a block from the site at Five Points where Coke was first served in 1886. In all, Woodruff and his foundations had given $250 million to the causes of health, education and the arts in Atlanta over the years. Now the company wanted a favor in return. From Coca-Cola's headquarters on North Avenue, CEO Paul Austin could look out on Techwood Homes, the nation's first public housing project, long occupied by white tenants, and watch it turning black. Once the transformation was complete, he believed, the crime rate in the neighborhood would triple, endangering his employees. He wanted to relocate the residents to a new facility on the outskirts of town and to fill the 50-acre site with middle-income housing, parks, a shopping mall, and a theater.

Austin approached the mayor with his proposal, and Jackson initially agreed to help him. Once word of the plan became public, however, Jackson instantly backed off, fearing the black community would never forgive him for participating in another episode of "urban removal." Austin considered the mayor's reversal a stab in the back. Adding to the discord, Austin kept prodding Jackson to let the Rand Corporation perform an efficiency study at City Hall, an intrusion the mayor was not about to allow.

The city's political mood changed dramatically. Small matters took on exaggerated significance. Visitors to City Hall noticed that the mayor's office had been redecorated in an African motif with zebra stripes and leopard spots, and concluded that Jackson must be making some kind of radical political statement. The fabric "seemed ready to spring on passing small prey," one reporter noted ominously. Actually, the new decor had been installed during the last days of Massell's administration. Even the mayor's hair became an issue, when he switched from a straightened style to a modest Afro. The *Journal* and *Constitution* doubled their coverage of

City Hall, making banner headlines of the mayor's every misstep. Finishing an interview with a reporter one night, Jackson said wistfully, "In the words of *Tea and Sympathy*, 'When you think of me later — and you will — be kind.'" But the newspapers were not kind.

Adding to the mayor's woes, he picked the summer of 1974 to save money in the city budget by eliminating backyard garbage collection. Atlanta's homeowners had to begin hauling their trash out to the sidewalk, a chore that provoked yet another split along racial lines. With greater wealth and bigger houses, whites tended to have longer driveways than blacks, making curbside pickup a greater inconvenience. To assist people in handling their garbage, the city supplied households with hefty plastic containers on wheels called "Herbie-the-Curbies," which grumbling whites promptly renamed "Maynards." Blacks found it hard to empathize.

Far from retreating in the face of the white community's disapproval and criticism, Jackson redoubled his determination to forge change. He referred to himself as "large and in charge," and as if to prove it he issued his most controversial directive yet, an executive order that minority firms be awarded 25 percent of all city contracts. The quota included the next major project on the city's drawing board, the construction of a new, $400 million terminal at the airport. "Unless I am assured of minority participation in the construction of the facility," Jackson stated flatly, "it will not be built."

For Atlanta's white business leaders, Jackson's joint-venturing ultimatum was the final straw. They could clench their teeth and endure most of his activities; they had even listened one day as he threatened to close the city's accounts and move the money to banks in Alabama unless they began appointing women and blacks to their boards of directors. But tampering with the airport, the city's aorta, scared them in an entirely new way.

In 1971, the airport had finally earned the title "International" (though just barely) when Eastern Airlines won a route to Mexico City. Bill Hartsfield died the same year, and his name was given to the aviation center he had done so much to create and nurture — Hartsfield International Airport. Before succumbing to a massive heart attack, the old mayor had the immense satisfaction of traveling to Birmingham, Alabama, where he gave a speech to the Kiwanis Club and explained how he had finagled the federal air-mail route for Atlanta more than forty years before. Much to his amusement, he was picketed, and the editors of the Birmingham *Post-Herald* labeled him the "great airport hijacker."

By 1974, the Atlanta airport had become the second busiest in the nation, just behind Chicago's O'Hare. Handling more than 400,000 flights a year, the old terminal was completely overrun, its notoriously long concourses jammed with speed-walkers racing to make connections. Talk of building a second airport bogged down in a dispute over where to put it, and in the meantime the airlines, led by Delta, pushed for construction of a mammoth new terminal in the midfield between the runways. The city agreed to build the facility with revenue bonds underwritten by the airlines. Under Jackson's order, a quarter of the spending — some $100 million — would have to go to black firms. The requirement would create delay, whites feared, and possibly endanger the whole project.

Had he faced no other difficulties beyond the struggle to gain some of the white power structure's money for his black constituents, Jackson's first year in office would have been daunting enough. As it was, he also had the bad luck of serving during the worst recession to hit the country since the 1930s. After decades of unfettered growth, Atlanta's bankers and builders suddenly found themselves dangerously overextended. The go-go lending practices that made Mills Lane rich and famous at C&S Bank pushed his protégé and successor, Richard Kattel, to the brink of ruin. New skyscrapers continued going up, but tenants began vanishing. By one account, eight million square feet of office space lay vacant in Atlanta at one point during the mid-'70s, pitching the city's developers into deep trouble.

Tom Cousins was one of them. Cousins and his partners had undertaken a hugely ambitious program to build a hotel, office, and retail complex next to the Omni and World Congress Center. They were spending lavishly on a glittering showcase with ten movie theaters, indoor and outdoor swimming pools, an ice-skating rink, and expensive specialty shops — something to match the wonders Cousins's rival, Portman, had created uptown. In all, Cousins planned to spend $600 million in the area. "It's a real estate man's dream," he said when ground was broken for the project in 1972. "To miss, you'd almost have to try." Two years later his company was bleeding money, and the fate of the venture looked uncertain.

As the economy worsened, so did unemployment. From a record low of one percent, the city's jobless rate shot to 9.5 percent and reached well into double digits in the black community. Poverty bred crime. Accustomed to superlatives and rave reviews, Atlantans found their hometown tagged with a harsh new nickname, "the murder capital of America," as the city suffered the highest homicide rate in the nation in 1974. The ranks of the victims included Martin Luther King, Jr.'s mother, Alberta, gunned down by a deranged man one Sunday morning as she played the "Lord's Prayer" on the organ at Ebenezer Baptist Church.

In October 1974, as if to preserve in amber the old days of glorious press coverage, *Town & Country* carried an article that managed to ignore almost all of the new realities. Atlanta, the magazine said, was booming and vibrant. "Money is flowing in," the article reported, "from Wall Street, Chicago, Texas, Japan, and even Kuwait in a constant stream as steady as the current of the Chattahoochee River." That the money was spilling out just as fast, down a sewer of bad loans, went unremarked.

A truer picture came out soon afterward. The January 1975 issue of *Harper's* magazine ran a story listing Atlanta as one of the nation's worst cities, based on crime, poverty, and health statistics. "To be frank," the author said, "I was surprised." Like most people, he had read only positive stories in recent years. But measured against an objective set of standards, Atlanta fell short. One of the most discouraging findings, refuting the city's image as a black promised land, was the relative poverty of the city's black families. Atlanta, it seemed, was closer to Newark than Nirvana.

By almost any measure, the city had fallen on hard times. In an especially lousy piece of timing, its marketers unveiled a new ad campaign — "Atlanta, the World's Next Great City" — that would have sounded overblown even in the best of circumstances. Given the sour economy, the crime wave, and the wretched relations between City Hall and the business community, the claim triggered open ridicule. With the sports teams performing abysmally, one journalist suggested that "Losersville" might make a more suitable slogan.

Adding a final layer of indignity, the city's police leaders behaved as if they had been hired for roles in a Keystone Kops comedy. A squad car belonging to Eldrin Bell, the mayor's police aide, was torched when he parked it overnight in the driveway of a female friend. Reggie Eaves, the new superchief, was caught trying to wrangle a public service job for his nephew and then was found to have hired a convicted felon as his personal secretary. The city was dropped from a statewide criminal intelligence network. The misadventures were reported in great detail on the front pages of Atlanta's dailies, the *Journal* and *Constitution*.

By the early months of 1975, it began to appear that Sam Massell had been right after all and that Atlanta might be about to die young. Concerned about the spate of bad publicity, John Portman called on publisher Jack Tarver and asked for a "lull" in coverage of Eaves and the Police Department in the Atlanta newspapers. Tarver refused. Instead, disgusted by the growing menace of crime in downtown Atlanta, Tarver commissioned a series of articles called "A City in Crisis," in which the days of Mayor Allen were recalled as "Camelot" and the loss of white political power was bemoaned in terms that bordered on apocalypse. The final story described Atlanta as "increasingly a city of blacks, of welfare recipients, of crime victims and crime perpetrators. . . ."

The mayor and his close advisers were genuinely disturbed by the series, seeing for the first time just how thoroughly the white power structure had become alienated. Several meetings of the Action Forum were devoted to the problem of degenerating race relations, to no avail. Whites believed Jackson was recklessly endangering the city's future greatness, while blacks believed as fervently that whites meant to keep the city's wealth clutched in their bony fingers unto death.

It took a random act of nature to remind blacks and whites alike how inseparably their lives and fortunes were tied together. On the morning of Monday, March 24, 1975, the city was devastated by the worst tornado in its history, a howling black funnel that sheared an eight-mile path of destruction across the map, from the Perry Homes housing project to the manors of West Paces Ferry Road. No disaster has ever evidenced a more egalitarian attitude. The same wind that knocked down the walls of Liza Mae Amos's apartment at Perry Homes tore the roof off the Governor's Mansion. Three people were killed, one black, two white, all from different walks of life.

Like all storms, it helped clear the air.

CHAPTER 9

THE ATLANTA "STORY"

On November 7, 1975, six top executives from the nation's largest insurance companies came to Atlanta to see for themselves how bad the economic and political crisis had become. With $1.4 billion invested in real estate in the city, they had a giant stake in Atlanta's future. After a day-long meeting with state and local officials and members of the business community, John T. Fey, the chairman of the Equitable Life Assurance Society of the United States, emerged and made a pronouncement. "We don't," he said, "regard things as being out of control here."

As votes of confidence go, it was pretty pale stuff. Yet the verdict of the insurance men marked the beginning of Atlanta's slow recovery from the ravages of the mid-1970s. For a time, it appeared the state might take drastic action to pry Maynard Jackson out of City Hall, possibly by creating a "District of Atlanta" to be run by the General Assembly. "We need some place to train the National Guard," one south Georgia lawmaker told the *Atlanta Journal*, "so why not use Atlanta to give the Guard battlefield experience?" Others talked of reducing City Hall to a ceremonial office, allowed only "to issue library cards, pick up garbage, and hand out parade permits." On a less ominous note, former Governor Carl Sanders championed the idea of consolidating Atlanta with its white suburbs, an idea the mayor said might have merit — provided it occurred after he ran for a second term in 1977.

All the talk of restoring a white majority in Atlanta came to naught, partly because blacks were loath to surrender political power so soon after gaining it, and mostly because whites in Atlanta's suburbs stood united in adamant opposition to rejoining the city so many of them had fled.

Creating a metro-wide government threatened to trigger widespread school busing, which white parents simply refused to accept. Rumors popped up occasionally that the state planned to create various authorities that would seize control of the airport or MARTA or other vital assets, but the fact was that white business leaders had very little interest in turning the city's crown jewels over to the Legislature. Better, they figured, to deal with the devil they knew.

For his part, the mayor admitted that he had moved too quickly at first, alienating the businessmen. "I don't need you guys to get elected," he told Richard Kattel, the head of Citizens & Southern Bank, "but I've learned that I certainly need you to govern." After a delay of several months, the contracts for the new midfield terminal at the airport were finally let, causing relief on all sides.

In many parts of town, especially the well-to-do white enclave of Buckhead, Jackson remained a reviled figure. According to the *Northside News*, a weekly for the social set, "many sound-minded, unprejudiced Atlantans are saying that Maynard Jackson, Atlanta's Negro mayor, is well on his way to bringing ruin to Atlanta as devastating as was the fire started by General Sherman." Racial tensions ran high at City Hall. Two of the liberal white members of the City Council, Charles Helms and Panke Bradley, created a brief stir when they announced that they no longer intended to cast votes on the basis of "white guilt."

The black community watched in discomfort as Jackson tried to push Reggie Eaves, the controversial public safety commissioner, into quitting. He had known Eaves only casually in college, the mayor declared in a newspaper interview, striking a defensive note. "We were in the glee club together. We never ran together. He was never a buddy." Eaves was just a "temporary" appointment, he insisted. Jackson nearly talked Eaves into resigning at one point, only to have the deal unravel when the council president, Wyche Fowler, issued a public demand for Eaves's ouster. Rather than appear to be caving in to a white politician, Eaves clung to his job. And he continued to embarrass the mayor. Eaves ordered a new car at city expense, loaded with options, and when the newspapers stirred up criticism, he responded angrily, "I'm giving too much time and effort to this city to try to prove that I'm the 'good nigger.' If I can't ride in a little bit of comfort, to hell with it."

Still, for all the continuing racial friction, the city fathers could point to hopeful signs that the worst was over. In December 1975, Atlanta voters approved an $18.9 million bond referendum for a new central library, a modest but welcome show of faith in Atlanta's future. The failure of three other issues on the ballot — for new sewers and streets and improvements at the Atlanta Zoo — simply indicated that the city's convalescence would be a lengthy one.

The most significant contribution to the improvement in Atlanta's damaged reputation came from an unlikely source, the state Capitol, where Governor Jimmy Carter astonished friends and detractors alike by announcing that he planned to run for president. The first hurdle Carter faced, in the eyes of the national media and many Democratic Party regulars, was to prove that he did not harbor racist tendencies. Despite the talk of a New South, white politicians from the region were still considered suspect on the issue of race, and in Carter's case the ugliness of his campaign for governor in 1970 made close scrutiny inevitable. He got his big break in 1974 when Bob Strauss, the party chairman, named him "national campaign manager" for the midterm elections, a role that allowed Carter to travel the country making contacts and winning converts.

In December 1974, Carter attended the Democratic Party's post-election "mini-convention" in Kansas City, where he visited various state delegations in the company of Atlanta's black congressman, Andrew Young. Though Young made no formal endorsement, he spoke well of Carter and gave him an instant stamp of approval by his mere presence. Their friendship had begun in 1970 at Paschal's restaurant in Atlanta, where Carter tried to convince a group of black leaders that he was not as hostile to their interests as his campaign strategy suggested. He failed to allay their suspicions, but Young noticed afterward how Carter went back to Paschal's kitchen and shook hands with the staff, pausing to chat warmly with each worker. In 1972, Carter's mother, Miss Lillian, gave Young a contribution in his bid for Congress, and Young returned the favor at the Democratic Convention by mentioning Carter to George McGovern as a possible running mate.

During his years as governor, Carter kept in touch with Young and solicited his advice on a wide range of political issues, not just race relations. When Carter decided to try for the presidency, Young lent him a stack of a thousand index cards containing the names of black leaders across the country, guaranteeing Carter a hearing in the black community. With a civil rights leader of Young's impeccable credentials standing by his side, Carter could pursue his campaign for the White House free from lingering accusations of being a "seg" sympathizer.

Lester Maddox performed a similar service for Carter, though not intentionally. Unable to forgive Carter for abandoning the white man's cause, Maddox spent his four years as lieutenant governor squabbling with Carter on an almost daily basis. When Carter revealed his presidential ambitions, Maddox took to the road, denouncing Carter at every stop as "the biggest fake and the most dishonest man I have ever known." Seeing the advantage of having Maddox as an enemy, Carter and his aides subtly encouraged the attacks. "Being called a liar by Lester Maddox is like being called ugly by a frog," Carter's press secretary, Jody Powell, said in a famous retort.

During his service as lieutenant governor, Maddox opened a concession at Underground Atlanta, where he sold pick handles, "Phooey" T-shirts, alarm clocks that said "Wake Up, America," and a novelty item called McGovern Pantyhose ("They'll never run again"). He often manned the counter himself, signing autographs and chatting with customers. When he made a sale of $3.12, he would call out, "That's three dollars for the merchandise and twelve cents for health, education, graft, and welfare."

"No, sir! I don't think it detracts from the dignity of the office," Maddox told a reporter who questioned the seemliness of the enterprise. "I think the only way you can do that is to be a cheater or a liar or a hypocrite." In truth, Maddox had become an act, one whose appeal was increasingly threadbare. With Carter's term ending in 1974, Maddox made a bid to succeed him and return to the governor's office. He lost decisively, closing the door once and for all on the segregationist era in Georgia politics. Fittingly, the winner was George Busbee, the state legislator who had sponsored the creation of the Sibley Commission, the panel whose hearings dampened the rush to close the state's public schools in the early 1960s.

The jumble of events — Maddox's loss, Carter's gathering momentum as a presidential candidate, Young's tacit support — created an impression of Georgia and its capital city that dispelled some of the dismal reports that had been flowing from Atlanta in recent months. Carter's emergence on the national scene coincided with a growing recognition that all areas of the country, not just the South, had serious difficulties coping with issues of race. Compared with Detroit, say, or Boston, Atlanta's racial travails did not seem quite so hopeless. It was a matter of perspective. By displacing George Wallace as the South's favorite son, Carter advanced the idea that the whole region was making progress, with Atlanta leading the way.

Of course, not everyone bought this interpretation. Carter's habit of exaggerating his accomplishments provoked considerable skepticism, highlighted by a notorious article, "Jimmy Carter's Pathetic Lies," that appeared in *Harper's* magazine. Carter called himself a farmer when he actually ran a peanut warehouse, called himself a nuclear physicist when he was not, and promised never to lie when all politicians do. Among those who kept him at arm's length was Maynard Jackson. When Carter committed a celebrated gaffe by pledging to protect the "ethnic purity" of America's neighborhoods, "Daddy" King and other black leaders in Atlanta rushed to defend him, but Jackson did not. Even after he beat Gerald Ford and captured the presidency, doubts remained about Carter's attitude toward race.

Those misgivings burst into a fierce national debate when Carter nominated an old friend and neighbor from south Georgia, Griffin Bell, to be his attorney general. Bell's confirmation hearings turned into a trial, not just of Bell as an individual, but of Georgia's entire white leadership, including the Atlanta power structure, and the actions they had taken during the civil rights era. The case for the prosecution was articulated with scathing brilliance by Calvin Trillin in the *New Yorker*, as he heaped scorn on the self-styled "moderates" of the South who claimed to have worked "behind the scenes" to bring about desegregation — always, it seemed, as slowly and grudgingly as possible. A moderate, in Trillin's view, was a segregationist with good manners, a racist without a sidearm. Expressing the view of the liberal establishment, Parren Mitchell of Maryland, the chairman of the Congressional Black Caucus, said of Bell, "We're going after his hide."

The charges against Bell fell into three broad areas. He had served as Governor Ernest Vandiver's top legal adviser during the "no, not one" period. Then, after President Kennedy appointed him to the U.S. Fifth Circuit Court of Appeals in 1961, Bell had spurned busing as a remedy in scores of school desegregation cases, including Atlanta's. And finally, he belonged to a pair of all-white social clubs in Atlanta.

During 12 days of hearings before the Senate Judiciary Committee, Bell defended himself with uncommon patience and candor. He described his role in creating the Sibley Commission to relieve Vandiver of his foolish vow and keep the schools open. He freely admitted his distaste for busing, but pointed to a 15-year career on the bench enforcing desegregation in other ways. He had intervened in the Atlanta case to urge a compromise, even though the case had not yet reached his court, but he made no apology. The black leadership of Atlanta had accepted the settlement, and it had freed the schools from endless litigation. He agreed to quit his social clubs, leaving it for others to reflect that restrictive clubs were hardly a problem unique to the South.

As he endured 13 hours of testimony, sitting by himself without counsel, speaking without notes, Bell enjoyed a personal triumph that also served as an acquittal of other white Southerners who had grown up when segregation was a way of life, and who had changed their thinking, often with difficulty. In an editorial advocating his confirmation, the *Washington Post* looked back on the South of the 1950s and '60s and argued that "in the context of that region at that time, Mr. Bell was a constructive influence." The Atlanta "story," of pragmatic cooperation between the leaders of the black and white communities, gained renewed luster.

Bell's ordeal had the effect of exposing a rift that had been building for some years between white liberals from the North and black leaders in the South. Some of the South's civil rights leaders opposed Bell, but many more admired him and believed they could trust him. As Andy Young explained to the *New York Times*, he preferred Southern white men who had struggled with the issue of race to Northern "intellectual liberals" who had little personal acquaintance with black people, and whose views were theoretical, untested, and all too often patronizing.

To appreciate the peculiar nature of Atlanta's economic revival, one had to climb aboard an eight-story, 205-foot-long escalator, overcome vertigo, ride to the top of the new Omni International complex, and enter the World of Sid & Marty Krofft.

Developer Tom Cousins and his partners completed the Omni International early in 1976. Scaled back only slightly because of losses during the recession, the ambitious project included a hotel, two office towers, six movie theaters, an indoor skating rink, several restaurants, an International Bazaar, and upscale retail shops including Pucci, Hermès, Lanvin, and Givenchy. Atop it all sat the world's first indoor, high-rise "fantasy" park.

How these various parts would fit together — whether, for instance, secretaries would buy Hermes scarves during their lunch break, or ice-skaters would go to the movies — was largely a matter of guesswork. With a price tag of $14 million, the World of Sid & Marty Krofft represented by far the biggest risk. Would Atlantans, who lived in a warm climate, near a genuine amusement park, Six Flags Over Georgia, go downtown and pay money to visit an attraction inside a building? The answer, in a word, was no.

The Krofft brothers, who produced a children's TV show, created an eight-story "world of family fun," as they called it, in which visitors were greeted at the end of the escalator ride by mimes and costumed puppets, guided to a village of giant hats called Lidsville, and subjected to various live performances in a 1,000-seat theater. The main ride was a six-foot pinball that clattered around hitting flippers and bumpers. During the opening ceremonies, one guest found himself riding a crystal carousel with Bert Lance and Kate Smith, wondering, literally as well as figuratively, if the venture would hold up. Six months later, the World of Sid & Marty Krofft closed.

The fate of the whole Omni International complex fell into doubt. People were impressed with the facility — one account called it the "brightest star" to shine in downtown Atlanta since the opening of the Polaris Lounge — but it struggled against a tide of change in the city's habits of work and play. Until the early 1970s, white Atlantans had the streets of downtown Atlanta pretty much to themselves. Office workers picnicked every lunch hour on the greensward of Central City Park, and at night, Underground Atlanta drew an audience of local revelers along with out-of-towners. Blue laws kept the surrounding counties dry, providing a ready clientele for Atlanta's bars and restaurants.

Aside from northern DeKalb County, white flight had yet to create much of a suburban boom. The metropolitan population had grown to 1.3 million by 1973, up only a modest 30 percent since reaching a million on "M Day" in 1959. The whites who fled tended to be working-class parents, not the wealthy. A few office parks germinated in DeKalb and Cobb counties, but most companies kept their headquarters inside the city limits.

Then, inevitably, the complexion of downtown Atlanta began to change. Law and evolving customs made blacks more welcome at stores and on the sidewalks. With the advent of a black mayor and police chief, blacks no longer felt obliged to keep out of parks and plazas. At the Capitol, City Hall, and the Fulton County courthouse, blacks found new opportunities for employment. These developments caused little consternation for the white business leadership. But the recession of the mid-1970s also placed quite a number of unemployed blacks on the streets, and in time parts of the central business district began to report sharp increases in crime. Attendance at Underground Atlanta plummeted after a couple of nearby muggings. The leaders of Central Atlanta Progress, the business lobbying group, set up a scale model of downtown Atlanta with pins marking crime sites and used it to persuade the mayor to beef up police protection.

In the minds of most planners and developers, including Tom Cousins, the city's future would be shaped by MARTA, the rapid transit system. In Toronto and other cities with modern subways, urban "clusters" had sprouted around the rail stations, spurring high-rise development. In Atlanta, the theory went, MARTA stops would lure white residents into the core of downtown, reducing crime and reviving the central business district. Far from despairing, Cousins hoped to secure the Omni International as a frontier on the southwest edge of downtown, and then to hook up to Rich's and eventually to Underground Atlanta, Georgia State University, and the Capitol complex beyond, all by following MARTA.

Looking at a map, the master plan was obvious. Blacks now lived to the west, south, and east of downtown Atlanta, as if holding the central business district in a cupped hand. To keep businesses from leaving downtown, MARTA would connect the dots of downtown's major institutions and supply them with a steady stream of white people. These calculations were discussed mostly in euphemism, because it was easy to misunderstand the strategy as one of racial exclusion. The point was not to force blacks out of downtown, but to lure whites there in numbers adequate to maintain their "comfort" level.

But MARTA did not work as anticipated. Part of the problem was money. Even with an initial budget of $1.4 billion, most of it coming from the federal Urban Mass Transit Administration, the project proved too rich for Atlanta's blood. To save on condemnation costs, MARTA's rail lines had to follow the right-of-way of the old railroads, which meant positioning the main station at Five Points, near the original Zero Mile post where Atlanta was founded. One immediate drawback was that MARTA claimed land from several of Underground Atlanta's pubs, restaurants and shops, forcing them to close. Construction disrupted many other establishments there, until the complex eventually went out of business, eliminating one of the institutions MARTA was meant to save.

A more fundamental difficulty lay in the politics of MARTA's completion schedule. From the white community's point of view, the smart move would have been to build the north-south line first, so that white commuters from the northside could ride downtown to work. One of the early plans for the Five Points station envisioned "a glistening hub of activity, serving as a transportation center with airline ticket offices and space for unloading bus and limousine passengers. . . ." The line would reach south of the city all the way to Hartsfield International Airport, giving visitors cheap, direct access to the convention hotels that speckled the downtown area.

But black voters had given MARTA its margin of passage, and they were bearing the heaviest burden of the penny sales tax that provided the system's local funding. Political fairness dictated that the east-west rail line be built first, giving blacks a quicker return on their investment. As a result, MARTA began life as a largely "black" enterprise, while white commuters remained tucked snugly inside their cars driving to and from work. As late as 1975, city planners predicted that the area around Five Points would flourish as a "city center," with "a 'street culture' assortment of kiosks, gaily colored bus shelters, and cross-walks, trees and other landscaping, street lighting and storefront lighting." And they were right, except that the patrons turned out to be black, not white.

MARTA was further handicapped by the refusal of suburban whites to join the system. Confined to two counties, Fulton and DeKalb, the buses and rail lines had no way of reaching the other parts of the metropolitan area. When the great wave of national migration to the Sun Belt began in the late 1970s, filling Atlanta's suburbs with new arrivals from the North and Midwest, growth followed the interstate highways — I-75 north to Cobb County and I-85 north through DeKalb to Gwinnett County. The northern arc of I-285, the perimeter highway that builder Ben Massell once mocked as the dividing line between "chicken salad" and "chicken shit," became a magnet for development.

Demographics ruled the day. White people who moved to Atlanta did not wish to live with blacks or send their children to black schools, so they bought houses or rented apartments as far away from the black community as they could get, which meant going north. Political decisions contributed to the trend. Though they had little else in common, Maynard Jackson and Jimmy Carter both opposed the construction of additional highways through Atlanta's established neighborhoods. Together, they helped kill a pair of developmental roads, I-485 and the

Stone Mountain Tollway, that might have fostered growth on the east side of Atlanta. As a result, the Downtown Connector remained the city's major artery, a north-south conduit that funneled traffic and development in a single direction — north.

At the Omni International, these larger forces had a severe impact. With office space in the downtown area still woefully overbuilt, the 600,000 square feet in the complex's twin office towers proved hard to peddle to tenants. The hotel, designed to house sports fans attending events at the Omni coliseum, did poorly until it was refurbished for conventioneers visiting the World Congress Center. The hotel ballroom, an afterthought, was built across the railroad tracks, reachable only by an enclosed pedestrian bridge. The retail shops suffered because convention visitors tended not to be upscale shoppers. No one went to the movie theaters. The skating rink and an adjacent video arcade attracted youngsters who annoyed the other patrons. Interest on the $76 million construction loan went unpaid.

Still, Cousins had no intention of giving up. He convinced MARTA's administrators to plan a station at the Omni. He talked Morgan Guaranty and the other lenders out of foreclosing. He moved his personal offices into the complex as a show of faith. And he continued drawing up blueprints for Omnisouth, a 22-acre, $265 million final phase that would link his empire to the rest of downtown. He even talked of spending $39 million on a giant space needle as Omnisouth's signature piece.

Cousins believed downtown Atlanta had a future, and others in the white business community shared his dogged optimism. MARTA might not be turning out as they expected, but it was bound to transform Atlanta *somehow*. The trick was to guess what changes lay ahead and try to exploit them. During the planning stages of MARTA, John Portman foresaw a triple-decked pathway coming straight up Peachtree Street from Five Points through his Peachtree Center complex, with the rail line underground, cars on the pavement above, and a pedestrian mall on top. Though that futuristic vision now seemed overly ambitious, the north line of MARTA still offered opportunities. A rail station would serve Peachtree Center eventually, and Portman believed it would foster growth. Picking up where he left off in the tug-of-war over the World Congress Center, he tried to get Rich's executives to move their department store to his end of town. Cousins lobbied just as hard to keep Rich's where it was, near Five Points.

For his part, Mayor Jackson labored mightily to assuage the business community and to keep Atlanta's big corporations from picking up stakes and moving. If Five Points had lost its appeal, he argued, at least companies could stay within the city limits. He counted it a success when Paul Austin decided to build Coca-Cola's new office tower on the company's old site on North Avenue. And Jackson helped persuade the executives of Southern Bell, the giant telephone utility, to build their new headquarters in Midtown, next to another planned MARTA stop. His relations with the white power structure, having nowhere to go but up, gradually improved.

As he prepared to run for re-election, the mayor could count on virtually unanimous support from the black community, and he found himself in surprisingly good shape with some white voters as well. His ardent resistance to building new highways in the city earned him a devoted following in several reviving neighborhoods, while the business community grudgingly embraced him out of simple fear that a more radical black politician might come along in his place. Eager to make a strong showing, Jackson tilted to the right. Like other mayors before him, he confronted an election-year strike by the city's garbage collectors, and like his predecessors, he took a hard line against them. In a gesture to the city's ministers — black as well as white — he made a point of declining to issue a proclamation celebrating Gay Pride Day in Atlanta.

In a variety of ways, the mayor seemed to be a new man. He divorced, went on a diet, lost more than 100 pounds and revealed quite a handsome fellow beneath the baby fat. He began squiring an attractive airline executive named Valerie Richardson around town. A year shy of his fortieth birthday, he showed signs of mellowing. One of the issues near and dear to white voters was the restoration of the Cyclorama, a massive, 360-degree painting and tableau that depicted scenes from the Battle of Atlanta. Jackson agreed to spend city funds repairing the canvas and the building that housed it, even though many of his black constituents questioned the use of their tax dollars on an attraction that glorified the Confederacy. "Heck, the right side won," Jackson said, ending the debate with a terse reminder of the Civil War's outcome.

One subtle aspect of the mayor's race of 1977 was a growing recognition on the part of white Atlantans that Jackson, for all the political differences they had with him, nonetheless was a fellow Atlantan, and one of estimable lineage at that. The mayor's limousine bore a plate on its front bumper that said "Talk Up Atlanta," and he lived by the slogan. He promoted the city vigorously, sometimes shamelessly, sounding very much like the civic boosters who had come before him. The former mayor, Ivan Allen, Jr., made a point of endorsing him for re-election, as did the editors of the *Atlanta Constitution*.

The final hurdle for Jackson turned out to be his nemesis, Reggie Eaves. In August 1977, just weeks before the election, four policemen accused the commissioner of involvement in a cheating scandal in which certain officers — supporters of Eaves — were given advance copies of the written examinations for promotion to sergeant and captain. The city attorney's office conducted a quick investigation that cleared Eaves of wrongdoing, but suspicions remained. Jackson survived the crisis, largely on the weight of his own reputation for personal integrity, winning re-election with 63 percent of the vote. But as he prepared for his second inaugural, he faced growing pressure to reopen the case and resolve the lingering questions about Eaves's involvement.

Jackson agreed to appoint a special panel to examine the police cheating scandal in depth, and the resultant probe kept Atlantans in thrall for months. According to his accusers, who were also black, Eaves personally ordered favored treatment for several of his allies in the Afro-American Patrolman's League, seeing that they got copies of the promotional exams ahead of time. Eaves denied having done so. He submitted to a lie-detector test, which he then attempted to confound by breathing at the abnormally low rate of five or six breaths per minute, or about a third of the ordinary frequency, and by holding his breath so hard before exhaling that his blood pressure readings literally jumped off the chart. The non-plussed examiners tried four times to get Eaves to finish the test properly, but each time his breath-holding pattern grew more exaggerated. In their final report, the investigators cited Eaves's evasive behavior during the polygraph test, along with other evidence, in concluding that he had "expressly authorized" the cheating.

Not surprisingly, these revelations got the mayor's second term off to a rocky start. Hoping to avoid the spectacle of firing Eaves, Jackson urged him to resign, but Eaves resisted. If he quit, he said, it would be an admission of guilt. He insisted he was innocent. After two weeks of stalemate and mounting criticism in the local media, Jackson arranged for time on local television, saying he planned to announce a resolution of the matter. He prepared two speeches, one saying that Eaves would stay on, the other that Eaves would go.

On the night of the speech, Jackson's staff placed small wagers on which version he would deliver. As he began speaking on live TV, backers of the "keep him" speech started to collect their bets. Then, about halfway through, Jackson switched to the "fire him" speech. He rattled on at length, alternating texts, until at last he said the issue required "more attention" and would remain unsettled for an indefinite period. In the meantime, he assigned an outside administrator to run the police department on a day-to-day basis, leaving Eaves in limbo.

Many who watched his 40-minute performance that night thought Jackson had slipped a cog. Actually, he hoped that Eaves would quit in the aftermath of the speech, which is more or less what happened. The mayor talked Eaves into signing a letter of resignation, effective in June, three months off, and then suspended him for 90 days, effective immediately. Eaves tried to retrieve his letter, but Jackson kept it stashed under lock and key in the city vault. The Eaves regime was over at last.

At the price of enduring a considerable amount of mockery, Jackson managed to get rid of Eaves without having to go through the mess of an impeachment trial before the City Council. But the collateral damage was high. The episode gave the impression of a city divided along racial lines, with whites calling for Eaves's head while many blacks wanted to exonerate him. Just a few months after leaving the police department, Eaves ran for a seat on the Fulton County Commission from a black district and won easily, proving himself a force to be reckoned with in city politics in the future.

At the same time the Eaves fiasco was unfolding, one of Atlanta's most visible business leaders watched his career end in disgrace. Dick Kattel, the chairman of C&S Bank, thought he had weathered the worst of the recession by early 1978. After four years of losses from a mounting pile of "non-performing" real estate loans, he was prepared to announce that C&S had enjoyed a modest profit of $3 million in 1977. But on February 24, 1978, a federal bank regulator looked over the books and refused to accept the figures, saying the bank still had a large backlog of bad loans to pay off. Badly shaken, Kattel resigned the next day, citing fatigue, frustration, and errors of judgment. A writer from *Fortune* magazine, reviewing Kattel's tenure, called him "incompetent" and "clearly out of his depth," though the real culprit seemed to be the legacy of Mills B. Lane, Jr., and the wide-open days when every officer in the bank was authorized to lend the legal maximum of $10 million without so much as a supervisor's okay.

Kattel's downfall jolted the mayor. As president of the Chamber of Commerce during the election, Kattel had been Jackson's biggest political supporter, a trusted adviser who smoothed his relations with the other members of the white business leadership. Now Kattel was gone, just when Jackson needed him most in helping to repair the misunderstandings of the Eaves affair.

The exposure of C&S's continuing financial difficulties brought renewed attention to the condition of Atlanta's economy, which remained fragile. By one estimate, 150 small and medium-sized businesses had closed their doors or left the city during the previous five years. Only one sector, the hospitality industry, was fully recovered. Hotel rooms had doubled in 10 years and more space was needed. Thanks to the World Congress Center, Atlanta held its rank as the third busiest convention city in the country.

President Carter, whose administration did few other favors for Atlanta, saw to it that Delta Air Lines finally got the overseas routes necessary to justify Hartsfield International Airport's middle name. Delta gained approval for a London route in 1978, after having applied unsuccessfully for flights to European cities since 1967. But observers cautioned that the city was not yet prepared to cope with an influx of world travelers. Signs were posted exclusively in English. Few hospitality workers spoke a second language. Only central bank branches changed foreign currency. In one awkward encounter, a delegation of Chinese visitors complained when a hotel clerk, unaware that the Chinese place their family names first, registered them under their given names.

Atlanta's provincialism became a favorite topic of conversation. Emory University offered a course on what Atlanta should do to become truly international, as if the city were an untutored student. In downtown Atlanta, one local critic lamented, echoing Mencken, one could not find "a recording of a Mahler symphony, a Bach cantata, or a Puccini opera because there simply are no good well-stocked record stores there. Zilch. Except for the big department stores, until a few years ago there were no really good bookstores downtown. Even now, Atlanta has many pretty good restaurants scattered all over the place, yet the only one famous beyond our own environs is the world's biggest drive-in hot-dog stand" — the Varsity. Others complained about a proliferation of adult movie houses, yellow-front adult bookstores, and strip joints.

After years of lavish praise from the national media, city leaders girded themselves for coverage that now seemed uniformly negative, often unfairly so. In the fall of 1978, the Los Angeles Times ran an infamous article by Robert Scheer that savaged Atlanta as "a 60 percent black city that floats in a sea of white suburbia whose inhabitants desperately avoid contact with the untouchables." Scheer's description of an inner city beset with poverty and violence appeared just as the Georgia-Pacific Corporation, the forestry giant, announced plans to move its headquarters from Portland, Oregon, to a site in downtown Atlanta a few blocks north of Five Points. Worried employees had to be reassured that they were not being transferred into a war zone.

Scheer's piece contained a memorable account of his attempt to visit Perry Homes, the huge public housing project on Atlanta's west side, during an afternoon outing with black leaders John Lewis and Julian Bond. Lewis and Bond got lost trying to find the place, which gave a laugh to Atlantans of both races and suggested that white suburbanites were not the only guilty parties when it came to avoiding contact with the poor. Still, there was nothing amusing about the tone or content of the article. Others followed, including a *Wall Street Journal* article saying Atlanta's "Scarlett O'Hara act . . . may be wearing thin."

The news staff of the *Atlanta Journal*, taking a hard look at their hometown, concluded that race permeated every aspect of life in the city. Whites were 40 percent of the city's population and had 95 percent of its wealth. A survey of 53 white-owned businesses showed that blacks held only three of the 458 seats on their boards of directors. And one man, Jesse Hill, filled two of the spots. Meanwhile, the city now contained 15,252 units of public housing, many in poor condition and infested with rats.

Hosea Williams, the black activist, lashed out at the black middle class. "They don't really believe they're black," he spat. "They talk about art rather than the rats and the roaches in the projects. They don't want to eat at Paschal's anymore. They go to the Midnight Sun. Atlanta has always been the home of the richest and most powerful Uncle Toms in America." A reporter pressed Williams to name them. He refused, saying sheepishly, "I've gotten too Uncle Tom myself to call their names."

There were random acts of kindness. In the summer of 1978, when he was 88 years old and hobbled by a pair of strokes, Coca-Cola's grand old man, Robert Woodruff, made a show of donating $7 million of his company's stock to the Atlanta University Center for a new library. Woodruff invited the center's chancellor, Charles Merideth, to his office and pointed to a thick envelope containing the stack of certificates. "If you can lift them," Woodruff said, "you can have them."

"Needless to say," Merideth reported later, "I found the strength to remove them from his desk."

More and more, though, the mood of the races was one of edginess. In 1978, FBI statistics showed Atlanta to have the highest crime rate in the nation. The city regained the unwanted title of America's homicide capital. Whites became increasingly leery of the downtown area, complaining of incidents of aggressive panhandling, jostling, and ugly remarks from loitering black men. (Many black women had the same complaints.) Housewives had long since stopped coming downtown to shop. White-collar jobs were dwindling as well, as more and more companies moved to the suburbs. A survey showed that by the late 1970s, only one employee in nine in metropolitan Atlanta worked downtown. At night, the central city became a place of white conventioneers and poor blacks.

On the evening of Thursday, June 28, 1979, Dr. Marc Tetalman was walking south on Piedmont Avenue with his wife and a small group of friends, returning to their hotel after dinner at the elegant Abbey Restaurant. The Tetalmans had been celebrating their eleventh anniversary, and it was late — 10:45 p.m. — when they passed the Civic Center on their way to the Hilton. Two black assailants approached them with pistols drawn and demanded their valuables. Dr. Tetalman refused. He was shot in the chest at point-blank range and died an hour later.

As such incidents often do, the Tetalman shooting brought the city's growing tensions into clear focus. Dr. Tetalman was the director of nuclear medicine at Ohio State University, in town for the annual meeting of his peers. The death of a distinguished visitor in a sidewalk holdup represented exactly the kind of crime city leaders everywhere dread, but this one had an extra dimension. When Mayor Jackson went to see Dr. Tetalman's colleagues the next day to apologize for the incident, they told him their group already had reported more than *forty* crimes to the police, including a dozen other muggings. In an unusual breech of decorum, the head of the World Congress Center, where the doctors' convention was being held, described police protection at the facility as "pathetic." The *Wall Street Journal* labelled downtown Atlanta a "war zone."

Contrary to popular memory, Dr. Tetalman's death did not provoke a frenzy of recriminations against the mayor on the part of the white power structure, at least not openly. Coverage in the local newspapers was restrained. Behind the scenes, however, a cold fury was building among whites, a belief that the city's streets now belonged to a black riffraff that the Jackson administration refused to control. The mayor did not have the will, it seemed, to preserve Atlanta's civil order. The Tetalman killing awakened a feeling of rage, one that erupted four months later after a second horrific crime.

Unlike the murder of Dr. Tetalman, the death of Patricia Barry could only be considered one of those freak accidents of the human condition, the meeting of an innocent woman and a madman. Barry, a secretary in former governor Carl Sanders' law firm, planned to celebrate her twenty-sixth birthday by going to lunch with a co-worker. She was in the midst of a crowd of people walking along Peachtree Street at high noon on October 17, 1979, when a demented Vietnam veteran shot and killed her. The man, Raymond Bunting, immediately put the pistol to his own head and pulled the trigger. He was dead by the time a mounted policeman on patrol nearby could draw a bead on him.

In the cool light of reason, it was hard to blame the mayor for Patti Barry's slaying. But as news of the incident spread, the pent-up frustrations of recent months exploded in a mood that could fairly be described as hysteria. The *Constitution* ran a package of front-page stories accompanied by a drawing that depicted Bunting, the perpetrator, as a snarling animal with exaggerated Negro features. Lewis Grizzard, a local columnist better known for his folksy, often extremely funny ruminations on life in the South, lost his grip and wrote a bitter attack on the mayor, saying Jackson was more interested in his political career "than the welfare of the citizens of this city." Atlanta was in a state of war, Grizzard wrote, with "the drunks and the punks against the rest of us. And we're losing, goddammit! We're losing." He advocated calling out the National Guard. A switchboard operator reported hundreds of calls in support of Grizzard and only one complaint.

The newspaper's editorial page was equally unrestrained. A cartoon showed Jackson shrugging and saying, "Oh, this could happen in any city," while corpses lay strewn behind him and a policeman casually twirled his nightstick. The mayor, an editorial charged, had allowed an "aura of permissiveness" to infect the streets of downtown rather than conduct "no-nonsense law enforcement." Sanders called a press conference and demanded "less jawbone and more backbone" from City Hall. "The reason every kook, nut, and crackpot in the country comes to Atlanta," he said, "is that they feel they can get away with things here that they can't do elsewhere."

The lava heat of the reaction left Jackson utterly stunned. He protested that Barry had died in an "insane shooting" that his administration could not possibly have prevented. The killer, who suffered a long history of mental imbalance, had only recently moved to Atlanta from New Jersey. He had bought his handgun illegally, lying on the federal form that asked about his record. Stricter gun control might have kept him unarmed, Jackson noted, but no one seemed to be advocating that sort of crackdown.

Had the order of the two killings been reversed, so that the outpouring of anger came in response to Dr. Tetalman's death, race relations in the city might have fared better. Police protection for conventioneers was a perfectly defensible demand, the sort of issue any chamber of commerce would pursue. But taking back the streets from "undesirable elements," as Sanders put it, presented an altogether different question. It raised the specter of a return to the days when white police harassed blacks and rousted them from parts of downtown. A black mayor could not easily countenance such a campaign.

The desire of the business community to preserve a white presence in the city took on a desperate edge. Worried because their roster of bus drivers was now majority black, MARTA administrators secretly adopted a quota system giving preference in hiring to white applicants. White leaders began talking in earnest about recapturing City Hall in the next mayoral election.

Naturally, blacks recoiled at this onslaught, believing the mayor — and themselves — to be the targets of racism. Far from sharing the white community's dismal view of Jackson, many blacks believed he had gone too far trying to mollify the crowd at the Chamber of Commerce. Hosea Williams labeled him a "tool" of the power structure, a charge that illustrated the vastly different perceptions of the two races.

As the new decade of the '80s dawned, hopeful signs could be found in Atlanta: The new central library neared completion, as did the giant midfield terminal at the airport, on time and within budget at that. Commercial and industrial construction revived. Still, crime remained the leading topic of conversation among blacks and whites alike. The city finished 1979 with a record 231 homicides, up an alarming 61 percent from 1978, itself a record year. As always, most of the victims were black. And a disquieting number were children.

Atlanta's "missing and murdered" children, as the cases came to be known, tested the city in a new and unique way. By the early part of 1980, people in the black community were whispering anxiously about a rash of disappearances and grisly discoveries. Over a period of eight months, the bodies of five children were found in various spots around town. All of them had been murdered.

At first, the police doubted any connection between the cases. A teenage boy had been shot, a nine-year-old boy strangled, a 12-year-old girl sexually assaulted and choked. Some of the slayings might be linked, a homicide detective conceded, but there was no proof. Then, in the late spring and early summer of 1980, three more children disappeared and another three were found dead. At a press conference in July 1980, Camille Bell, the mother of one of the victims, brought the issue to public attention with an anguished demand that the police take action.

The city's new police commissioner, Lee P. Brown, soon admitted that a serial killer appeared to be at work. He formed a task force whose members went about the grueling task of sifting clues, trying to establish a pattern and find a suspect. Their work was aided, and in some instances hindered, by an army of volunteers who spent weekends combing the city's vacant lots and canvassing door-to-door.

It is impossible to exaggerate the terror that gripped black parents in the ensuing weeks, as the number of victims on "the list" reached a dozen and kept growing. One mother, whose two sons were late getting home after their school bus broke down, told a reporter, "I almost went out of my mind."

Given the already tense racial atmosphere in Atlanta, some blacks were ready to believe that a grand conspiracy was in place, aimed at exterminating black children. On one of the first cool days of autumn, a faulty furnace exploded in the basement of a day care center at the Bowen Homes housing project, killing four children and an adult supervisor. An angry, panicky crowd gathered in the street outside, jeering when Mayor Jackson arrived and tried to reassure them that the disaster had been an accident. Hosea Williams did the city a great service that day by leading a march on City Hall — a march that took several hours to complete and dissipated the fury of the protesters along the way.

Inevitably, as time passed without an arrest, Commissioner Brown became the target of criticism. Not everyone believed that a mass murderer was at large. The local media, having contributed to the frenzy that greeted the Barry killing, took a far more cautious approach to the "missing and murdered" cases. The business community, fearful of permanent damage to Atlanta's reputation, discouraged the view that a single serial killer was prowling the black community snatching large numbers of children. Privately, police investigators admitted that some of the victims on the list might have been killed by acquaintances or family members.

In the black community, however, any attempt to discount the scope or seriousness of the reign of terror was met with outrage. Understandably, some blacks took the view that the life of one white secretary, Patti Barry, seemed to count more with the white establishment than the lives of a dozen black children. The city's racial divide, never easy to bridge, grew wider. Many whites openly expressed the hope that the killer would turn out to be black. Many blacks found it impossible to believe that one of their own could be responsible.

The mayor announced a $100,000 reward for the capture of the killer. The City Council imposed a seven o'clock curfew on children under the age of 16. Still the string of homicides continued. By the spring of 1981, the child murders were a major national news story. "City of Fear," proclaimed a headline in *Time*. A fevered, freak-show atmosphere gripped parts of Atlanta. A character in dreadlocks named Chimurenga Jenga organized the tenants of Techwood Homes into a "Bat Patrol" armed with baseball bats. New York's controversial Guardian Angels sent a contingent, even though Commissioner Brown made it clear they were not welcome. Hucksters in several cities were discovered soliciting money for the families of the victims and pocketing the funds. The mother of one victim spent part of her charitable receipts having a cosmetic "tummy-tuck."

The drumbeat of discoveries of young corpses took an emotional toll on everyone in the city, not least Mayor Jackson. "It got to the point," one of his aides recalled later, "that I wouldn't have to say anything — just, 'Mr. Mayor . . .' And he would say, 'Oh, God, oh, God.'" But Jackson did not give in to despair. On the contrary, he found a reservoir of strength during the ordeal and helped restore the composure of those around him. He heaped scorn on the con men who tried to exploit the tragedy and on the visiting reporters who exaggerated the trauma. "These things are upsetting people who are already distraught," he admonished. "This is rubbing salt in the wound."

Without saying so directly, Jackson made the point that black elected officials were now running the city, with a black police commissioner in charge of the investigation. Any suggestion that the city of Atlanta stood on the verge of chaos reflected badly on black governance and thus tended to arouse a defensive tone among black leaders. When the *Washington Post* described Atlanta as "about to crack" under the pressure, Tyrone Brooks, a black activist, responded disgustedly, "Where do they *get* this stuff?"

Reflecting on what might have happened, had a white mayor still held office, or if John Inman had remained chief of police, one could conjure up dire scenes of serious disruption, with black Atlantans taking extreme measures to protect their children from what might have seemed a pogrom. Instead, most blacks trusted Jackson to do all in his power to stop the wave of killings. When white leaders underwrote a TV ad campaign showing blacks and whites side by side, with the slogan "Let's Keep Pulling Together, Atlanta," cynics dismissed the effort as a public relations ploy meant to gloss over the city's racial frictions. But no one could credibly accuse Jackson of putting the city's image ahead of the lives of its children.

The strange resolution of the case began with a splash, literally, on the night of May 22, 1981. A police recruit staking out a bridge over the Chattahoochee River heard a heavy object hitting the water. He radioed his colleagues, who stopped a station wagon moments later and discovered a would-be talent agent named Wayne Williams behind the wheel. Williams was interrogated, then released. Two days later, the body of another victim was discovered downstream, and Williams was placed under surveillance.

For nearly a month, the FBI and Atlanta police played a game of cat-and-mouse with Williams, questioning him and following him wherever he went, but not formally charging him with any crime. Events took on a slapstick air. At one point, Williams held a press conference, proclaimed his innocence, and passed out his résumé to reporters. Later, he led police on a merry chase past Mayor Jackson's house. Finally, he was arrested and arraigned on charges of murdering the last two of the 23 victims on the list.

From a criminal justice point of view, the case against Williams was more than adequate. The police assembled convincing evidence tying him to many of the victims through carpet fibers and dog hairs, and several witnesses said they had seen him with some of the victims. A jury convicted him, and most Atlantans agreed with the verdict for the simple reason that the string of killings stopped after he was in custody.

In terms of Atlanta's reputation, though, Williams presented a problem. A short, baby-faced, 23-year-old black man, he did not look or act like most people's conception of a serial murderer. The two victims he was accused of killing were adult men in their twenties, not children. Many of the other cases on the list were "cleared" after his conviction, but the fact remained that Williams was not tried for their murders. A curtain was drawn on the slain children when no one had been convicted of killing them.

Even before the trial, skeptics charged that Williams was being railroaded to put an end to the crisis atmosphere in the city. A disparaging article in *TV Guide* said Atlanta "comes across as awkwardly self-conscious and tinged with guilt," as if the city itself were some kind of skulking culprit. When CBS announced that it planned a "docudrama" on the murders, many in Atlanta feared the worst. "I oppose it," the mayor wrote in a letter to the network's executives. He listed his objections: "Rotten timing, profoundly bad taste, and rank, avaricious exploitation. The door of my administration is closed to this project and to anyone peddling it. I urge you to reconsider your plans. Our city, still in mourning, needs no added burden."

The project, guided by the award-winning producer Abby Mann, went forward anyway. As Jackson and others feared, "The Atlanta Child Murders" presented the city in an unflattering light and strongly suggested that Wayne Williams was innocent. But the film had a fatal flaw. It implied that Jackson and other black officials had knuckled under to the white power structure in rushing to convict a scapegoat. To the actual members of Atlanta's business elite, reflecting on their constant clashes with the mayor during the past several years, the very idea was laughable. Mann, a white liberal, had made the mistake of tossing black officials into the old stewpot of brute stereotypes that had long haunted Southern whites.

In a way, the docudrama about the child murders served as a parallel episode to the grilling of Griffin Bell. In Bell's case, white liberals from the North assumed that they had a right to condemn the actions of a Southern white man, even though the Southern blacks who knew him vouched for him. In the case of the missing and murdered children, a white liberal filmmaker asserted that Southern blacks, having achieved political power, would remain subservient to Southern whites. Both notions were wrong.

One simple statistic was adequate to prove the latter point. When Maynard Jackson took office, black-owned firms participated in less than one percent of the city's business. By 1981, the final year of his second term, the figure had risen to 28 percent.

Another strong piece of evidence was the behavior of the white business community as the mayor's race of 1981 approached. If black elected officials had been as obliging and complaisant as the caricatures in "The Atlanta Child Murders" suggested, white leaders might have been expected to support a black candidate as Jackson's successor. Instead, the white businessmen searched for a "great white hope" and prepared for political war.

In winning three straight elections to Congress in the mid-'70s, Andrew Young displayed a remarkable ability to appeal to white voters. He got a higher share of the white vote each time he ran, culminating with 38 percent in 1976. His old colleague from the civil rights movement, Hosea Williams, marveled at Young's smooth, reassuring manner with white audiences. "Andy could do more with white people," Williams loved to say, "than a monkey could do with a peanut. That's the truth."

In 1977, President Carter rewarded Young for his support by naming him U.S. ambassador to the United Nations. Many blacks considered it a paltry prize. "I can't imagine Andy going to the U.N. to succeed Pearl Bailey," Julian Bond scoffed. But Young accepted the job eagerly, hoping to make a contribution on the world stage. He got off to a strong start, so much so that the *Journal-Constitution*'s Sunday magazine suggested he might one day run for president. Visiting Africa, in particular, Young was treated as if he were America's black secretary of state.

Then the gaffes began. Young liked to speak his mind, a habit that served him well enough as a minister and a congressman but undid him as a diplomat. The Swedes, he observed, were "terrible racists." The Cuban mercenaries fighting in Angola were a "stabilizing" influence on the region. The Ayatollah Khomeini was a kind of saint to the Iranian people. Jails in the United States held "hundreds, perhaps thousands" of political prisoners. It did not matter that much of what Young said contained an element of truth, or at least the kernel of a legitimate political argument. The media treated him as a loose cannon. Forced to resign after holding an unauthorized meeting with a representative of the Palestine Liberation Organization, Young returned to Atlanta, wounded but unrepentant.

Mayor Jackson, barred by the new city charter from running for a third consecutive term, wanted very much for Young to succeed him. The reason, having little to do with Young himself, was Jackson's ardent determination to keep Reggie Eaves from winning the office. Jackson saw himself as a centrist in the mold of mayors past. Just as Hartsfield and Allen had held off Lester Maddox and kept City Hall out of the hands of radical whites, Jackson believed he had an obligation to block the candidacy of a radical black like Eaves. Young, with a proven record of biracial appeal, seemed the perfect antidote.

In Jackson's view, the era of white mayors was over. During the decades when whites held a majority in Atlanta, blacks had provided a swing vote, choosing between white candidates. Now the roles were reversed. Whites were in the minority, and Jackson figured they would accept the task of picking between black candidates. But he figured wrong.

There is no easy way of explaining the mass delusion suffered by Atlanta's white business leaders in the months before the mayoral election. Their dislike for Jackson, their dream of a "pro-business" environment at City Hall, their discouragement over crime and incivility on the city's streets, their misreading of the mood of black Atlantans — all these things combined to convince the power structure that a white candidate could be elected mayor. Instead of backing Young, they searched their own ranks for a recruit, and when none could be found they threw nearly unanimous support behind a state representative named Sidney Marcus, a little-known liberal whose political profile could be adduced from the fact that he had been former Mayor Sam Massell's roommate in college.

Tagged with the nickname "great white hope," Marcus recoiled. "I'm not going to be a 'white' candidate," he insisted. "Don't want to be, am not going to be." In fact, Marcus had worked well with his black colleagues in the Legislature, where he chaired the Fulton County delegation, an unruly group whose districts ran from the suburbs to the inner-city. He and his allies, Gerald Horton, John Greer, and Grace Hamilton, often cajoled their rural counterparts into doing favors for the city of Atlanta. Like Young, Marcus had the natural instincts of a mediator, someone comfortable soothing his adversaries and finding common ground. Marcus often let meetings drone on for hours, allowing everyone to speak at interminable length. When exhaustion finally set in, he would nudge the parties toward compromise.

Circumstance pitched Young and Marcus, two born conciliators, into a campaign full of racial ugliness. In theory, at least, each man had qualities that should have appealed to voters of the other race. With his broad global experience and his popularity in many of the world's capital cities (except, perhaps, for Stockholm), Young seemed the perfect choice to lead Atlanta to international prominence, a goal long sought by the city's white business leaders. Marcus, meanwhile, emphasized his interest in the nuts and bolts of local governance, which should have appealed to black citizens dependent on city services. "You know," Marcus liked to say, "the reason cities were started in the first place was because people wanted to band together to provide these basic services — water, sewer, fire, police. And people are concerned about their garbage being picked up." Marcus had been a tireless worker at the state Capitol, attending to the nitty-gritty of local taxes, MARTA, and the World Congress Center.

Unhappily, the campaign quickly devolved into code words and name calling. Marcus began billing himself as a "day-to-day, hands-on administrator," a way of suggesting that Young was a giddy jet-setter unlikely to be able to run an office at City Hall. When reporters discovered that Marcus was not quite the model of efficiency and business acumen he claimed — that, in fact, he owed back taxes to the city and county on numerous small parcels of real estate — Young's supporters trumpeted the disclosure as evidence that the white business community was backing a white deadbeat over an accomplished black man. Only one white leader of prominence, Charles Loudermilk, the chairman of a furniture rental company, joined Young's campaign, and he was greeted with suspicion at first by some of Young's advisers who thought he might be a spy for the power structure.

In the primary, voting followed racial lines. Whites went overwhelmingly for Marcus, blacks for Young. The good news, from Jackson's point of view, was that Eaves came in a distant third and lost. The bad news was that Young failed to capture an outright majority. With a runoff between Young and Marcus scheduled three weeks later, Jackson feared that some of Eaves's supporters and other blacks might climb aboard the Marcus bandwagon and give him a margin of victory over Young. Jackson's fear had little basis in reality, given the city's racial composition, yet it was real enough to push him into the most disgraceful act of his political career.

Speaking at the Hungry Club, the venerable forum for addresses to the city's black leadership, Jackson referred to the blacks who supported Marcus as "Negroes" — he drew the word out, making his derision plain — and accused them of "grinning and shuffling" around the Marcus camp in hopes of political reward. He suggested that they might be acting out of racial "self-hatred" akin to that of ex-slaves who had returned to their plantations after emancipation.

The venom of Jackson's attack left his listeners dazed. At Marcus headquarters, one of his targets, state Representative Douglas Dean, responded with icy anger, "I would rather him to call me a nigger. That's what he meant." Another black legislator, Billy McKinney, threatened to get in his car, go to City Hall, and punch Jackson out. The editor of the *Constitution*, Hal Gulliver, a white liberal who often took Jackson's side, accused him bluntly of delivering "a racist speech."

Jackson refused to back down. He spurned the idea that any sane black person could possibly consider Sidney Marcus better qualified to be mayor than Andy Young. It was that simple, and in the end the mayor's view prevailed. Young almost certainly would have won the runoff anyway, but Jackson's speech helped guarantee a big turnout of black voters. Late on the afternoon of election day, some of the mayor's aides stationed themselves at the exits along I-20 in the black section of Atlanta, holding up hand-lettered signs that said, "Heavy turnout on the northside!" — a warning that whites were voting in big numbers. Thus incited, black commuters stopped at their precincts on the way home and pulled the lever for Young, who won easily.

Jackson's speech might have been consigned to the same dustbin as his predecessor Sam Massell's ill-advised warning of "a city too young to die," except that it did have one positive aspect. If someone, somewhere, still believed that the mayor of Atlanta was a quiescent, namby-pamby tool of the white business community, that notion stood thoroughly, exhaustively, and completely discredited.

CHAPTER 10

"IT'S ATLANTA!"

When MARTA opened its West Line, no one felt a greater sense of relief and excitement than Tom Cousins. The developer's ambitious plans for downtown Atlanta depended on a steady flow of people in his corner of the city, and the new rail station at the Omni promised to deliver them.

For five years, the Omni International complex had struggled to attract tenants and customers. Now, Cousins believed, rapid transit would draw them in from the suburbs by the tens of thousands, filling the empty office space with workers and the boutiques with well-heeled shoppers. Cousins staged a series of events in 1980 meant to break the ice and get the party started. There were plays, a recital by the Alvin Ailey dancers, celebrity appearances by Gene Kelly and the cast members of "Dallas" — even Rula Lenska showed up, the obscure British actress who gained fame in America doing hair-color commercials.

Cousins remained convinced that MARTA held the key to the future. He acquired several parcels of land between the Omni and the main MARTA station at Five Points and applied to the federal government for $60 million in grants to help finance a corridor of development along the southern edge of downtown Atlanta. Still dreaming of an empire that would equal or even surpass John Portman's on the northern fringe of the central business district, Cousins pushed ahead with plans for a mammoth shopping mall, Omnisouth, to be anchored by the downtown Rich's department store. Rich's executives were so excited by Cousins' vision that they talked of building a skyscraper of their own as part of the project.

The problem was that Cousins guessed wrong. The MARTA station at the Omni got a fair amount of traffic, but it came from the other stations along the West Line. The passengers were black, and they had little interest in shopping at Hermès or Givenchy or dining at the French Restaurant. MARTA's North Line, which might have provided the crowds of suburban whites needed to sustain the shops and restaurants of the complex, was not yet open. The white Atlantans who did come to the area arrived by car, parking at the Decks at night to attend Hawks games and concerts at the Omni coliseum. They typically left without bothering to peek inside the vast retail complex next door.

Unlike his great rival Portman, who drew criticism for the forbidding, wall-and-moat exteriors of his developments, Cousins had designed the Omni International to be extremely accessible. It had dozens of doors at street level, leading to the skating rink and video arcade inside. Black kids loved to hang out there after school, or to cut classes and spend the whole day. MARTA made it easy for them to do so. As one of the architects admitted, the rink and arcade "didn't bring in people who could support the other uses" of the complex.

As the weeks and months passed in 1980, the expected surge of white patrons at the Omni International failed to materialize. Cousins held out as long as he could, clinging to his fantasy, until at last the harsh realities of life in the heart of downtown Atlanta overtook him. Lenders disappeared. Federal grants withered with the advent of the Reagan era. Omnisouth languished on the drawing board. The block of land Cousins had assembled next to the Five Points station fell into foreclosure.

The lone viable role for the Omni International, it seemed, was to service the convention traffic that continued to pour into the nearby World Congress Center. Bowing to reality, Cousins decided to close the skating rink, expand the hotel, and otherwise try to cater to the tastes of trade-show visitors from out of town.

This disappointing outcome might have been of interest only to Cousins, his partners, and shareholders, except that his experience mirrored what was happening in the city as a whole. The gush of growth that Mayor Hartsfield and other visionaries long anticipated came to pass, but it was happening outside the city limits. In 1968, the city's planning department had presented an official forecast to the Board of Aldermen, predicting that metropolitan Atlanta would reach a population of two million by the early 1980s. The number turned out to be accurate. The planners expected, however, that the city proper would contain 670,000 of those people, a guess that proved woefully wrong. Atlanta actually was losing residents. Its population tumbled below 450,000, making it one of the nation's smaller core cities. The 1968 study had projected 156,000 students in Atlanta's public schools by the '80s; the actual number was half that, and 95 percent of them were black.

Atlanta, in the phrase of *Atlanta Journal* columnist Dick Williams, had become "the Incredible Shrinking City." As white flight completed its course, middle-class blacks joined the exodus too, eager to find bigger houses, safer streets, and better schools in suburbia. The northern tier of neighboring DeKalb County had blossomed with white subdivisions in the 1960s and early 1970s, displaying the same profusion of office parks, shopping malls, softball leagues, and garden clubs that characterized bedroom communities elsewhere in the country. By 1980, thanks to a parallel black migration to the southern part of the county, DeKalb's population was fully a third black. Like Detroit, it seemed Atlanta might be on the verge of emptying out.

As he prepared to assume the mayor's office in January 1982, Andrew Young viewed these trends with deep alarm. During the campaign, the city's white leaders had treated him as a sort of latter-day Karl Marx, likely to bring socialism to City Hall. And it was true that in the '60s and '70s, Young had flirted with radical ideas. His résumé of gaffes included disparaging remarks about capitalism and western values in general. But Young's friends knew him as a free-market conservative at heart. Dr. King often teased him, calling him the "house Republican" of the civil rights movement. Young recognized that money — the wealth controlled by the white men in Atlanta's boardrooms — represented the last, best hope of saving the city and its growing segment of poor black citizens.

On the day after his election, Young went to a luncheon on the top floor of the Merchandise Mart to call a truce with the businessmen who had tried so desperately to defeat him. Like Maynard Jackson before him, Young spoke of plain truths. "I didn't get elected with your help," he told the group, "but I can't govern without you." Unlike Jackson, he meant it.

Following through on his promise, Young gave an inaugural speech brimming with enthusiasm for the role of the private sector. "The challenge of the '80s," he said, "is economic— jobs — and Atlanta must once again lead the way." In the early days of his administration, Young took several steps to appease the white business leaders who had spurned him. As a way of relieving their property taxes, he agreed to support a one-cent hike in the local sales tax, even though critics complained that poor blacks would suffer a disproportionate burden. After opposing the construction of a new highway through the neighborhoods of east Atlanta when he was a congressman, he now reversed field and revived the project as part of Jimmy Carter's plan to build a presidential library and center. He enlisted in an effort to rebuild Underground Atlanta.

Driving around town one day in his blue Cadillac Seville, Young explained his thinking to an interviewer from *Esquire*. "My job," he said, "is to see that whites get some of the power and blacks get some of the money." Speaking to a black group, he was even more succinct. "I've made peace with capitalism," he said. Though he never uttered the phrase, Young, a lifelong Democrat, basically accepted the "trickle-down" premise of the Reagan administration's economic policies. If Atlanta encouraged a thriving business climate, he believed, blacks would get their share of the new jobs.

Part of Young's approach stemmed from his background as a minister. He loved to soothe and anneal the angry passions that divided people. During the civil rights movement, Dr. King had sent him into countless towns where street demonstrations and boycotts fomented crisis, and Young — handsome, articulate, reassuring — had negotiated with the white leaders and found common ground. Many years later, he titled his memoirs A *Way Out of No Way*, which aptly described his vision of things.

As Young readily admitted, Maynard Jackson had fought and won many battles for Atlanta's black community. A lawyer and fierce advocate, Jackson had relished the challenge. "We tried the easygoing ways, and they flunked," Jackson observed shortly after leaving office, "so what we had to do was put the pressure on to get the change." Believing the state of alert could now be relaxed, Young reverted to the easygoing ways. He instituted a "one-stop" permitting process for construction projects that cut the Jackson administration's notorious red tape. During the next three years, as Atlanta joined in the national economic recovery, City Hall issued a record 20,000 building permits.

Not that Young spent much time in City Hall himself. He believed his diplomatic contacts could be exploited to attract investment from abroad, especially from black-led nations in the Caribbean and Africa. That ambition, combined with his legendary disdain for deskwork, kept him on the road constantly. His travels earned the predictable mockery. Once, displaying a sunny ignorance of municipal reality, he assured reporters at a press conference that Atlanta's streets were in perfect repair. "If you have a pothole," he bragged, "come see me. I'll fix it myself.

There are so few of them that I can make that promise." His office fielded 60 calls that day alone. The next morning, smiling ruefully, Young donned coveralls and a hard hat and got busy wielding a jackhammer.

Despite the teasing, Young's travels paid off. Avoiding the indiscreet remarks that marred his diplomatic career, he became an ambassador for Atlanta and was received in the world's capitals as a visiting celebrity. In one telling episode early in 1983, Young went to New York to help introduce Georgia's new governor, Joe Frank Harris, to the investment community. When a reporter asked about Harris's background, Young vouched for him. "He's really a nice guy," Young said. "Very quiet and serious. Not the normal rabble-rousing Georgia good ol' boy." The mayor of Atlanta was now acting as a spokesman for the whole state of Georgia.

Around the time Young took office, Rand McNally & Company brought out a book called *Places Rated Almanac* that ranked Atlanta as the finest place to live in the United States. As always in such matters, the listing depended on an arbitrary set of criteria that tended to ignore esthetics and intangibles. Still, appearing in the wake of the city's agony over its murdered children and the trench warfare between Maynard Jackson and the business community, the survey's findings came as a pleasant surprise. The authors credited Atlanta with the nation's best transportation system and gave high marks for its climate, colleges, and local economy. The trick, though, was that *metro* Atlanta won the accolades, not the central city.

Young's salesmanship helped attract new business to Atlanta, but the day was long gone when he or any other politician could lasso the growth and keep it inside the city limits. By the early 1980s, metropolitan Atlanta sprawled over a 15-county chunk of north Georgia that contained 40 percent of the state's people. Newcomers arrived by the tens of thousands each year, turning the northern suburbs into a congested hodgepodge of offices, businesses, malls, and apartment complexes — what the demographers called an "edge city." With its dwindling population, Atlanta became a smaller and smaller part of the equation. As mayor, Young presided over fewer people than did the chairman of the DeKalb County Commission, a wily, sharp-tongued tavern-owner named Manuel Maloof.

A vague sense of disorientation seemed to overcome many Atlantans as the building boom accelerated and the metropolitan area surged in size and shapelessness. An Atlanta Braves pitcher named Pascual Perez gained a measure of fame one afternoon in the summer of 1982 when he got lost on the perimeter highway, I-285, trying to find Atlanta Stadium. Like Charlie on Boston's MTA, the "man who never returned" of folk song renown, Perez spent hours driving the 61-mile circumference of the highway without finding the right exit to downtown. He missed his start in the baseball game that night but found a place in the hearts of thousands of empathetic Atlanta commuters. Carrying an average of 84,000 cars per mile per day, the city's highways had become the second busiest in the nation.

In the counties north of Atlanta, people began massing in huge numbers — "beyond anyone's imagination," in the words of one local official — creating a population explosion that choked the roads and schools and threatened to overwhelm the sewer systems and drain the water supply out of Lake Lanier. During a five-year period beginning in 1982, metropolitan Atlanta led the nation in job growth. Gwinnett became the country's fastest growing county. The area's white-collar economy drew well-educated migrants at such a rapid rate, one study found, that native Georgians soon were outnumbered by Yankees and other non-Georgians.

Atlantans had never been much for nostalgia. Like others in the Deep South, they could look back on a history of strife and second-class citizenship and be glad to have escaped. Mayor Young was especially scornful toward the city's preservationists. He taunted them for trying to save various landmarks, notably an eccentric old rookery called the Castle that he dismissed as "a hunk of junk." A campaign to renovate Margaret Mitchell's old apartment building was hindered by the fact that she herself had referred to it as "the Dump" and urged its demolition.

But the 1980s brought a wave of remembrances of things past — the Crackers baseball team, the "Gray Ghost" rollercoaster at the Southeastern Fair, the railroad terminals, the downtown movie theaters. An account in the *Journal-Constitution* actually lamented the passing of the days when state legislators met in "Parlor A" at the Georgia Hotel and raffled off prostitutes. As to the newspaper itself, readers mourned the end of a long and spirited competition between the news staffs of the morning *Constitution* and afternoon *Journal*. After 1982, the two newsrooms were combined into one, and only the papers' editorial pages remained separate.

Critics complained that the new metropolis lacked personality. "What's Atlanta About?" asked a headline, and the answer seemed to be: commerce. The strength of Atlanta's economy lay in its emphasis on providing services, from lawyers and accountants to software programmers and money managers. Only seven of the Fortune 500 companies were headquartered in Atlanta— a legacy of the city's lack of heavy industry — but 432 of the Fortune 500 maintained regional offices.

Since Atlanta's principal business activity was office work, its landscape tended to be dominated by office buildings, a fact of life that disappointed some visitors. "Other than buildings," a *Wall Street Journal* reporter observed, "Atlanta produces very little." Even the city's friends had trouble explaining its appeal. One writer, straining for a word to describe the evolving quality of life in Atlanta, came up with "nebulosity," which was pretty vague — though hardly any worse than the city's official new slogan, "Look at Atlanta Now."

The truth of the matter was, Atlanta's greatest glory lay in her neighborhoods, so thick with trees that it appeared someone had nestled the city into the midst of a virgin forest. If you had an office in one of those featureless glass-and-steel skyscrapers, you could look out on a sea of green stretching to the horizon, knowing your home was hidden out there somewhere under a canopy of pines, oaks, and magnolias. The old cliché about New York, that it was a fine place to visit but you wouldn't want to live there, could be neatly reversed and applied to Atlanta. Atlanta was a wonderful place to live, not so great to visit.

The problem was that thousands upon thousands of people, more than a million a year, *did* visit Atlanta. Thanks to Hartsfield International Airport, with its 2,400 flights a day reaching 135 cities in the United States, Atlanta remained the third busiest convention center in the country, the point of destination for what one writer called "a badge-wearing army." The vast majority of these visitors seemed content to split their time between the newly expanded World Congress Center and the web of first-class hotels a few blocks away, with an occasional taxi ride to dinner or shopping trip to Lenox Square as a diversion. The city also boasted some of the finest strip clubs in the nation, another selling point (albeit a whispered one) for convention organizers. An argument could be made that June 1, 1981, the day the U. S. Supreme Court ruled that communities could not ban nude dancing, deserved a special place in Atlanta history.

From a sightseer's point of view, though, the itinerary was limited. One still visited Stone Mountain, Six Flags, and the Cyclorama. The Atlanta Zoo, in serious decline since the defeat of a bond issue a decade earlier, became the focus of a national scandal after an administrator was caught shipping a sick elephant to a traveling circus. By way of new attractions, the High Museum moved into a stark, stunning new home (whose arresting design helped disguise the modesty of the permanent collection inside). And the King Center opened in 1982, adding a somber memorial that eventually drew more than three million visitors a year.

What got some people angry was Atlanta's lack of a teeming, 24-hour street life full of ethnic enclaves, diverse entertainments, and the cultural amenities offered by other, older cities. Sitting smack in the middle of the Sun Belt, Atlanta lacked a sidewalk ambience because it was simply too hot to eat, drink, stroll or even sit still outdoors during long stretches of the summer. Life took place inside, in the air-conditioning. If Atlanta's boosters could be blamed for anything, it was their insistence on claiming a temperate climate when they knew full well that from Memorial Day to Labor Day the sun hung low over their city and belched forth the fires of Hades.

———————

During the last week of November 1984, many of the city's leaders gathered for a series of discussions called the "Atlanta Future Forum," hoping to make sense of the rapid changes swirling around them.

The fundamental instrument shaping Atlanta's growth was hardly a mystery: the car. As Michael Lomax, the bearded, elegantly tailored chairman of the Fulton County Commission, put it, Atlanta had become a city "not of walking distances, but of automobiles to one enclosure or another." Government had tried to control the pattern of development in metropolitan Atlanta, and for the most part, it had failed. MARTA grew to maturity in the mid-1980s, as the North Line opened in stages and gave whites in Atlanta's northside neighborhoods the chance to use rapid transit. They spurned it in vast numbers.

After 13 years and $1.7 billion in construction costs, MARTA remained a predominantly black system. In a metropolitan area of more than two million people, MARTA rail cars carried fewer than 200,000 riders a day, well under half the original projections. Studies found that four-fifths of those riders were "transit dependent" (a bureaucratic term for carless), meaning that only one rider in five used MARTA voluntarily for convenience or to save money.

Residents in the suburban counties continued to resist all entreaties to join the system. A survey by the *Journal-Constitution* in 1985 found

MARTA's prospects "cool" in Clayton County, "chilly" in Gwinnett, and "icy" in Cobb. Those attitudes were reinforced by a flurry of crimes in MARTA stations and on trains and buses, culminating in early 1986 with the slashing of a Georgia State University student by a knife-wielding robber who demanded her purse.

It could not be said that MARTA was a complete flop. One of its anticipated effects came to pass almost exactly as the city's planners hoped, as developers built skyscrapers and high-density complexes at several stops along the North Line. Looking up Peachtree Street from Five Points, one could see a succession of mountain tops: the Georgia-Pacific Building at the Peachtree Center Station, Southern Bell's headquarters at North Avenue, AT&T's Promenade at Midtown, the IBM Tower at the Arts Center. The station at Lenox Square inspired several office towers and a mile-long row of condominiums and apartments along Lenox Road (with some of the rezoning expedited by a city councilman who was later convicted of taking bribes from a developer).

The problem was that *only* Peachtree Street inspired these sorts of high-rise clusters. Most of MARTA's other stations stood in not-so-splendid isolation. As Michael Lomax reminded the Future Forum, greater Atlanta had become a linear metropolis, following a narrow corridor north and south along the Peachtree ridge, with a downtown that stretched from Five Points north to Buckhead. One day soon the city might be 80 miles long.

Far from helping, MARTA had inflicted severe damage in several places. In Decatur, College Park, and East Point, three of the dozens of existing small towns overtaken by Atlanta's urban sprawl, rail construction had put countless small merchants out of business, many of them permanently. The area around the main MARTA station at Five Points lost some 4,000 jobs from 1980 to 1985. The station at Garnett Street, just south of Five Points, might have attracted development in the black community, except that the city built a huge new jail there, squelching interest in commercial or residential projects.

The saddest truth about MARTA was that it proved inconvenient. In theory, riding the trains was supposed to liberate commuters from bumper-to-bumper traffic and get them to the workplace quickly and comfortably. But people typically had to walk or drive to the nearest station, wait for a train, switch lines or transfer to a bus, then walk again to reach the office. The result, one study found, was that commuting by MARTA actually took a little longer on average than driving. Completing an unhappy cycle, MARTA's sluggish ridership meant fares had to be increased to cover expenses, which in turn reduced MARTA's appeal as a money-saver and further discouraged use.

Seeing that rapid transit would not provide much relief for Atlanta's congested roads, the state Department of Transportation reverted in spirit to its former name — the Highway Department — and undertook a program to "free the freeways" by expanding their capacity. The Downtown Connector, originally six lanes wide, was broadened to 10 lanes, 12 in some spots, to handle the crush of traffic. The perimeter highway, I-285, was similarly widened along its northern arc. As a monument to the triumph of automobile traffic, engineers devised an intersection at I-85 and the perimeter that piled a dozen entrance and exit ramps atop each other, criss-crossed and cantilevered and nearly reaching the sky.

While the highway system stood as the most visible symbol of change in shaping the Atlanta of the 1980s, other agents were at work, too, only harder to see. Identifying the city's leaders, once a simple task, became tricky. In their February 1984 issue, the editors of *Atlanta* magazine listed a "New Power Elite" — and began in shopworn fashion by naming Coca-Cola's Robert Woodruff, who was then 94 years old, deaf, almost blind, confined to a wheelchair, often disoriented, and completely retired from his company's affairs. The next rung, labeled as having "mega-clout," consisted of builders, bankers, utility executives, and developers, including John Portman and Tom Cousins. Next came the "heavy hitters," another familiar roster of businessmen and politicians. Only at the bottom, among "others" gaining honorable mention, did one find the name of Ted Turner.

As late as the mid-'80s, many people assumed that Atlanta's economy was the same as it had always been, just bigger. By the old conventions, bankers were accorded top status because they doled out capital and made growth possible. Three bank chairmen — Bob Strickland of Trust Company, Bennett Brown of Citizens & Southern, and Tom Williams of First National Bank of Atlanta — were listed ahead of Turner in *Atlanta*'s pecking order.

But the city's banks were suffering an undiagnosed illness that made them considerably weaker than they appeared. For decades, state law had clamped severe restrictions on Atlanta's big banks to keep them from swallowing up their smaller rural counterparts. With 159 counties, Georgia had scores of tiny, independent banks, whose directors enjoyed considerable clout with their local state legislators. Bending to the wishes (and campaign contributions) of the small-town bankers, the General Assembly consistently refused to allow statewide branch banking, with the result that Atlanta's banks failed to keep pace with the growth of their counterparts in North Carolina and Florida.

In the early 1980s, anticipating the eventual advent of national banking, and fearful of domination by the financial centers of New York and California, the legislatures of several Southern states including Georgia agreed to allow interstate banking mergers within the region. The idea, a modern incarnation of a sentiment at work 120 years earlier, was that by joining together in a confederacy, the Southern states would be powerful enough to keep Northern predators at bay. In June 1985, the U. S. Supreme Court ruled the Southern banking compact legal, thereby giving a green light to unions among banks in Georgia, Florida, Tennessee, Virginia, and the Carolinas.

Most observers, recognizing Atlanta's commercial dominance of the region, expected C&S, First National, and Trust Company, the three big Atlanta banks, to leap into action and begin acquiring partners in other states. The *Journal-Constitution* assured readers that the Supreme Court decision "ensures Atlanta's role as the financial capital of the Southeast." But the years of overregulation had left Atlanta's banks ill-prepared to compete. In a move that surprised the business community, First National Bank of Atlanta was snapped up by Wachovia, a North Carolina bank headquartered in the relatively small city of Winston-Salem. The fact that Wachovia had $2 billion more in assets than First National was evidence of the strength that came from statewide branch banking. C&S, once the South's premier bank, found itself in a similar bind fending off a takeover bid from Wachovia's main competitor, North Carolina National Bank. Only Trust Company managed to prevail in the newly unsettled banking arena, merging with Sun Banks of Florida to become SunTrust and keeping the headquarters in Atlanta.

Atlanta's shortage of capital was a chronic problem. It meant, among other things, that developers had to look elsewhere — insurance companies, pension funds, New York banks, Texas oil millionaires — for the cash to build the new skyscrapers, office parks, and shopping malls needed to accommodate the city's rapid growth. With Mayor Young's help, international money also found its way to Atlanta, as Europeans looked to protect their capital by investing it in the American South. By 1983, 37 foreign governments had representatives in Atlanta, including a dozen full-time consuls, and 19 foreign banks opened offices.

The drawback of relying on outside money, of course, was that Atlantans did not have the final say in spending it. The city's two premier developers, Portman and Cousins, had a lifelong commitment to the survival of downtown, but many other developers preferred building on the fringes of suburbia, where land prices were cheap. Others built within the city limits, but not downtown. At the same time he served as president of Central Atlanta Progress, the downtown lobbying organization, developer Frank Carter built several major projects in the Midtown area — a sharp irony that left Portman and Cousins scratching their heads.

The intense pride that the city fathers of the 1960s took in the gleaming new accouterments of downtown Atlanta — the stadium, Peachtree Center, the Omni, and the Arts Center — did not pulsate quite as strongly with investors from elsewhere. The attitude of some of the new people in town was best expressed by Ross Johnson, the entrepreneur immortalized in the book *Barbarians at the Gate*, after he merged R. J. Reynolds and Nabisco and moved the headquarters to Atlanta. Speaking to a meeting of the Atlanta Rotary Club, Johnson informed the members that he did not wish to be bothered with requests for contributions or volunteer work. "I told them I can't support every organization from the United Way to the Seven Jolly Girls Athletic Club Beanbag competition," he told an interviewer. "If it pisses them off, I can't help that."

Other newcomers, notably the executives of United Parcel Service, were better corporate citizens. But with the old lions of the native-born power structure either retired, dying, or dead, it fell to a younger generation of Atlantans to champion the interests of downtown and worry about the city's long-term health. The most improbable member of this emerging group, as reflected by his low ranking in *Atlanta* magazine, was Ted Turner, the owner of a media empire that was just beginning to circle the globe.

Today, the story of Turner's rise is widely known: how the hyperactive college dropout inherited a collapsing outdoor advertising business when his father committed suicide, then bought a shabby local UHF station and turned it into a "superstation" on national cable television. At the time, because he acted like an overheated 16-year-old, it was difficult to appreciate the extent of Turner's genius. The author, then a reporter for the *Constitution*, can recall handling the press release that announced Turner's plan to put WTCG on satellite and thinking it was no big deal.

Showing re-runs of "Leave It to Beaver," selling Slim Whitman

Above: Sam Massell (*right*) won the mayor's race of 1969 despite being denounced by Ivan Allen. Massell's brother Howard (*far left*) and his new police chief, John Inman (*left*) got him into political trouble.

56

57

58

60

59

Left: Carl Sanders and Jimmy Carter began the Georgia governor's race of 1970 with smiles. But Carter ran a mean campaign, as his aides tried to hurt Sanders with white voters by distributing a photo of him (*above*) being dowsed with champagne by Hawks star Lou Hudson.

61

62

After running as a George Wallace sympathizer, Carter switched course and served as a progressive governor, signing legislation (*above*) that created MARTA, Atlanta's rapid transit system. MARTA construction (*left*) turned downtown Five Points into an open pit.

63

Above: On October 6, 1971, Mayor Massell made a fatal political blunder when he urged an influential black audience, including educator Benjamin Mays (*left*) and builder Herman Russell, to "think white."

Below: By defeating Massell in the 1973 mayor's race, Maynard Jackson (standing between his mother and wife) became Atlanta's first black mayor.

64

65

Police misconduct during this demonstration (*above*) in 1974 led Mayor Jackson to appoint a political crony, A. Reginald Eaves (*far left*) as public safety commissioner.

66

67

On this swing in 1974, Hank Aaron hit his 715th home run and broke Babe Ruth's record. "Just wanted to get it over with," he said.

At his first game as owner of the Braves in 1976, Ted Turner jumped onto the field (*top*) to celebrate a home run. Among his other antics, he led the crowd (*left*) in singing "God Bless America." Inaugurating CNN in 1980 (*right*), he started on a path to world prominence.

71

72

Above: After his gaffe about protecting the "ethnic purity" of neighborhoods, presidential candidate Jimmy Carter needed an embrace from "Daddy" King to recover.

Left: Griffin Bell, Carter's nominee as attorney general, got a hero's welcome in his hometown of Americus, Georgia, after winning Senate confirmation.

A grim Mayor Jackson displayed some of the reward money raised during the investigation of Atlanta's "missing and murdered" children.

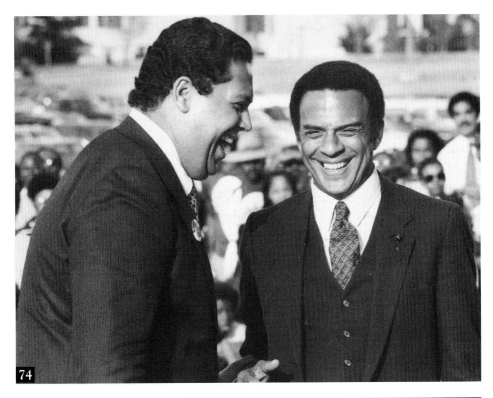

74

Above: In the 1981 mayor's race, Jackson endorsed Andrew Young (*right*) as his successor.

Right: A day after denying that Atlanta's streets had any potholes, a perspiring Mayor Young was out helping fix them.

75

76

Above: In 1987, responding to a racial incident in Forsyth County, Georgia, twenty thousand people, black and white, marched in support of civil rights.

Below: Though the business community spurned him at first, Young was gung-ho for development during his two terms as mayor. "He never   met a building permit he didn't like," said one critic. Here he poses above Woodruff Park, a gift to the city from Coca-Cola's Robert Woodruff.

Next page: Atlanta's skyline in the 1990s.

77

79

80

Above: In 1990, Olympic chieftain Juan Antonio Samaranch announced the name of the host city for the 1996 Summer Games. "It's … Atlanta!" he said, bringing organizer Billy Payne (*left*) to his feet in triumph.

81

In 1992, serving his third term as mayor, Maynard Jackson seemed exhausted by the city's social problems. "I'm so tired I can't think," he told a friend.

82

Bill Campbell took office as mayor in 1994. Giving fresh meaning to the term "crumbling infrastructure," he posed under a dilapidated viaduct and urged passage of a bond referendum in time for the Olympics.

records and Ginsu knives, Turner gradually built a profitable business. His first important civic gesture came in 1976 when he bought the Atlanta Braves. With the team's dismal record and poor attendance figures sparking talk of a possible relocation to Toronto, Turner paid nearly $10 million to keep them in town. As with so many aspects of Atlanta history, his motive was as much pecuniary as altruistic. His station televised more than 60 Braves games a season, and he stood to lose a crucial source of inexpensive programming if they moved away.

For a time, it appeared Atlanta had been spared the embarrassment of losing a major league sports franchise only to endure the spectacle of a team owner out of control. Among his other antics, Turner put on a uniform and tried managing the Braves himself, staged an ostrich race as a promotion, and tried to push a baseball around the infield with his nose. He ran afoul of the commissioner's office and was briefly suspended from the game. Accepting his punishment with more than a touch of megalomania, he told an interviewer, "The world has gotten along without Abraham Lincoln, John Kennedy, and Jesus Christ. Baseball can get along without me for a year."

Off the field, Turner's behavior was equally bizarre. An accomplished sailor, he defended the America's Cup in Newport, Rhode Island, in 1977, and then celebrated by getting knee-walking drunk at the award ceremony. He picked up nicknames — "Terrible Ted," "Captain Outrageous," "the Mouth of the South" — the way velvet picks up lint. He tended to see his ventures as military campaigns. "I'm having about as much fun as somebody might have had marching with Patton to relieve the boys at Bastogne," he said in Newport. "I mean, the atomic bomb looked great from the Enola Gay. But if you were in Hiroshima, it was hell."

Given his flamboyance, it was easy to overlook the contributions Turner made to the city's well-being. A year after buying the Braves, he acquired another troubled franchise, the Hawks. Owner Tom Cousins gave him little choice. "[He] told me if I didn't take 'em over, they were gone. Moving. He was getting out," Turner said. "And I had, you know, two days to make up my mind. And I said, well, hell, I'll go ahead and try and save it."

Turner exaggerated the one-sidedness of the negotiations. Once again, he preserved an important source of programming for his cable channel at a fairly low price. But of far greater significance, he was drawn into involvement with the Hawks' arena, the Omni, and the money-losing complex next door, the Omni International. In 1980, Turner christened the Cable News Network, the 24-hour news operation whose jury-rigged sets and frequent glitches would eventually mature into a world-class product with a name almost as familiar as Coca-Cola's. By 1985, CNN had outgrown its headquarters in an old country club, and Turner was looking for a new home. He found it in the Omni International.

In buying the complex, Turner brought to an end Cousins' 20-year crusade to create an urban domain in downtown Atlanta. As Cousins pulled up stakes and moved out, his legacy was a pair of public arenas, the Omni and World Congress Center, and a public facility, the MARTA station, that suggested his political clout might have exceeded his vision as a builder. His office towers, retail spaces, and movie theaters had never succeeded. Still, he left behind a solid base for Turner to build on in years to come. And thanks to some clever financial maneuvering along the way, Cousins had not lost much money.

For nearly a full decade, four huge balconies at one end of the complex had stood empty, the dusty vestiges of the demise of the World of Sid & Marty Krofft. Now they would house the studios of CNN and Headline News. The symbolism was perfect. In the *new* New South, telecommunications would be as important an ingredient as the traditional enterprises of banking, transportation and general commerce in making Atlanta the hub of the region. The Omni International, having proven an abject failure in so many guises and for so many reasons, all tied to the difficulties of the downtown area as a whole, gained a new life as CNN Center. Before long the eight-story escalator was running again, carrying visitors on tours of the world of Ted Turner.

In February 1987, the Democratic Party announced it would hold its 1988 national convention in Atlanta. The *Wall Street Journal*, tongue more or less in cheek, responded with a page-one story whose headline wondered, "Will Top News Topic in World Next Year Be Atlanta's Taxis?" In an era when conventions had turned into political rallies offering little news, many members of the national press corps treated them as an opportunity to play travel guide and judge the shortcomings of the host city. According to the *Journal*, many of Atlanta's cabs were driven "by men from all continents who are strangers to English, to Atlanta and to ethics."

The awarding of the convention signaled open season on Atlanta, and some of the reviews were scathing. Arthur Frommer, the travel writer, launched a blistering attack in a speech to the members of the Atlanta Historical Society, indicting their city as "characterless and without charm, dull, and exceedingly devoted to business and finance." As for night life, Frommer said, "evening in Atlanta is a graveyard, a scene of death and desolation, a nullity as far as the life, culture, and camaraderie that is present in numerous other cities." Apparently, he had not discovered the Limelight discotheque. Another sharp-tongued critic, the novelist Pat Conroy, dismissed Atlanta as "the Ollie North of cities," a vortex of aggression and greed.

The problem was that the name "Atlanta" did not immediately conjure up a positive mental image. Other cities were linked with popular attractions — New Orleans and jazz, New York and Broadway, San Francisco and its cable cars and Golden Gate Bridge. Atlanta did not fare as well in a game of free association. One study found that the single most familiar idea evoked by Atlanta was *Gone With the Wind*, a work of fiction.

Atlanta did, however, have a story to tell. As the home of Martin Luther King, Jr., and many of his associates, it could lay claim to being the birthplace of the civil rights movement. Its display of common sense and conciliation in the '50s and '60s was a matter of record. The inaugural celebration of the King federal holiday on January 15, 1986, focused the world's attention on Ebenezer Baptist Church and reaffirmed Atlanta's position as the capital city of American race relations.

Not that Atlanta was free of bigotry. In the same month the convention was announced, the aging but ever defiant activist Hosea Williams led a small band of marchers through Forsyth County, 40 miles north of Atlanta, an area known historically for violent antipathy toward blacks, and was showered with rocks and gobs of mud by a small band of jeering whites. The TV news footage of angry rednecks, shouting racial epithets and waving rebels flags, made for a painful spectacle. Still, the real news occurred one week later, when more than 20,000 people, black and white, gathered side by side in response and marched through Forsyth County in support of civil rights, shaming the few hundred race-baiters who confronted them by sheer force of numbers.

Most profiles of the city accepted its "too busy to hate" legacy at face value. Atlanta, said an article in *National Geographic*, "prides itself on a degree of racial harmony and cooperation rare among large U. S. cities." Certainly Mayor Young's re-election in 1985, with broad support from white voters, gave evidence of a city at peace. Young openly urged whites to move back into the city, telling the Atlanta Rotary Club, "I don't think anybody is anxious to see a city become 70 percent black anymore." He maintained close relations with the business community, so much so that one critic, a neighborhood activist, observed tartly, "He never met a building permit he didn't like."

Young greeted visiting journalists as if he were the city's chief of protocol, charming them as he charmed everyone. This was a man, after all, who gladly dressed up as "Andy Claus" at Christmas, who did not mind spending a day working as a city garbageman, who modeled hair-care lotions for M & M Products under the caption "the Look of a Leader," and who once danced to the beat of Michael Jackson's song "Bad" on a stage in front of hundreds of city employees — all the while maintaining a perfect sense of dignity.

But Young's magnetism was not enough to hide the fact that black Atlanta, for the most part, remained a place of poverty, with an unemployment rate three times higher than the white community's, and of violence, with one of the nation's highest crime rates. Fully 50,000 people, more than 12 percent of the city's population, lived in public housing, much of it abysmally substandard. The Atlanta Housing Authority suffered chronic mismanagement and once was labeled "the city's worst slumlord" by a disgusted inspector. More than 90 percent of the families in the projects were headed by unwed mothers. The average age of grandmothers in Atlanta public housing was 32. Crack cocaine and AIDS ran through the underclass like twin revisitations of the black plague.

No one in Atlanta tried to deny these bleak facts. And no sensible visitor expressed much surprise upon learning them, since every city in America with a large black population struggled to cope with the same problems. Even so, some of the coverage of the city in the period leading up to the Democratic convention made a point of Atlanta's failure to live up to its reputation as a "black Mecca." The *Wall Street Journal*, returning for another look (and evidently having lost its sense of humor), excoriated Atlanta as a city of avarice, with little compassion for its underclass. "When the Democrats pick a presidential candidate here in July," the *Journal* reported, "delegates will find shanty homes nearly in the shadow of the convention center." One wondered if a city existed somewhere that had no poor people or shanties, or a convention center that cast no shadow.

Many observers, noting the gulf between black and white, spoke of

Atlanta as two cities. But really it was three. On any given day, the World Congress Center itself qualified as a city — one of Georgia's 10 largest — as tens of thousands of trade show visitors roamed its cavernous reaches. There were 32,000 hotel rooms in metropolitan Atlanta available to lodge these temporary residents at night, and the convention and tourism industry employed some 82,000 workers to minister to their needs. The city's legendary Southern hospitality was real enough, since it oiled the whole enterprise.

The key to a successful Democratic convention was to tuck the delegates safely into this third city while limiting their contact with the other two. The Democrats were in town to use the Omni as a big TV studio and to stage a smooth show in nominating Michael Dukakis for president. They had not come for sightseeing or slumming. They cared about logistics, not legacies.

As it happened, few delegates wandered off in search of shanty homes, and few Atlantans, black or white, trespassed on the proceedings at the Omni and World Congress Center. In the convention's climactic moment, Dukakis entered the Omni to the strains of Neil Diamond's "Coming to America," an anthem that glorified immigration and Ellis Island and had not a thing at all to do with the Atlanta story or the American South.

Members of the media were free to critique the host city, and did. The *Constitution*'s editorial cartoonist portrayed Atlanta as Scarlett O'Hara, desperate for embrace, and the visiting press as a scornful Rhett Butler, saying, "Frankly, my dear, I don't give a damn." The truly important reviews, however, came from the Democrats, who pronounced complete satisfaction with their care and feeding. They did not even blame Atlanta for the outcome of the general election.

Atlanta's hospitality industry, its city within a city, earned a gleaming gold star in front of a national audience.

———

Not many people recall the quixotic venture of the amateur athlete who once dreamed of bringing the Olympic Games to Atlanta.

No, not Billy Payne. This was a fellow named Dennis Berkholtz. A native of Milwaukee, Berkholtz played college basketball at Kansas State and then discovered a new sport, team handball, while serving in the

Army. He and three teammates represented the United States in Munich in 1972 and considered themselves a success for winning one round before being eliminated.

Berkholtz moved to Atlanta in 1974, one of the wave of new arrivals to the city, and began a career as a marketer. He coached the U.S. handball team that went to Montreal in 1976, and returned thinking Atlanta ought to host the summer Olympics in 1984. He set out to make it happen.

One of Berkholtz's first stops was the Atlanta Chamber of Commerce, where he got a positive response from Tom Hamall, the president. A friend at the Georgia Department of Industry and Trade gave him free office space. Maynard Jackson, then enjoying a lull in his battles with the business community, expressed cautious enthusiasm. So did Dick Kattel of C & S Bank, the mayor's top ally in the power structure. Ron Hudspeth, a popular *Atlanta Journal* columnist, tried to drum up public support.

Taking the project one step further, chamber officials asked Research Atlanta, a local think tank, to make a formal study of staging the Olympics. The ensuing report, issued in the summer of 1978, was devastating. Final numbers had come in from Montreal, showing the Games there as a financial disaster that left taxpayers on the hook for a billion dollars in losses. The Research Atlanta report described the risks of playing host city in highly discouraging terms. Within days, Paul Austin, the chairman and CEO of the Coca-Cola Company, sent word that he wanted the Olympic bid killed, and it was. A former Olympic rower himself, Austin did not believe the city was ready to take on an event of such magnitude.

A decade later, things had changed. The midfield terminal was open, allowing Atlanta to handle a crush of passengers from around the globe. The World Congress Center had doubled in size. Thousands of additional hotel rooms were available. Most important by far, Peter Ueberroth and the city of Los Angeles had proved in 1984 that the Games could be funded by corporate sponsors, at a profit, without placing a burden on the taxpayers.

Even so, Billy Payne found himself facing the same kind of skepticism that confronted Dennis Berkholtz. In the winter of 1987, Payne was a man in search of renewed purpose for his life. A former defensive lineman for the University of Georgia Bulldogs, he had become a real estate lawyer with a medium-sized firm, earning a comfortable salary of

$250,000 a year. A success by most people's standards, he felt restless and yearned for more.

Like Ted Turner, Payne was driven by a fear of dying young. His father, Porter Payne, had died of a heart attack at age 55. Billy underwent triple-bypass surgery in 1982, when he was 34, and the doctors found evidence that he had suffered a heart attack at 26. Impatient by nature, unsure of his longevity, Payne wanted to leave his mark, and quickly.

On a Sunday morning in February 1987, Payne experienced what he later described as an "extraordinary sensation." He and his wife, Martha, had just led a successful fundraising campaign for a new sanctuary for their church, St. Luke's Presbyterian Church in Dunwoody. He felt a glow of accomplishment that had eluded him in his law practice, and he turned his thoughts to what he might do next to repeat and enhance the emotion. Early the next morning, sitting at his desk, he scribbled the phrase "1996 Olympics" on a scrap of paper.

Payne has insisted that his vision was not some form of religious experience, yet it is difficult to explain what possessed him to make the considerable leap from raising money for St. Luke's to stalking the Olympic Games for Atlanta. Many people assumed he had gone giddy. His wife, for one, urged him to talk to his most level-headed friend, Peter Candler, before proceeding with the venture. Candler, an executive with an insurance company (and one of the many distant relatives of Coca-Cola's founder, Asa Candler, who proliferated in Atlanta), surprised the Paynes by endorsing the idea. He and Billy formed an organization called the Georgia Amateur Athletics Foundation and started making contacts.

The early days were discouraging. Payne wrote a letter to Rankin Smith, the owner of the Falcons, soliciting advice and support, and did not get a response. He tried to get an appointment with Mayor Young and failed. Eventually, with a friend interceding on his behalf, he was booked for a 15-minute interview on WGST Radio. "This guy says he's going to bring the Olympics to Atlanta," talk-show host Tom Houck told his listeners, barely able to keep from laughing. The *Journal-Constitution* treated Payne, in the words of one writer, "as a screwball with a hare-brained scheme."

Payne desperately needed an entree to the corporate leaders who could bankroll his bid, and Candler believed he knew where to turn. The lawyer representing Candler's insurance company was Horace Sibley, a senior partner at King & Spalding and a son of John Sibley, the city's elder statesman. The Sibley family had close connections with SunTrust

Bank and the Coca-Cola Company, the pillars of the power structure, and Horace Sibley agreed to open whatever doors he could for Payne.

Even with Sibley's backing, though, the purse strings remained drawn tight. Payne went to see Don Keough, the president of Coca-Cola, and got the legendary Keough treatment — a greeting so warm and effusive, an expression of interest so sincere, that only later, when he was driving home, did Payne realize he had come away empty-handed. Coca-Cola would make no contribution to bringing the Olympics to Atlanta. A sponsor of the Games since the 1928 Summer Olympics in Amsterdam, the company was content to peddle its soft drinks anywhere. Wouldn't it be great, Payne asked Keough, to have the Olympics in your own back yard? And Keough answered gently, "Billy, the whole world is our back yard."

What frustrated Payne the most was his certainty that Atlanta had the ability to handle the Games. For as little as $50,000, he believed, his group could put together a presentation that would impress the United States Olympic Committee, which was then in the process of selecting an official American bid city. But Payne fell victim to a piece of bad timing. In the summer of 1987, Atlanta's business leaders were preoccupied with the impending Democratic convention. Everywhere he turned, people gave Payne the same polite, negative answer. They were "tapped out." They had no money for him, not even pocket change.

According to Horace Sibley, the low moment came one afternoon in the summer of 1987, when Payne gathered his small circle of friends for lunch at the OK Cafe and explained that he had failed to secure outside backing. He was discouraged and talked of giving up. Instead, the group dug into their own pockets and furnished the $50,000 needed to continue the campaign.

Payne's organization at that point consisted entirely of volunteers, including three energetic women — Ginger Watkins and Linda Stephenson, who were fresh from staging the "Festival of Trees," the annual fundraising event for the Egleston Children's Hospital, and Cindy Fowler, a professional party organizer who ran an outfit called Presenting Atlanta. Billy and the Girl Scouts, as the group was dubbed, did not have the resources of the Chamber of Commerce at their command. But they did have one vital strength, a knack for party-giving, and they put it to good use in the autumn of 1987. Purely by coincidence, the U. S. Olympic Committee scheduled one of its meetings in Atlanta. Payne's group rented the High Museum for the evening, wined and dined the USOC visitors in the atrium, and put on a show featuring students from

Northside High School's program for the performing arts. George Steinbrenner, the New York Yankees' principal owner and a longstanding USOC member, called it "the finest event like this I've seen."

The Atlanta organizing committee began picking up steam. Once he became convinced the Olympics could be staged without costing the city any money, Mayor Young threw his full support behind the bid. A talented sprinter in college, Young had considered trying out for the U.S. Olympic team before turning to the ministry, and he had a lifelong interest in the Games. He revered Jesse Owens, the black track star who won four gold medals in Berlin in 1936, making a mockery of Hitler's claim of Aryan supremacy.

As the deadline approached for USOC's designation of an American bid city, it became clear that Atlanta had a very good chance of winning. Payne's circle expanded, and corporate money began to appear. BellSouth, the telecommunications giant, paid for a promotional film that Payne took to Colorado Springs to show USOC officials. The most important decision, in hindsight, may have been to keep two of Atlanta's most prominent citizens completely *out* of the process. Jimmy Carter had outraged the Olympic community by ordering the American boycott of the 1980 Games in Moscow. And Ted Turner, by staging the alternative Goodwill Games, had threatened the lucrative Olympic franchise. Neither man's name was whispered when Atlantans lobbied USOC.

Atlanta's main competition turned out to be Minneapolis-St. Paul, which did not match up as well on the list of criteria — hotel rooms, highways, airport — that USOC used to gauge a city's capacity for hosting the Games. Leaving nothing to chance, Payne's group put on another lavish party in the spring of 1988 when USOC met in Washington, D. C., to pick the bid city. The Atlantans rented a townhouse, had butlers in tuxedos greet guests and serve champagne, and arranged for 10 strolling violinists to work the room playing "Georgia on My Mind." Atlanta won, and it made a fine irony that the credit went not so much to the city's vaunted power structure, or to its carefully groomed image or "story," but to three women schooled in the art of putting on charity balls.

Once Atlanta became the American bid city, the pace of activity and enthusiasm quickened dramatically. Now Atlanta was competing internationally, up against five other cities — led by the sentimental favorite, Athens, Greece — for the honor of holding the centennial modern Olympics. The International Olympic Committee, headquartered in Lausanne, Switzerland, and headed by an imperious Spaniard, Juan

Antonio Samaranch, would make the choice.

Playing on the global level had its quirks. One of Payne's early con-
scripts was a lawyer from King & Spalding named Charlie Battle, a sports
enthusiast who simply stuck his head in Horace Sibley's office one day
and insisted on joining the effort. Giving up the lucrative drudgeries of a
municipal bond practice, Battle joined Payne full time and became
Atlanta's emissary to the world courts where IOC politics were played
out. Days after winning the American bid, the Atlantans received an
invitation to go to Malta for a planning session on the international
selection process. Writing to say he planned to attend, Battle realized
that the freshly organized Atlanta Committee for the Olympic Games
did not yet have any stationery. He used his law firm's letterhead instead,
and was tickled upon arrival to see that places had been reserved for King
Faisal, King Constantine, and King & Spalding.

Money was no longer a problem. The Woodruff Foundation, formed
from the estate of Robert Woodruff after his death in 1985, chipped in
$1 million, and the Coca-Cola Company had its bottling subsidiary,
Coca-Cola Enterprises, contribute $250,000 and the use of a corporate
jet. Bob Holder, one of Atlanta's foremost builders, signed on as the
Atlanta committee's vice chairman, signaling the blessing of the Chamber of Commerce. In all, Atlanta raised $7.3 million — only half the
amount spent by some of the other bid cities, but more than enough to
go courting. The IOC had 88 voting members, and the Atlantans set out
to meet and woo every one of them.

One of Payne's smartest decisions was to limit his group to roughly its
original size. Other cities, notoriously Athens, flooded various IOC
meetings with hundreds of delegates, who jammed hotel lobbies and
made a great deal of noise without making a good impression. One of
Samaranch's friends gave the Atlantans a good piece of advice: Keep
your numbers small, target the IOC members individually, befriend
them, and make sure they recognize you and know you by name. Payne,
Young, and a handful of others made all of the contacts with IOC members, and the strategy paid off. Young was especially helpful with Third
World members, who recalled his days at the United Nations. At one
meeting, an IOC member from Senegal thanked Young for having
helped him gain an appointment to the World Court and asked what he
could do in return.

Payne showered the IOC members with gifts, provoking inevitable
complaints that the United States was trying to buy the Games. Actually,

most of the presents were fairly modest — compact disc players with recordings of the Atlanta Symphony, photographs taken by Young, in one case a pet bulldog — and in any event other cities gave out similar favors. Of greater impact was the close personal attention Payne, Young, and the others paid to the IOC members. The Atlanta committee opened dossiers on all of the IOC members, keeping notes about their families, hobbies, interests, and idiosyncracies. Payne got 78 of the 88 members to visit Atlanta, where they were entertained in Atlantans' homes and given the warm, personal reception by the city's social elite that most convention-goers never got to experience.

The campaign went on for two years, until at last the IOC gathered in Tokyo to choose the 1996 host city. By then Atlanta had a new mayor. With Young barred from seeking a third consecutive term, Maynard Jackson had left the private sector and announced that he wanted to return to City Hall. As a mark of the exceptional changes in attitude that occurred during the 1980s, a poll measured Jackson's favorable rating with voters at a sky-high 76 percent, while his negative response was only 11 percent. Quite a number of whites, it seemed, had changed their minds about Jackson. A group of rich Republicans actually endorsed him.

Jackson's lone opponent in the 1989 mayor's race was Hosea Williams — "unbought and unbossed," as he called himself, still as militant as ever. Williams kept a poster in his office showing Aunt Jemima raising her fist in a black-power salute, and that pretty well summed up his political philosophy. He considered Jackson a fat cat who deserved opposition, even if only of the token variety.

For his part, Jackson brought a much mellower personality back to public life. He was in his fifties now, his baby fat nicely marbled into portliness. He liked to quote a friend who said of him, "When Maynard steps on a cigarette, that sucker is definitely *out*." He had moved from the old neighborhood to a quiet cul-de-sac in Buckhead, a block from the Governor's Mansion, where he was raising his children in a 15-room, $600,000 French provincial mansion. His law practice paid him some $300,000 a year, enough to employ a pair of identical twins to chauffeur him around town. "I've waited tables, picked tobacco and sold encyclopedias," Jackson insisted in his campaign brochure, straining to strike a common touch. He won in a landslide anyway.

Back in office, Jackson joined the Olympic quest. He was in Tokyo with Payne and a large contingent of boosters on September 18, 1990, when Samaranch, the IOC's president, stepped to a ballroom micro-phone to announce the results of the secret balloting. In Atlanta, where it was just before eight o'clock in the morning, thousands of people gath-ered downtown to hear the news together. "The International Olympic Committee," Samaranch intoned, "has awarded the 1996 Olympic Games to the city of . . ." He paused, heightening the suspense. "Aht," he said, lingering on the first syllable. Many people still expected Athens, the sentimental favorite, to win. ". . . Lanta!"

Payne hugged Young and Jackson and then leapt on the stage with Samaranch and was mobbed by TV crews and reporters. Young had tears streaming down his face. In the ballroom of the New Takanawa Prince Hotel in Tokyo, the Atlantans hollered and embraced each other and echoed the stunned euphoria of Charlie Battle, who said, "I'm excited, I'm elated, I'm shell-shocked! I can't express it, I'm at a loss for words." In the streets of Atlanta, fireworks lit the morning sky, and the cheering and partying went on for hours. In a special souvenir edition, the Journal-Constitution proclaimed that Atlanta's ambitious old slogan, "the World's Next Great International City," had become prophecy.

Not everyone shared Atlanta's joy. In the losing bid cities, notably Athens, many cried foul and accused American television and the Coca-Cola Company of rigging the vote to bring the Olympics to Atlanta. "Bullshit! Bullshit!" chanted an unhappy crowd of 70,000 in Melbourne. Yet by all accounts, Atlanta won fairly, its success built on civic enthusi-asm, biracial cooperation, and the impressive size and quality of its hos-pitality industry. Athens was doomed by an unstable government, chok-ing traffic, and a rickety airport — precisely the problems Atlanta had worked so hard during the past several decades to overcome.

In Tokyo, as he listened to his friends express amazement over win-ning the Games, Billy Payne grew mildly irritated and finally admon-ished them to stop using words like "stunned." The outcome, he reminded them, was not completely unexpected. Nor was it the least bit undeserved.

It has become commonplace over the years to assert that Atlanta's sig-nature characteristic as a city is its habit of making impossible boasts and then managing somehow to live up to them. People in Savannah, who ordinarily do not speak in such vulgar terms, like to say that if Atlantans could suck in as hard as they blow out, their city would have a seaport of its own on the Atlantic Ocean. Atlanta's civic pride, an otherwise friendly observer once remarked, "has acquired an almost religious quality, as if on the seventh day God hadn't rested at all, but decided to make Atlanta instead, and saw that it was surprisingly good."

Payne took to referring to the upcoming Olympics as "the greatest peacetime event of the 20th century," exactly the sort of bravado that made people in other cities grit their teeth. He represented the cocky side of Atlanta's personality, the voice that said, "We're just as good as anybody," while refusing to admit to any underlying twinge of apprehension.

Looking through a darker prism, critics often portrayed Atlanta as a city on the make — the "Big Hustle," as the *Wall Street Journal* once called it — full of Babbitts and consumed with the almighty buck, as if other places did not have chambers of commerce or convention bureaus or advertising budgets. A *Washington Post* reporter greeted the awarding of the Olympics with particular disdain, calling Atlanta "a town for sale . . . a peddler's paradise, the capital of commercial seduction and voluptuous rhetoric, a raw plutocracy that can make a deal faster than you can say, 'a Co'Cola, please, ma'am.'"

The problem with these heavy-breathing summations of Atlanta's soul was that they missed some important subtleties. Atlanta was a center of commerce because the region around it suffered crippling poverty after the Civil War and looked to Atlanta as a source of capital and salvation. The city had a reputation for good race relations because Ralph McGill and Martin Luther King, Jr., calibrated the pace and led the way to slow, certain change. The airport was a gateway to the Southeast because Bill Hartsfield saw it that way at a time when barnstormers still flew biplanes. The city was united in support of the Olympics because its people and its leaders had learned, occasionally with great difficulty, to trust each other over the years.

And, of course, it helped to have a visionary or two in town. From Henry Grady to Billy Payne, Atlanta could claim its share.

EPILOGUE

The ticker tape had barely been swept from Peachtree Street when Atlantans began worrying about staging the Olympic Games. Billy Payne and Andy Young returned from Tokyo in triumph and rode at the head of a parade while 200,000 people cheered and threw confetti. Mayor Jackson spoke grandly of "the spirit of Olympism." Then reality set in.

In 1990, downtown Atlanta faced disturbing prospects. John Portman's global empire teetered under the weight of $2 billion in accumulated debt, and he lost control of his crown jewel, the Peachtree Center complex, to lenders in Japan and New York. A white-collar exodus from Five Points was underway, as the big banks pulled out and moved several miles north, taking their law firms, architects, and accountants with them.

One episode in particular had grave consequences. In 1983, the executives of Citizens & Southern National Bank had hoped to assemble a full block next to Woodruff Park, just north of Five Points, for the eventual site of a new high-rise headquarters. The sellers all agreed on a purchase price, but the deal fell through at the last minute when the chairman of Muse's, a men's clothing store that owned the largest parcel, held out for more money at the closing, killing the contract. As a result, seven years later, bank officials decided to build their new skyscraper on North Avenue, away from downtown. The old, familiar initials C&S disappeared, as the bank was swallowed up by North Carolina National Bank, headquartered in Charlotte, and renamed NationsBank.

Disappointing signs abounded. Underground Atlanta reopened, thanks to a revitalization effort that included $85 million in bonds guaranteed by the taxpayers, but attendance fell short of expectations, and the tenants were struggling. The collapse of Eastern Airlines threatened the primacy of the airport. Gwinnett County held a referendum on joining MARTA, and the voters said no. The Braves finished the 1990 season in last place, as they had so many times before.

In the spring of 1991, one of downtown Atlanta's most durable institutions, Rich's Department Store, closed its doors forever. For thousands of Atlantans who had grown up riding the "Pink Pig," the little monorail train on the store's roof, the loss of Rich's underscored the decline of the central city in a sharp, personal way that other changes did not. The census showed the city's population had fallen below 400,000.

Not all was despair. The Braves of 1991 pulled off a rare "worst-to-first" coup, won the National League pennant and played in the most exciting World Series ever, losing a climactic seventh game in the final inning. Rooting for the home team (and doing the notorious "Tomahawk Chop" that riled some Indian activists) became a unifying experience for the whole metropolitan area. In 1995, on their third try in five years, the Braves finally won the Series, defeating the Cleveland Indians four games to two. The hapless Falcons kept losing, but the state built them a new arena anyway, the $215 million Georgia Dome, to keep them in town. The city's list of museums, theaters, and cultural amenities improved and expanded. The zoo was rebuilt into a nationally renowned attraction. And for those seeking enlightenment about carbonated sugar water, a commercial museum called the World of Coca-Cola opened near Underground Atlanta, drawing a million visitors a year.

On New Year's Eve, 1991, the *Journal-Constitution* ran a remarkable color photograph that covered two-thirds of the front page, a shot from a helicopter that showed a rich, ochre sunset mirrored in the glass of the city's skyscrapers. The upbeat headline said, "A Changing Year, A Golden City." Still, the accompanying story carried a disquieting note. Celestine Sibley, a widely admired columnist who had been covering the news in Atlanta since the 1940s, rode in the helicopter and beheld an urban behemoth that was now strange to her. "It spread before me," she wrote, "in cubes and towers and stadium circles and concrete ribbons of expressways. And I knew it not." The state Capitol, once a familiar landmark, now looked to her "as small as a child's play-pretty."

Just as Atlanta's sprawl overwhelmed an old chronicler, the rapidly worsening conditions of the inner-city neighborhoods and housing projects left the mayor dismayed, sounding unsure of himself for the first time in his public career. "When I left office, there was no crack [cocaine]," Jackson told an interviewer. Now, he said, there was "crime, guns, dope, lack of values, lack of direction among those who are caught up in the dope world, communities being undercut. . . ." Once the staunchest of liberals, he advocated the death penalty for drugs dealers and gunrunners.

Atlanta crept back into the nation's number-one spot for violent crime, thanks in part to the work of teenage gangs. In May 1992, in the wake of the Rodney King case in Los Angeles, Atlanta suffered a serious riot of its own, as angry black youths surged through Underground Atlanta and around CNN Center, breaking windows, overturning trash containers and benches, jostling white bystanders, and in one instance beating a white businessman nearly to death. Police engaged in a pitched battle outside CNN Center for control of the streets.

The city's economy sagged, part of the national recession, and Delta Air Lines suffered steep losses after acquiring Pan Am's European routes and operations. A corruption scandal enveloped Hartsfield International Airport, as federal prosecutors caught several concessionaires paying bribes and kickbacks to city officials, including one influential councilman whose illicit take over the years came to nearly $1 million. Former President Carter, expressing shock at the misery of the city's underclass, organized an ambitious volunteer effort called the Atlanta Project to try to help.

The deluge of discouraging news appeared to leave "Action" Jackson, as the mayor once styled himself, in a state of paralysis. "I'm so tired I can't think," he told a friend after one especially grueling day at City Hall. Jackson underwent major bypass surgery to unblock six arteries near his heart in the summer of 1992, and not long afterward he announced that he would pass up the option of running for another term. As if to mock him in retreat, a 70-year-old sewer collapsed one morning beneath a Midtown parking lot, creating a huge sinkhole that sucked two people to their deaths. Warnings that the city might have to spend $100 million or more repairing its infrastructure suddenly became real.

At first blush, winning the Olympics was seen as the icing on Atlanta's cake, recognition that the city had achieved its aspirations and could sit back and enjoy the hosannas. Two years later, the Games had become a necessity, the catalyst that was needed to revive downtown, spark an economic recovery, and dispel the mood of lassitude that swirled around the city like ground fog. Billy Payne and others in the Atlanta Committee for the Olympic Games began to complain that too many people were loading up their 17-day track and field meet with impossible expectations.

The infusion of money associated with the Games, variously estimated at $3.5 billion and up, rivaling the entire MARTA system in overall economic impact on the Atlanta region, caused widespread envy and created inevitable frictions. The Olympians promised to leave a generous legacy — a new baseball stadium for the Braves, dormitories for students at Georgia Tech, Georgia State, and the Atlanta University complex, a new central city park, various athletic facilities, even a complete transformation of aging, crumbling Techwood Homes into a middle-class neighborhood. These gifts, gratefully received at first, soon became mired in squabbles about jurisdiction, fine print, and financial risk and reward.

Not surprisingly, Payne and company made some beginners' mistakes. One awkward moment came at the Summer Olympics in Barcelona in 1992, when the Atlantans unveiled their official mascot, a pop-eyed, wormlike morph nicknamed "Whatizit." Not only did the art critics howl, so did the Coca-Cola Company: Izzy's primary color was Pepsi blue. A campaign to sell Olympic bricks sank like one. Members of the International Olympic Committee professed surprise that it was scorching hot in Atlanta in the summer, and accused Payne of misleading them when he said the average July temperature was 79 degrees. "I didn't say what time of day," Payne answered innocently. Other problems were more serious, including a design flaw in the Olympic Stadium that caused a huge light stanchion to collapse during construction, killing a worker.

Inevitably, politics broke out. The Legislature refused to change the state flag, even though it was certain to draw protest during the Games. The Cobb County commissioners, a group whose raw-boned conservatism exceeded even that of their congressman, Newt Gingrich, issued a resolution condemning "the gay lifestyle." A proposal by ACOG to stage a demonstration of Olympic golf at Augusta National, the home of the Masters, ran aground over the club's prior history of discrimination against blacks and women. Among the losers were members of the Ladies Professional Golf Association, who viewed the Olympics as a way of competing in a women's Masters.

Still, the Olympics loomed as a glorious opportunity to fix the many things that ailed Atlanta and its spreading suburbs. In the early 1990s, it seemed almost every sentence spoken in north Georgia ended with the phrase, ". . . in time for the Olympics." Everyone had a project, from repaving the expressways to reviving the old stadium neighborhood, Summerhill, to renting out their homes to rich visitors for windfall profits. Businesses, local governments, neighborhood associations, individual citizens, all behaved as if they had gone on a simultaneous treasure hunt and spring housecleaning binge.

In the autumn of 1993, a city councilman named Bill Campbell won the Atlanta mayor's election and took his place on the roster of remarkable men who had guided the city during the previous half-century. Like Maynard Jackson and Andy Young, Campbell was black, but in other ways he more nearly resembled Bill Hartsfield — a feisty lawyer with a hot temper, a ward politician with a keen feeling for the interests of the city as a whole. After botching the paperwork on his first try, Campbell called a bond referendum in 1994 for $150 million in repairs to the city's streets, sewers, and viaducts — in time for the Olympics, of course — and was given a resounding thumbs-up by the voters.

As the Games drew closer, Hartsfield's legacy came very much to mind. His successes were widely appreciated, but his little-known failures carried an imporant lesson as well. Just as he had foreseen the importance of the airport, Hartsfield also struggled to create a port in Atlanta. He spent years trying to get Congress to pay for dredging operations and dams that would make the Chattahoochee River navigable, only to be foiled by the city fathers of Columbus, Georgia, who jealously guarded their status as the head port of the river. Led by Robert Woodruff's notoriously stubborn first cousin, Jim Woodruff, the men in Columbus never stopped to think how much more traffic they might have enjoyed had they joined forces with Atlanta.

There was a similar confusion of interests between Atlanta and its suburbs. In the famous Plan of Improvement, the act that expanded Atlanta's city limits in 1952, an obscure clause gave the city the right to annex adjacent land lots once they reached a certain population density, without any further legislation or public referendum. In essence, the clause said Atlanta could grow at will. But the mechanism went unused for years because Mayor Hartsfield and his city attorney believed it was unconstitutional and refused to try to enforce it. In the 1960s, Mayor Allen finally tested the provision. By then racial attitudes had hardened, and the Georgia Supreme Court overturned it. Had the court upheld the clause, Atlanta might have become a metro-wide government, with blacks and whites forced to live together under a single municipal roof, working out their problems as they went along.

Instead, the rift between city and suburb had become a chasm. Some 86 percent of greater Atlanta's population growth during the '80s and '90s occurred north of the city limits, and the new arrivals rarely ventured south of I-285, the perimeter highway. In 1994, Roberto Goizueta, the ordinarily reticent chairman and CEO of the Coca-Cola Company, made an unusual public appeal to his fellow businessmen to commit themselves to the health and well-being of downtown Atlanta. His com-

pany, he reminded them, had built the World of Coca-Cola next door to
Underground Atlanta, within a stone's throw of the Zero Mile post
where the city was founded, when it would have been cheaper and easier to put the attraction in the suburbs. Coca-Cola had made a commitment to the "future vibrancy" of the central business district, Goizueta
said, and he expected others in the power structure to follow suit. As
always, when the head of Coca-Cola spoke, others paid heed.

In the final year before the opening of the Games, downtown Atlanta
began to look like one giant construction pit, with new parks and buildings dotting every corner. By far the most ambitious project was a master
plan to save downtown Atlanta and turn it into a safe, thriving, 24-hour
city, full of visitors and office workers by day, and college students and
loft-dwelling artists by night. The dream hatched by Robert Troutman,
Jr., nearly 40 years before, and pursued with such relentless zeal by Tom
Cousins for so many years afterward, now seemed attainable.

If — if — all went just so, you might finally be able to connect the
dots. You could go south from the Coca-Cola tower on North Avenue
through a refurbished Techwood Homes to a new Olympic Centennial
Park, and reach all the way to the front door of CNN Center and the
adjacent Omni, World Congress Center, and Georgia Dome. Then you
could take a dogleg left, to the east, and run along the old railroad gulch
to Five Points and Underground Atlanta, and beyond that hook up with
Georgia State University and the government complex — the state
Capitol, City Hall, the Fulton County courthouse, and the federal buildings. You could turn north to the Georgia-Pacific building, now the
southernmost anchor of big business, and past that reach the convention
hotels, stores, and restaurants, then follow MARTA up Peachtree Ridge
to Buckhead and the suburbs beyond. You could, in effect, reconnect
Five Points with the three million people who live outside the city limits but still like to call themselves Atlantans.

The city's newest slogan, "Atlanta — Come Celebrate Our Dream,"
was unveiled early in 1995 to generally ho-hum reviews. The thought
occurred that it might more accurately have been rendered as "Atlanta
— Come *Fulfill* Our Dream," because so much was left to be done and so
much was riding on the Olympics. The Games were driving the city on
a spending spree, a big gamble whose payoff was due at the Opening Ceremony on July 19, 1996, and whose success would mean that 50 years of
striving had been worth it.

Mayor Hartsfield would have loved it.

ACKNOWLEDGMENTS

Asking for help in the research and writing of a book seems to bring out the best in people. I am grateful to all who answered the call, starting with Dr. Linda Matthews, director of Special Collections at Emory University, who guided me to several valuable new collections. Her success in obtaining the papers of sociologist Floyd Hunter was a particular coup for Emory and a great benefit to me. The archivists in Emory's Special Collections Department, Beverly Allen, Virginia Cain, Stephen Enniss, Kathy Knox, Barbara Mann, and Ellen Nemhauser, were helpful, knowledgeable, and good company.

Similarly, I appreciate the advice and assistance given me by Anne Salter, directory of Library and Archives at the Atlanta History Center, and her staff: Frank Wheeler, Tammy Galloway, Helen Matthews, Sara Saunders, Priscilla Pomazal, Jennie Williams, and Bill Hull. The center's visual arts archivist, Ted Ryan, directed me to several of the photographs that appear in this book. Franklin Garrett, Atlanta's venerable historian, proved as always to be a walking wellspring of information.

Dorothy Shea, Richard Hallman, Valerie Lyons, and Kathy Drewke of the *Atlanta Journal-Constitution*'s News Research department guided me through their photo archives and helped me find the striking images that fill most of the book's photo sections.

At the Georgia Department of Archives and History, Director Ed Weldon and archivist Joanne Smalley dug out their files on the state flag, which helped shed new light on a contentious piece of Georgia's history. I am also indebted to Michael Thurmond, director of the Georgia Division of Family and Children Services, for sharing his research on the flag's origins.

Rob Aaron of Aaron-Smith Associates, Inc., provided prompt, professional assistance with some of my research.

Many people made unwitting contributions to this book by helping me with *Secret Formula*, my history of the Coca-Cola Company. Scores of vital decisions about Atlanta's future were made in Robert Woodruff's private dining room on the fourth floor of Coca-Cola headquarters, and I appreciate the accounts given to me by some of the participants. I'm especially grateful to the family of Hughes Spalding for granting me access to his private papers, a rich lode of background material and good gossip.

Over the course of my fifteen years with the *Atlanta Constitution*, hundreds of people contributed to my understanding of how the city works (and occasionally doesn't). In particular, I value the lessons taught to me by the late Dr. Clarence Bacote of Morehouse College, the savviest political scientist Atlanta has ever produced.

Jed Dannenbaum and Kathleen Dowkey, the producers of "Dawn's Early Light," an excellent documentary on Ralph McGill, created an important oral history archive by giving the transcripts of their interviews to Emory. I also appreciate the decision by my friends Joe Cumming and Bill Emerson to give their *Newsweek* bureau files to Emory. I borrowed freely.

Several knowledgeable people gave the manuscript of *Atlanta Rising* a close, critical reading, among them George Goodwin, Gerald Horton, Claude Sitton, and Dana White. Any surviving errors are mine, not theirs. Valued members of my "Board of Literary Advisers" include Peggy Galis, who gave the book its title, and Pam Meredith, who read and smoothed several difficult passages. Others who contributed were Sam Brownlee, Bob Coram, Cliff Graubart, Judy and Bennett Kight, Dawn and Doug Mullins, and Gerry Woodruff.

My colleagues at "The Georgia Gang," Atlanta's oldest and most contentious TV talk show, made valuable contributions to the book. Bill Shipp, my former city editor at the *Atlanta Constitution*, covered many of the events of the period and shared his first-hand recollections with me. Dick Williams has already heard the audio cassette of the book, as I called on him to listen to my daily output and critique it. Tom Houck, a close friend and confidant of the family of Dr. Martin Luther King, Jr., and other civil rights leaders, gave me the benefit of his knowledge. Jeff Dickerson contributed his thoughtful observations on modern urban life.

Every city deserves a watering hole like "Mr. C's," where wonderful stories are told and retold (and occasionally prove to be true). George

Berry, Tom Boller, Tom Watson Brown, Chuck Driebe, Wyche Fowler, Hal Gulliver, Windsor Jordan, Rebekah Stewart, and many other regulars are preserving Atlanta's folklore. I appreciate their accepting me into the fold.

My agent, Kris Dahl of International Creative Management, and her assistant, Dorothea Herrey, provided therapy for me along with first-rate representation.

Working with Longstreet Press has been a genuine pleasure. Publisher Chuck Perry, senior editor John Yow, sales director Ruth Waters, designers Jill Dible and Neil Hollingsworth, and publicists Jeannie Ringo and Bethany Moreton — all have been generous with their time and skills, making *Atlanta Rising* a book we are proud to put on the new release table (or better yet, right next to the cash register).

As always, my greatest thanks go to my wife, Linda, who has served as my personal Maxwell Perkins during this whole project. She has endured the inevitable moodiness of a writer at work and has spent a lot of time pushing me uphill. We'll be celebrating our twentieth anniversary as this book is published; its successful completion is only the latest of her many gifts to me.

A NOTE ON SOURCES

Most of the material in this book comes from the private papers of individuals who were intimately involved in forging Atlanta's history from World War II to the present. In several instances, the materials have only recently become available for review.

Manuscript Collections

Emory Special Collections, Emory University, Atlanta
  Helen Bullard Papers
  Calvin Craig Papers
  James C. Davis Papers
  William B. Hartsfield Papers
  Floyd Hunter Papers
  Ralph McGill Papers
  Newsweek Atlanta Bureau Files
  Robert Woodruff Papers

Atlanta History Center, Atlanta
  Atlanta Bureau of Planning Files
  Herbert T. Jenkins Papers
  Long-Rucker-Aiken Family Papers
  "Sunday News Conference" Tape Collection

Hughes Spalding Papers, Rare Books Department, University of Georgia, Athens, courtesy of the Spalding family.

State Flags Collection, Georgia Department of Archives and History, Atlanta

Oral Histories

"Dawn's Early Light: Ralph McGill and the Segregated South," transcripts of interviews for documentary on McGill, 1988, Jed Dannenbaum and Kathleen Dowkey, Emory Special Collections.

William B. Hartsfield, 1/6/66, by Charles T. Morrissey, Kennedy Library.

Ralph McGill, 1/6/66, by Charles T. Morrissey, Kennedy Library.

John A. Sibley, May/79, by Chester Goolrick, AJC.

Herbert T. Jenkins, 5/14/69, Lyndon Johnson Library, Austin, Texas.

Author Interviews

The following people granted interviews specifically for this book and are cited in the endnotes:

Ivan Allen Jr., Maurice Alpert, Luther Alverson, Charles Battle, Griffin Bell, John Sammons Bell, Dennis Berkholtz, George Berry, Furman Bisher, John Blackmon, Henry Bowden, Harold Clarke, Tom Cousins, Don Farmer, Cindy Fowler, David Franklin, Franklin Garrett, George Goodwin, Denmark Groover, Hal Gulliver, Peyton Hawes Jr., Harold Henderson, Bob Holder, Gerald Horton, Tom Houck, Joseph Jones, Michael Lomax, Lester Maddox, C.T. Martin, T.M. "Jim" Parham, Carl Sanders, Clarence Seeliger, Bill Shipp, Horace Sibley, Claude Sitton, Jerry Stargel, Jack Tarver, Michael Thurmond, Norman Underwood, Ernest Vandiver, Dana White, Dick Williams, Hosea Williams, Sam Williams, Dick Yarbrough.

These individuals, also cited in the text and/or endnotes, were interviewed by the author either during his career with the *Atlanta Journal-Constitition* or during his research for *Secret Formula*:

T.M. Alexander, Ellis Arnall, Jeane Austin, Clarence Bacote, Eldrin Bell, Julian Bond, William Holmes Borders, Charlie Brown, Lee P. Brown, Helen Bullard, George Busbee, Bill Campbell, Jimmy Carter, Clint Chafin, Rodney Cook, John Cox, Ovid Davis, A. Reginald Eaves, Wyche Fowler, Roberto Goizueta, Marvin Griffin, R.A. "Cheney" Griffin, Roy Harris, John Inman, Maynard Jackson, Herbert Jenkins, Leroy Johnson, Dick Kattel, Don Keough, Coretta Scott King, Martin Luther "Daddy" King Sr., John Lewis, Manuel Maloof, Dillard Munford, James Paschal, Robert Paschal, John Portman, Sidney Marcus, Sam Massell,

Donald Ratajczak, Hughes Spalding Jr., Jack Spalding, Herman Talmadge, Ted Turner, Charles Weltner, Q.V. Williamson, Andrew Young.

Abbreviations Used in Notes

AC	*Atlanta Constitution*
AJ	*Atlanta Journal*
AJC	*Atlanta Journal-Constitution*
AP	Associated Press
NYT	*New York Times*
UPI	United Press International
WSJ	*Wall Street Journal*
int	Interview by author
oh	Oral history
A&E	*Atlanta & Environs*
AHC	Atlanta History Center
CCP	Calvin Craig Papers
DEL	"Dawn's Early Light" Transcripts
FHP	Floyd Hunter Papers
HJP	Herbert Jenkins Papers
HSP	Hughes Spalding Papers
JSP	John Sibley Papers
RMP	Ralph McGill Papers
RWP	Robert Woodruff Papers
SNC	"Sunday News Conference" Tapes
WHP	William Hartsfield Papers

BIBLIOGRAPHY

Allen, Frederick. *Secret Formula*, Harper Business, New York, 1994.

Allen, Ivan, Jr., with Hemphill, Paul. *Mayor: Notes on the Sixties*, Simon and Schuster, New York, 1971.

Anderson, William. *Wild Man from Sugar Creek*, Louisiana State University Press, Baton Rouge, 1975.

Bartley, Numan V., *The Creation of Modern Georgia, Second Edition*, University of Georgia Press, Athens, Ga., 1983 and 1990.

Bisher, Furman. *Miracle in Atlanta*, World Publishing, Cleveland, 1966.

Braden, Betsy, and Hagen, Paul. *A Dream Takes Flight*, University of Georgia Press, Athens, Ga., and the Atlanta Historical Society, 1989.

Branch, Taylor. *Parting the Waters*, Simon & Schuster, New York, 1988.

Brown, Charlie, and Bryant, James C. *Charlie Brown Remembers Atlanta*, Bryan Company, Columbia, S.C., 1982.

Bryant, James C. *Capital City Club, the First One Hundred Years*, Capital City Club, Atlanta, 1991.

Carney, Robert. *What Happened at the Atlanta Times?*, Atlanta, Business Press, 1969.

Carter, Jimmy. *Why Not the Best?*, New York, Bantam, 1976.

Cook, James F. *Carl Sanders: Spokesman of the New South*, Macon, Ga., Mercer University Press, 1993.

Coulter, E. Merton, *Georgia, a Short History*, Chapel Hill, University of North Carolina Press, 1933 (1945, 1960.)

English, Dr. Thomas H. *Emory University, 1915-1965: A Semicentennial History*, Atlanta, Emory University, 1966.

——*From Thurmond to Wallace: Political Tendencies in Georgia, 1948-1968*, Johns Hopkins Press, Baltimore, 1970.

Galphin, Bruce. *The Riddle of Lester Maddox*, Camelot Press, Atlanta, 1968.

Garrett, Franklin. *Atlanta & Environs*, 2 vols, University of Georgia Press, Athens, Ga., 1954.

Garrow, David J. *Bearing the Cross*, Morrow, New York, 1986.

Goldberg, Robert, and Goldberg, Gerald Jay. *Citizen Turner*, Harcourt Brace & Co., New York, 1995.

Henderson, Harold Paulk. *The Politics of Change in Georgia: A Political Biography of Ellis Arnall*, University of Georgia Press, Athens, Ga., 1991.

Kennedy, Stetson. *I Rode With the Ku Klux Klan*, Arco Publishers Ltd., London, 1954.

Jenkins, Herbert T. *Atlanta and the Automobile*, Atlanta, Center for Research in Social Change, Emory University, 1977.

——. *My Forty Years on the Force, 1932-1972*, Atlanta, Center for Research in Social Change, Emory University, 1973.

Jenkins, James S. *Murder in Atlanta*, Atlanta, Cherokee Publishing, 1981.

King, Coretta Scott. *My Life With Martin Luther King, Jr.*, New York, Avon Books, 1970.

Logue, Calvin McLeod. *Notes on Eugene Talmadge: Rhetoric and Response*, Greenwood Press, Westport, Ct., 1989.

Martin, Harold. *Atlanta & Environs*, vol III, University of Georgia Press, Athens, Ga., and the Atlanta Historical Society, Atlanta, 1987.

———. *Georgia: A History*, W.W. Norton & Co., New York, 1977.

———. *Ralph McGill, Reporter*, Boston, Little Brown, 1973.

———. *Three Strong Pillars*, Atlanta, Trust Company of Georgia, 1974.

———. *William B. Hartsfield, Mayor*, Athens, University of Georgia Press, 1978.

Mathias, William J., and Anderson, Stuart. *Horse to Helicopter: First Century of the Atlanta Police Department*, Atlanta, Community Life Publications, Georgia State University, 1973.

Mays, Benjamin. *Born to Rebel*, Scribner, New York, 1971.

McGill, Ralph. *A Church, A School*, Abingdon Press, New York, 1959.

———. *No Place to Hide*, Mercer University Press, Macon, Ga., 1884.

Miller, Paul W., ed. *Atlanta, Capital of the South*, American Guide Series, Oliver Durrell Press, 1949.

Raines, Howell. *My Soul Is Rested*, Putnam, New York, 1977.

Raper, Arthur F., and Reid, Ira De A., *Sharecroppers All*, University of North Carolina Press, Chapel Hill, N.C., 1941.

Roland, Charles P. *The Improbable Era, the South Since World War II*, University of Kentucky Press, Lexington, 1975.

Rothschild, Janice O. *As But A Day: The First Hundred Years, 1867-1967*, Atlanta, Hebrew Benevolent Congregation, 1967.

Shavin, Norman and Galphin, Bruce: *Atlanta: Triumph of a People*, Atlanta, Capricorn, 1982.

Shavin, Norman. *The World of Atlanta*, Atlanta, Capricorn, 1983.

Sibley, Celestine. *Dear Store*, Garden City, N.Y., Doubleday, 1967.

———. *Peachtree Street, U.S.A.*, Garden City, N.Y., Doubleday, 1963.

Spritzer, Lorraine Nelson. *The Belle of Ashby Street: A Political Biography of Helen Douglas Mankin*, University of Georgia Press, Athens, Ga., 1982.

Stone, Clarence. *Regime Politics: Governing Atlanta, 1946-1988*, University of Kansas Press, 1989.

Talmadge, Herman, with Winchell, Mark Royden. *Talmadge: A Political Legacy, A Politician's Life*, Peachtree Publishers, Atlanta, 1987.

Trillin, Calvin. *An Education in Georgia*, University of Georgia Press, Athens, Ga., 1991, paperback. (Originally published by Viking Press, New York, 1964.)

Wallace, Robert B., Jr. *Dress Her in White and Gold: A Biography of Georgia Tech*, Atlanta, Georgia Tech Foundation, 1969.

Watters, Pat, and Cleghorn, Reese. *Climbing Jacob's Ladder: The Arrival of Negroes in Southern Politics*, Harcourt, Brace and World, Inc., New York, 1967.

White, Theodore. *The Making of the President, 1960*, Athaneum House, New York, 1961.

ENDNOTES

AUTHOR'S NOTE

[vii] Sherman's visit: Recounted by McGill in *National Geographic*, Feb/69. "Babbittry over bigotry": *The New Yorker*, 3/7/73. [viii] Benjamin Harvey Hill: Cited by Grady in his "New South" speech. Julian Bond: Remark to author, ca. 1975.

[x] Meteorologist's report: Forecaster George Mindling, 3/7/40, cited in the original manuscript of *A&E*, Vol. III. McGill quote re "citizen of medieval walled city": Harry Ashmore int, DEL.

CHAPTER 1

[1] Ramspeck resigned: Letter, Ramspeck to Hartsfield, 5/6/49, WHP. Mankin wanted to run: *Record, Contested-Election Case, Helen Douglas Mankin v. James C. Davis, 5th Congressional District of Georgia*. A "cussin', whiskey-drinking ... lawyer:" Spritzer, p. 55. Stood five-foot-nine, shot pistol, played baseball: *Ibid.*, p. 10. "Look a hole": *Augusta Herald*, 12/3/46. Enemies called her communist: Flyer, James C. Davis campaign. Whispered she was lesbian: Spritzer, p. 29.

[2] Special election rules: *Record*. Court challenges to Georgia's whites-only primary: Henderson, pp. 142-143.

Black registration swelled to 7,000: AC, article by author, 9/25/78. Candidates invited to Butler Street YMCA: Bacote int. Walden and Dobbs unified: AC, 9/25/78. C.A. Scott quote: issue of 2/10/46, cited by Spritzer, p. 71. Events of election eve and election night: Bacote int; AC, 9/25/78. *Time* and *Newsweek* citations: Spritzer, p 72.

[3] Gene Talmadge's purge of University of Georgia: Columbus News, 7/17/41. [4] The principal target was Dr. Walter D. Cocking, dean of the university's College of Education. A good contemporary account, including an interview with Talmadge, appeared in the St. Louis *Star-Times*, 7/26/41. Sherwood Anderson: Cited in text, speech by Mark Etheridge, 12/4/58, RMP.

Arnall's reforms: Henderson, pp. 53-55. Quote from *Collier's*: Issue of 7/24/43, RWP. (Arnall's greatest accomplishment was a successful attack on the discriminatory railroad freight rates that kept the South in colonial status by making it cheaper to export raw materials than finished products. Stephens Mitchell, Margaret Mitchell's brother, often remarked that the two greatest forces in modernizing the South were the equalization of freight rates and air-conditioning.)

Talmadge wrote in *Statesman*, gave nickname: Spritzer, p. 74. Mankin called timing "unfavorable": *Christian Science Monitor*, 2/21/46, cited by Spritzer, p. 73.

[5] Talmadge kept a cow on the grounds: Anderson, p. 83. New Deal brought "liquor,

popcorn": *Statesman*, 1/21/36. "Used to help out with a little whipping": Letter, McGill to John Bartlow Martin, 4/11/57, RMP. **[6]** "Self-made illiterate": *The Reporter*, 10/20/55. "I believe in white supremacy": Letter, Talmadge to McGill, 12/20/43, RMP.

Blacks placed double-V signs: *The American Mercury*, Dec/44. Veterans marched with flyers: Flyer, WHP. Head of NAACP wrote manager: Letter, Victor Backus to Burt T. Wellborn, 11/13/45, WHP. Spending on black pupils a third white level: AJ, 12/13/45. **[7]** "Sour mattresses": Hunter, *Atlanta Letter*, 8/1/46.

Columbians: Memo, Keeler McCartney, AC police reporter, 12/2/46, RMP. Sides confronted each other: *Atlanta Letter*, 12/1/46. Supreme Court overturn Georgia primary: Henderson, pp. 142-43. "I will not be a party": *Ibid.*, p. 144.

Talmadge counterattack; "unfettered": Anderson, p. 222. A good explanation of the county-unit system appears in *The Reporter*, 10/20/55. **[8]** Democratic leaders inflicted mischief on Mankin: Brief for Contestee, *Contested Election Case*. Voters tripled to 24,000: *Atlanta Letter*, 6/1/46, FHP. Davis's qualifications: Flyer, RMP. **[9]** "I was raised among niggers": Anderson, p. 230. Recording of Talmadge and storm: Transcript, Logue, p. 283.

Klan rebirth, *Constitution* reporter re handkerchiefs: AC, 5/9/46, cited by Anderson, p. 224. IRS infiltrated Klan: Manuscript, untitled, by Harold Martin, ca. 1950, RMP. (Stetson Kennedy posed as Klan member "John Perkins" for years, then revealed his true identity in his book, *I Rode With the Klan*, in 1954.) Kennedy re "Superman": Kennedy, p. 92. **[10]** Kennedy briefed McGill on Yellow Cab drivers: Memo entitled "Notes on talk with SK May 11," RMP. Rumor about 5,000 babies: Informant report, 4/1/47, RMP.

Titles of investiture: Letter, unnamed "faithful Kligrapp" to Craig, 4/17/63, CCP. "Split his tongue": Informant report, 4/1/47, RMP. Sam Roper: Confidential memo, Hartsfield to Chief Hornsby, 6/7/46, WHP.

Spalding, "It is the Negro issue": Spalding to Robert Woodruff, 5/23/46, RWP. **[11]** Carmichael re "our Southern traditions": Anderson, p. 225. "Honey, is you bin down": Card, RMP. Carmichael look-alike rode with black men: PM, 8/8/46.

Talmadge denounced Mankin as "nigger candidate"; she told police, "I am proud": Spritzer, pp. 97-99. She got 53,882 votes, Davis "won": Brief, Wyman C. Lowe, *Contested Election Case*. Talmadge, Carmichael totals: Anderson, p. 232. **[12]** Concluding episode, visit to McGill: Martin, *McGill*, pp. 117-18.

NYT re "misfortune": Henderson, p. 168. Herblock: *Washington Post*, 7/19/46.

Lynching in Walton County: Louisville *Courier-Journal*, 7/28/46. **[13]** Sheriff Gordon, "They hadn't ought": *Ibid. Post* denounced "mobocracy": Editorial, issue of 7/29/46. Eleanor Roosevelt: Column, 7/29/46. PM, "Portrait of a Lynch Town": Issue of 8/5/46. Columnist re "red-soiled desert": Mac Williams, Dunkirk [N.Y.] *Evening Observer*, 7/29/46. **[14]** Benjamin Mays: PM, 8/8/46. A.T. Walden: *Ibid.*

Cirrhosis, ruptured vein: Anderson, p. 235. Herman Talmadge's write-in scheme: Talmadge, pp. 74-75. **[15]** McGill disclosed succession plan: AC, 12/20/46. Thompson claimed governor's chair: Henderson, p. 173.

Gathering at Capitol on 1/14/47: *Newsweek*, 1/27/47, cited by Henderson, p. 176; *Time*, 10/15/56. Talmadge's friend relied on .45-caliber revolvers: Talmadge, p. 85. Paper ballots carted in hamper: Goodwin int. Herman finished third: Henderson, p. 177. **[16]** "If they are stupid enough": *Ibid.* p. 178.

Telfair write-ins: Goodwin int. (Goodwin won a Pulitzer Prize for his discovery that the dead had voted, alphabetically.) Talmadge's confrontation with Arnall; chauffeur's jaw broken: Talmadge, pp. 87-88. **[17]** Talmadge returned, changed locks; supporter threw firecracker: *Ibid.*, pp. 89-91.

Washington Post: Editorial, issue of 1/20/47. Arnall re "King Herman": Henderson, p.

185. Talmadge moved out of mansion: *Time*, 10/15/56. Gallup poll: Henderson, p. 188.

[18] Hartsfield prowled Capitol: Harris in *Augusta Courier*, 8/5/57. Hartsfield disliked those "stirring up racial questions": Letter, Hartsfield to Rep. Martin Dies, 3/13/44, WHP. Asked Congress to investigate NAACP: *Ibid.*

Hartsfield got briefing from Attorney General's office; warned Hornsby: Memo, marked "confidential," Hartsfield to Hornsby, 6/7/46, WHP. [19] Cawthon advised: Klan informant's report, 6/30/47, RMP. Hartsfield visit from Borders, Scott: Master's thesis, "The Issue of Employing Black Policemen in Atlanta," Charles L. Rosenzweig, Emory University, 1980. Eight black patrolmen: See endnotes, Chapter 2.

CHAPTER 2

[20] Hartsfield's barnstorming episode, dropping dog out of plane: Jesse Outlar column, AC, 5/12/67. Son of a tinsmith: Martin, *Hartsfield*, pp. 7-8. Hartsfield passed bar: *Ibid.*, p. 10. Elected alderman: *A&E*, vol. II, p. 788. [21] Asa Candler, Jr., built raceway: Obit, AP, 1/12/53. (Several accounts mistakenly credit Asa Sr. with building the track.) Hartsfield saw Moisant: *Atlanta*, Jun/65, WHP. A fine account of early days at the field is "Pioneering in Aviation in Atlanta," an article by James H. Elliott in *Atlanta Historical Bulletin*, Jul/40.

The account of Col. Danforth's activities, including his lobbying of local governments, Mayor Key's veto and the argument with Hartsfield, is from a "The Selection of Candler Field 1924-25," a manuscript by John N. Gibbs, Jr., submitted for the Honors History Program at Emory University, 5/26/69. Danforth's map: Chamber of Commerce report, 6/1/28, WHP. [22] "He got my goat": *Atlanta*, Jun/65. Hartsfield quote, "the city that makes its port": Birmingham *News*, 10/13/70, WHP.

Hartsfield found Blevins and Davis: Letter, Hartsfield to Henry Maddox, Jr., 5/7/68, WHP. Candler offered use of land: Gibbs. Hartsfield got bird's eye view: *Atlanta*, Jun/65. [23] Hartsfield got $5,000 for grading: Gibbs. Completed job using steam shovel and convict labor: Jack Gray, Sr., quoted in AJC, 6/27/71, WHP. Mayor Sims's flight, trip to Washington: Gibbs.

Hansell brought in manure: Unidentified newspaper clip, WHP. Dairy farmer: *Atlanta*, Jun/65. [24] Hartsfield's resolution praising the Candlers: Minutes of the Atlanta City Council, 12/7/25, cited by Gibbs. Asa Jr.'s eccentricities: AC, 1/12/53; Sibley, *Peachtree*, pp. 153-154. Birmingham's bid; "looked at a map": *Atlanta*, Jun/65. Assistant postmaster visited, had escort, sumptuous dinner: AJ, 5/30/26. "No east Indian potentate": Birmingham *Post-Herald*, 10/14/70. Government designated Atlanta: Braden and Hagen, p. 37. (Braden and Hagen say a second federal official, William P. MacCracken, head of the Bureau of Aeronautics in the U.S. Commerce Department, also got the royal treatment and was responsible for Atlanta's designation.)

[25] City bought Candler Field, renamed it: Letter, Hartsfield to Henry Maddox, Jr., 5/7/68, WHP. Lighting, hangars: AJC, 6/27/71. Ranked third in flights: *A&E*, vol. II, p. 851. Chamber award: Martin, *Hartsfield*, p. 15. Hartsfield went bankrupt: Letter, Mayor Key to a Miss Baker, 9/21/36, WHP. Invested in mining: Martin, *Hartsfield*, pp. 15-16. Lived with mother: *Ibid.*, pp. 10-11. Drove around the streets at night: *The Reporter*, 7/11/57, WHP.

Hartsfield accused Key of a "one-hour a day administration" and winking at vice: Text, speech on WSB radio, 9/1/36, WHP. Key found $86 doctor's bill: Key letter to Miss Baker, 9/21/36, WHP. Hartsfield asked people who owed money to vote for him: Memo, unidentified, 1949 mayoral campaign file, WHP.

[26] Hartsfield's early accomplishments as mayor, naming new chief: Martin, *Hartsfield*, pp. 21-23, 26; A&E, vol. II, p. 950. Opened Hurt Park: AC, 5/13/42, WHP. Harllee Branch anecdote: *Atlanta*, Jun/65. Hartsfield wanted to dredge Chattahoochee, make Atlanta a port: Letter, Hartsfield to John Cooper, 5/3/45, WHP. Wanted dam: Letter, Hartsfield to Ed Hughes, 11/3/61, WHP. Wanted to annex Buckhead for "decent folks": Letter, Hartsfield to John Carlton, 10/22/42, WHP.

Hartsfield's attitude toward *Gone With the Wind*, quote about "magnolias and beautiful ladies": *Time*, 8/17/62, RWP. [27] Hartsfield lobbied Selznick, Junior League planned ball, Hartsfield "leapt eight feet": Martin, *Hartsfield*, p. 27-28. Description of premier: A&E, vol. II, pp. 977-991. Invitations embossed with Confederate flags: Martin, *Hartsfield*, p. 29.

[28] Letter from associate warning Hartsfield "you have no friends": Letter, Clint W. Hager to Hartsfield, 6/2/39, WHP. Hartsfield lost to LeCraw: AC, 9/6/40, WHP. "You could pave the streets with gold": AJC magazine, 12/10/61. Hartsfield turned to Woodruff for help, called him "number one friend": Letter, Hartsfield to Woodruff, 12/28/67, WHP. [29] Business community cool toward Hartsfield: Letter, Hager to Hartsfield, 6/2/39, WHP.

Hartsfield pulled over with woman in car: Martin, *Hartsfield*, pp. 33-34. Hartsfield pushed Bell plant: AC, undated but May/42; letter, Hartsfield to Frank Etheridge, 4/13/68, WHP. Lengthen runways for B-29s: Letter, Hartsfield to Christie Bell Kennedy, 9/15/43, WHP.

LeCraw resigned: A&E, vol. III, p. 80. Hartsfield swept field: *Ibid.*, p. 81. Hartsfield used 16-millimeter camera: Martin, *Hartsfield*, pp. 40-41. "A soldier could come ... not be robbed": *Ibid.*, p. 38. [30] Called city editor: Letter, Hartsfield to John Carlton, 10/22/42, WHP. Got permission to repair auditorium, asked newspapers not to report story": Letter, Hartsfield to AC and AJ, undated but 1942, WHP.

Government designated Atlanta as military supply center, "Little Washington": A&E, vol. III, p. 56. Population swelled to 500,000: *Ibid*, p. 84. Bell plant attracted Northern investors: Shavin and Galphin, pp. 250-251. Telephone exchange: A&E, vol. III, p. 149. LeCraw returned, promised to make Atlanta great: Speech text, 7/26/45, WHP. Hartsfield trounced: AC, 9/7/45. Hartsfield got 10,131 votes, LeCraw 6,892.

High Museum's "Memory Lane": AJ magazine, 4/6/41, cited in *Atlanta History*, Spring-Summer 1994, p. 32. Budget of $25,000: Art Association files, JSP. Association could not afford $600 fee: Letter to E.R. Hunter, 1/23/52, JSP.

[31] Description of Municipal Auditorium, "Buster" Caruso story: AJC, 2/11/73; AJC magazine, 4/4/65. William Oliver building: Garrett int. Traffic lights not synchronized: Jenkins in AJC magazine, 11/13/77. 50,000 visitors: *Atlanta Letter*, 9/1/47, FHP. Winecoff Hotel fire: A&E, vol. III, pp. 128-130.

South had $7 million in capital: Text, Sibley speech, 3/1/51, JSP. Regained economic ground by 1946: Memo, *Newsweek* files, 11/17/54. [32] "Cotton Ed" Smith: *The American Scholar*, Mar/51. Boll weevil: Text, undated, article by Carson McCullers for *Holiday*, ca. 1954, RMP; AJC, 7/10/94. Topsoil erosion: Text, speech, Mark Etheridge, Executives Club, Meridien, Miss., 9/28/46, RMP. Black migration; state spent $1 billion; illiteracy rate; Mississippi teachers' pay: *ibid.*

Delta moved to Atlanta in 1941: A&E, vol. III, p. 32. Trains still passed through: *Ibid.*, p. 191. Hartsfield unveiled map of "Downtown Connector": Draft letter to Hartsfield from city planner, 3/7/46, WHP. [33] "Airmindedness": AJ, 6/18/51. City opened terminal: A&E, vol. III, p. 138. Grounds muddy; Gray's ploy: AJC, 6/27/71, WHP.

Bridges ran supermarket: Master's thesis, "The Issue of Employing Black Policemen in Atlanta," Charles L. Rosenzweig, Emory University, 1980. Hartsfield condoned lottery: Letter, Hunter to Dr. Gordon W. Blackwell, 11/27/50; AP, 5/4/57; Jenkins memo to police, 4/21/57; Shipp int. **[34]** Condoned liquor: Letter, Reuben Garland to Hartsfield, 5/13/48; *Birmingham News*, 10/13/70, WHP.

Hartsfield protected Capital City Club: Bryant, pp. 320-321. Hartsfield kept out organized crime: *A&E*, vol. III, p. 82. Jenkins's reforms: Rosenzweig; Jenkins int. Jenkins's background, "Daddy" King story: AJC, 11/17/79; Jenkins, DEL. **[35]** Hornsby threatened to resign: Rosenzweig. Picked eight recruits, their names: Program, Greater Mount Calvary Baptist Church, 4/30/48, WHP.

Jenkins answered, "Hell, no": AC, 5/31/65. Sent detractor to Pittsburgh; hundreds cheered: Rosenzweig. NAACP celebration: Program, 4/30/48. Jenkins gave black police permission to make arrests: *Atlanta Letter*, 9/1/47, FHP. Same guns and pay: Rosenzweig.

[36] Herndon: *A&E*, vol. II, pp. 609-610; Shavin & Galphin, p. 207. Could stand on sidewalk and watch: Hunter draft, 1973. "Chief" Aiken: Photo, Aiken Papers, AHC. Letter at Christmas: Leon Eller to Aiken, 12/19/47, Aiken Papers, AHC. Rutledge quote: Draft, *American Mercury*, 11/17/44, WHP.

[37] Brown called Hartsfield "old and tired": AJ, 6/5/49. Hartsfield letter warning "time is not far off": 1/7/43, WHP. Hartsfield went to Auburn merchants: AC, 3/1/68. Brown attacked Hartsfield for "pet project": Brown flyer, WHP. "Look up in the air": Memo, unidentified, WHP.

Brown recalled broken-down Hupmobile: Brown, p. 230. **[38]** Called Hartsfield "fixer": *Ibid.*, p. 228. Hartsfield studied at library: Martin, *Hartsfield*, p. 9. Said Brown would "shake the corpse's hand": *Newsweek* telex, undated but 1961.

Suspend construction: Memo, Hartsfield to Clarke Donaldson, 8/3/49, WHP. Advice to "keep on an even keel": Letter, G. Everett Millican to Hartsfield, 8/17/49, WHP. Bess, wonder horse story: Letter, Hartsfield to John W. Hazard, *Kiplinger* magazine, 7/12/47, WHP. Margaret Mitchell struck, Gravitt's record: Ad, AJ, 8/14/49.

McGill defended Hartsfield: McGill column, undated but Sep/49, WHP. Woodruff and Robinson backed Hartsfield: Letter, Robinson to Hartsfield, 9/16/49. Brown's slogan: Letterhead, Brown campaign.

CHAPTER 3

[39] Admirer of Lenin: Hunter's handwritten notes, 4/17/48. ("One of the most impressive moments of my life," Hunter said, "was standing before a tomb at midnight — the tomb was that of Nicholae [sic] Lenin on the Red Square in Moscow.")

Hunter's background: Planning council newsletter, 2/1/46, FHP. Support for Wallace: Resolution of support, People's Progressive Party, Macon, Ga., 4/17/48. Hunter's meeting with Spalding: Letter, Hunter to Dr. Gordon W. Blackwell, 11/27/50; and transcript of interview, FHP. **[40]** Spalding liked gossip: Letters to Robert Woodruff, HSP; letter, Arch Avary to Robert L. Steed, undated but 1985, JSP.

[41] Hartsfield christened plane with Coke: *A&E*, Vol. III, p. 167. Kept portrait of Woodruff on wall, Elliott, p. 187.

Georgia tax on securities: "Crackerland" column, AJ, 11/16/34. **[42]** Woodruff moved to Wilmington: Letter, Harold Hirsch to John Sibley, 8/22/35, RWP. "All these people": Letter, Hughes Spalding to Jack Spalding Sr., 1/20/37, HSP. Talmadge asked Coca-Cola executive; was "pretty much" in good graces: Letter, Carl Thompson to Robert Woodruff, 7/26/46, RWP.

"He would have been economical": Letter, Spalding to Woodruff, 12/23/46, HSP. Spalding's deathbed promise: Letter and draft article, McGill to Helen Fuller, *New Republic*, 5/20/47, RMP. **[43]** Woodruff invited Talmadge to lunch, quail hunting: Talmadge int.

Spalding appointed to regents: Letter, Spalding to Woodruff, 10/16/48, HSP. Talmadge opposed Klan: Letter, McGill to Fuller, *New Republic*. Talmadge on "binge": *Ibid*.

[44] Woodruff believed blacks needed rest: Letter, Robert Mizell to Woodruff, 4/27/44, RWP. Spalding concentrating on hospital: Letter, **[45]** Spalding to Woodruff, 9/21/49, HSP. "You probably do not like our governor": Transcript, Hunter int with Spalding, FHP.

Senator George and Coca-Cola: Allen, p. 228-230. Spalding meeting with Talmadge, "told him as frankly": Letter, Spalding to Woodruff, 9/12/49, HSP. Herman Talmadge wanted to build: Talmadge, pp. 129-130. Spalding made deal with Talmadge: Allen, p. 315. "Best governor": *Time*, 6/26/50.

State budget nearly doubled: Talmadge, p. 108. Blacks filed suit; "'separate but equal' theory is a myth"; Mays speech: Article, Benjamin Mays, *New South* newsletter, Sep-Oct/50. **[46]** Talmadge spent $452 million on public education: *Harper's*, Jan/55.

Hartsfield pushed $200,000 to build black course: *A&E*, Vol. III, p. 186. McGill supports employer's right "to hire whom he pleases": Letter, McGill to W.L. Bell, 2/17/49, RMP. Impossible to hire black reporter: Letter, McGill to Walter C. Johnson, 6/16/49, RMP.

[47] Cox background: Shavin & Galphin, p. 246. First priority hiring editor to fight Talmadge: Letter, Cox to Ralph Hayes, 1/4/40, RWP. Cox accused McGill of "conniving": Letter, Cox to McGill, 7/14/55, RMP. Shingles: Letter, Maynard Kniskern to McGill, 7/21/55, RMP. Woodruff arranged private party: Letter, Spalding to Woodruff, 12/7/51, RWP. Woodruff asked no paving: Talmadge int.

[48] Mencken essay: McGill article in *Clip*, Jun/63. Symphony on NBC: *A&E*, Vol. III, p. 208. Parks and Recreation sponsored kite contest, etc.: *Ibid.*, p. 182. Kress offer, refusal: Letter, Robert F. Maddox to John Sibley, 4/21/52, JSP. **[49]** Association bickered, "mentality of four-year-old": Memo, Walter C. Hill to file, 10/29/54. (He was referring to a Mrs. Whitman.)

Atlanta a "city of salesmen": Jack Spalding, AJ, 6/18/51. *Engineer* criticized city's spending: Issue of Nov/49. Apologized: Issue of Jan/50. Groundbreaking of Buford Dam: Program, 3/1/50, WHP. **[50]** Dedication, Hartsfield late: AJ, 7/30/76. Voters tripled city size, added 100,000 citizens: Plan of Improvement; AJC magazine, 3/22/53. Hartsfield friend accosted by teacher: Letter, Joe Prendergrast to Hartsfield, 3/31/53, WHP.

Hartsfield's "go slow" policy: Martin, *Hartsfield*, p. 48. Addressed blacks as "Mr."; left signs unpainted: *Ibid.*, p. 49. Dobbs broke with Hartsfield: *Daily World*, 5/7/53. Flyer accused Hartsfield of plotting to fire white firemen; perpetrator questioned: Report, Sgt. J.L. Moseley to Chief Jenkins, 1/2/52, WHP.

[51] Hartsfield advanced election: AC, 2/26/53; AJC, 2/10/57. Spalding defended Clement: Flyer, Hartsfield campaign, WHP; paper by Henry Lee Moon, 7/10/53, Fisk University, WHP. "No concession" to bigots: Memo, unidentified adviser, WHP. Brown's friends sounded out Talmadge: Account of Harry Phillips, campaign file, WHP. Hartsfield elbowed Brown: AC, 2/23/71.

[52] *Newsweek* lauded Atlanta as "showcase": Issue of 3/8/54. McCullers: Draft article, May/54, RMP. Elks held parade: *A&E*, Vol. III, p. 209. Delta merged with Chicago and Southern: *Ibid.*, p. 194. "Municipal" dropped: AJ, 4/20/54. C&S lent money: Letter, Mills Lane to McGill, 1/5/55, RMP.

McGill concluded segregation "finished": *Time*, 12/14/53. Warned against integrating schools: Letter, McGill to Dr. Colgate W. Darden Jr., 5/14/53, RMP.

Talmadge speaking in Lafayette; quote on "Mixing of the races": *Newsweek*, 5/31/54. **[53]** Georgia historian: Coulter, p. 465. Talmadge on "Meet the Press": AJ, 6/7/54. *Harper's* chided: Issue of Jan/55. Talmadge answered phone: *Ibid.*

[54] Dr. Clement advocated "go slow": *A&E*, Vol. III, p. 206. Brochure "Pending Tragedy in the South": RMP. **[55]** *New York Times Magazine* estimated; quote about marrying daughters: Issue of 10/13/57. McGill quote re those "willing to insult": Letter to Garland Porter, 11/22/55, RMP.

Carter admitted he failed to notice disparity: Transcript, DEL. [56] Hosea Williams recalled ducking: *Ibid.* Woodruff's valet and chauffeur kept account: Joseph Jones int. Lonnie King story: DEL. [57] Woodruff and Sibley believed in "natural" segregation: Letter, Sibley to Woodruff, 8/9/54, JSP. Sibley wrote Vinson: Letter, 1/30/56, JSP. McGill on train with Talmadge: Letter, McGill to Eisenhower, 2/23/59, RMP.

Newsweek correspondent found "football-watching...mood": Bill Emerson draft, 11/17/45. [58] NAACP "gratified": *A&E*, Vol. III, p. 223. *Constitution* called it "a relief"; McGill wrote Warren: Report, Southern Regional Council, RMP.

CHAPTER 4

[59] Marvin Griffin background: Profile [by author] AJC, 12/17/77. Hosea Williams anecdote: Williams int. [60] Firing secretaries: Cheney Griffin int. Voters agreed to turn schools private; [61] legislature outlaws integrated schools: Report, Southern Regional Council, RMP.

Griffin crony sold "gas savers": *Newsweek* telex, 12/17/60. Officials sold paint to state: *Ibid.* Boats that wouldn't float; *Reader's Digest* quote; Batista story: AJC, 12/17/77. Called reporters "jorees": Memo to file, *Newsweek*, 6/6/64. Turned up volume for distraction: Gulliver int.

Court outlawed segregation in parks; Griffin announced state would stop operating: *A&E*, Vol. III, p. 224. Account of Sugar Bowl: A complete account is given in *Atlanta History*, Spring/1995. [62] Library board acquired bookmobile: *A&E*, Vol. III, p. 224.

Hartsfield's strategy on desegregating golf course: *The Reporter*, 7/11/57, RWP; *The Police Chief*, Jun/63. [63] *North Side News*: Issue of 12/29/55. AJ editorial: Issue of 12/27/55. Cook on intermarriage: Letter to McGill, 9/16/55, RMP. Woodruff's views: Allen, *Secret Formula*, p. 285. [64] White Citizens Councils: *Saturday Evening Post*, 6/15/57. Cook traveled: Text, speech at Old Point Comfort, Va., 4/23/56; *Newsweek* telex, May/56.

Flag: John Sammons Bell int. Depositions and testimony from several participants in the 1956 Legislature are in a federal case, 1:94-CV 1673 ODE, *Coleman v. Miller*, filed in U.S. District Court in Atlanta. Origin of "Stars and Bars": E. Merton Coulter, "The Flags of the Confederacy," *The Georgia Historical Quarterly*, Sep/53. [65] Stephens favored flag resembling Old Glory: "The History of Confederate Flags," a monograph published by M. Jemison Chestney, Macon, Ga., 1925. Problem with Stars and Bars, use of battle flag: Coulter.

Craze over battle flag: Author's column, AC, 4/9/87. [66] Cheney Griffin made reproduction: AC, 1/15/56. Davis introduced: Affidavit, Jefferson Lee Davis, Jr., *Coleman* case. Mrs. Kibler objected: AJ, 2/10/56. *Constitution* on esthetics: Author's column, AC, 4/9/87. Flag's legal description: Senate Bill 98, Georgia State Archives. "Mullets": Bell int. [67] "Stainless Banner": Coulter, Chestney. "White Man's Flag": I am indebted to Michael Thurmond, director of the Georgia Division of Family and Children Services, for his research on the subject, reported in AJC, 3/13/88.

Legislators wondered who might profit: Groover affidavit, Mackay testimony, *Coleman*; Bell int; Groover speech to Georgia House, 3/9/93. Pou story: AJ, undated clip, Georgia State Archives. [68] Bell offended: Bell int. Bell's purpose, flag at conventions: Robert G. Stephens, Jr., affidavit, *Coleman*; AC, 4/9/87. Passage of bill: Legislative record, Georgia State Archives. Groover's floor debate: AJ, 2/10/56.

[69] Elections of 1956: Dan Carter int, DEL; Branch, p. 183. Lockheed, Scripto hired black workers: Letter, McGill to Roby Robinson, 4/17/56, RMP. Atlanta's wealth, trolley riders discuss market: *Newsweek* telex, undated but mid/55. "Too busy to hate": Hartsfield interview, AJC, 1/18/70. (There are other accounts of the first use of the phrase, but this was Hartsfield's final explanation, just before he died.)

Airport passengers doubled; highways attracted traffic: *U.S. News & World Report*, 1/29/56. Plans for I-285: AJ, 10/9/56. Grady went up: AJC magazine, 2/27/67. Fulton National building: AJ, 9/8/57. Parking space up 72 percent: A&E, Vol. III, p. 248.

Jaycees: *Newsweek* telex, mid/55. Two of five newcomers from outside South: A&E, Vol. III, p. 236. [70] Alexander proposed World's Fair: *Ibid.*, pp. 241-242. Griffin spoke in New Orleans: *Newsweek* telex, May/56. Borders in *Daily World*: Issue of 1/9/57. Hartsfield angry: Martin, *Hartsfield*, p. 118; *The Reporter*, 7/11/57. Bus driver pulled down wires, scrolled up "Special sign": Shavin & Galphin, p. 259. [71] Hearn asked Jenkins: AJC, 1/18/81. Arrest of Borders: *The Reporter*, 7/11/57.

Hartsfield beat Lindsey: AP, 5/4/57. Fluoridation: Martin, *Hartsfield*, p. 168. Nelson exposed police and lottery: AC, 5/28/57. Nelson complained: Nelson, DEL; Shipp int. Hartsfield beat Lindsey with black vote: AP, 7/1/57.

[72] T.M. Alexander background: *Business Atlanta*, Aug/81; draft introduction, Jimmy Sibley, 1963, JSP. "Atlanta Negroes want ... progress": *The Reporter*, 7/11/57. Griffin backed Summers: *Business Atlanta*, Aug/81.

[73] The account of Faubus's dealings with Griffin and Harris is from an excellent article in *Look*, 11/12/57. (A sidebar, "Georgia: Rallying Point of Defiance," has interviews and quotes from Griffin and Harris.) [74] Events of 9/2/57 through the mob violence at Central High: *Arkansas Gazette*, 10/6/57; text, Faubus's TV speech, 9/20/57. [75] Faubus's meeting with Eisenhower: *Time*, 9/23/57. [76] Eisenhower held his temper in check: Letter to McGill, 10/9/57, RMP. [77] Faubus charged troops entered locker room: *Newsweek* telex, 10/21/57. "Naked bayonets": Memo, Cook to Griffin, 10/15/57, JSP. Harris quote on "beatings"; Griffin on "No Georgia boy": *Look*, 11/12/57. Gallup poll: *Miami Herald*, 10/6/57.

[78] Hartsfield wanted "a showdown": Memo, Hartsfield to McGill, 9/23/57, RMP. Brown considered running: AJ, 6/26/57.

Maddox ran Pickrick: AC, 7/4/64. Skillet-fried chicken, "You PICK it out": Ad, AC, 7/3/64. The best overall exploration of Maddox's personality is Bruce Galphin's *The Riddle of Lester Maddox*, cited in the Bibliography. "Divine right to discriminate": *Newsweek* telex, undated but Nov/63. Flonnie believed in Second Coming, quote: AJC, 12/3/67. Maddox one of seven children, description of father: Galphin, pp. 5-7.

Lester dropped out of school, opened "beaner": *Newsweek* telex, undated but Sep/61. Ad against "amalgamation" of races: AJ, 9/16/57; *The Nation*, 5/1/67. Point about Willie Highgrass; Maddox's strongest epithet was "jigaboo": *New York Times Magazine*, 11/6/66.

[79] Maddox couldn't remember names, called people "buddy boy": *New Yorker*, 1/19/68. Hartsfield quote about race relations: AJ, 9/23/57. Episode at City Hall; Maddox arrived with 6,200 signatures: *Atlanta Citizens' Weekly*, 11/7/57. Hartsfield opened first headquarters: *Atlanta* magazine, Nov/61. [80] Episode facing down rednecks: Undated memo by Joe Cumming in *Newsweek* files.

[81] Hartsfield lost white vote: Letter, George Goodwin to Hartsfield, 10/5/59, WHP. *The Reporter*: Issue of 7/11/57.

Airport grew: Text, Hartsfield's state of city address, Jan/57. Caravelle: A&E, Vol. III, p. 267. "...heaven or hell" in minutes: *Ibid.*, p. 258, citing chamber minutes of 5/8/57. Matron explained; status symbols: *Newsweek* telex, 8/15/58. [82] Rucker family background: Papers of Mrs. Lucy Rucker Aiken, AHC; profile, AJC, 12/9/79.

Vandiver background: *Newsweek* telex, 8/20/57, Vandiver, Shipp ints. Norfolk incident: *Christian Science Monitor*, 1/30/59; 11/22/59. **[83]** "Aren't we lucky...": Letter, Spalding to Woodruff, 9/17/58, HSP. Bombing of Temple: *Newsweek* telex, 10/12/58. McGill greeted by wife: Martin, *McGill*, p. 157. "Let us face": Text from McGill, *A Church, A School*, pp. 9-11. Griffin statement: *Newsweek* telex. Four suspects arrested: AC, 9/30/88. Eisenhower praised: Letter to Hartsfield, 10/20/58, WHP.

[84] Census Bureau added Gwinnett: *A&E*, Vol. III, p. 294. "M" Day: Press release, Chamber of Commerce, 10/10/59. Little Rock cost $1 million: *Tennessean*, 5/31/59. Hartsfield testified: *U.S. News*, 5/4/59. Buses, libraries desegregated: *A&E*, Vol. III, p. 299. Hooper asked plan for schools: *Ibid.*, pp. 310-311.

[85] Ed Noble, Lenox Square: Text, Richard Rich speech, Atlanta Rotary, 5/18/59; press release, Chess Lagomarsino & Associates, 8/3/59; *Newsweek*, 10/19/59. Special section: AJC, 10/11/59.

CHAPTER 5

[86] Hooper ordered desegregation: Text, Sibley speech, AC, 3/4/60. Bell background, commission idea: Letter, Bell to John Sibley, 1/5/84; Hal Gulliver column, AC, 2/8/77; Bell, Vandiver ints. **[87]** Sibley description: Allen, *Secret Formula*, p. 115, p. 294. Sibley liked physical labor: *Atlanta*, Feb/62. Busbee introduced: Letter, Bell to Sibley, 1/5/84.

[88] Harris vowed "crusade," blamed "Rastus": AJ, 2/16/60. Sibley elected chairman: Minutes, Sibley Commission, 2/17/60. Sibley denounced *Brown*: Text, Sibley remarks, AC, 3/4/60. Started in Americus: *Atlanta*, Feb/62. Sibley's performance: Transcript, meeting of 2/26/60. "No speeches": *Atlanta*, Feb/62. **[89]** "Opening of a steamcock": Gene Patterson column in AC, undated, JSP. Harris, "have to stand": Text, Sibley Commission testimony.

Norfolk: *Esquire*, Mar/61; *Christian Science Monitor*, 1/30/59. Sibley held woman's baby: Photo, JSP. Sibley to black man, "I might not mind": *Esquire*, Mar/61. Dorsey: AJ, 3/23/60. **[90]** Final report: Report of the General Assembly Committee on Schools, JSP. Hooper announced another year, "one last chance": Booklet, "Background: Atlanta, A Handbook for Reporters Covering the Desegregation of Alanta Public Schools," prepared by OASIS, the Organizations Assisting Schools in September.

Atlanta's speed most deliberate in Dixie: Letter, Hamilton Lokey to Saunders Jones, 6/30/61, AHC. McGill re "citizen of medieval walled city": Harry Ashmore, DEL. Alabama tried King, he concentrated on defense: Branch, p. 269, pp. 277-278. Single day of Atlanta sit-ins: *Ibid.*, p. 286. **[91]** Jenkins and Alabama patrol captains; told FBI, "If you want to raid him": Jenkins, DEL. March on Capitol, Vandiver's response: Branch, pp. 301-302. Jenkins turned students aside: Jenkins, DEL.

[92] Hartsfield and blockbusting: Unless otherwise noted, material on the activities of the "housing coordinator" is from the files of the Atlanta Bureau of Planning, AHC. City gained 38,000 blacks: Report of housing coordinator, 8/26/60. Cards asking, "Who will be": AC, 12/12/61. Adamsville bombing: Letter, Parham to R.E. Little, 4/22/60. Hartsfield asked no "sold" signs: Letter, M. DuQuince Davis to Hartsfield, 6/21/60.

Hartsfield paid coordinator off budget: Letter, Hartsfield to Milton Farris, 9/14/59. (According to an unsigned letter to the file, the coordinator worked at the Metropolitan Planning Commission, his salary paid by "special appropriation.") "When I learned to pray": Parham int. Parham sent questionnaires; responses from Kirkwood residents: Kirkwood folder, 1960, 1961. **[93]** Empire Real Estate: Report of housing coordinator, 6/1/61. Parham saw "insatiable" demands: Parham report, 8/26/60. "A Negro may not ride": NYT magazine, 2/14/60.

[94] Rich's background: Sibley, *Dear Store*. Corsets: A&E, Vol. I, p. 764. Sales of $75 million: *Newsweek*, 10/19/59. Some 400,000 had charge plates: Sibley, p. 21. "You're nobody": *Holiday*, May/61. Rich's in 1917, Depression: Sibley, pp. 14-15. Neely: *Ibid.*, pp. 61-62. Clerks called blacks "Mr.": Harold Fleming, DEL. Store segregated: AC, 10/21/60.

[95] Rich considered himself liberal: Lockerman int, DEL. Bond, King saw Rich's as inviting target; "Rich's was the gem": Bond, King ints, DEL. Bond, King backgrounds: Raines, p. 83. "Close out your charge account"; meeting of Rich, Jenkins and King: *Ibid.*, p. 88. Rich fumed: Lockerman int, DEL. **[96]** Bond, King wanted to influence presidential election: Lonnie King int, DEL. Martin King showed little enthusiasm; Lonnie said, "Martin, hear me out": *Ibid.*

Black students descended on downtown stores; King arrested at Rich's: AJ, 10/19/60. Klan protested: Lonnie King int, DEL. Maddox formed G.U.T.S.: AJ, 11/4/60. Jenkins had patrol cars circling: *Detroit Free Press*, 5/31/61.

[97] Hartsfield called Western Union: Hartsfield oh, 1/6/66, Kennedy Library. Older blacks appointed Hill intermediary: Garrow, p. 142. Hartsfield invited black leaders to City Hall: Hartsfield oh, Kennedy Library. (Full accounts of the Saturday meeting, Wofford's role, and Hartsfield's maneuvering are in Branch, pp. 353-356, and Garrow, pp. 144-145. My conclusion that Hartsfield was more interested in the local situation than presidential politics is based largely on his attempt to enlist Richard Nixon in the plan along with Kennedy. Hartsfield's offer to let Calhoun use the phone is from Hartsfield oh, Kennedy Library.)

[98] Borders re "best meeting": Branch, p. 356. Mitchell issued warrant; detectives shackled King: *Ibid.*, pp. 356-358. **[99]** "Atlanta had nothing to do with this": *Newsweek* telex, undated. Vandiver's role in King's release: Vandiver int. Kennedy called Coretta: Branch, p. 362. SCLC chartered plane: Garrow, p. 148. **[100]** Daddy King re "suitcase"; outcome of election: White, p. 363.

Hartsfield's "laughing" campaign: AJ, 11/4/60. Rich refused to budge; Hartsfield wrote Sibley: Letter, 11/16/60, RWP. **[101]** Chains volunteered to desegregate; Klan marched: Photo, Dec/60, CCP. Klan meetings at Dinkler: Atlanta police report, 12/1/60, HJP; photo, Dec/60, CCP.

Visitors found Hartsfield napping: Parham int. Hartsfield overly energized: *Look*, 4/25/61. Hartsfield blamed "ignorant rabble": AC, 12/13/60. Wanted to remarry: Martin, *Hartsfield*, p. 147. Allen mediated desegregation; Walden anecdote; difficulty with details: Allen, pp. 37-39.

[102] Vandiver had go-between sound out Kennedy: Gulliver int. (Vandiver denied seeking the appointment, but it seems highly unlikely such an approach would have been made without his blessing.) McGill reported to Kennedy; wanted Byrd governor: Letter, McGill to Bobby Kennedy, 1/5/61, RMP. Vandiver leaked news: *Ibid.*; Shipp, Gulliver ints. **[103]** Vandiver's comments on Brazil: AC, 12/2/60. Salinger tried to warn; McGill begged for modest position: Letter of 1/5/61.

Trial in Athens, Bootle's order: Trillin, pp. 42-43. Ward drafted: Shipp int. **[104]** Description of Hunter and Holmes arriving: *Newsweek* telex, Cumming, 1/9/61. Vandiver on "saddest duty": AC, 1/10/61. Allen contacted legislators outside Atlanta, used bankers: Letter, Allen to Sibley, 1/12/61, JSP.

[105] Disturbance at university: UPI, 1/11/61. Tate grabbed students: Trillin, p. 52. Vandiver played ostrich: Cook, p. 70; Shipp, Gulliver ints. Hunter carried madonna: Trillin, p. 54. Students reinstated: NYT, 1/17/61. Vandiver got Legislature to revoke law: Cook, p. 70.

[106] Poll of Southerners: *Esquire*, Mar/61. "Rather be pushed off sidewalk": Letter,

Eleanor Joslin to Sibley, 1/30/60, JSP. HOPE: Subject file, AHC. Maddox sent HOPE a
Confederate $10 bill: Letter, Maddox to HOPE, Mar/59, AHC. Allen reached compro-
mise with Walden: Allen, p. 39; minutes, Plans and Procedures Committee of the Chamber of Commerce, 5/18/61, JSP.

Lonnie King frustrated: King int, DEL. "Clarification" meeting: Branch, p. 396.
(Some accounts mistakenly place the meeting at Wheat Street Baptist Church.) Borders
called "Uncle Tom": Bond int, DEL. [107] Daddy King; "That's the problem": Branch,
pp. 396-397. Nurse re "charge card": Bond int, DEL. King Jr.'s speech: Allen, pp. 41-42;
Lonnie King int, DEL.

Opening of new terminal: AJ, 2/2/61. [108] Photo of Hartsfield leaping: AP Wirepho-
to, 3/30/61. Lane sent postcards: Allen, pp. 46-47. Hartsfield resisted stadium: Letter,
Hartsfield to Sibley, 4/20/61, JSP; AJ, 12/26/61. "Civic furniture movers"; "culls, misfits":
Atlanta, Nov/61. Quote in Holiday: Issue of May/61.

[109] Allen's appointment with Hartsfield: Allen int, Allen, pp. 48-49; Martin, Hartsfield, p. 148. Mayor announced retirement: Atlanta, May/61. "So long, old tiger": Gene
Patterson, AC, 6/8/61. "When you say you're through": Celestine Sibley, AC, 6/9/61.

Jenkins organized screening, police interviewed parents, students: Report, undated,
Det. J.D. Hudson to Jenkins, HJP. [110] AP reporter subjected to background investiga-
tion: Ibid. Klan flyer, surveillance: Atlanta Daily World, 6/11/61. Mayor stayed close with
Marshall: Letter, Hartsfield to Marshall, 7/30/61, WHP.

City warned "spectators, sightseers": Draft letter, 8/17/61, WHP. Telephone hookup:
Notice, undated, signed by Hartsfield, WHP. Jenkins put force through dry run: Order,
8/21/61, HJP. Guards "better get blown up with them": NYT, 8/30/61.

[111] Team of four: Herald Tribune, 8/29/61. Booklet: OASIS. Man wearing Nazi
emblem: AP, 8/30/61. FBI undercover agents: New York Post, 8/31/61. "A mob sizes you
up": Look, 4/25/61. Mayor gave tour: Notice by Hartsfield. Times commended Atlanta:
Issue of 8/31/61. Kennedy press conference: Goodwin int. Hartsfield desegregated Biltmore: Martin, Hartsfield, p. 154.

CHAPTER 6

[112] Allen's rattlesnake story: Allen int. Allen at first debate: Allen, p. 54. "I inher-
ited money": Atlanta, Dec/69, FHP. [113] Allen advocated sending blacks to Africa:
Shipp, Gulliver ints. Advocated segregated counties: Horton int. Raised $175,000:
Allen, p. 60.

Maddox squealed "Lookee": The New Yorker, 12/31/73. Hartsfield late to Allen's inau-
gural: AC, 1/3/62. $80 million bond issue: AJ, 1/2/62. Jet from Los Angeles: A&E, Vol.
III, p. 332. Portman and merchandise mart: Ibid., pp. 333-334. [114] Debut of Atlanta:
Ibid., p. 331. Detroit Free Press: Issue of 5/31/61. Atlanta third on Kremlin's list: Holiday,
May/61.

Airport busiest: A&E, Vol. III, p. 332. Cabana description: Holiday, May/61. "Theater
owners asked": Minutes, meeting of 12/18/61, WHP. "One man, one vote"; Hartsfield
filed suit: Newsweek, 4/9/62.

[115] Crackers: Bisher int. Art school charged double tuition: Letter, Ivan Allen Sr.
to Jimmy Carmichael, 11/23/62, JSP. "Timeless Wedgwood": Minutes, trustees meeting,
10/17/56, JSP.

Mills Lane description: Bisher, p. 7. [116] Woodruff bailed out Crackers: L.F. Montgomery papers, AHC. Spalding predicted "baseball will go the way of bustles": Letter,
Spalding to Woodruff, 8/14/59, HSP.

Woodruff favored arts center: Jones int. Weltner martini story: Hughes Spalding Jr. int. "Bois d'Atlante": Letter, Weltner to Woodruff, 5/27/62, RWP. Woodruff offered $4 million: Allen int. [117] Allen briefed editors: Memo, Allen to Woodruff, 6/19/62, RWP. "Start a groundswell": Letter, Weltner to Woodruff, 5/17/62, RWP. Ballerinas: AJ, 5/23/62.

Art Association background: An excellent series of articles on the history of the arts appears in Atlanta History, Spr-Sum/94. Ivan Sr. wanted "museum only": Letter, Allen to Carmichael, 11/23/62, JSP. Carmichael supported art school: Atlanta History. Carmichael hired curator: Memo, Carmichael to trustees, 5/9/62, JSP. [118] Orly crash, Allen's actions, trip to Paris: Newsweek telex, 6/8/62; article, 6/18/62.

Carmichael called emergency meeting: Atlanta History. [119] "In no way to be confused": Minutes, trustees meeting, 6/26/62, JSP. Rumor re Herndon foundation: Atlanta History. "Redneck elements": Allen, p. 70. Park lost 2-to-1: AC, 8/3/62. Woodruff in rage: Jones int. "I hate to quit": Letter, Weltner to Woodruff, 8/7/62, RWP. [120] Weltner began "to mozie": Letter to Woodruff, 2/6/63, RWP.

Griffin's campaign: Author's profile, AJC, 12/17/77. No-bill: AC, 12/22/60. Griffin quotes re King, activists: Cook, p. 91. Klan burned cross: Program, Klan rally, 7/7/62, CCP. Craig endorsed: Valdosta Daily Times, 7/13/62, CCP.

[121] Power structure behind Sanders: Sanders, Jones ints. "Not a damned fool": Cook, p. 93. Raised $750,000: Ibid., p. 89. (Sanders won enough counties to claim victory under the old county-unit system, but it is not clear whether he would have won those counties had the old system remained in place.) "Ate my barbecue": Griffin to author, 1977 int.

Davis lost to Weltner: A&E, Vol. III, p. 342. Leroy Johnson: Author's profile, AJC, 4/18/76. Peyton Road barricade: Photo and story, AC, 12/19/62. "Berlin Wall": Saturday Evening Post, undated but early 1963, JSP. [122] "Never make a mistake": Newsweek telex, undated but 1963. AJ cartoon: Issue of 1/10/63. Sam Williams quote: Allen, p. 72.

Town & Country: Issue of Feb/63. Wall issue ignored: Patterson column, AC, 2/8/63. Lovett School: AJ, 3/15/63. McGill quit: Kitty Ross int, DEL. GASPA: A&E, Vol. III, p. 392.

[123] Birmingham background: Birmingham News, 1/18/62; Newsweek telexes, 5/1/62; 5/5/63; 5/8/63. "Too late": Look, 12/3/63. Weibel: Newsweek telex, 6/27/63. Chuck Morgan anecdote: Raines, p. 180. [124] Use of children: Branch, pp. 752-754.

Sibley formed Atlanta Civic Enterprises: Draft, profile of Alexander, JSP. Alexander background: Business Atlanta, Aug/81. "Chief" Aiken overextended: Letter, Sen. J. Allen Frear to J.B. Aiken, 4/26/56, Lucy Aiken Papers, AHC. Waluhaje: Sibley, Peachtree, p. 93.

Allen and Pruden Herndon: Allen, pp. 86-87. (Allen mistakenly renders Mrs. Herndon's first name as Prudence.) Chamber of Commerce and Russell: A&E, Vol. III, p. 345. Leroy Johnson incident at Commerce Club: Cook, pp. 240-241. Allen and Woodruff: Allen int.

[125] "Retreat of the Rednecks": Saturday Evening Post, undated but early 1963, JSP. McGill's meetings with Kennedy: McGill memo, 10/2/63, RMP; oh, 1/6/66, Kennedy Library. Cox philosophy: Newsweek memo to file, 6/6/64; Tarver, Shipp ints. Tarver re Rich's: Tarver int, DEL.

[126] McGill meeting with JFK re Russell: McGill oh, Kennedy Library. McGill opposed public accommodations: McGill, No Place, Vol. II, p. 445. Kennedy phoned Allen: Allen, pp. 104-106. Sibley expressed disgust: Text, Sibley speech to Southern CPAs, 6/15/64, JSP. (He called the bill "a step toward a police state.")

[127] Proprietors wanted bill: Jenkins oh, 5/14/69, Johnson Library. Allen talked with

wife: Allen, p. 109. Restaurants had re-segregated: Confidential memo, Greater Atlanta Council on Human Relations, 8/27/63, JSP. Allen and Woodruff: Allen int; Allen, p. 108. Grilling by Thurmond, cold shoulder at home: Allen, pp. 111-116.

Allen wanted Woodruff to buy stadium land: Letter, Allen to Woodruff, 5/22/63, RWP. [128] Finley visit: Bisher, pp. 15-16. "We offered [Finley] a stadium": Bell & Stanton release, undated, *Newsweek* files. Allen and Lane: Allen, pp. 156-157. $700,000 in unsecured loans: Bell & Stanton release.

Weltner complained, land "jerked out from under us"; [129] "Jimmy is dead set": Letter, Weltner to Woodruff, 6/21/63, RWP. Woodruff's luncheon meeting with Carmichael: Letter, Carmichael to Woodruff, 6/25/63; memo, Joseph Jones to Woodruff, 6/25/63, RWP. Two-week deadline; Weltner's complaint: Letter, Weltner to Rutherford Ellis, 6/26/63, RWP. Woodruff enlisted Chiles, Rich: Letter, Carmichael to Woodruff, 6/25/63. [130] Carmichael embraced idea: *Atlanta History*.

Allen and Lane recruited Montgomery: Bell & Stanton; AJC magazine, 4/4/65. News from Cronin: Allen, p. 157. Talks with Braves: Bisher, p. 30. Woodruff declined again: Letter, Montgomery to Woodruff, 9/19/63, RWP. "Let me run this show": Allen, p. 158.

[131] Background of stadium land: AJC magazine, 4/4/65. Civic center in Buttermilk Bottom: Letter, Allen to Woodruff, 5/22/63, RWP. Blacks from 31 to 36 percent: Report of housing coordinator, 8/26/60, AHC. Hartsfield predicted black majority, worst elements: *A&E*, Vol. III, p. 339.

[132] Forman took control of SNCC: *Newsweek* telex, 1/30/64. Allen announced desegregation agreement: *A&E*, Vol. III, p. 403. Episode at Leb's: AJ, 1/27/64. Leb had evicted black customers in past: *Newsweek* telex, 6/25/63. Baugh's role; Klan: *Newsweek* telex, 1/30/64. [133] Craig description: Townsend column, *Atlanta*, Nov/65. "Klonvocation": Letter, L.B. Holland to Craig, 4/26/62, CCP.

Blacks mocked Klan: *Newsweek* telex, 1/30/64. Pointed at shoe: *Atlanta*, Nov/65. Dick Gregory: Sitton int. "Just like the niggers": *Ibid.* [134] Allen vowed "full protection": AJ, 1/27/64. Jenkins arranged deal; blacks reneged: *Newsweek* telex, 1/30/64. Walden and Forman; Lebedin's quotes; arrests: *Ibid.* [135] AP analysis: 1/30/64.

"Fouled the nest": AC, 1/30/64. "Wrong-headed": AJ, 1/30/64. Hartsfield wrote friend in Birmingham: Letter to W.G. Hastings, 12/14/61. Sibley wrote Russell: Letter of 3/18/64, JSP. Walden retired: AJ, 2/6/64. King backed SNCC: *Newsweek* telex, 1/30/64.

[136] "Danger flags": Note, typed on newsclip, AC, 1/26/65, JSP. Jack Spalding on Atlanta "U.S.A.": AJC magazine, 4/4/65. "Tearin' up Peachtree": *A&E*, Vol. III, p. 447. Playboy Club: *Ibid.*, p. 389.

Value of real property $1 billion: Letter, Hartsfield to John White and Milton Farris, 12/28/61. Ben Massell quote: George Goodwin to Floyd Hunter, 1973, FHP. Executives of AJC pressured: Tarver int.

[137] Woodruff renewed pledge: AJ, 3/13/64. Allen re "broken away from the old small-town": Allen, p. 159. Delta fifth largest; profile of Woolman: UPI, 3/17/63; *Newsweek* telex, 12/14/62. [138] "International": *Atlanta*, Aug/64.

CHAPTER 7

[139] Johnson signed act: Garrow, pp. 337-338. Account of confrontation at Pickrick: AJC, 7/4/64; report, Morris Redding to Chief Jenkins, 7/3/64, HJP; Galphin, pp. 57-59. Victors as "Maddox's friends": *Esquire*, Oct. 1967. Maddox snared in justice system: Galphin, pp. 59 *passim*.

[140] McGill warned Johnson of "ugly mood," Humphrey booed in Moultrie: Letter,

McGill to Johnson, 9/30/64, RMP. Woodruff groused about "outside agitators": Memo, Robert Woodruff to file, 8/26/65. Woodruff's associates criticized his ties to McGill: Memos to Robert Woodruff, authors's names torn off, file marked "Boycott Data 1963," RWP.

[141] Business leaders angry with King over Scripto strike: NYT, 12/29/64. Hartsfield likened situation to Grand Slam: Time, 2/5/65. Four leaders organized dinner: Letter to Robert Woodruff, 12/16/64, RWP. Maddox had formed P.A.S.S.: Letter, Maddox to Arthur Montgomery, 8/17/63, RWP. McGill considered calling event off: Time, 2/5/65. Allen went to see Woodruff: Allen int.

Woodruff instructed Austin: Allen, Jeane Austin ints. [142] Episode involving Duvalier: Author int with Helen Bullard, 1977; Raines, pp. 412-13. New York Times story: 12/29/64 issue. A thousand tickets sold at $6.50: AC, 1/13/65; Newsweek telex, 1/28/65. Hoover launched attack: Garrow, p. 360; Jenkins oh, HJP. Deputies contacted newsmen: Raines, pp. 368-70. Description of dinner: AC, 1/28/65; Atlanta Times, 1/28/65; Allen, pp. 98-99. [143] King wrote Hartsfield: Letter, 3/15/65.

Kirkwood school episode: AC, 1/26/65. [144] Hooper's order; board's vote: A&E, Vol. III, p. 428. Braves' exhibition: Newsweek telex, 4/10/65. [145] Football franchise: [N.Y.] Daily News, 6/9/65; NYT, 6/9/65; Cook, pp. 271-272. Beatles: A&E, Vol. III, p. 442. "Allen's Coffin": Allen, p. 160. Hartsfield booed: Bisher, p. 8.

Unemployment 2 percent: A&E, Vol. III, p. 419. Hotel rooms doubled: Nation's Business, Apr/76. Yellow Pages: AJC, 3/23/75. "We're building": Text, King speech, 5/1/65, RMP.

[146] Xernona Clayton: Clayton int, DEL. Julian Bond denied seat: A&E, Vol. III, p. 464. Carmichael seized SNCC: Newsweek telex, 5/20/66. [147] "When I see a Tarzan movie": AJ, 7/14/66. No longer welcome whites: Village Voice, 8/25/66. McGill tip to FBI re VISTA: Letter, McGill to Charles Harding, 7/6/66, RMP.

Sandy Springs vote: AJ, 5/12/66. Blacks 44 percent: NYT magazine, 10/16/66. "Mugsy" Smith worried: Letter to North Side News, 9/10/65.

Maddox placed coffin: Photo, Allen, p. 121. Poll showed Maddox trailed: Galphin, p. 110. Maddox drove Pontiac: NYT magazine, 11/6/66. [148] Jotted speech on sign, nailed to tree: Book proposal, Bob Cohn and Steve Ball, to Michael Korda, Simon & Schuster, 8/28/70, Newsweek collection.

[149] Department of Industry and Trade ad: NYT, 5/15/66. Police shot suspect, account of riot: WSJ, 9/9/66; NYT magazine, 10/16/66; Allen, pp. 174-192; report, "Perspective on the Atlanta Rebellion," by Julius Lester, Movement Press, 1967. Courts quote: int ca. 1973, FHP.

Republicans crossed party lines: Some analysts have disputed allegations of such a strategy, but see persuasive argument by Galphin, p. 115, that in many counties Maddox's vote in the runoff was higher than in the general election.

Allen denounced Maddox: Allen, pp. 139-140. Friend told NYT: Magazine, issue of 10/16/66. [150] Conditions in Summerhill, Allen, p. 179. Weltner withdrew, Woodruff sent Davis: Davis int. McGill wrote Johnson, called Maddox "psycho"; called Callaway "arrogant": Letter, 11/4/66, RMP.

Woodruff pledged Callaway $100,000: Memo, Joseph Jones to Woodruff, 3/23/66, RWP. Maddox liked to press flesh: author's observations. [151] Called Lane "fat cat": Newsweek, 1/18/71. Callaway "amused": Galphin, p. 122. Maddox attacked Life ad: Letter, McGill to LBJ, 11/4/66. Maddox promised "little people's day": Newsweek, 1/18/71. Called Callaway "puppet": Galphin, p. 140.

Davis went to work: Series of confidential memos to Woodruff, 1966, RWP. New York Times explained: Magazine, 11/6/66 issue. Goldwater interview with Cronkite: Galphin,

p. 164. [152] Supreme Court upheld legislators' right: *ibid*, p. 162-63.

Portman observed: *Louisville Times*, 12/22/72. Description: Author's observation. Portman designed self-contained environment; calculated 7.5-minute walk: *National Geographic*, Feb/69. Catwalk: *A&E*, Vol. III, p. 502. Not many used catwalk: White int. [153] Influence of Tivoli; "a little Peeping Tom": *Esquire*, Feb/ 75.

Critics attacked Portman: *Saturday Review*, 5/14/77, called his structures "urban dinosaurs." Portman viewed downtown as "strong, vibrant core": *A&E*, Vol. III, p. 548. "Shiny-suit crowd": Berry int. [154] Troutman's deal: Alpert int; Cousins int, FHP. Cousins' background: *Ibid.*; AJC magazine, 7/22/79; *Georgia Trend*, Jun/95.

[155] Maddox in charge of National Guard: *The Nation*, 5/1/67. Maddox's inaugural: NYT magazine, 11/24/68. Inmate drowned, Maddox's quote: AP, 7/30/67; Galphin, p. 182. Maddox met "Daddy" King, other black leaders: Maddox int. Appointed blacks to boards, named Burson to head welfare: NYT magazine, 11/24/68. Maddox rebuked by Klan leader: AC, 1/27/68.

[156] Media proclaimed "new" Maddox: Galphin, p. 171. Maddox advised "flatten the tires": *Newsweek*, 1/18/71. Maddox agreed not to call out guard: Galphin, p. 207. AP analysis: 7/30/67.

Maddox rode bicycle backwards: Photo, Galphin, after p. 106. Maddox cracked down on Sunday drinking, quote about conventioneers not "cutting up": *New Yorker*, 1/19/68. Maddox's mother saw hippies as portent of Millennium: AJC, 12/3/67. Maddox re "bums, criminals": *A&E*, Vol. 3, p. 576.

[157] Catacombs; first issue of *Bird*: *Newsweek* telex, 2/11/71. Coffin quote: *Great Speckled Bird*, March 15-28, 1968. Writer attacks city's "defects": *The Courier*, Sept. 21-27, 1973. (The writer, Bill Winn, was a former managing editor of *Atlanta* magazine.) Hartsfield underlined dirty words: Copy of *Bird*, WHP. Wrote friend: Letter, Hartsfield to Spiro Agnew: 10/31/69, WHP. McGill denounced: *Bird*, March 15-28, 1968.

Newsweek reporter on Atlanta's reputation: Telex, undated but Oct/69. "Triumph of Babbittry over bigotry": *New Yorker*, 3/7/73. (The quote was attributed to local wits by the writer, Calvin Trillin.) [158] Description of SNCC: *National Observer*, 11/27/67.

Klan situation: Memo signed "W.S." and dated 8/20/66, CCP. Last 75 stamps: Letter, "faithful Kligrapp" to Craig, 4/17/63, CCP. Craig guilty of contempt: Transcript, Report No. 1242, House of Representatives, Proceedings Against Calvin Craig, 10/28/65; letter, office of Probation Officer, U.S. District Court, District of Columbia, to Craig, 1/16/69, CCP.

Maddox responded to MLK death by holing up in Mansion: Galphin, p. 207. Allen drove to King's home: Allen, p. 197. Police aides met him: *Ibid.*, p. 199. [159] Woodruff and Sanders at White House: Jones, Sanders ints. "Ivan," he warned: Allen, p. 205; Allen int. Belafonte offered: Houck int.

Six schools held march; Abernathy arranged funeral: Allen, pp. 206-211. Mays felt son had died: Text, Mays's eulogy, Mays, p. 357. Maddox flag anecdote: NYT magazine, 11/24/68. Eastern record for charters; dignitaries: Allen, pp. 213-214. Shut off liquor sales: Proclamation, 4/8/68. [160] Security arrangements: Allen, p. 214.

Maddox's behavior: Galphin, pp. 208-210. Maddox tried to call out Guard: Jenkins oh, 3/8/77, Billy Graham Center. Funeral description: AC, 4/10/68. "I remember glancing": Allen, p. 216. "Red, White and Maddox"; NYT magazine, 11/24/68.

[161] Jordan quote re Woodruff: int, DEL. Austin urged black Coca-Cola director: Memo (marked "private and confidential, by hand only"), Austin to Woodruff, 9/27/73, RWP. MARTA failed; Rich embittered: AC, 3/28/75.

Townsend proclaimed "Atlanta's decade": *A&E*, Vol. III, p. 487. [162] Cousins and Sanders bought Hawks: AC, 5/8/68. Marriott built, enlarged: *A&E*, Vol. III, p. 492. Seventh in convention-goers: *Ibid.*, p. 552. Added 160,000 jobs: *National Geographic*, Feb/69.

Citizens Trust; Cochrane quote: Cochrane int, FHP. Paschal's: Author's profile, AJC, 10/21/78.

75,000 blacks out of homes: A&E, Vol. III, pp. 535-536. Sibley orchestrated campaign to "lessen" black population: Draft, history of Atlanta Civic Enterprises, Inc., JSP. [163] Blacks jumped from 45 to 57 percent of student population: A&E, Vol. III, p. 502. "Melancholy truth": Gulliver, AC, undated but Aug/71. 60,000 whites moved out, 70,000 blacks in: Speech by Milton Farris, 8/16/77.

Black officer described beating: A&E, Vol. III, p. 576. Spalding warned "no Joshua": Memo, Spalding to Woodruff, 4/29/64, HSP. Lane warned of lack of leaders: Holiday, May/61. Elite supported Cook: Allen, p. 224.

[164] Voters League disbanded: AC, 9/25/78. "Black Young Men on the Go": AJC, 10/21/78. Herndon reclusive, gay: Franklin int. Group had Cameron Jackson transferred: AJC, 10/21/78.

Massell ran against "glamorous" projects: AJ, 1/18/70. Massell charged anti-Semitism: NYT, 10/23/69. Nightclub scandal: AC, 10/23/69; Allen, pp. 226-231. [165] Massell described as "just failed to catch on to a joke": Newsweek telex, undated but Oct/69.

Massell admitted "bad judgment": Ibid. Allen urged Massell to withdraw: Gulliver column, AC, 10/23/69. Account of debate; Massell's remarks the next day; election night scene: Newsweek telex. [166] Racial breakdown of vote: Tally sheet, JSP. Strategist muttered, "Sam's brother": Newsweek telex, 10/23/69.

CHAPTER 8

[167] People wondered aloud: Author's mother. Description of hippies, bikers: Newsweek telex, 2/11/71. "Singles" complexes: Farmer int. Median age 26: Esquire, Feb/75. Women "mostly in miniskirts": Sunday News, 4/25/71. "Sauciest, swingingest city": National Observer, 2/22/71. Article on restaurants: Esquire, Feb/75.

[168] Maddox's favor re Underground: Saturday Evening Post, Nov/74; Hawes, Blackmon ints. Massell bought ties: AJ, 1/18/70; Hunter notes, FHP. Broke garbage strike: AC, 3/20/70. Crackdown on drug use: Newsweek telex, 2/11/71. Airport figures: A&E, Vol. III, p. 550. Second airport: Letter, Hartsfield to Massell, 12/5/69, WHP.

"Oh, no," Allen answered: AJC, 2/20/72. Cousins and Massell reached agreement on Omni: AJ, 5/10/70. [169] Cousins' plans: Time, 8/4/72; AJ, 1/16/74. Portman re "private urban renewal program": Interiors magazine, Sep/71.

Rivalry over the World Congress Center: AJC magazine, 7/22/79; Berry, Cousins, Sanders, S. Williams, Underwood ints. Jehovah's Witnesses, American Legionnaires: A&E, Vol. III, p. 551. Portman re "over there in the hole": S. Williams int.

[170] Carter's campaign of 1970: New Republic, 4/12/75; Shipp int. Maddox approval rating of 62 percent: NYT magazine, 11/24/68. [171] Ad re "This is the door": Cook, p. 325. Nickname "Cufflinks Carl": Cook, p. 324. "I say to you quite frankly": Carter, p. 120. Massell unveiled sign, buried hatchet: Newsweek telex, 11/9/71.

Business Week called Portman leading architect: Issue of 2/17/73. [172] "The burden of what he said": AJC magazine, 7/22/79. Carter tried to steer project: AC, 10/19/83. WCC doubled in size: AJC, 4/26/85.

[173] Maynard Jackson background: AC, 10/7/77; campaign bio, AHC; Peter Ross Range article, NYT magazine, 4/7/74, FHP. Jackson description: Author's observations. "Negro Attorney to Face Talmadge": AC, 6/6/68. "We reject the vapid, jejune trappings": Range. Whites assumed Jackson was Greek: Franklin int. Photograph was darkened: Seeliger, Franklin ints. Editors of Constitution almost endorsed: Memo, Eugene Patterson to

staff, AC, 9/27/68.

Jackson carried Atlanta by 6,000 votes: Range. Announced for vice mayor (3/7/69): A&E, Vol. III, p. 572. "Who'd he check with?": Range. [174] Jackson got 98 percent of black vote: Tally sheet, JSP.

Jackson joined garbagemen's picket line: AJC magazine, 9/30/73. Black leader called Massell a good "one-term" mayor: Newsweek telex, int with Andrew Young.

MARTA fare fixed at 15 cents: AC, 11/9/71. Perry Homes promise; list of "concerns": Author's column, AJC, 4/15/86. [175] Threat of backlash: Newsweek telex, 8/2/71. Massell's "think white" speech: Newsweek telex, 10/29/71. Action Forum; Massell in helicopter: Ibid. "Abolish Atlanta": AC, 12/3/69; Clarke int. Maddox killed measure: AJC, 10/7/73.

[176] Schools 71 percent black: New South magazine, Spring/72. Mays quote: Christian Science Monitor, 3/21/70. School compromise: Newsweek telex, Oct/72; The New Yorker, 3/7/73. NYT on "falling out": Issue of 4/8/73. NAACP ousted King, suspended Jackson: Newsweek telex, Oct/72. King, "The people in New York": Newsweek files. King argued: DEL.

[177] School population 85,000, 84 percent black: AC, 3/30/75. "Fighting over a dead body": Raleigh Bryans, quoted in Newsweek files.

Hill and Russell supported Johnson; Caddell poll; Franklin quote: Range article, FHP. Johnson a "hustler": Hunter draft for Newsday, 1973. NYT called him "Machiavelli": AJC, 4/18/76. Raised $325,000: AJC, 3/23/75. [178] "Power Structure Deal": Atlanta Voice, 6/30/73. (The author covered the election for the AC.)

Young captured Fifth: Charlotte Observer, 12/17/72. [179] Howard Massell description, photo: AJC magazine, 8/25/74. Inman background: AC, 4/19/74. Massell on TV re "gangsters": Text, Massell speech, 9/29/72. Wolcoffs planned to "go straight": AJC magazine, 8/25/74. Massell gave tongue-lashing: AC, 4/19/74.

[180] Inman investigated alderman: AC, 3/1/73. Massell almost fired Inman: AC, 4/4/73. Gellerstedt reluctant to back Jackson: Atlanta Voice, 6/30/73. Mitchell finished third: AC, 10/3/73. "Lifts the hood": Unidentified sheet, Helen Bullard Papers.

"Too Young to Die" ad: AJ, 10/10/73. [181] Gulliver headline: AC, undated but Oct/73. Runoff results; Williams quote re "coats and ties": AC, 10/17/73. "Crime is his issue": AC, 10/15/73. Jackson dismissed "desperation": Text, Newsweek int, 10/18/73. Jackson's inaugural; "black Mecca": Range article; AJC, 3/23/75.

[182] Cleage quote: Newsweek telex, undated but 1974. Saturday Evening Post: Issue of Nov/74. "Specious, illogical": Author's recollection. "Scatological": Author's int. "I prayed for it": AC, 4/10/74. Aaron's quote: Saturday Evening Post, Nov/74.

Jackson's limousine: AJC magazine, 7/24/77. "People's administration": Text, inaugural address, 1/7/74, AHC. Inman filed suit: AC, 4/19/74. [183] Jackson fired Inman; description of showdown: AC, 5/7/74; author's recollection. [184] Constitution called on Inman to resign: Issue of 4/19/74.

Munford endorsed Inman: AJ, 6/5/74. Jackson warned of "plot": AC, 6/6/74. Spy at Atlanta Voice: AC, 6/6/74. Orkin indicted: AC, 6/24/74. [185] Gibson killing; fracas involving Hosea Williams: AC, 6/27/74. Jackson condemned "overreaction": AJ, 6/27/74. Supreme Court ruled: AC, 7/4/74.

Jackson picked Eaves: AC, 8/19/74. Eaves appointment "wrong": AC, 8/19/74. [186] Brockey letter: Copy, AHC. Woodruff had given $250 million: Speech, Boisfeuillet Jones to Atlanta Rotary, 9/11/78. Austin re Techwood: Memo, Austin to Woodruff, 6/11/71, RWP. Austin approached mayor: S. Williams, Franklin ints. Austin re Rand: series of memos, Austin to Woodruff, 1974-6, RWP.

Decor "seemed ready to spring": AJC magazine, 11/11/79. Mayor's afro: Franklin int.

[187] *Tea and Sympathy*: Author's int. Curbside garbage: AC, 9/13/77. "Unless I am assured": AC, 12/7/81. Threatened to move bank accounts to Alabama: AJC, 12/13/87.

Eastern won Mexico City route: Ad, AJC, 6/27/71. Hartsfield in Birmingham: *Birmingham News*, 10/14/70; *Post-Herald*, 10/14/70. [188] Atlanta second busiest: AJC, 8/3/75.

Kattel, C&S pushed to brink: AJC, 4/16/78; *Fortune*, 6/5/78. 8 million square feet vacant: AC, 11/1/77. Cousins in financial trouble: AJ, 3/29/78. "Real estate man's dream": *Time*, 8/4/72. Unemployment to 9.5 percent: AC, 3/30/75. [189] Highest homicide rate: AJ, 4/1/75. King's mother: AC, 7/4/74.

Town & Country: Issue of Oct/74. *Harper's*: Issue of Jan/75. "Next Great City": *Real Estate Atlanta* magazine, special issue, 1976. "Losersville": Ron Hudspeth.

Bell's car torched; Eaves's troubles: AJC, 3/23/75. [190] Portman called on Tarver: *Ibid*. "City in Crisis": Series ran in AC 3/23/75 to 3/30/75. (The author was a member of the team of reporters who wrote the series.) Tornado: AC, 3/25/75.

CHAPTER 9

[191] Six top executives: *Nation's Business*, Apr/76; *Real Estate Atlanta* magazine, special issue, 1976. "District of Atlanta"; "place to train the National Guard"; "to issue library cards": AJ, 10/20/75. Sanders re consolidated government: Cook, p. 343. Maynard re after second term: AC, 10/2/75.

[192] "I don't need you guys": AJ, 4/14/77. *Northside News*: Issue of 11/27/75. Helms and Bradley re guilt: *Creative Loafing*, 6/5/76. Jackson says Eaves "never a buddy": AJC, 3/23/75. Eaves "temporary": AC, 12/7/81. Eaves' resignation unraveled: AC, 6/6/76. "I'm giving too much time": *Time*, 3/22/76. Voters approved library bond: AC, 12/7/81.

[193] Carter got break from Strauss; traveled with Young: *New Republic*, 4/12/76. Young, Carter at Paschal's; Miss Lillian gave contribution; Carter mentioned as McGovern running mate: NYT magazine, 2/6/77. [194] Maddox re Carter as "most dishonest": UPI, 4/16/75. "Called ugly by a frog": AJ, 2/20/76.

Maddox at Underground: AJC magazine, 5/7/72. Busbee sponsored Sibley: Letter, G. Bell to Sibley, 1/5/84, JSP. [195] *Harper's*: Issue of Feb/76. "Ethnic purity": AJC, 7/16/78.

Trillin, *The New Yorker*: Issue of 3/21/77. Parren Mitchell: AP analysis, 12/26/76. Charges against Bell: *National Observer*, 1/29/77. [196] Testified 13 hours: AJC magazine, 11/4/79. *Washington Post* called Bell "constructive influence": Issue of 1/25/77. Young explained to NYT: Magazine, 2/6/77. (The article's author, Joseph Lelyveld, later the newspaper's executive editor, seemed surprised at Young's criticism of Northern "intellectual liberals." Young's top aide, Stoney Cooks, was quoted as explaining, "Liberals want to do it for you. Southerners want to do it with you.")

World of Sid and Marty Krofft: *Atlanta*, May/76; AJC promotional insert, undated; brochure. [197] Bert Lance and Kate Smith: AJC, 1/6/85. "Brightest star": *Ibid*.

Population reached 1.3 million: Chamber of Commerce booklet, 1975. [198] Muggings near Underground: *Newsweek* telex, 12/1/72. CAP set up model with pins: *Nation's Business*, Apr/76.

Cousins hoped to hook up to Rich's, beyond: AJC magazine, 7/22/79; AJC, 7/19/87; Cousins int, FHP. MARTA followed railroad right-of-way: "Anatomy of Atlanta," paper by Dana White and Timothy Crimmins, 2/14/75. Claimed land from Underground: AJ, 10/15/76.

[199] "A glistening hub": *Atlanta*, Jul/66. Five Points as "city center": AJ, 6/20/75. Demographics: Two excellent studies of population growth in Atlanta, provided to the author by Sam Williams of CAP, are "Overview of Atlanta's Economy Relative to Real

Estate Demand," by Gregg T. Logan of Robert Charles Lesser & Co., Jun/95; and "The Changing Location of Development and Investment Opportunities," by Christopher B. Leinberger, *Urban Land*, May/95.

[200] Carter, Jackson killed I-485, Stone Mountain Tollway: AJ, 12/15/72; *Atlanta*, Oct/75; *Buckhead Atlanta*; 12/28/79. Problems at Omni International: AJC, 7/19/87. Space needle: *Ibid*. Portman saw tripled-decked pathway: AJ, 1/16/74. Portman tried to get Rich's: AC, 6/4/79.

[201] Southern Bell in Midtown; Jackson's relations improved: AC, 10/3/77. Jackson took hard line against garbage strike: AC, 8/17/77. Declaimed Gay Pride proclamation: AC, 12/26/77. Jackson dieted, squired Valerie Richardson: AJC magazine, 7/24/77. Cyclorama; "right side won": Jackson to author.

"Talk Up Atlanta" plate: AJC magazine, 7/24/77. [202] Allen endorsed: AC, 6/7/77. *Constitution* endorsed: Issue of 10/3/77. Eaves accused in cheating scandal: AC, 9/29/77. Jackson won with 63 percent: AC, undated.

Special panel investigated Eaves: AC, 11/2/77. Eaves and polygraph: Text, report of panel, 2/21/78. Jackson's TV speech: Text, AC, 3/8/78. [203] Staffers bet on version: Berry int. Eaves signed letter of resignation, was suspended: AC, 3/11/78.

Kattel resigned: *Fortune*, 6/5/78. Kattel supported Jackson: AJ, 4/14/77. [204] 150 businesses closed doors or left: AC, 10/31/77. Hotel rooms doubled: *Nation's Business*, Apr/76. Carter got overseas approval for Delta: AC, 10/3/77. Delta had applied since 1967: AJC, 6/27/71.

Atlanta unready for world travelers: Jasper Dorsey column, AJC, 4/16/78. Emory offered course: AJC, 10/6/74. No good record stores: AJ, 11/3/77. [205] Scheer article: *Los Angeles Times*, Dec/78. Worried Georgia-Pacific: Gulliver column, AC, 12/18/78. WSJ warned Scarlett act wearing thin: Aug/79, cited in *Chicago Tribune* profile, 4/6/80.

AJ concluded race permeated life; Hosea Williams quote: Series beginning 2/18/79. Woodruff gave $7 million: AJC, 9/2//78; memo, B. Jones to Woodruff, 9/1/78.

[206] Highest crime rate: AJC, 4/6/80. Only one employee in nine worked downtown: AJC, 9/4/80. Tetalman murder; Jackson's meeting with colleagues: AJC, 6/30/79. WSJ labeled downtown "war zone": D. Williams int.

[207] Patricia Barry killing; AC response: Issue of 10/19/78. Sanders, Jackson quotes: *Ibid*. [208] MARTA quota for white drivers: AJC, 7/3/85. Williams called Jackson "tool": *Chicago Tribune*, 4/6/80. City had 231 homicides: *Ibid*.

[209] Details of the early days of the "missing and murdered" children: Series in AJC beginning 2/15/81. Terror gripped black parents: Author's ints at the time. [210] "City of Fear": *Time*, 3/2/81. Jenga; Guardian Angels; bogus fundraising: *Time*, 4/6/81. Tummy tuck: *TV Guide*, 10/17/81.

"It got to the point": AC, 12/8/81. "Rubbing salt in the wound": *Time*, 4/6/81. [211] *Post* said Atlanta "about to crack"; Brooks response: *Ibid*. "Let's Keep Pulling": *TV Guide*, 10/17/81. Wayne Williams: AJ, 6/16/81; AJC, 6/22/81. Jury convicted him: AJC, 2/28/82. [212] Disparaging article in *TV Guide*: Issue of 10/17/81. (The article's author, Jeff Prugh, the Atlanta bureau chief of the *Los Angeles Times*, later co-wrote a book attacking the credibility of the case against Williams.)

Mayor wrote CBS: AJC, 8/12/84. "Atlanta Child Murders": Review, AC, 2/8/85. [213] Blacks had 28 percent of city business: AC, 12/9/81.

Young got 38 percent in 1976: AJ, 10/7/81. "Andy could do more": Williams int, DEL. Bond scoffed: NYT magazine, 2/6/77. AJC magazine said Young might run for president: Issue of 8/7/77. Young's gaffes: *Atlanta Inquirer*, 6/4/77 (re Swedes); AJC, 3/19/78. (Dean Rusk, the former U.S. secretary of state, remarked to the author at the time that he thought Young was correct about the Swedes.)

[214] Jackson's support for Young: Author ints with Jackson, Franklin at the time. Marcus background: Obit [by author], AJC, 10/28/83. "Not going to be 'white' candidate": AJ, 3/25/80. Marcus let meetings drone: Horton int. [215] "Reason cities were started": AJC, 10/28/83. "Hands-on": *Ibid.*

Loudermilk suspected as spy: Franklin int. [216] Jackson re "Negroes ... grinning and shuffling": AC, 10/15/81. At Marcus headquarters: Author recollection. Gulliver: AC, 10/16/81. Signs on I-20: Franklin int.

CHAPTER 10

[217] Events at Omni International: AJC, 1/6/85; ad, AC, 11/26/80. Cousins acquired land, applied for grant: AJC, 7/19/87. Rich's talked of skyscraper: AJC, 4/18/91.

[218] Blacks frequented Omni: Author's observations; AJC, 12/25/80. Architect admitted complex "didn't bring in people who could support": AJC, 7/19/87. Block fell into foreclosure: AJC, 6/8/83. Cousins catered to convention traffic: AJC, 6/13/81.

Planning department forecast: AJC magazine, 2/18/68. [219] Schools 95 percent black: *Business Atlanta*, Mar/86. "Incredible Shrinking City": D. Williams int. DeKalb a third black: *Atlanta Business Chronicle*, 10/2/78; series in AJ starting 5/26/80.

King called Young "house Republican": Houck int. Luncheon at Merchandise Mart: AJC, 8/11/87. "The challenge of the '80s: AJC, 1/4/82. [220] Explained thinking to *Esquire*; "made peace with capitalism": Issue of Jun/85.

"We tried the easygoing ways": AJC, 11/7/82. "One-stop" permitting; 20,000 permits: Text, Young's state of city address, 1/21/85. Young and potholes: AJC, 4/6/83; 4/7/83. [221] Young introduced Harris: AJC, 3/29/83. *Places Rated*: AJC, 12/5/81. Pascual Perez: AJC, 8/20/82. [222] 84,000 cars a day: AC, 1/10/82.

"Beyond anyone's imagination": Manuel Maloof, quoted in AJC, 5/1/84. Metro Atlanta led nation in job growth: WSJ, 2/29/88. Gwinnett fastest growing county: AJC, 4/21/88. Native Georgians outnumbered: 1980 census, cited in *Sky* magazine, Oct/82; AJC, 5/19/87.

"Hunk of junk": AJC, 12/31/89. The "Dump": Author's recollection. Remembrance of Crackers, "Gray Ghost": AJC, 4/18/82. The same issue mistakenly asserted that "Parlor A" was in the Henry Grady Hotel; it was in the Georgia Hotel. Merger of newsrooms: Author's recollection.

"What's Atlanta About?": AJC, 10/15/84. [223] 432 of Fortune 500: *Reader's Digest*, Jun/75. "Other than buildings": WSJ, 2/29/88. "Nebulosity": *Sky*, Oct/82. "Look at Atlanta Now": AJC, 11/7/84. Hartsfield's 2,400 flights: *National Geographic*, Jul/88. 135 cities: AJC, 8/10/87. "Badge-wearing army": *Sky*, Oct/82.

Supreme Court re nude dancing: AJC, 6/2/81. Zoo scandal: AJC, 10/1/87. [224] King Center drew three million: King Center spokeswoman.

"Atlanta Future Forum": AJC, 11/25/84; Lomax int. MARTA carried fewer than 200,000 riders: AJC, 5/3/85. "Transit dependent": AJC, 12/14/87. [225] Survey on MARTA prospects: AJC, 8/4/85. Crime, knife-wielding robber: AJC, 5/6/86. High-density complexes: AJC, 12/9/84; 9/8/85.

Decatur, College Park, East Point: AJC, 6/30/89. Five Points lost 4,000 jobs: AJC, 12/7/87. Garnett Street: AJC, 7/1/85. Commuting by MARTA took longer: AJC, 3/3/87. [226] "Free the freeways" program: Jerry Stargel, DOT spokesman.

Atlanta re "New Power Elite": Issue of Feb/84. Banking background: AJC, 6/26/94; S. Williams int. (The author covered the bank legislation fights of the 1970s.) [227] Southern banking compact: AJC, 10/14/85. Supreme Court ruled compact legal: AJC, 6/11/85.

"Ensures Atlanta's role": *Ibid*. First National snapped up by Wachovia: AJC, 10/14/85.

Shortage of capital: S. Williams, Donald Ratajczak, quoted in AJC, 10/23/83. 37 foreign governments had representatives: AJC, 8/26/83. **[228]** Carter left Portman and Cousins scratching heads: S. Williams int. Ross Johnson anecdote: WSJ, 2/29/88; *Barbarians*, p. 85.

Turner background: *TV Guide*, 8/22/81; AJC, 5/21/76; author int with Turner, 1977. **[229]** Turner and Braves: *Citizen Turner*, p. 174 *passim*. "The world has gotten along": NYT, 1/19/77, cited in *Citizen Turner*. Turner in Newport: Author's observations, int with Turner, 1977. Turner bought Hawks from Cousins: AJC, 2/24/80. **[230]** Turner bought Omni International: AJC, 7/19/87.

"Will Top News Topic?": WSJ, 2/13/87. **[231]** Frommer: AJC, 7/4/88. Conroy quote: *National Geographic*, Jul/88. Most familiar idea was *Gone With the Wind*: AJC, 4/21/91. Forsyth County: Author's recollection. *National Geographic*: Issue of Jul/88. **[232]** Young at Atlanta Rotary: AJC, 3/3/87. "Never met a permit": Richard Ossoff, quoted in AJC, 12/31/89.

"Andy Claus": Photo, AJC, 12/22/83. Work as garbageman: AJC, 12/5/84. "Look of a Leader": AJC, 8/3/83. Sang "Bad": AJC, 8/12/88. Public housing: *Atlanta Business Chronicle*, 12/16/94. WSJ excoriated Atlanta: Issue of 2/29/88. **[233]** 32,000 hotel rooms: *Sky*, Oct/82. 82,000 workers: AJC, 11/7/84. "Coming to America": Underwood int. Cartoonist portrayed Atlanta as Scarlett: AC, 7/3/88.

Berkholtz: Berkholtz, H. Sibley ints. **[234]** Austin killed bid: Berry int. Payne background; **[235]** Olympic bid: *Sports Illustrated*, Aug/90; AJC, 9/28/90; H. Sibley, Battle ints. Payne on WGST: Houck int. "Screwball with harebrained scheme": William Oscar Johnson in *Sports Illustrated*, Aug/90. **[236]** Payne and Keough: H. Sibley int. Payne and Girl Scouts: Battle int. **[237]** BellSouth paid for film: Yarbrough int.

[238] International bid strategy: H. Sibley int. Young and member from Senegal: AJC, 9/16/90.

[239] Maynard Jackson at 76 percent: AJC, 8/17/89. Republicans endorsed: AJC, 5/17/89. H. Williams and Aunt Jemima poster: AJC, 9/24/89. "Sucker is out": AJC, 11/1/87. Mansion, salary, twin chauffeurs: AJC, 9/24/89.

[240] Samaranch's announcement: AJC, 9/19/90. "I'm excited, I'm elated": *Ibid*. Unhappy crowd in Melbourne: *The* [Melbourne] *Age*, 9/19/90. Athens' problems: *Sports Illustrated*.

[241] Civic pride "almost religious": *National Geographic*, Jul/88. "Big Hustle": WSJ, 2/29/88. "A town for sale": *Washington Post* National Weekly Edition, 10/1/90.

EPILOGUE

[243] Ticker-tape parade: AJC, 9/24/90. Portman's empire teetered: WSJ, 9/11/90; AJC, 6/25/95. Muse's episode: S. Williams int; AJC, 2/2/95. Underground struggled: AJC, 5/20/95. Gwinnett voted no on MARTA: AJC, 9/26/91.

[244] Rich's closed: AJC, 4/18/91. "Pink Pig": AJC, 12/17/87. Population below 400,000: AJC, 1/4/91. Georgia Dome: AJC, 8/16/92.

Mayor dismayed, quote about "crime, guns": AJC, 1/15/92. **[245]** Number one in violent crime: SNC transcript, 5/5/91. Atlanta riot: Author's observations from CNN Center. Airport corruption: *Georgia Trend*, Jan/94. "So tired I can't think": C.T. Martin int. Jackson surgery: AJC, 9/8/92. Jackson passed up another term: SNC transcript, 6/13/93.

Sinkhole: AJC, 6/19/93. **[246]** "Whatizit" offended Coca-Cola: Confidential source. "I didn't say what time of day": Yarbrough int. Golf at Augusta National: Battle int. **[247]**

Campbell botched paperwork: SNC transcript, 3/13/94. Referendum passed: SNC transcript, 7/24/94.

Hartsfield tried to create port: Letter, Hartsfield to John Cooper, 5/3/45, WHP. Woodruff of Columbus fought idea: Letter, Hartsfield to Charles Weltner, 3/12/63; letter, Hartsfield to Caughey Culpepper, 1/14/65, WHP. Clause in Plan of Improvement: I'm indebted to George Berry for directing my attention to the clause and lending me his copy of the act. City attorney thought it unconstitutional: Bowden, Alverson ints. Court overturned it: *Jamison et al v. City of Atlanta et al*, 165 SE2d 647.

86 percent of growth north of city: AJC, 1/30/84. **[248]** Goizueta speech: Text, Coca-Cola Company. Master plan to connect dots: AJC, 8/5/92; AJC, 8/5/95.

INDEX

PHOTOGRAPHS COURTESY OF:

Atlanta Journal-Constitution, photograph numbers: 1, 3, 5-7, 9-11, 14, 15, 18-27, 31-33, 36, 38, 39, 43, 44, 47-60, 63-82

Atlanta History Center, photograph numbers: 2, 12, 13, 16, 30, 35, 37, 40, 41, 42, 45, 46, 61, 62

Associated Press, photograph numbers: 4, 8, 17, 28, 29, 34